GEORGE WASHINGTON'S FINAL BATTLE

ROBERT P. WATSON

★ ★ ★

GEORGE WASHINGTON'S FINAL BATTLE

★ ★ ★

THE EPIC STRUGGLE TO BUILD A CAPITAL CITY AND A NATION

GEORGETOWN UNIVERSITY PRESS / WASHINGTON, DC

The publisher is not responsible for third-party websites or their content. URL links were active at time of publication.

Library of Congress Cataloging-in-Publication Data

Names: Watson, Robert P., 1962– author.
Title: George Washington's Final Battle : The Epic Struggle to Build a Capital City and a Nation / Robert P. Watson.
Description: Washington, DC : Georgetown University Press, 2021. | Includes bibliographical references and index.
Identifiers: LCCN 2019032707 (print) | LCCN 2019032708 (ebook) | ISBN 9781626167841 (hardcover) | ISBN 9781626167858 (ebook)
Subjects: LCSH: Washington, George, 1732–1799. | City planning—Washington (D.C.)—History—18th century. | Washington (D.C.)—History—18th century. | United States—Capital and capitol—History.
Classification: LCC F197 .W315 2020 (print) | LCC F197 (ebook) | DDC 973.4/1092—dc23
LC record available at https://lccn.loc.gov/2019032707
LC ebook record available at https://lccn.loc.gov/2019032708

♾ This book is printed on acid-free paper meeting the requirements of the American National Standard for Permanence in Paper for Printed Library Materials.

22 21   9 8 7 6 5 4 3 2   First printing

Printed in the United States of America
Jacket design by Jeff Miller, Faceout Studio
Production assistant, Sienna Brancato

Cover images: Cartwright, T., Artist, and George Beck. *George Town and Federal City, or City of Washington.* Georgetown Washington D.C, 1801. London and Philadelphia: Atkins & Nightingale. Photograph. https://www.loc.gov/item/2002695146/.
Royalty-free stock illustration ID: 423235858 George Washington, by Gilbert Stuart, c. 1803–05, American painting, oil on canvas.
Washington and Hoban inspect DC, 1798 by N. C. Wyeth, 1932.
Courtesy of the White House Historical Association.

A great city would really and absolutely be raised up, as if by magic.

—*Maryland Journal and Baltimore Advertiser*, 1789

CONTENTS

PART IV. Conflict and Compromise

PART V. Building the Capital

PART VI. Legacy

Illustrations follow page 164.

PREFACE

Millions of Americans and tourists from all around the world enjoy visiting the city named for George Washington. The majestic governmental buildings, tree-lined National Mall, world-famous museums and galleries, touching memorials, and imposing monuments are sites to behold. Indeed, the federal government has certainly done a commendable job preserving its history, commemorating the wars and events that shaped the nation, and celebrating the country's heroes. Today the city is full of splendor, but this was not always the case.

The remarkable events and political struggles that led to the creation of a national capital are not well-known.[1] Rather, the founding debates about the city's location, design, and size, along with the numerous challenges of building an entirely new city out of a landscape of farmland, small towns, and woodlands, are often omitted from the pages of textbooks, at times ignored by scholars, and generally taken for granted by the American public. Yet these very same issues proved even more contentious for the founders than the debates at the Constitutional Convention over a system of governance. In fact, on several occasions, these "other founding debates" nearly tore the young nation apart.

General Washington emerged victorious from the Revolutionary War and was the fledgling republic's most revered citizen. After the long conflict he looked forward to a quiet retirement from public life and domestic tranquility "under vine and fig tree," but his work was not done. The new experiment in popular government for which he had shed blood was a work in progress. Indeed, it was on shaky ground—bitterly divided, in debt, and paralyzed by a weak, ineffectual, and ad hoc system of governance.

Washington would need every bit of his considerable esteem and surprising political shrewdness after the war to convince his peers that a grand capital city was necessary—and then enlist them in building such a capital. He understood that it was not simply a matter of building a city. The general and his fellow founders were proposing an entirely new form of government based on radical ideas whereby the people would lead. Thus, the location and design of the capital mattered; they would shape the development of the nation politically and economically. Building the capital would therefore be an exercise in building the republic.

Washington hoped the city would imbue his fellow citizens with a sense of nationhood and American identity while also uniting the raucous states behind an energetic and stable federal government. The city would therefore help forge a "political culture" of democracy and both reflect and host the lofty ideals of self-government. It would not be easy.

A note to the reader on spelling and word use: when quoting letters and other historic documents, the original spelling and grammar are retained wherever and whenever possible. Only in a few instances have changes or corrections been made, and only when the meaning of the original writing might be unclear. In addition, during the founding period, political factions emerged that would soon form the nation's first political parties. The "federalists" and "antifederalists" played a central role in many of the important debates and developments discussed in this book. They first debated whether or not to ratify the Constitution, with the federalists being for it and the antifederalists against it. The federalists believed the country needed a stronger federal government than what the Articles of Confederation had provided, while the antifederalists advocated for a small federal government of very limited powers. Thomas Jefferson, with his concerns for individual liberty, became the leading light of the political movement. As political parties they were also known by other names. For instance, the anti-federalists became known as the Jeffersonian "Republicans" in 1791, and then the formal "Democratic-Republican Party," which may sound quite confusing to us today. The federalists became the formal Federalist Party of Alexander Hamilton, John Adams, John Jay, and others who gained the upperhand in American politics during the 1790s until President Adams's defeat for reelection in 1800. To uncomplicate the matter, the terms "federalist" and "antifederalist" are written in lowercase when referring to political factions. When political parties formed, the terms are capitalized, and the names of the nascent parties are used.

One additional clarification: even though the historian Kenneth Bowling notes in his book *Peter Charles L'Enfant* that the famous French-born architect used the name "Peter" or "P. Charles" while in America, this book will use "Pierre" because most readers continue to know him by that name, which was his birth name. The goal here is to avoid confusion while still being historically accurate.

In honor of the city that Washington built, quotations open each chapter in the book. Some of these comments about the capital city can be found etched or engraved onto the walls and public spaces of government buildings and monuments throughout the capital city as well as in the Capitol Building itself. Other quotes provide insights into the process of building a capital and nation by the Founders themselves. These words, like the magnificent structures in the city, define the ideals and promise of the nation.

ACKNOWLEDGMENTS

The book would not have been possible without the assistance and support of many people. Over the past few years I have had the pleasure of lecturing and conducting research at several wonderful historical sites. These include the Brooklyn Historical Society, Fraunces Tavern Museum, George Washington's Mount Vernon, James Madison's Montpelier, the Museum of the American Revolution, the National Archives, the National Museum of the US Navy, and the Smithsonian's National Museum of American History, to name but a few. Numerous administrators, archivists, and librarians at these sites and others were helpful. In a larger sense much of history would have been lost but for their dedication and attention over the years. Librarians and archivists make historians' work a lot easier. Thank you!

Additionally, I have had the good fortune of interviewing several leading historians of the Revolutionary era as part of a public program on America's founding hosted by the Society of the Four Arts in Palm Beach and C-SPAN. These conversations with Richard Brookhiser, Ron Chernow, Joseph Ellis, David McCullough, Richard Norton Smith, Gordon Wood, and others further stimulated my thinking about important stories from the founding that are not widely known. The work of two other historians—Kenneth Bowling, preeminent scholar of all things pertaining to the capital city, and Bob Arnebeck, a freelance writer—was enormously helpful. Last, I found the letters of William Maclay of Pennsylvania and Fisher Ames of Massachusetts to be irresistible. These two members of Congress were diligent—if not impertinent and churlish—in chronicling the early nation and the political debates surrounding the capital. They were never at a loss for words or their opinions!

These experiences and individuals inspired me to think deeper about such questions as how the national capital was built and how a people galvanized by revolution and a distrust of monarchy came together as a nation. The answers revealed George Washington to be a vastly more formidable political strategist, visionary, and bold risk taker than he is credited with being. In addition, the one constant in discussing nearly any legacy of the founding is the primacy of George Washington. He was the driving force behind the creation of the capital city.

I am indebted to Katrina Carter-Tellison, academic dean and vice president, and Gary Villa, dean of the College of Arts and Sciences at Lynn University, for their support of my research endeavors; Jared Wellman, my campus's resource librarian, who was again invaluable in tracking down and obtaining obscure historical documents; and both Alan Fruman, former parliamentarian of the US Senate, and Matthew Gilmore, historian of all things related to the District of Columbia and fellow at the DC Policy Center, for their sage advice. My friends Nancy Katz, Dr. George Goldstein, Bob Seidemann, and Samuel Stockhamer took the time to read an early draft of this book and provided helpful feedback. I would also like to thank Peter Bernstein, my literary agent, for his guidance, and Georgetown University Press—Donald Jacobs, senior acquisitions editor; Glenn Saltzman and Elizabeth Crowley Webber, production managers; Virginia Bryant, marketing and sales director; Stephanie Rojas, publicist; Caroline Crossman, marketing coordinator; Sienna Brancato, production assistant; Jessica Flores and Hannah Greco, publishing assistants; and the entire staff—for their interest in this book. It has been a pleasure to work with them! A special thank you to copyeditor Julie Kimmel for her careful attention to detail. Any errors, of course, are mine alone.

Mostly, I would like to acknowledge my family—Claudia, Alexander, and Isabella—for their many insightful ideas and feedback on this and all my books and projects.

And to you the reader, I hope you enjoy this story.

CHRONOLOGY

September 5, 1774	First Continental Congress meets in Philadelphia.
April 19, 1775	War breaks out when militiamen meet the British at Lexington and Concord.
May 10, 1775	Second Continental Congress meets in Philadelphia.
June 15, 1775	Washington selected as commander in chief of the Continental Army.
July 4, 1776	Congress adopts Declaration of Independence.
March 1, 1781	Articles of Confederation ratified.
September 3, 1783	Treaty of Paris ending the war signed between Great Britain and the United States.
December 23, 1783	Washington surrenders his commission to Congress.
May 25, 1787	Constitutional Convention begins in Philadelphia.
September 17, 1787	Constitution signed.
June 22, 1788	Constitution ratified by nine states.
September 13, 1788	Congress votes for New York City to be the temporary capital.
January 10, 1789	Washington unanimously elected first president.
March 4, 1789	Constitution and new government take effect.
April 30, 1789	Washington is inaugurated as the first president.
July 16, 1790	Washington signs the Residence Act establishing a seat of government.
December 6, 1790	Congress officially moves to temporary capital in Philadelphia.
January 21–22, 1791	Washington appoints commissioners for federal district and capital.
January 24, 1791	Washington announces the location of the federal district and capital.

March 9, 1791	Pierre Charles L'Enfant is commissioned as the architect for the capital.
April 15, 1791	Cornerstone laid for federal district's boundary.
September 9, 1791	Commissioners announce the capital city will be named for Washington.
February 26, 1792	L'Enfant resigns as the capital city's architect.
July 16–18, 1792	James Hoban wins a design contest for the presidential residence.
October 13, 1792	Cornerstone for the presidential residence is laid.
March 4, 1793	Washington begins his second term as president.
September 18, 1793	Washington lays cornerstone of US Capitol.
March 4, 1797	Washington ends his presidency, refusing a third term and retiring.
December 14, 1799	Washington dies at Mount Vernon.
May 15, 1800	President John Adams orders government offices to relocate to Washington.
November 1, 1800	John Adams moves into the "White House" in the new capital.
November 17, 1800	Congress officially moves to the new capital in Washington.
January 1, 1801	The presidential residence is opened to the public.

The "Other" Founding Debates

This place is the mere whim of the President of the United States.
During his life, it may out of compliment to him be carried on in a slow
manner, but I am apprehensive as soon as he is defunct, the city, which
is to be the boasted monument of his greatness, will also be the same.

An immigrant stonemason, 1795

Against all odds George Washington and the Continental Army managed to win the war. The cessation of military operations in 1783 brought a long-awaited peace to the former colonies and freedom from the Crown. But the struggle for independence was not over. Far from it. Most revolutions in history, after all, end in disaster. For the colonists it would not be a simple matter of transitioning from soldier to citizen or from revolutionary to American. The civic vacuum created by the end of British rule posed a number of immediate and daunting challenges, most of which the fledgling nation was ill prepared to address. The question on everyone's mind was, most assuredly, "What happens next?"

Referred to by scholars as "the critical period" in the nation's history, the 1780s would be the decade that determined if the nascent experiment in popular government would endure. (The experiment would again be challenged during the Civil War.) The newly formed states, after all, distrusted one another and were about to discover that, with the departure of so many loyalists during and after the war, the country had been left with few trained physicians, builders, architects, or other vital professions. It had relatively few banks, institutions of higher learning, libraries, and museums, or even many roads or widely circulating newspapers to connect rural communities across the vast countryside.

There was little manufacturing in the states. Everything from plows to paint to printing presses came from Europe. Indeed, the colonies had been utterly dependent on trade with England, but that partnership was now in jeopardy, and with the economy in shambles from the war, most Americans lacked the finances to ship goods to or buy from other European powers. In fact, with multiple currencies still in use and rendered largely worthless, even trade among the states was problematic. So too did interest on the states' debts greatly exceed the entire federal budget. Despite the dire financial situation, efforts to levy taxes in 1781 and again in 1786 failed, largely owing to ideological inflexibility, leaving some veterans unpaid, the military unprepared, and the new confederation of states deeply in debt.[1]

There were also still threats to security. The British remained at forts along the border with Canada and in the northwestern territories, while the Royal Navy continued to harass American shipping and block full access to the West Indies. American merchant ships operating along the North African coast no longer enjoyed the protection of the powerful Royal Navy and found themselves routinely harassed by pirates who seized their cargo and held their crew hostage for ransom. Relations with Native Americans, many of whom had backed the British during the war, were unsettled, and the Spanish controlled Florida and the important mouth of the Mississippi.

Quite simply, America was an "undeveloped backwater" without a standing army, with little infrastructure, and with even less credibility among the powers of Europe.[2] In the wry observation of the intellectual Thomas Law, the new nation was home to little more than "radicals and rye coffee, slavery and green peas, bugs and statistics."[3] To be sure, America's few cities were little more than towns by European standards and were separated by vast expanses of wilderness.

A political culture was developing, but slowly, and there remained much uncertainty as to how this new form of government would work. The First Congress, much as had been the case with the Continental Congress during the war, was limited in its effectiveness but did manage to compromise and establish important institutions of government. However, some members read newspapers during the proceedings and showed little interest in their job or even a basic understanding of what it was they were to do. In fact, the job was so thankless that, during the new nation's first decade, fully one-third of the members either resigned or decided not to seek another term.

The public was equally curious about, but often dismayed by, their representatives. In one case, spectators arrived in the gallery to observe the First Federal Congress in action but were met by Congressman James Jackson of Georgia who allegedly pointed pistols at them and threatened to shoot anyone who made too much noise. The firebrand from Georgia was known to "hurl ad hominem attacks" strewn with biblical allusions at his colleagues, the press, and the public. Things did not get much better. Just a few years later, Roger Griswold of Connecticut and Matthew Lyon of Vermont attacked one another on the floor of the House with a wooden cane and steel tongs from the fireplace. The embarrassing scuffle occurred in response to Congressman Lyon spewing tobacco spit on Griswold.[4] The nation was off to a rough start.

There were other challenges in establishing a republic. Questions remained about basic rights, courts had to be built and staffed, and the roles and responsibilities of elected officials were still being defined. Each state had different requirements for holding public office and for voting, and women and nonwhites remained disenfranchised. In some states even white men who failed to satisfy the requisite property qualifications were unable to vote. For instance, in Pennsylvania a white man could vote if he paid taxes, but other states, such as Virginia, required ownership of a certain number of acres of land, whereas South Carolina required proof that an individual had a minimum net worth. Either way, others simply did not know when, how, or where to vote, and there were inadequate systems for announcing elections, counting votes, and certifying election results.

One of the main challenges to developing a republican political culture for the new nation, however, was sectionalism. The northern and southern regions of the country seemed to be separate nations to the extent that it was not certain that, should there be a foreign invasion, either side would come to the assistance of the other. The same could be said for many of the states whose citizens remained far more loyal to them than to the new nation. When a Virginian, for example, referred to his "country," he meant *Virginia* rather than the *United States*. Thomas Jefferson, himself a staunch critic of a strong national government, went so far as to ponder whether "these separate independencies, like the petty States of Greece, would be eternally at war with each other, & would become at length the mere partisans & satellites of the leading powers of Europe." Others, such as individuals newly arrived in America, retained deep cultural ties with their country of birth.[5]

The most immediate matter involved the development of a government. It had become apparent that creating a government and then running one would be just as difficult, if not more so, than winning a war for the right to do so. Fortunately, a patchwork system had formed rather quickly in the new states. New Hampshire and South Carolina, for instance, had begun preparing initial state constitutions even before the Declaration of Independence was drafted. Other states followed suit, and by 1777 most of the remaining states, such as Georgia and New York, had constitutions. That same year, after six drafts and considerable debate, the Second Continental Congress finally approved a rudimentary system for governance—the Articles of Confederation. Nevertheless, support was not a foregone conclusion. It would take until March 1, 1781, before the last of the holdout states ratified the Articles.

Ironically, this very system of government was one of the main barriers preventing the budding republic from moving forward after the Revolutionary War. The Articles, which had grown out of wartime urgency, proved to be ineffectual in large measure because of their ad hoc nature and pièce de résistance—their organizing principle was a near paranoia about centralized power. Article III of the "League of Friendship," for instance, specified that the states would remain sovereign and independent and that the one branch of the national government established would do little more than provide "for their common defence, the security of their liberties, and their mutual and general welfare."[6]

While Congress was empowered to make treaties, run a postal service, and coin money, there was no provision for the national legislature to levy taxes, regulate commerce, maintain a standing army, or perform most of the vital functions necessary to recover from the war and build a nation. Washington's former artillery general and friend, Henry Knox, summed up the situation as follows: "The source of all evils of which we complain, and of all those which we apprehend was [the Articles]," which he deemed one of the "weakest and most inefficient [systems] . . . that ever nations were afflicted with."[7] Indeed.

Troublingly, while most leaders recognized that the existing system was unsustainable, there was no agreement on how to improve things or whether to replace the Articles. The founding generation now seemed utterly paralyzed by an early version of ideological inflexibility. For instance, James Madison and Alexander Hamilton tried to address the problem by organizing a convention in Annapolis in 1786. Only a handful of states sent delegates and little was accomplished. After disagreeing, they simply went home. But the Convention built momentum to try again in 1787.

It would take four long years after the Treaty of Paris ended the war before the framers undertook the extraordinary challenge of creating a constitutional system rooted in bold, untested, and liberal ideas. Remarkably, with the glaring exception of not ending slavery, they succeeded spectacularly. Their handiwork remains a beacon of hope and liberty as well as a model for democracy and self-government to countless millions of people around the world.

Obviously much has been written about the "great debates" that both prompted the Constitutional Convention and played out during the momentous summer of 1787. This moment in American history is well-known to most and is rightly celebrated to the present time. However, other debates and pressing challenges were not fully resolved by the framers in Philadelphia. Both before and during the convention, bitter internal political rifts were forming. The most problematic political divide featured, on one side, those who might be said to be "nationalists" in that they supported the establishment of a national (or federal) government and a constitution. Recognizing the pending financial and governing crises, they attempted to resolve them by strengthening the federal government and empowering it to act. On the other side were those who were ideologically opposed to a strong national government and nearly all forms of centralized government. They wanted governing power to be restricted to the states and then only in the narrowest of ways.

These "federalist" and "anti-federalist" factions were named over the issue of whether to ratify the Constitution (1787–90) and sharp disagreement over whether to have a relatively strong federal government (the federalist position) or a government with very limited powers (the anti-federalist position). This general political divide persisted after the debate over ratification of the Constitution and would later become the basis for the first political parties. After the Constitution was ratified, they battled over nearly every issue, including what to do about the states' war debts and whether the country needed a permanent seat of government and, if so, where. As we will see, these two issues became intertwined.[8] All these concerns, along with a growing sectionalism between northern and southern states and a worsening animus between those living on the Eastern Seaboard and those in the more rural western communities, would, regrettably, form enduring divisions in American society.[9]

General Washington attempted to remain above these partisan and sectional frays and did not publicly state his preferences, even though he was in favor of the federalist positions on the need for a constitution, a strong federal government, and other issues, such as paying veterans. During the bitter debate in which anti-federalists criticized the Constitution, Washington countered by heralding the document as "a new phenomenon in the political and moral world, and an astonishing victory gained by enlightened reason over brute force."[10] He was joined ideologically by several other Founders, including John Adams, Benjamin Franklin, John Jay, John Marshall, and Alexander Hamilton, who soon thereafter backed Washington's presidency and government and helped to organize the Federalist Party. This faction enjoyed a base of support largely in the North and in more populated areas.

The anti-federalists were led by such Founders as Patrick Henry, George Mason, and James Monroe. Although the anti-federalists drew some support in New York, Massachusetts, and Rhode Island during the ratification fight, over time the base of their support became more closely identified with rural communities, especially in the South and in the growing West. Thomas Jefferson and James Madison later became the most notable advocates of states' rights and a small federal government, and the anti-federalist coalition evolved into Jefferson's Democratic-Republican Party. The Constitutional Convention of 1787 occasioned a rift in the anti-federalist movement, with Patrick Henry, who proclaimed he "smelt a rat," and others turning down invitations to Philadelphia. They were joined by the state of Rhode Island, which was the only state to refuse to send delegates and whose actions rattled the usually unflappable Washington, who complained that the state "still perseveres in that impolitic, unjust, and one might add without much impropriety scandalous conduct, which seems to have marked all her public councils of late."[11]

Recognizing the inevitability of political parties, James Madison described their centrality in the *Federalist Papers*, explaining, "The regulation of those various and interfering interests forms the principal task of modern legislation, and involves the spirit of party and faction in the necessary and ordinary operations of the government."[12] Sure enough, many former anti-federalists who backed Jefferson would in 1791 form the nucleus of the Jeffersonian Republican Party, commonly referred to as "Republicans" (and named for the form of government known as a republic). They later reorganized as the Democratic-Republican Party.[13] These political divisions hardened and nearly destroyed the new experiment.

Throughout the critical postwar years, Washington discreetly bemoaned the anti-federalist and southern reservations about building a capital city and resolving the country's debt problem, believing the argument that any role for government was a threat to basic liberty to be unfounded. The man who longed for national unity worried that loyalties to faction and ideology might supplant love of country and Constitution. He also correctly predicted the problems that would be created by these nascent factions, writing, "However [political parties] may now and then answer popular ends, they are likely in the course of time and things, to become potent engines, by which cunning, ambitious, and unprincipled men will be enabled to subvert the power of the people."[14] In the postwar years the main challenges to the struggling nation came not from abroad by a foreign power but from within through factions.

The war had just ended, but the future of the new experiment in popular government was already in jeopardy such that Washington, usually guarded about his political opinions, felt it necessary to encourage his countrymen to support the struggling government. Throughout the ensuing debate, however, one unlikely issue in particular threatened to tear it apart, but that same issue also held the promise of saving it.

Historians point to two events as being among the seminal moments in the nation's early history: the act of declaring independence and the drafting of a Constitution. One was messy and violent, the other an attempt to build something new. Both were from the founding period, and both were successful. However, these actions alone did not form the character or course of the United States of America. Rather, there were additional debates that occurred at the end of the war. These "other" debates ended up shaping the drama of democracy in far-reaching ways.

Undeniably, the republic was far from complete in the years after the war, and it was not certain that the United States would even survive those initial months or years. For all their collective wisdom and vision, the Revolutionary generation had not fully planned beyond the fighting. The result was that several potentially ruinous and complicated issues were put off. Unlike the more famous debates of 1776 and 1787, these other debates were so tumultuous that they remained unresolved throughout the war and during both the confederation period and the Constitutional Convention. In fact, the debates continued through the decade and into Washington's two terms as president. Ultimately, they proved to be so divisive that they gridlocked the Congress in 1790, contributed to the rise of the political parties, and proved to be among the most contentious in the country's history.[15]

So what were these other debates? One of the main controversies after independence involved a permanent capital city and all its attending questions.

The idea of a capital had been debated since at least December 1779, but with little progress. That year, with the struggle for independence raging, Congress found itself embroiled in a fight over the location for a temporary capital. Needless to say, the inability to agree on a location from which to lead a revolution was a major embarrassment and nearly undermined the cause of liberty.

The legislative body had been convening in Philadelphia but was seeking another location for the upcoming year. Cities from Burlington and Princeton in New Jersey to Fredericksburg in Virginia and others were considered. But vote after vote failed to get a majority, with southern delegates typically vetoing proposals out of concern that Congress might meet in the north (thus affording northern states added political influence). After a long and fruitless debate, Congress decided simply to remain at the Pennsylvania State House in Philadelphia, the site where it had been meeting since 1775.[16]

When the war ended and Congress was forced to begin planning the details of the new government, it again found its effort "hung up by a debate over what city should be selected as the provisional capital."[17] The upstart colonists had announced their independence, fought a long war, signed the Treaty of Paris ending the long conflict, and then framed a constitution, all without a capital city or even a plan for a permanent seat of government. It was hardly the way to ensure that the new experiment in self-government would work. Lacking a capital city and the basic machinery of governance, the new political experiment was a nation in name only.

Complicating matters was that the Founders were going far beyond the ideas of liberty and self-government contemplated by the classic Greek philosophers or practiced by the Roman Senate. Creating an entirely new system of government that worked would be a precarious undertaking; doing so without a vibrant capital would be a long shot. Moreover, the capital's location and design would have important consequences for the future of slavery, the host city's economy, and perhaps most important, the type of nation the United States would become. It would be a laboratory for republican government. These factors, of course, contributed to the bitter nature of the debate, one that was so foul that it spilled over into nearly every other issue and continually prevented agreement on a home for the new government.

Early on, Philadelphia was a leading contender. It was the cradle of American independence and was the largest and most sophisticated city in the nation. Yet roughly thirty different sites were, at one point or another, proposed as a possible location. These included Annapolis and Baltimore in Maryland; Burlington, Elizabeth, New Brunswick, Newark, Princeton, and Trenton in New Jersey; Albany and New York City in New York; Bethlehem, Easton, Lancaster, Philadelphia, and York in Pennsylvania; Fredericksburg in Virginia; and others.

The District of Columbia and the city of Washington did not exist at the time. Embarrassingly, because of the paralyzing debate over a capital, from 1774 to 1800 Congress ended up convening in nine different cities. At times Congress was chased out of the host city by British forces; at other times their own bickering and indecisiveness caused the relocation. Most of these interim capitals had homes to use as temporary residences and courthouses that could serve as meeting places for Congress, but all of them lacked the public infrastructure necessary for running a national government. The situation remained contentious and far from resolved.

Washington was beginning to recognize the need for a federal capital that would function as a commercial and political hub of the country. This city, he would later hope, would be a beacon for freedom, unite the bickering states, and promote a sense of nationhood. It would end up being built alongside a river he knew well and greatly admired.[18]

It was a novel and audacious, if not wholly unpractical and unrealistic, plan. Washington eventually would need to build support for his vision, unite the squabbling factions, identify the exact location, contend with parochial interests that opposed any site other than one in their home state, convince landowners in the area to sell their property, contend with land speculators eager to monetize every opportunity, raise a considerable amount of funds, hire architects and find enough builders and tradesmen, and see to the capital's construction.

As if that were not enough, this new city would need forts, roads and infrastructure, warehouses and a port, residential housing and residents, and much more. It would certainly not be the small, pastoral "town" the Jeffersonian faction favored; no, the new city's scope would be the most ambitious yet seen on the continent. It would be the physical home of the new nation, but much more—it would shape the future of the republic and be the embodiment of self-government.[19]

Time was of the essence. After so many years without a permanent capital, the fledgling republic desperately needed one. Yet it was a huge challenge to build an entirely new capital. Only a few capitals in history, such as St. Petersburg, Russia, had been built from scratch. In contrast, the great capitals of Europe—Rome, Paris, London—had long histories. It made far more sense to simply select an existing city, such as Philadelphia or New York, as a capital. The effort to build a new capital would likely jeopardize everything the Americans had fought for.[20]

Although he did not enjoy politics, through the struggle over the capital city George Washington would also reveal his skill as a gifted political dealmaker who was not always above wallowing in the political mud or twisting arms for votes.[21] To achieve his goals for the capital city and new nation, Washington pulled an array of political rabbits out of his hat. He is therefore not unlike his successor Abraham Lincoln, who is now appreciated as a political chess master who knew when to be magnanimous and when to act with force. And so did Washington. Lincoln staffed his cabinet with, in the words of his noted biographer Doris Kearns Goodwin, a "team of rivals" and solicited advice from a wide array of perspectives. He also took the long view through short-term setbacks and, to paraphrase the old saying, saw the forest while others bickered about the trees. Yet long before Lincoln, Washington exhibited these same political attributes.[22]

Washington is frequently, though inaccurately, depicted as a leader who never entered a political or partisan fray. In the words of Washington biographer and Pulitzer Prize–winner Ron Chernow, "Sometimes it's portrayed that George Washington somehow floated above the fray, that he was a figurehead and that Hamilton was running it. Not at all. Washington was absolutely on top of everything that was going on."[23] However, when necessary, like Lyndon Johnson, Washington proved to be quite effective lobbying, or sending surrogates to lobby, members of Congress and bringing the full weight of his reputation to bear on an issue. He was even known to play two aides off one another, much as Franklin Roosevelt did. In addition, like John Kennedy, he was always aware of his charisma and used his enormous popularity to achieve his goals. Washington knew when to stand back and let events play out to his advantage. As scholars have said about Dwight Eisenhower's presidency, Washington's could be a "hidden-hand" presidency.[24] At other times, like Theodore Roosevelt or Harry Truman, he knew when to act unilaterally and with expediency and force. He surrounded himself with highly capable men he trusted and let them act, a management style applauded by fans of Ronald Reagan. Yet like Bill Clinton and Barack Obama, he took much personal interest in the details of the issue at hand. Washington was a formidable politician, one who possessed a number of positive traits attributed to those esteemed leaders who followed him in office.[25]

In short, he was the right person for the job of building a capital city. Washington, after all, had a penchant for architecture and was an experienced surveyor. These were his passions. Throughout his adult life, he continually renovated and tinkered with the design of his Mount Vernon home and pursued every opportunity to survey and acquire vast tracts of land. These skills would end up serving him well when dealing with the minutiae of planning a capital city.

In fact, Washington's fingerprints would be on nearly every decision and detail involving the development of a capital city—he would help to select the site, raise the funds, purchase the land, hire the architects, and oversee the city's construction. It was apparent to the members of Congress, who noted that the project "more than anything else had his attention." It became a near obsession for him, consuming his energy and attention such that Washington biographer Douglas Southall Freeman even quipped, "[Washington] scarcely could have found the future seat of government more time-consuming."[26]

After winning the war for independence, presiding over the creation of the Constitution, and establishing a new government as the first president, this struggle would be Washington's final battle and perhaps his most challenging. This book tells that dramatic story. It is, however, first necessary to understand the formative experiences and events in Washington's life that fashioned the skills he would one day need to create a grand capital city and honed his passion for doing so. The initial chapters of the book do just that; the later chapters tell the story of the debates and struggle to build the capital.

The American experiment in republican government was altogether new, meaning there was, one might say, no script to follow after the war. The capital city, like the nation, would be built from scratch. In that respect, the city's birth paralleled the forging of the nation and Washington's own story. Their histories—and their fates—were connected.

PART I

GEORGE WASHINGTON'S EARLY LIFE AND AMERICAN VISION

CHAPTER 1

Surveying a Future

Wisdom is the principal thing; therefore get wisdom:
and with all thy getting get understanding.
Proverbs 4:7

In 1792 an English nobleman approached George Washington and inquired about his ancestry. For a man as sensitive about his image and appearance as Washington, the answer he gave was surprisingly flippant: "I confess I have paid very little attention," responded the president. He went on to explain, "My time has been so much occupied in the busy and active scenes of life from an early period of it that but a small portion of it could have been devoted to researches of this nature."[1]

It may be that Washington's response was simply his way of sidestepping the fact that, although he was the product of a family that enjoyed a degree of prosperity, the Washingtons had not commanded the upper echelons of either English or colonial society. Yet perhaps this seeming indifference to his lineage by the "Father of His Nation" was not surprising at all. America was a new experiment, one that held the promise of new ways of thinking and new ways of organizing society. In the social order that was forming, a person's status would have less to do with pedigree than with merit. What is apparent is that the spirit of adventure and entrepreneurship along with a commitment to justice and public service coursed through the bloodline of the Washington family.

These traits date to at least Washington's great-great-grandfather Lawrence, an Oxford-educated Anglican minister from Oxfordshire. The Reverend Washington

3

enjoyed a degree of notoriety; however, he was forced from his pulpit when puritanical passions reigned in England under Oliver Cromwell. It was his son John, likely motivated by his father's predicament and the English Civil War, which began in 1642, who came to America in search of a better life. Like many other young men in England, he was probably attracted to the many and varied opportunities Britain's North American colonies offered. Thus, in 1656 John crossed the Atlantic to trade tobacco.

During one voyage the ship on which he was sailing, the *Sea Horse*, ran aground in the Chesapeake Bay. John simply decided to stay. A brother named Lawrence joined him in Virginia, and both Washingtons settled in Westmoreland County near the Potomac River.[2]

John Washington did well for himself. He married Anne Pope, the daughter of a wealthy planter, and accumulated vast tracts of land for his tobacco farms. Later, the act of hiring indentured servants from England to work his lands provided him the opportunity to pursue public service as both a politician and military officer. In this capacity he participated in the various military campaigns along the frontier against the native inhabitants. The first Washington to live in the New World ended up burying two wives and marrying three times. By the time of his passing in 1677, at the age of forty-six, John Washington had become part of Virginia's "second-tier gentry" and had amassed thousands of acres of land.[3]

Both John Washington's son and grandson would follow his example, accumulating land, raising tobacco, owning slaves, prospering as traders, pursuing political office, and marrying well. John had a son named Lawrence (both "John" and "Lawrence" were popular family names) who returned to England to be educated. Back in Virginia he married into money, wedding Mildred Warner, whose father served on the King's Council. Like other Washington men, Lawrence was a planter and served in public office. He too would die young. His second son, who was just a boy at the time of Lawrence's passing, was named Augustine and would one day have a son who would lead the colonies to independence.

Lawrence's widow remarried—to an English shipping captain—and returned to England with Augustine and her other children. The historical record is thin, but it appears she died in childbirth and her son Augustine sailed back to Virginia. It would have been a difficult and lonely time for the boy, sailing across the ocean with a stepfather he barely knew and who spent most of his time away at sea.

Unfortunately, there is little we know about George Washington's father other than that he was a tall and strong man. One historical claim suggests that he could "raise up and place in a wagon a mass of iron that two ordinary men could barely raise from the ground." Such stories match those that would later be told about his strapping son.[4] Augustine Washington was also said to be a disciplinarian. Like his predecessors, he married well—to Jane Butler—acquired even more land along the Potomac River, held local public office, and was a trader who did business in England. Augustine Washington and Jane Butler had two boys, Lawrence and a son named for the father, as well as a daughter named for the mother.

Upon his arrival back in Virginia after another business trip to England, Augustine received devastating news. His wife of several years had died. As was the custom of the time, the thirty-seven-year-old widower remarried and did so rather quickly—in 1731—to Mary Ball, who was fourteen years his junior. Yet at twenty-three Mary was considered rather old by eighteenth-century standards to be a first-time bride. A number of descriptions remain about the woman who would be George Washington's mother, but nearly all of them describe her as headstrong, pious, bothersome, and dour. She might be forgiven any personality kinks, however, given her tumultuous upbringing.

Mary's own father, Joseph Ball, was a successful trader from England who died when she was only three. Mary and her mother—Mary Johnson—struggled financially (as did many widows at the time) and socially from an embarrassing family scandal. Joseph, it seems, was a ripe fifty-eight when he married his much younger, illiterate mistress. Mary's mother also died. The orphaned child ended up being placed in the care of George Eskridge, a family friend.[5]

Augustine Washington and Mary Ball lived in a large farmhouse on a few thousand acres near Pope's Creek in eastern Virginia's Westmoreland County.[6] The land was worked by roughly fifty slaves, and despite what appears to have been a strained marriage, the family prospered and had six children—two girls and four boys—of which George was the eldest.[7] Life was precarious in the New World in the eighteenth century, and a younger sister died in infancy. None of George's three older half siblings would reach an advanced age. However, four of George's siblings lived to maturity: Betty, Samuel, Charles, and John Augustine, whose son Bushrod would one day become George's favorite nephew and a member of the US Supreme Court.

George Washington was born on February 11, 1732, a date that would later be altered to February 22, 1732, in the new calendar (in 1752, Britain adopted the Gregorian calendar in order to more accurately reflect the length of a year). Yet Washington always celebrated the former as the date of his birth.[8]

Taking after his father, young George was an exceptionally large baby and was named by his mother in honor of the man who had adopted her when she had been orphaned. When George was three his father moved the family sixty miles to another comfortable plantation at Little Hunting Creek near the Potomac. Little else is known about the young boy's upbringing except that it was marked by hard work and little interaction with his father, who frequently traveled to find markets for his tobacco and produce. Nevertheless, as the son of a family considered "lower Virginia gentry," the burly youth had good prospects. He could count on a formal education, including the possibility of travel to England, and would likely stand to one day inherit several slaves and a sizable plot of land. Fate intervened.

Augustine passed on April 12, 1743, at the age of forty-nine. George was only eleven at the time. As the future president would later describe, "Tho' I was blessed with a good constitution, I was of a short-lived family."[9] The event would dramatically change the boy's life and possibly the course of American history. It was also not the only loss young Washington experienced—his older half sister, Jane, and an infant sister named Mildred also passed away at around the same time.

The sons from Augustine's first marriage inherited the Mount Vernon estate and the Pope's Creek farm, leaving the widow and her children with little. Mary was forced to move to Ferry Farm, a smaller home by the Rappahannock and Potomac Rivers in nearby Fredericksburg. Despite having a large family in her care, Mary Ball Washington never remarried, which was quite uncommon for the time. One consequence of this was that young George had responsibility thrust on him at a tender age in the form of caring for his younger siblings and overseeing the farm. The boy's future prospects were further derailed because of Mary's marginal education and frugality; she did not prioritize her son's education or support new opportunities for him. Whereas Augustine's two sons from his first marriage were educated in England and well traveled, George had only passing instruction that allowed him to learn basic reading, writing, and mathematics. Unlike most of the other Founders, he never attended college and was poorly traveled.

The prudish and private widow also avoided social events. The result was that her son grew up with very limited exposure to the world beyond the farm and their relationship would never be affectionate or close; rather, with the son overly sensitive to criticism and the mother quite prone to offering it, their rapport was always strained. Not surprisingly, as an adult Washington would become somewhat emotionally detached from his overbearing mother.

Mary Ball Washington, like her late husband, was also a disciplinarian. George's childhood contained little in the way of frivolities or amusements. Stern lessons about honesty and hard work were ingrained in her son, traits that would define the man in the years to come. Despite her frugality—or perhaps because of it—in her later years Mary Ball Washington would make constant, unreasonable requests of her eldest son. Although he provided for her financially, she publicly embarrassed him by claiming throughout her eighty-two years that he did not.

Aside from his father's passing, one of the earliest profound influences on the young boy was his half brother Lawrence, fourteen years George's senior, who stepped into the role of surrogate father. Lawrence inspired the teen with stories of his adventures as a naval officer serving under Adm. Edward Vernon. His head filled with swashbuckling tales of honor, naval battles, and faraway lands, George longed to run away and join the navy, but his mother forbade it. Ever dutiful, the fourteen-year-old honored his mother's request that he stay home. It would be milking cows, rather than sailing the seven seas, for young Washington—for the time being. However, a spark had been lit inside the boy. His adolescent yearning for adventure would grow into a burning ambition as a young man.

There was another key influence on the restless teen forced to spend long days working his mother's farm. Her name was Sally Cary Fairfax, and she was two years George's senior.[10] Washington longed for something more, and likely his first glimpse of a better life came courtesy of the wife of George William Fairfax, one of the colony's leading aristocrats.

The Fairfax home—the impressive Belvoir estate—was located not far from Washington's home geographically, but a world apart socially. Young George's luck changed in 1747, when Lord Fairfax employed his teenage neighbor on a survey mission to the unexplored wilderness of the Virginia frontier. The event gave Washington a new occupation. One year later, he was working as the county surveyor for Culpeper County, courtesy of a referral from Fairfax. But the expedition also brought Washington into contact with Sally.

Attractive, witty, social, traveled, well-read, and flirtatious, the daughter of two of Virginia's most prominent families was clearly an unattainable object of young Washington's admiration. Surviving accounts strongly suggest that he was captivated by her beauty and intellect, just as she seemed keen on her young neighbor's charisma and potential.[11] It was Sally, the wealthy, sophisticated socialite, who introduced the brawny and guileless teen to literature, theater, and the art of social discourse. Sitting by her side as she hosted the region's most popular salons, young Washington met and observed the Tidewater's leading citizens and began to visualize new possibilities. Thanks to Sally, he was exposed to the kind of people he would later need to know in order to rise in status.

It was also around this time that the sixteen-year-old surveyor's assistant copied 110 "rules of civility" from a well-known book on etiquette. The maxims, which dated to the sixteenth century, were a great influence on the studious and ambitious teen in terms of honing the development of his character and aiding in his desire to pass himself off as a gentleman who knew how to behave when in good company.[12] One can see the makings of Washington's fondness for etiquette, social ambition, and entry into the ruling class in his time with Mrs. Fairfax. A new door of possibilities had been opened.[13]

Perhaps inspired by Sally's beauty, wealth, and social standing, the young man attempted to court women from the Tidewater who resided well above his social position. He was unsuccessful—initially—and even put pen to paper to express his frustrations:

> Ah! Woe's me, that I should love and conceal,
> Long have I wish'd, but never dare reveal,
> Even though severely Loves Pains I feel.[14]

The other side of history's courageous, indomitable, and seemingly unflappable hero was that Washington had become keenly aware of the clothing he wore, his image, and the fact that he possessed stature and was graced with a natural charisma. George Washington would grow up to be an excellent dancer and a natural in the saddle; a hard worker with a fondness for social events, salted cod, exotic pineapples and Brazil nuts, and madeira; and a leader who was surprisingly guarded and thrifty. Thanks to the Fairfax family, the young surveyor began to survey a better future.[15]

CHAPTER 2

Western Adventures

*A rising nation, spread over a wide and fruitful Land, traversing
all the seas with the rich production of their Industry.*
Thomas Jefferson

In so many ways Washington's life as a planter, his relentless pursuit to acquire more land, and his time spent in the westernmost edge of the colonies—first as a teenage surveyor, then as a soldier fighting on Britain's westernmost possessions, and eventually as an investor—shaped his character. But the future president's passion for developing the American West and his vision for the future of the new nation were also forged during his youth.[1]

The socialite Sally Fairfax exposed the young Washington to high society and nurtured his potential, but it was her husband, George William Fairfax, who introduced the teenager to the West. Born into affluence in the Bahamas, Fairfax was the son of a British lord and colonial governor. In 1747 he sailed to Virginia, where he established the vast Belvoir plantation near the Potomac River. The Washington and Fairfax families, although occupying different rungs within Virginia's Tidewater aristocracy, were close; William Fairfax's older sister, Anne, had married George Washington's older half brother, Lawrence.

It was from the Belvoir estate that Fairfax hired young Washington to assist him in surveying his western land holdings and those of his cousin, Lord Thomas Fairfax. And so at sixteen Washington was part of a monthlong surveying expedition that changed his life. The party journeyed through the rugged highlands of Virginia and the scenic Shenandoah Valley, camping in the wilds as they traveled. The adventure taught Washington a trade but also infatuated the teenager to the extent that surveying, acquiring land, and settling the West would become lifelong passions and later figure prominently in his plans for the nation.

Fairfax would further help Washington in 1749 by securing for him the job of surveyor for Culpeper County. That next year the young man purchased his first tract of land. Washington, who was quite smitten with Mrs. Fairfax and owed much to Mr. Fairfax, would later be devastated when the couple, along with countless other loyalists, returned to England just before the start of the fighting in the Revolutionary War. However, this early expedition and experience forever formed Washington's belief in the potential for the colonies to grow westward.[2]

Meanwhile, with his marriage to a Fairfax and his own aggressive acquisition of lands, George's older half brother, Lawrence, rose through Virginia's political, social, and military ranks. He served in the colony's House of Burgesses and was made adjutant general in the colonial militia. Like his younger half brother, Lawrence would also look westward, tying his economic and political future to the new Ohio Company and his land acquisitions in the fertile Ohio region.

However, Lawrence's health deteriorated, the result of an illness—most likely tuberculosis—he had contracted years before while serving as a colonial officer under Adm. Edward Vernon off the coast of Cartagena in South America. Desperate for a cure, the older Washington brother traveled to England, the warm springs of present-day Berkeley in West Virginia, and elsewhere. Nothing worked; he was dying.[3]

Still seeking relief from his malady, Lawrence heeded the advice of a physician who suggested the tropical climate of Barbados. Therefore, in 1751 Lawrence set sail for the island, taking his younger half brother with him. It was George's first and only trip outside the original thirteen colonies and their western borders, and it was not without consequence. The younger Washington contracted smallpox in Barbados. However, the journey was a blessing in disguise, for the malady likely saved him and the revolution. When smallpox ravaged the countryside during the war, Washington, having suffered the disease, was immune. He had also learned in Barbados the importance of inoculating himself and others in a procedure then known as variolation. Moreover, with Lawrence too ill during the visit to Barbados, teenage George was sent in his place to meet with officials and military commanders on the British-controlled island, an opportunity that stoked George's passion for a career in uniform and bolstered his confidence. As for Lawrence, the climate did not help. He died in 1752 from the ailment at just thirty-four.

Lawrence had named his estate overlooking the Potomac River for his former naval commander. It sat on land Lawrence's great-grandfather had acquired eight decades earlier and enjoyed a commanding view of the Potomac. By the 1750s the Mount Vernon estate was titled at five thousand acres, including twenty-five hundred acres bordered by the Dogue and Little Hunting Creeks. On his passing, Lawrence's widow, Anne, inherited the plantation, but after she had remarried, George purchased Mount Vernon. The young man would later obtain the other twenty-five hundred acres of the original tract of farmland, eventually acquiring an additional thirty-five hundred acres.

Young Washington had grown up idolizing his older half brother and wanting to pursue a similar life for himself. That was about to happen. Because Lawrence had been an officer and thanks to both his business investments in the new Ohio Territory and partnership in the enterprise with the colony's lieutenant governor, Robert Dinwiddie, George was offered a commission as an officer in the Virginia militia—by none other than Dinwiddie. His first major assignment would be to secure his late half brother's investments in the West. The mission was of much importance, for the western lands figured prominently into the plans to develop and assert English influence in the region and enrich the pockets of leading citizens of Virginia. The resulting fight over these western lands would mark one of the lowest and highest moments of Washington's career, but it would also shape his future and that of the United States.

Twenty years before the signing of the Declaration of Independence, Benjamin Franklin raised the prospect that Europeans would settle in America in great numbers and expand westward across the new land. The result, Franklin predicted in a pamphlet, was that the great wilderness continent would influence the politics of the colonies and open an array of new economic and social possibilities for those of European heritage. Tragically, it would also lead to the decimation of Native Americans. One of the readers of Franklin's essay was a young John Adams. He, like George Washington and so many other Founders, was intrigued by the West and the way it might shape the future of the country. Adams even wondered if global political power would begin to shift to North America or if the British throne would relocate to her American colonies. After all, the colonies were viewed by many in Europe as a utopia—an agrarian paradise that attracted many Europeans.[4]

Both the British and French saw the political and economic benefits of controlling the vast western region beyond the Appalachians, starting with Ohio. By the 1750s the choice land by the Allegheny, Monongahela, and Ohio Rivers (near present-day Pittsburgh) was attracting traders, investors, and the new Ohio Company, which began aggressively acquiring land in the region. However, their investments were jeopardized by French encroachment in the region. Attempting to check British ambitions, French forces had moved from Fort Niagara on Lake Ontario into the Ohio River Valley and had begun forcing English settlers out of their homes and erecting small forts in the region, including Fort Presque Isle near Lake Erie and Fort Le Boeuf near the Ohio River.

In October 1753 King George II responded by decreeing that the Ohio Valley belonged to Britain and non-English settlers must leave or be driven out by force. It was a direct warning to the French. To implement the decree, Lieutenant Governor Dinwiddie dispatched a diplomatic mission ordering the French to abandon the forts and leave Ohio. The man Dinwiddie picked to lead the mission was twenty-one-year-old George Washington. The young Virginian was given his late half brother's job with the rank of major in the colony's militia, although he lacked military experience. It would soon show.

Washington set off with a small party to Fort Le Boeuf in the Ohio Valley in December 1753 to inform the French of the king's order. The Virginians made it through Iroquois territory without incident and arrived at the French outpost on December 11 to deliver the ultimatum to the fort's commander. The reception was not what Washington expected. His warning was flatly rejected, and the young officer was given a letter saying that the English king had no influence over the French. Humiliated by the rebuke, Washington wanted to deliver the news to Williamsburg as quickly as possible, but freezing temperatures, thick forests, and deep snow delayed the group. To save time, their commander proceeded to race ahead with only one guide. The rash decision nearly cost him his life—twice. The two men were fired on by Indians, and later, while on the icy Allegheny River, Washington fell out of a raft and nearly drowned.

Washington made it back to Williamsburg on January 6, 1754, and delivered the bad news to the lieutenant governor. Dinwiddie requested a thorough written report on the situation, which the young officer was happy to submit. Eager to protect his own investments in the Ohio Territory and build British support for defending the region, Dinwiddie published Washington's somewhat embellished narrative under the title "The Journal of Major George Washington" and then propagandized the British "cause" in the West by having it reprinted throughout the colonies and in London. The young major who had just celebrated his twenty-second birthday found his name being spoken everywhere. He was promoted to the rank of lieutenant colonel and was about to become a pawn in the struggle for the American West.[5]

In response to the French slight, Dinwiddie promptly ordered small fortifications be built by the junction of the three rivers and along the important western trade route. However, in April a numerically superior French force drove the British out and commandeered one of the partially built forts, which they renamed in honor of the Marquis de Duquesne, the governor of "New France." The act heightened tensions and prompted Dinwiddie to send a small, armed force back to the region to monitor French activities. For the task, he appointed an English-born, Oxford-educated former professor at the College of William and Mary named Joshua Fry. But Fry died on the eve of the mission because of injuries sustained from being thrown from his horse.

Command passed to Washington, who enthusiastically accepted the opportunity. Dinwiddie knew Washington shared his view of the importance of the Ohio region; the lieutenant governor also correctly believed his new officer to be loyal and fearless. Therefore, Washington returned to what is now western Pennsylvania in May 1754 in command of roughly forty sparsely provisioned and undisciplined militiamen and a few native scouts. Eager to legitimize his command, the young officer obtained red uniforms for his men, attire usually reserved for British regulars, not militiamen, and reflecting the importance of the mission and larger interests in the Ohio by both Dinwiddie and the British.

The inexperienced commander pushed his men at a relentless pace, marching westward at nights and even through a downpour. As might be expected, during the dark, moonless nights the men became disoriented in the forests. By the time the unit found its way to Fort Duquesne, a few men were missing; presumably they had either gotten lost or wisely abandoned their relentless and reckless young lieutenant colonel.[6]

Washington finally allowed the men to rest and set up camp at a place known as Great Meadows. But only briefly. After discovering that French soldiers were nearby, Washington boldly—or perhaps foolishly—went in search of them on the evening of May 28. That night he encountered a Mingo-Seneca chief named Tanaghrisson, more commonly known as Half King.[7] The chief helped the Virginians locate the French; his reason for doing so would soon become apparent.[8]

At dawn the colonials and their Indian allies spotted the small French unit camped in a ravine surrounded by boulders. Surprisingly, the French had not posted sentries, allowing Washington to surround the camp. What they saw in the dim, predawn light was a detachment of roughly thirty French soldiers, either asleep or stirring from their slumber and beginning to prepare breakfast. Against orders that he was only to *monitor* French movements, Washington directed his men to open fire.

The ensuing skirmish lasted only about fifteen minutes and was a lopsided victory for the Virginians, who suffered only one dead and two wounded. There were, according to Washington, ten French killed, and the remaining twenty soldiers, including the commander, Joseph Coulon de Villiers, a thirty-five-year-old diplomat holding the title of Sieur de Jumonville, were captured. One Frenchman escaped the ambush and managed to make it back to Fort Duquesne to tell the story. His escape ended up changing history because of what happened next.[9]

Both sides claimed the other had started the fight. The French, whose version seems more plausible, maintained that Jumonville's men were part of a diplomatic mission, but Washington believed they were lying and were actually preparing to attack the British. Washington reported, "They informed me that they had been sent with a summons to order me to depart. A plausible pretense to discover our camp and to obtain the knowledge of our forces and our situation!"[10] Lieutenant Governor Dinwiddie, of course, accepted Washington's version of the story and claimed the incident was a military victory, writing to his young officer, "I heartily congratulate you, as it may give a testimony to the Ind[ians] that the French are not invincible w[he]n fairly engaged with the English."[11]

Although the details are unclear, it also seems that the unseasoned Washington failed to control his Indian allies and settle the terms of the surrender appropriately and according to custom. It turned out that Chief Tanaghrisson had a history with his enemies such that, when Jumonville was detained in a manner unbecoming an officer, the chief seized the opportunity to kill the French aristocrat with a hatchet, splitting open the man's head and then scalping him. Washington described Tanaghrisson's intention: "To knock the poor, unhappy wounded on the head and bereave them of their scalps."[12] What's more, not only was the French officer treated like a common prisoner and murdered under Washington's watch, but the naive Virginian callously vacated the battlefield without seeing that the enemy dead were properly buried.[13]

Young and overly eager, Washington described the clash in brash terms, not initially realizing the gravity of his mistakes. To his younger brother, he wrote, "I fortunately escaped without any wound, for the right wing, where I stood, was exposed to and received all the enemy's fire, and it was the part where the man was killed, and the rest wounded." He then added indelicately, "I heard the Bulletts whistle, and, believe me there is something charming in the sound." Years later, when the British were at war with their former colonies, Washington's boast was published in London and became a source of ridicule. Even the king scoffed about his foe's reference to the sound of bullets as "charming," writing, "He would not so, if he had been used to hear many."[14]

The so-called Jumonville affair, which occurred not far from the forks of the Ohio, was the spark that ignited the French and Indian War. It ended up being a global struggle that claimed over a million lives and was known in Europe as the Seven Years' War. Ironically, the debt amassed winning the war was a key factor behind Britain's decision to tax its North American colonies, which, in turn, prompted the colonials to revolt. Alternatively, in the poetic words of the English historian and politician Horace Walpole, "The volley fired by a young Virginian in the backwoods of America set the world on fire."[15]

Yet Washington was not relieved of command for his mistake, nor was he ridiculed back in Virginia. Rather, he was promoted. The young Virginian's unprompted attack on the French diplomatic party played into Lieutenant Governor Dinwiddie's ulterior motives. Eager to assert English control in the Ohio region and protect his own investment, the scuffle was the pretext he and others needed for war.

The next month Washington was promoted to the rank of colonel, given command of over 150 men, and sent back to the region. The mission now called for the defense of English settlements and investments in the area as well as making a show of force designed to deter French ambitions. Washington also undertook the task of building a road across Virginia and Pennsylvania to the three rivers, the beginning of a lifetime of efforts to enhance transportation and trade with the region.

In late May 1754 Washington's regiment arrived at Great Meadows not far from the site of the Battle of Jumonville, which is just over fifty miles southeast of what is today Pittsburgh. Over a hundred British regulars arrived from South Carolina on June 9 to supplement Washington's small army. Nevertheless, these gains in strength were offset when Chief Tanaghrisson and his native scouts, impatient with their inexperienced commander and alarmed by reports of a sizable French and Indian force on the march from Fort Duquesne, abandoned the effort.

The young commander assumed the French would attack, so he ordered a fort be built. Washington's "fort" was not much of one—a small wooden palisade measuring roughly fifty-three feet in diameter. The circular stockade protected a storage shed filled with supplies, but not much more. A few low earthworks and trenches were dug around the fortress, and nine swivel guns were mounted on wooden blocks to supplement the meager defenses. The commander also ordered that a fifty-yard "field of fire" around the stockade be cleared of trees and brush. The problem was that muskets could reach farther than that distance, especially if they were fired down from higher ground, which would soon be the case.

Washington's defensive measures were surely constrained by time, as he likely assumed the French would attack at any moment, but also by his inexperience and stubborn unwillingness to listen to the seasoned veterans within the ranks. The location of the camp could scarcely have been worse—it was in a low-lying, marshy field surrounded by thickly forested woods. The French would be shooting fish in a barrel from the high ground and from behind the protection of trees.

The fortifications were completed on July 1, and Washington wrote confidently to Dinwiddie two days later, "We have just finish'd a small palisaded fort, in which, with my small numbers, I shall not fear the attack of 500 men." He named his handiwork Fort Necessity.[16]

Sure enough, reports that the French were marching from Fort Duquesne proved true. Around six hundred French regulars, Canadian militia, and Indian allies arrived in the woods surrounding Fort Necessity on the morning of July 3. It was about to get worse—it started to rain. The ground on which Washington's men camped was soon a swamp. Moreover, it turned out that the commander of the French army was none other than Louis Coulon de Villiers, brother of the dead French diplomat, and he was determined to have his revenge.

The fighting began amid heavy rain. The French had the advantage in terms of troop strength, supplies, terrain, and weather. French sharpshooters in the trees picked off Washington's men one at a time. Washington's army put up a determined defense, but it was futile. They were losing far more men than the French, and the outcome was inevitable. Washington had little choice but to surrender.

The terms of the agreement, signed around midnight on July 7, were generous. The British troops and their colonial allies could go free, back to Virginia with their muskets. However, they would have to surrender their swivel guns, and their commander would have to sign a document admitting that he had "killed" Jumonville. Washington signed the negotiated settlement but claimed he did not understand the French translation. He had affixed his name to an admission that he had actually "assassinated" the French diplomat.

The Battle of Fort Necessity was a disaster for the British. It failed to secure the important Ohio River Valley and emboldened the French and their Indian allies. But it was even worse for Washington. His second mistake in two commands exposed him as inexperienced and headstrong. Washington was removed from his position, and his units were divided and placed under the command of various captains. Lest he be demoted in rank or fired, however, he quickly resigned. Washington was just twenty-two, and his fleeting dreams of military glory and western adventure appeared over.

CHAPTER 3

The Dispensations
of Providence

I hope I shall possess firmness and virtue enough
to maintain what I consider the most enviable of
all titles, the character of an honest man.

George Washington

Washington was given one more opportunity to redeem himself militarily, and it too came courtesy of the West. English investors, settlers, and political leaders were not happy with the French military successes in the Ohio River Valley. They petitioned for reinforcements and an expansion of the conflict. They got both. It was time to get serious: Maj. Gen. Edward Braddock, a career soldier with forty-five years in uniform, was appointed commander of all British forces in North America. He arrived in the colonies with two full regiments of infantry and announced that beginning in the spring of 1755 he would personally lead the attack on the western French forts, including Fort Duquesne.

However, there was a secondary motive behind the Braddock campaign. More than French and Indians were at stake—there was money to be made from a lucrative trade route westward. Five colonial governors met with General Braddock in Alexandria. Each one, along with leaders from Philadelphia, wanted a trade route to Ohio. They also worried about competing with Virginia's Potomac-Ohio trade alliance. The Pennsylvania delegation proposed a route across its state; leaders from Virginia and Maryland, along with Colonel Washington, countered by advocating the Potomac as the starting point for a western trail to link the two major river systems. Braddock also preferred a trade route to the Ohio using the Potomac, yet in an effort to appease both factions, his army marched west through Pennsylvania to establish another route to the Ohio region. The competition for the West only grew from there.

First, there were the usual social pleasantries expected by the aristocratic class to which Braddock had to attend. A grand ball was organized for the famous general in the colonial capital of Williamsburg. One of the special guests was Washington's muse and neighbor, Sally Cary Fairfax. The wealthy wife of Lord Fairfax needed an escort for the event, and Washington was happy to accompany one of the leading socialites of Virginia.

At the ball Washington observed with envy a lengthy line of fashionable women in queue for the opportunity to dance with the dashing British general in full dress uniform. One of them was Sally. The itch to be back in uniform—and perhaps to be Braddock—was such that Washington jumped at the opportunity to reenlist as a colonial aide, despite the general's dismissive view of the fighting abilities of the continentals. Washington was back in the game, and perhaps more important, Sally took notice.[1]

The year prior Washington had hacked and carved a trail—known as the "Namacolin Trail" for the Lenape Indian who originally founded the path—westward to the headwaters of the Ohio River Valley. Washington's trail would end up playing an important role in the politics of western expansionism. Correspondingly, as one of the few Englishmen to have actually been to Fort Duquesne and the one most familiar with the long trail, the young colonial aide proved valuable to the expedition. General Braddock not only proceeded along parts of this trail but also ordered his army to widen the road to twelve feet, thereby accommodating the wagons and artillery in tow.[2] The effort would later benefit transportation and trade but was time-consuming and slowed the attack.

A massive line of over two thousand British regulars and over four hundred colonial recruits, including a young Daniel Boone and Daniel Morgan, snaked for miles through the thick forests of western Pennsylvania. They passed the site where Washington had engaged the French, which must have evoked difficult memories for the young aide. One British officer noted, "We marched about two Mile the other side ye great Meadows. It was strongly imagined if we met with any opposition, ye Meadows would be ye place; but we marched through without any Molestation or alarm."[3]

As he was nearing the French stronghold, Braddock realized he needed to hasten the pace of his advance, so he split his army in two. In command of the front line, Braddock rushed forward with fifteen hundred men and a few cannons. Despite being so sick that he could barely march or ride, Washington so wanted to be a part of the attack that he joined Braddock. Braddock's senior officer—Col. Thomas Dunbar—followed some distance behind with the remainder of the troops and most of the supplies.

Overconfident and dismissive of the abilities of the French and Indians, Braddock foolishly continued through the thick forests in a long, exposed, thin column with the rear of his army too far behind the front line to be of any use if they were attacked. He also ignored the warnings of his junior staff and aides like Washington to post scouts in advance of the army and through the thick woods. This would prove to be his undoing.[4]

The expeditionary force neared the forks of the Ohio River in early July 1755, crossing the Monongahela on the ninth. The attack occurred later that same day. Braddock had unwittingly marched his army into a trap, one that would claim the lives of every officer in the forward column and hundreds of British soldiers. From the cover of the forest, a few hundred French defenders and a sizable force of Indians poured deadly volleys into the exposed red line. Braddock was among the first hit. Shot in the chest, the commander fell mortally wounded. The ambush quickly turned into a complete rout.

The exposed redcoats began to panic, putting the entire forward force in jeopardy. However, a fast-thinking Washington mounted a horse and rode between the army and its attackers, placing himself in harm's way. As he did, he drew enemy fire while shouting directions for an orderly retreat. A more mature Washington, one both tempered by war and humbled by nearly dying, later described the "horror" of losing hundreds of men and their commander, recalling, "The dead, the dying, the groans, the lamentation, and crys along the Road of the wounded for help . . . were enough to pierce a heart of adamant."[5]

Washington managed to orchestrate a somewhat orderly withdrawal, leading the British force back down the road to rejoin Colonel Dunbar's column. They paused long enough to bury their dead commander, placing the body in the path of the trail. Washington then ordered the army to march over it to obscure the resting place, lest the local Indians exhume and desecrate the corpse.

British captain Robert Orme, one of the officers in Dunbar's column, described on July 11 what happened next: "It was found necessary to clear some wagons for the wounded, many of whom were in a desperate situation; and as it was impossible to remove the stores, the Howitzer shells, some twelve pound shot, powder, and provision, were destroyed or buried." That done, what remained of the once-proud army hurried through hostile territory back to Maryland. Periodically, they passed abandoned Indian villages with fires still burning and heard from the thick forests the war cries of Indians celebrating the victory. Captain Orme observed of the macabre celebration, "They had marked in triumph upon trees, the scalps they had taken two days before."[6]

The only officer from Braddock's advance column to survive the attack, Washington rode back to Maryland at the head of the army. He wrote to his brother a few days later describing the battle: "But by the all-powerful dispensations of Providence, I have been protected beyond all human probability or expectation; for I had four bullets through my coat, and two horses shot under me, yet escaped unhurt, although death was leveling my companions on ever side of me." Washington had saved hundreds of soldiers from certain death or capture; he had also redeemed himself and salvaged his reputation. Once reckless and headstrong, the young officer showed himself capable of being courageous in the face of death and calm under fire.[7]

The Battle of Monongahela was an unmitigated disaster for the British; throughout Virginia the news of the defeat was met by shock. However, for Washington there was an upside. Promoted to the rank of colonel, he replaced Braddock and, over the ensuing three years, was sent back west to defend the vast frontier with his Virginia Regiment.

Thanks to a patriotic and opportunistic Presbyterian preacher with a penchant for hyperbole and oratory named Samuel Davies, the young Virginian's name and feats in battle were praised throughout the colonies. The reverend, who hailed from Hanover, Virginia, and later served as the president of the College of Princeton, delivered a series of sermons titled "Religion and Patriotism, the Constituents of a Good Soldier." They were published as a pamphlet and then read aloud throughout the colonies to citizens eager for good news and a hero. In his account Davies extolled Washington's bravery and heroics, suggesting, "I may point out to the Public that heroic Youth Col. Washington, who I cannot but hope Providence has hitherto preserved in so signal a Manner for some important Service to his Country."[8]

The war brought Washington experience and fame. He managed again to make it through bloody battles untouched, but after lodging numerous complaints about unfair treatment and longing unrealistically for further promotion and glory, he finally ended his service to the Crown in 1758. Washington had learned a lot about warfare and leadership but also about the potential of the undiscovered lands of the West. Another passion was now burning inside him.

The French and Indian War ended in 1763, quite favorably for the British. Their attention—and Washington's—naturally turned west to the lucrative Ohio River Valley. Lieutenant Governor Robert Dinwiddie had, in a 1754 proclamation, offered lucrative land deals totaling some two hundred thousand acres as a means of enticing soldiers to enlist. Washington petitioned the colony that the deal be available to officers as well. Dinwiddie and other colonial authorities agreed, and Washington procured fifteen thousand choice acres, even purchasing additional lands from other veterans, including another thirty thousand acres near the Ohio River and its tributary, the Kanawha River. His bold move angered some who accused the young officer of opportunism by preying on cash-poor veterans and securing the best lands for himself (it should be noted that the average soldier received four hundred acres). The Virginian defended himself, maintaining somewhat arrogantly that, without "my unremitting attention to every circumstance, not a single acre of Land ever would have been obtained." Perhaps.[9]

Washington now owned his late half brother's Mount Vernon estate and vast and lucrative lands in the West. Washington shared his late half brother's passion for Ohio, stating, "There is no richer, or more valuable land in all that Region." Yet he never seemed content. Although he had his military pension, investments, and later a considerable fortune courtesy of marriage, Washington was always trying to purchase additional land around Norfolk, along the Potomac, in the Mohawk Valley of New York, out west in Kentucky, and on the trail to the Ohio River.[10]

With the experience he had gained building a primitive road west to the Ohio River a few years earlier, Washington pushed to further open the West and supported an expansion of both the colony's and the western territory's system of roads and canals. By the 1770s he and other colonial leaders succeeded in linking the Potomac River to the Ohio. Truly, "no one had grander visions than George Washington" for the commercial development of a grand western branch of the American empire.[11]

His ambition and confidence stoked by his western adventures, Washington remained keenly interested in the political and economic importance of the West—investing in trade, selling his produce, and acquiring land. To his Revolutionary general and friend Henry Knox, Washington predicted the western territories would become the "fastest growing" part of not only the new nation but also of the world. There were, therefore, great political and economic benefits to be gained by developing the western lands. He also suspected that immigrants who might align themselves with Spain or Britain would largely settle the western lands. "They will become a distinct people from us, have different views, different interests," Washington worried, "and instead of adding strength to the Union, may in case of a rupture with either of those powers, be a formidable and dangerous neighbor."[12]

Therefore, prompted by both vision and self-interest, Washington proposed that routes such as the Potomac River and his western trails and roads be enhanced in order to provide social, political, and economic ties between the Eastern Seaboard and the new territories. These views also reflect Washington's understanding of the need for a strong and united nation.[13]

In his travels west as a young man, Washington had stumbled militarily, but he would emerge as a hero and wealthy landowner. Like the West he admired, he was raw, restless, and filled with potential. Still burning with ambition, his head filled with dreams of land and a "continental vision," Washington, it can be said, was growing up together with the American West. Quite possibly, had he not gone to the western edge of British North America as a young man, history may very well have turned out quite differently.[14]

CHAPTER 4

Potomac Fever

*The heavens declare the Glory of God, and
the firmament showeth His handiwork.*
Psalm 19:1

The young Washington had a keen interest in land acquisition and development in the western border of the colonies, but perhaps his main passion
was the Potomac River. In hindsight it seems obvious that Washington would
desire to place the capital city on the banks of his beloved river.

The ambitious vision for the new nation he formulated as an adult was
shaped by an understanding of the importance of rivers to trade, transportation,
and the future development of the colonies. Washington recognized that several
waterways and regions in particular held the most potential to shape the future
of the country. Each was navigable, helped to connect the Atlantic Ocean to
the inland west, and passed through important population centers and fertile
lands. They would, of course, require both the building of canals and continued
dredging and other efforts to improve and maintain their navigability.

The first waterways included the Hudson and Mohawk Rivers in New York,
along with the Great Lakes to the north and west. The second encompassed the
Delaware, Schuylkill, and Susquehanna Rivers. Importantly, the first two rivers
came together at Philadelphia and ran into the Delaware Bay and then to the
Atlantic, while the Susquehanna joined New York and central Pennsylvania along
with such important cities as Harrisburg. With its access to the Chesapeake Bay
and with canals and navigational improvements, these systems had the potential

to link Harrisburg, Baltimore, Annapolis, and other critical places in the mid-Atlantic region. The third water system included the James, Great Kanawha, and Ohio Rivers, all of which, with canals and navigational enhancements, might one day help to link the East Coast with the West. Finally, the fourth set of waterways included the Allegheny, Potomac, Monongahela, and Ohio Rivers, which also provided access to the interior part of the new country.

Washington had invested in land and development projects along some of these waterways and believed they were the key to the nation's future. In particular, he saw the Potomac as the most critical waterway in the nation and understood its potential to link the East Coast with the Ohio River Valley. He also just so happened to live on the banks of the Potomac, and this would later factor into the selection of the site of the new nation's capital.[1]

To say the Virginian was fascinated with the important waterway is an understatement. Quite simply, Washington had what one historian described as "Potomac Fever."[2] Another historian referred to his near obsession with development of the river as a "malady."[3] Washington proudly boasted that the Potomac would become the most important waterway in America—for several reasons: it would promote trade both within America and internationally, as it could be used to get agricultural goods to marketplaces and ports, and the river, along with canals and roadways, was the answer to uniting the people of the vast new country. Even as a young man, Washington both foresaw and advocated for the construction of canals and roadways radiating westward from the Potomac. Thus, a young Washington offered the heady wager that it would one day assume its place among the world's great rivers—alongside the Seine, Thames, Danube, and Rhine.[4]

Others shared Washington's enthusiasm, although perhaps not his prediction. John Ferdinand Smyth, an English traveler to Virginia in 1784, wrote of the Potomac that it was "certainly the most noble, excellent, and beautiful river . . . in the universe." He went on to gush, "every advantage, every elegance, every charm . . . is heaped with liberality and even profusion on the delightful banks of this most noble and superlatively grand river." Wow![5]

However, not everyone shared Washington's passion for the river, as he would later discover while promoting the location as the site for the capital city. The Potomac region was still extremely rural, prompting Thomas Sedgwick of Massachusetts to grumble, "The climate of the Patowmack is not only unhealthy, but destructive to northern constitutions. Vast numbers of eastern adventurers have gone to the Southern states, and all have found their graves there."[6]

Washington's vision and passion for the river is perhaps best captured in the famous 1796 painting by Edward Savage, which depicts the patriarch and his family sitting contentedly by a window, the Potomac appearing prominently in the background. With a large globe of the world nearby, the general's left hand rests atop a map of the new capital city. The painting depicts the role the river would have in forging George Washington's political views and vision for the nation.[7]

One of America's most historic rivers, the Potomac flows roughly four hundred miles from the Allegheny Mountains and through present-day West Virginia, Maryland, Virginia, and the District of Columbia before it empties into the Chesapeake Bay and Atlantic Ocean. Scientists date the river's origin to roughly two million years ago and believe it was given its shape by the rising and lowering of the ocean levels and through the force of the white waters that once coursed through much of her path. The Great Falls section of the river, however, was likely carved by retreating glaciers.

It is a diverse waterway with a South Branch and North Branch. The former begins as a small, meandering stream flowing across West Virginia and then into Virginia, including through wild forests and mountains. The North Branch begins at Fairfax Stone in West Virginia and winds through a variety of landscapes and waterways, including Jennings Randolph Lake, a dam, and the eastern Allegheny Mountains, before flowing through western Maryland.

Long before the arrival of Europeans, indigenous peoples visited the area and established communities along the length of the river. Archaeologists have unearthed tools and implements in significant numbers made from river stones dating back some four thousand years. Some of the earliest inhabitants were Algonquian people known as Nacotchtank, who established a major trading center along the river and lived in the present-day District of Columbia. The English fur trader Henry Fleet visited a Nacotchtank village, noting it was called Tohoga, and from his descriptions, it appears the settlement was on the site of Georgetown University today. The Nacotchtank and other people in the region spoke Algonquian and named the river Patowmeck (sometimes listed as Potowmack or Petomek). The name likely comes from the term for making an offering or tribute, which can also be loosely translated as "something brought." Other First Americans referred to branches of the river as Patawomke, Wappatomaka, or Wapacomo. The Anglicized name "Potomac" became official in 1931.[8]

When the English organized their first American colony in the region at Jamestown in 1607, they recorded that three major nations inhabited the Potomac and Chesapeake: the Powhatan, which also included the Patowomeck and Doeg tribes and settled primarily on the Virginia side of the river; the Piscataway, which occupied the Maryland portion of the river; and the Nanticoke. Most of the tribes in the area were part of these three chiefdoms, spoke a dialect of Algonquian, and built basic wigwams with a similar design.

These first residents in the region were likely attracted to the mild climate found for much of the year and the rich soil lining the shores of the river. Along the river's floodplains beans, corn, potatoes, and squash grew in abundance to supplement the many varieties of fish that inhabit the river. The region's dense forests teamed with turkey, deer, elk, and other game, providing a near limitless supply of fur, meat, and wood. The result was that the river could sustain a growing and prosperous population that later built wooden longhouses and communities up and down its banks.

The Potomac was also an early source of transportation for native peoples and facilitated the settling of the entire mid-Atlantic region. A natural crossroads between north and south as well as the coastal plains with the wooded interior, the river enabled them to trade throughout the Chesapeake and beyond. These natural advantages of the river later inspired George Washington. Like the native peoples before them, the earliest European explorers and settlers in the region were attracted by the fertile lands, the abundance of game, and the access the river gave them to both the coast and interior lands.

The Spanish, hoping to find gold, were the first to arrive. They began exploring the Chesapeake and Potomac in the year 1562, with the Spanish adventurer Diego Gutiérrez making perhaps the first detailed maps of the river and cataloguing the flora, fauna, people, and geography of the region he called Bahia de Santa Maria. Other early European visitors to the area were fur traders, many of whom were French. They scouted and plied the Potomac but did not establish settlements. One of the first Englishmen to visit the Potomac was Capt. John Smith of Pocahontas fame, who founded the English colony of Virginia farther south along the James River in 1607, a half century before George Washington's great-grandfather arrived by ship in the colony.[9]

Like Washington after him, Captain Smith appreciated the river's width and navigability and marveled at its falls and rapids. Part of the Virginia Company, the Jamestown Colony was established to find gold, organize trade, and stake an English claim in America. The ensuing years, however, were plagued by bad weather and a lack of planning, familiarity with the land, and skilled settlers. Many of the new arrivals died rather quickly, and the venture failed despite the assistance from the Powhatan, who initially fed the starving colonists.

Despite the setbacks, European exploration and settlement of the region continued through the seventeenth and eighteenth centuries. Tragically, the first and second centuries of contact were often defined by a clash of cultures as the

European colonists grabbed land and raided villages. Relations soured with the native inhabitants and led to a series of wars and violence, then to displacement and forced migrations. Europeans also passed along diseases for which the indigenous peoples had no immunity. The subsequent scourges soon decimated the local population, with historians estimating that, in just the first half century after European contact, native populations along the Potomac were reduced to one-quarter of their precontact size.[10]

Conflict and disputes continued over the next century and a half of the colonial period as colonists and the first residents clashed over everything from land and trade to fishing and grazing rights. Little that happened in subsequent years would help to resolve the problems or address the many claims of the native peoples.[11]

The river's history helped chronicle the history of the country and is marked by interesting and important events. Among the first white landowners along the river in the present-day capital city were Thomas Gerrard and George Thompson, who purchased land on the shores of the Potomac and Anacostia Rivers in 1662. Not much is known about these two entrepreneurs, but in 1670 Thompson sold part of his holdings to a man named Thomas Notley, who continued to promote development of the region.

Two of the most important cities along the Potomac's shores were established in the mid-eighteenth century—Alexandria in 1749 and Georgetown two years later—after the colonial legislature acquired sixty acres from two landowners—George Beall and George Gordon, who were paid just 280 pounds for the land. A few years earlier Gordon had built a tobacco facility on the banks of the Potomac. Others built wharves and warehouses for the lucrative crop, and the village soon emerged as a major trading center. Because of the river's strong current and untamed nature, Georgetown was also the farthest point upriver for ocean-faring ships. This dilemma, however, served to enhance the importance of the new city.

Concurrently, Leonard Calvert established Maryland and became the colony's governor, bringing settlers and promoting the development of the Chesapeake in the seventeenth century. Some of the new arrivals built along the Potomac, and many land patents were granted in subsequent years with such colorful names as Cuckold's Delight, New Troy, and Scotland Yard. Even a parcel of land known as Widow's Mite populated its shores.[12] The establishment of Alexandria and Georgetown later initiated a construction and trade boom.

The river's location factored into its importance in one additional way. Lying midpoint on the north-south boundary of the British colonies, while also running westward and thereby connecting the Eastern Seaboard with some of the western territories, the Potomac was indispensable to the country's growth and held the potential to help unite the vast land economically, socially, and politically. For instance, because the Potomac extended farther west than other rivers that flowed into the Atlantic, Thomas Lee, a wealthy Virginia planter, promoted the idea of the Potomac as the gateway to the West. In 1747 he enlisted the support of fellow residents of the Potomac, such as George Mason and Lawrence Washington, George's older half brother, to form the Ohio Company. They worked to improve the navigation of the westernmost reaches of the river while also encouraging the construction of a trail from the river's western headwaters and through the wilderness to the Ohio River.[13]

Although Lee died in 1750, his descendants Richard Henry Lee and Henry Lee, along with Lawrence Washington, became the major proponents for developing the river, improving its navigation, and attempting to connect East and West. Lawrence had also championed the idea of a major city along the Potomac, one that would dominate commerce in the region and country. He suggested a site roughly ten miles upriver from Mount Vernon by the harbor at the mouth of Great Huntington Creek. Lawrence was even able to get the Virginia Assembly to build a tobacco inspection and trading station there and to convince the colony to issue a charter to name Alexandria the seat of government for Fairfax County. The pieces were falling into place for the Potomac to dominate the region.

The Potomac's swift current proved to be a mixed blessing—it kept the mouth of the river largely free from debris, but the rocks, white waters, and falls limited trade and transportation. Lawrence Washington proposed a series of projects to improve navigability and channel the river to bypass the falls.

The plan, however, was dealt a blow when Lawrence died suddenly in 1752. Upon his death, more than merely his home and land at Mount Vernon passed to his younger half brother. George continued Lawrence's efforts. The younger Washington planned, built support for, and undertook development projects for the river, including the efforts to dredge and enhance navigability envisioned by his older half brother. Up and down the river, young Washington pushed to improve navigation, encourage settlements, construct ports, and remove rocks and boulders from the troublesome spots.

Like his half brother before him, Washington also enlisted the support of other leaders who lived along the river in promoting the idea that the Potomac was the key to both linking the East with Ohio and trading with Europe. In 1770 Washington informed leaders in Frederick County, Maryland, that they should join him in promoting improvements to the Potomac, which was, in his

words, "The channel of conveyance of the extensive and valuable trade of a rising Empire." The various projects were moving forward but faced continual opposition from Maryland, which had jurisdiction over much of the Potomac and
often refused to cooperate with Virginia, most probably because Marylanders
favored Baltimore emerging as the preeminent city in the region.[14]

Yet investors and politicians in the region soon realized the river was deep
enough for oceangoing ships to traverse inland. An array of products and produce benefited from the internal improvements, which, in turn, led to an increasing population in both cities and along the river. Alexandria later emerged
as the main port in the area. While the economic and social heart of Virginia
and Maryland were elsewhere at the time, the Potomac would soon change the
region's political landscape.[15]

The leadership on nearly all matters pertaining to the river came from
Virginians, most notably Washington. For example, with the support of Richard
Henry Lee, Washington promoted a Potomac navigation bill in the Virginia
Assembly in 1770, but it failed. Undeterred, the two boosters were back at it
again in 1772; with Washington on the committee that drafted the measure,
this time it passed. The bill married Washington's vision for the river with the
means to make it a reality.

Washington's advocacy for the river continued throughout his life and was
shared by fellow Virginian Thomas Jefferson, who realized that the new nation
needed to develop trade in the West if they were to settle the West. This required, the men agreed, investments and trade routes. The Potomac and perhaps
other waterways would be the key to the future and, equally important, vital for
the enrichment of Virginia and themselves. Wrote Washington, "The immense
advantages which [Virginia] would derive from the measure would be no small
stimulus to the undertaking."[16]

Shortly after the end of the war, in February 1784, Washington encouraged
James Madison to promote a measure in the Virginia Assembly to create an annual levy or tax that would help clear and maintain the Potomac. All three men
knew that Virginia lagged behind northern states in promoting trade. "From
trade our citizens will not be restrained," observed Washington, "and therefore
it behooves us to place it in the most convenient channels, under proper regulation, freed, as much as possible, from those vices which luxury, the consequence
of wealth and power naturally introduce."[17]

Jefferson and other Virginians understood that only Washington could bring
the plan to fruition and summarily played on the general's ego by noting that he

must lead the effort. Washington understood that a developed Potomac would be a great "monument" for the ages. So did Jefferson, who wrote, "This is the moment however for seizing it if ever we mean to have it. All the world is becoming commercial. Was it practicable to keep our new empire separated from them we might indulge ourselves in speculating whether commerce contributes to the happiness of mankind?" Jefferson and Washington agreed that "nature then has declared in favor of the Potomac, and through that channel offers to pour into our lap the whole commerce of the Western world."[18]

Washington sought investment partnerships in the river from Europe, principally through Jefferson and Lafayette in France. He even predicted to Lafayette that an investment in the river would yield profits more lucrative than "any speculation I know of in the world." Washington also pitched his ideas to his wealthy countrymen, like Robert Morris, to whom he boasted, "There is no place within my knowledge to which so much produce will, from the nature of things, be brought, as to the highest shipping port on this river."[19]

When the Revolutionary War ended in 1783, Washington, like his hero Cincinnatus, chose to retire from public service and return to private life and farming. Other than his efforts to restore Mount Vernon, which had been neglected during the years he was away at war, and his ongoing role in building the capital city, Washington's other main priority at the time was the Potomac. He continued promoting projects to improve the river's navigation and role in trade and commerce, even becoming president of the Potomac Company two years after the war.

Washington was often guarded and discreet when discussing politics and public affairs. For instance, in July 1790 he admitted that it was his "maxim rather to let my designs appear from my works rather than by my expressions." Yet this was not the case when it came to the Potomac River. He confided in Henry Lee, who shared his passion for the river, "For I hold it necessary that one should not only be conscious of the purest intentions; but that one should also have it in his power to demonstrate the disinterestedness of his words and actions at all times, and upon all occasions."[20] Washington was rarely quiet and frequently animated when the topic of the Potomac was raised.[21]

Washington had spent most of his life within the Potomac basin, an important factor behind his belief that the waterway was the finest in the world and one that would both shape the future of the new nation and enhance his own economic advancement. As early as 1754 he traveled nearly the entire length of the Potomac by canoe, conducting a careful survey of the river that included interviewing locals about everything from its tributaries to its currents, all of

which is reflected in his surviving notes and diary entries.[22] As one historian
noted, Washington was a "passionate believer in the future glory of the river."
The Potomac became a lifelong interest and project for Washington; the developed and vital river would also become something of a living memorial to the
man.[23] And to the nation.

By 1968 the river had succumbed to overdevelopment, prompting President
Lyndon Johnson to promote measures to protect it and other rivers around the
country. With raw sewage contaminating the capital city's river, he even declared
the Potomac "a national disgrace." The efforts worked. In 1998, on the thir-
tieth anniversary of Johnson's program, President Bill Clinton designated the
Potomac as an "American Heritage River." With a length and drainage area of almost fifteen thousand square miles, making it the fourth-largest river along the
Atlantic Coast and twenty-first in size among the country's rivers, the Potomac
has helped chronicle the history and growth of the region and, along with the
Mississippi, lays claim to being the nation's river.[24]

CHAPTER 5

Cincinnatus

I hold the maxim no less applicable to public than
to private affairs, that honesty is the best policy.
George Washington

Very little is known about Martha Dandridge's early years. Born in 1731, she was the first child of a reasonably prosperous family of Virginia planters and was known as "Patsy." The few descriptions of the young woman, along with a surviving portrait and family tradition, suggest she was anything but the frumpy, bonnet-wearing homemaker remembered by history. At seventeen she had caught the eye of Daniel Custis, who was twenty years her senior and one of the colony's wealthiest bachelors—and heir to the Custis tobacco fortune.

The problem for the couple was that Daniel Custis's tyrannical and opinionated father, John, opposed his son's marriage to the daughter of a family occupying a lower rung on Virginia's social ladder. It speaks volumes to young Martha's grit and character that, after meeting the formidable John Custis, the teen was able to change his mind. The elder Custis ultimately gave his blessing, and the couple was married in 1749.

A long and happy union was not in the cards. Tragedy struck repeatedly. Both Martha's father and father-in-law passed. The couple also lost their first two children in infancy. Then, in the summer of 1757, Martha's husband died. Even though her prospects for remarrying were good and her financial situation strong, widowhood was a harsh and unpredictable experience in the eighteenth century. Women lacked basic rights, and she was thrust into overseeing her late husband's farms and businesses. At twenty-six Martha was a widow and mother of two surviving infant children with an uncertain future. She was also one of the wealthiest women in the colony.

Widows tended to remarry quickly at the time, and so it was with Martha. History does not record where or when George and Martha first met, but it seems probable that they would have attended some of the same events during Williamsburg's winter social seasons. What is known is that in the spring of 1758, Washington was traveling from the western theater of conflict during the French and Indian War to Williamsburg for an important meeting with the lieutenant governor of the colony. While on route the young officer stopped to water his horse at a prominent attorney's house, and the attorney happened to be hosting the wealthy widow for dinner. Washington initially declined an invitation to join the attorney for dinner—until he discovered the identity of the other dinner guest. The rest, as they say, "is history." Washington courted Martha with gusto.[1]

The couple was married on January 6, 1759. Washington was nearly twenty-six at the time, an age rather late for a first marriage. His bride, Martha Dandridge Custis, was one year older. The bride brought almost eighteen thousand acres of land, many slaves, a plantation, homes, and a lucrative London bank account into the marriage. She also had two children—a boy and a girl, ages four and two—which provided Washington with a family. This was important, as he would never have children of his own. Washington described his marriage, writing that he was now "fixed at this Seat with an agreeable Consort for Life."[2]

Although the Washingtons' love affair may not have been the stuff of poetry and passion, it was a solid and productive union, which helped them deal with these challenges. Both partners remained loyal and committed to one another. The woman, who described herself as "an old-fashioned Virginia housekeeper, steady as a clock, busy as a bee, and cheerful as a cricket," was a dutiful, warm, and "worthy companion." Washington would be a good father for her two remaining young children and a responsible manager for her vast estate and finances. The marriage also catapulted Washington to social and financial prominence.[3]

With Mrs. Washington's wealth and Washington's work ethic, Mount Vernon prospered. Despite the generally poor quality of soil in the area, Washington proved to be an innovative and persistent farmer, experimenting with numerous new growing techniques and new varieties of seed, ordering the latest farming implements, and even delving into aquaculture and the production of alcohol. Selling tobacco in London was a mainstay for Virginia planters such as Washington, but unlike many of his neighbors, he continued to acquire land and diversify his agricultural endeavors.

Washington also purchased new slaves soon after marrying. His farm books show disturbingly that roughly ninety enslaved workers lived at Mount Vernon in 1770. He stopped acquiring additional slaves after 1772, although the population at his plantation continued to grow through births. In 1786, for example, Washington conducted a census of his slaves, counting 216 men, women, and children. This inhumane practice seems even more shocking and inconsistent knowing Washington was the man who would win the war for liberty. Surviving writings also show that, earlier in his life, he referred to the slaves that worked his and nearby plantations as a "certain species of property," dispassionately recording their work in his farm logs in a manner not unlike he did for his livestock.[4]

Washington did mature in his views. By 1786 he believed that slavery had to be abolished (in Virginia), although seemingly not so much on humane principle as on political necessity. Recognizing that slavery was a damaging sectional wedge that undermined the moral legitimacy of the new republic, Washington eventually broke from many of his fellow Virginian planters. He stopped buying and selling slaves and became less reliant on tobacco and other labor-intensive crops, noting in a letter in 1786 to a friend, "I never mean . . . to possess another slave by purchase it being among my first wishes to see some plan adopted, by which slavery in the Country may be abolished by slow, sure, & imperceptible degrees."[5]

Late in life Washington admitted that the "unfortunate condition of the persons, whose labour in part I employed, has been the only unavoidable subject of regret." Although he did not advocate immediate abolition, Washington was moving in that direction, even writing to his longtime personal aide of his plan "to liberate a certain species of property I possess, very repugnantly to my own feelings." That thought, Washington noted, "afforded some satisfaction to my mind, & could not I hoped be displeasing to the justice of the Creator." He also hoped the new nation would "lay a foundation to prepare the rising generation for a destiny different from that in which they were born."[6]

Regrettably, in the meantime Washington continued to rely on slaves both in his fields and his homes. All the while, he fretted, "To sell the overplus I cannot . . . because I am principled against this kind of traffic in the human species. To hire them out is almost as bad . . . What is to be done?" More than anything else, it seems to have been his passion to strengthen the nation that changed Washington's views on the "peculiar institution."

During the 1760s and 1770s it was not slavery but the repressive regulations imposed by the Crown that commanded Washington's attention. The imposition of taxes and duties from the Stamp Act of 1765 and the Townshend Acts two years later had mobilized opposition against the colonists' masters in London. These measures frustrated Washington, who had tired of dealing with unreliable traders across the Atlantic and worried about the debt he accumulated. Likewise, he remained disappointed at never receiving an appointment as a senior officer in His Majesty's military. Washington began to believe that British policies were unfair to the colonists and exploitative of America's planters. His politics reflected this realization; he wrote, "We cannot conceive that because we are Americans, we shou'd therefore be deprived of the Benefits common to British Subjects."[7]

Washington was becoming a revolutionary, saying of the Boston Massacre of 1770 and Boston Tea Party of 1773 that "the cause of Boston [is] the cause of America."[8] He came to believe that it was no longer possible to appeal to the king and Parliament, and he soon had a chance to act on it. In 1774 Washington was selected to chair a meeting at the Fairfax County Court House to discuss a response to British oppression. The result was that the assembly adopted what became known as the Fairfax Resolves, which recognized the colonists' right to self-government. Fairfax County soon became one of the hotbeds of resistance in Virginia and began boycotting British goods. Washington emerged as one of the leaders of the nonimportation campaign.[9]

Although George and Martha Washington enjoyed many happy years at Mount Vernon, domestic tranquility did not last. After fifteen years together at Mount Vernon, war interrupted the Washington marriage. And so did tragedy. Mrs. Washington, who never fully recovered from the loss of two young children, also suffered the passing of her daughter, Patsy, at seventeen after a severe and sudden epileptic seizure at the dinner table. In Washington's words Patsy had collapsed "suddenly" and "without uttering a word, a groan, or scarce a slight." A few years later, after long opposing her son Jacky's requests to join the Revolutionary War, Mrs. Washington finally acquiesced in 1781. Jacky joined Washington's headquarters at Yorktown that October but contracted a camp disease (possibly typhus) and succumbed quickly.[10]

If not a passionate love affair, theirs was a solid marriage and strong partnership. The couple shared a similar personality in that they were image-conscious hard workers and gracious hosts who refrained from the social vices of the time and were dutiful to one another. Later in life Washington provided a clue as to his marriage, advising a young relative, "love is a mighty pretty thing; but like all other delicious things, it is cloying . . . too dainty a food to live upon alone." It was, he counseled, best to base marriage on "friendship." Or money.[11]

Much of what remains about Washington's early years is, unfortunately, lore; this includes the oft-told tale of him chopping down the cherry tree and then not being able to lie about it to his father. The story is a legend attributed to the imagination of Parson Mason Weems, who was more interested in selling books than recording actual or accurate history.[12] Ironically, such fables are actually somewhat helpful in that they end up reflecting the kind of integrity for which Washington became famous. Indeed, stories of Washington's personality, charisma, and imposing physique are numerous. However, because he lived in an age without photography and audio recordings, one is left to rely on letters and paintings to try to gauge the man.

Even a cursory examination of the record reveals that many of the memorials to Washington depict him as larger than life, perhaps none more than the 555-foot-tall Washington Monument in the city that also bears his name. The Founder has also been portrayed in regal repose by the French neoclassical sculptor Jean-Antoine Houdon, seated commandingly atop his horse in a large bronze statue by the Massachusetts sculptor Thomas Ball, and enshrined in marble by Horatio Greenough on the centennial of the Founder's birth. In the latter depiction Washington sits bare-chested and cloaked in a Greek toga on a throne while raising his right hand to the heavens, an effigy inspired by Phidias's famous statue *Zeus Olympios*. In each image the general is remembered or cast as a demigod, making it a challenge for us today to assess the man behind the myths.[13] History is left to look elsewhere for clues to understand the general's character as well as his influences, passions, and vision for the nation.

The paintings of Washington are also both telling and deceiving, as are the insights of the artists who attempted to capture the great man. On canvas the general often towers over battlefields, horses, and cannons. He is depicted in exaggerated scope befitting the need to bestow on the young republic the necessary patriotic myths, symbols, and heroes. Such iconic imagery and heroism is necessary for forging a national identity, unifying diverse groups of people, and promoting a sense of patriotism and civic virtue—the very objectives Washington had for the new nation.

To be certain, all nations and peoples engage in such imagery and myth making. The Greeks had Zeus, the king of the gods of Mount Olympus; the Romans had Romulus, whose deeds led to the founding of Rome; the Britons had Arthur, who defended the island nation against Saxon invaders. Such tales inspire a people and promote a national identity. Americans embraced Washington. The difference, of course, is that, while other mythical leaders are just that—the stuff of legend—Washington was real but is too often the subject of exaggeration and folklore. While serving as the focal point of such whimsy, he seems to have understood such adulation and the importance of such imagery in developing a national identity.

The noted artist Gilbert Stuart completed one of the more famous paintings of Washington. Born in Rhode Island, Stuart had spent much of his life in London. Temperamental, controversial, and ambitious, the esteemed artist sailed back to America in 1793 eager to produce a celebrated portrait of Washington, one he hoped would "make a fortune." Stuart all but stalked his subject, even painting John Jay in hopes that a reference from one of Washington's close friends would earn for him the opportunity to paint the "Father of His Country" and advance his own fame. It worked.[14]

Stuart is a particularly adept artist when it comes to capturing the true nature of the famous people he painted, not only because of his talent with the brush but thanks to his penchant for getting subjects to let down their defenses. At least most of them. Accordingly, while painting Washington, the portraitist attempted to penetrate the general's inviolable exterior and soften his notoriously restrained demeanor through flattery and small talk. However, the artist who had a fondness for the bottle and snuff immediately discovered that his subject, who disapproved of Stuart's vices, was made of granite.

Stuart tried again, appealing to his subject, "You must let me forget that you are General Washington and that I am Stuart, the painter." However, Washington murmured that neither one need forget anything. Stuart was discovering the essence of the man, just not as he had hoped. But the session was not for naught for history's sake.[15]

The artist did provide useful observations about Washington, claiming, "There are features in his face totally different from what [I] ever observed in that of any other human being." Of the general's appearance, Stuart, known for an artist's attention to detail, elaborated, "The sockets of the eyes, for instance, are larger than [I] ever met with before, and the upper part of the nose broader." However, it was Washington's physique and strength that most affected Stuart, who noted, "All his features . . . were indicative of the strongest and most ungovernable passions, and had he been in the forests . . . [Washington] would have been the fiercest man among the savage tribes." The gifted painter captured these qualities in his famous painting by depicting Washington's intense eyes and formidable strength percolating just below the surface of a serene facade and clamped mouth.

Importantly, Stuart recorded in detail his impressions of Washington's legendary character, surmising that behind the general's aloofness and cool countenance was a volcano. Washington's calm, concluded Stuart, was a product of self-control, masking an intensity he had never before encountered in any subject. Stuart's Washington was "by nature a man of fierce and irritable disposition, but that, like Socrates, his judgment and great self-command have always made him appear a man of different cast in the eyes of the world."[16]

Ultimately, Stuart attempted to unmask the Founder through his portrait and personal observations but inadvertently ended up contributing to the mythical stature of an unknowable Washington as a hero. Indeed, Washington remains to us today more monument than man, more myth than flesh and blood. Among the Founders, Washington is, ironically, both the most recognizable yet perhaps the most difficult to know. Interestingly, those same Founders also found the general to be something of a mystery.

Many of those with whom Washington worked to create a new nation took it on themselves to attempt to figure out their complicated and often remote leader. Jefferson, who would be a part of Washington's cabinet, often disagreed with the president's decisions but saw him as an unmatched rival. The Sage of Monticello echoed Stuart's observation, writing of Washington, "His temper was naturally high-toned, but reflection and resolution had obtained a firm and habitual ascendency over it." As to his intellect, Jefferson wrote, "His mind was great and powerful, without being of the very first order; his penetration strong, tho' not so acute as that of a Newton, Bacon or Locke; and as far as he saw, no judgment was ever sounder."[17]

John Adams, who also greatly respected Washington but was at times irked by the man's formidable shadow, commented similarly about the dual traits of emotion and restraint. He noted that the general "had great self-command . . . but to preserve so much equanimity as he did required a great capacity." Adams remembered of Washington, "Whenever he lost his temper, as he did sometimes, either love or fear in those about him induced them to conceal his weakness from the world."[18] Similarly, Gouverneur Morris, the author of the preamble to the Constitution and a Founder who knew a thing or two about passions and personalities—he was also known for trysts at the Louvre, sexual affairs, and scandals—commented on Washington's temper, saying, "Those who have seen him strongly moved will bear witness that his wrath was terrible. They have seen boiling in his bosom, passion almost too mighty for a man."[19]

Scholars have also commented on Washington's perpetual struggle to control his temper, even suggesting that his stoic resolve and evenhandedness were the by-products of a lifetime attempting to suppress his volatility. Others point out that the general could be vain and obsessed with his public image. For instance, he was overly sensitive to criticism and, despite the power he projected, could wrestle with anxiety and uncertainty. When traveling throughout the new nation to meet his fellow countrymen, the president would stop his carriage outside each town in order to mount his white horse. It made for a far more dramatic entrance.[20]

The preeminent Revolutionary era historian Gordon Wood noted that the dual nature of Washington's personality pitted his conflicted passions of pursuing his boundless ambition with his love of the gentlemanly life of a planter. As a result, he was torn between remaining at his beloved Mount Vernon and his duty to serve. In short, Washington was a far more complex man and leader than is generally remembered.[21]

A sense of the man comes from his many achievements, which were marked by public displays of humility and magnanimity but also of firm resolve. For instance, the general once offered advice to a young officer: "Be easy and condescending in your deportment to your officers, but not too familiar, lest you subject yourself to a want of that respect which is necessary to support a proper command." Likewise, he wrote to his favorite nephew, Bushrod, advising him to be friendly and kind to everyone, but intimate with few. "True friendship," after all, counseled the reserved Washington, "is a plant of slow growth and must undergo and withstand the shocks of adversity before it is entitled to the appellation."[22]

Therefore, after two centuries, Washington's emotionally reserved, ambiguous gaze staring across time—a Rorschach test of his true personality—remains as enigmatic as the Mona Lisa.

What is clear about the man is that in many ways Washington was a most unlikely leader. He lacked many of the traits typically associated with greatness. Washington was not well traveled, nor was he a great orator; his speeches were known as much for their brevity and hushed tone as for their content. As Thomas Jefferson pointed out about the president, his "colloquial talents were not above mediocrity." Furthermore, he offered "neither copiousness of ideas nor fluency of words." Undeniably, his letters and diary entries on feeding his livestock and ordering seed are often longer and more detailed than his writings about commanding the army or running the government. As a result, unlike other Founders, he did not leave behind brilliant or even memorable writings.[23]

Washington's oratory paled in comparison to such contemporaries as Patrick Henry, just as his writing would never come close to the likes of Thomas Paine—in part, perhaps, because Washington lacked much in the way of a formal education. As an intellectual, he was vastly overshadowed by Thomas Jefferson,

Benjamin Franklin, Alexander Hamilton, and John Adams, and he lacked their creativity and broad command of disciplines. Nor was Washington a military genius. Unlike the legendary military commanders of history, Washington lost more battles than he won. He enjoyed only a few victories on the battlefield, some of which were unremarkable in terms of tactics.

The Founder was also an unlikely leader for a revolution. A comfortable planter owning vast lands and many slaves, Washington potentially had more to lose from a political and economic upheaval than most of his fellow colonials. What's more, he had struggled mightily to achieve a measure of success and had married into great wealth; yet he risked his home, plantation, wealth, and beloved "domestic tranquility" by supporting—then leading—an uncertain struggle for independence. It was a potentially ruinous gamble.

The Founder countered his limitations, however, with more than a fair share of admirable traits, including many that marked him for greatness. Washington was tall, strong, dignified, and extremely charismatic. In short, he looked the part and, lest others miss it, took great pains to always fulfill the expected image of himself. One of the earliest descriptions of the future president dates to his teenage years and reads, "Straight as an Indian, measuring 6 feet 2 inches in his stockings, and weighing 175 pounds." He was broad shouldered and muscular with large hands, but a childhood pulmonary illness had left him with a sunken chest. Even as a teen, he towered over his peers; the young man's physique was such that one acquaintance gushed, "His frame is padded with well developed muscles, indicating great strength. His bones and joints are large as are his hands and feet. He is wide shouldered. . . . His movements and gestures are graceful, his walk majestic and he is a splendid horseman."[24]

As was the case with Gilbert Stuart, the distinguished painter, a number of people who met Washington were compelled to comment on his formidable stature. Complimentary descriptions abound, as is evident in another account: "His head is well shaped, though not large, but is gracefully poised on a superb neck. A large and straight rather than a prominent nose; blue-grey penetrating eyes which are widely separated and overhung by a heavy brow. A pleasing and benevolent tho a commanding countenance." Enough evidence has survived history for us today to know that Washington's face was scarred by a teenage bout with smallpox and highlighted by a prominent Roman nose and bluish-gray eyes. Light-skinned with long chestnut-reddish hair, he was easily sunburned, but a life spent outdoors left him deeply tanned. During his presidency Washington's hair began to turn white, but he often opted not to wear a wig, as was customary for the day and a man of his rank.[25]

Washington also had a rare ability to learn from his mistakes and an indefatigable commitment to self-improvement.[26] Later during the war he surrounded himself with men of varying opinions, as during his presidency he staffed his cabinet with the best and brightest, and was, in both positions, open to their advice. As perhaps the Founder most noticeably lacking a classical education, and never an intellectual, Washington nonetheless showed himself to be a quick study. Driven by a desire for social and economic advancement, he realized early on that to transcend his lot in life he would need to overcome his personal liabilities. In the words of one scholar, "More than most, Washington's biography is the story of a man constructing himself."[27] His life was a constant struggle not so much to *reinvent* himself but to *self*-invent, to become who he saw himself becoming. The result: Washington consciously forged the monumental character for which he would later be known.

While he possessed many admirable qualities, Washington achieved greatness not because he was a competent manager of his household and farms or because he was free from many of the social and economic vices that afflicted the upper class of his times. Nor was his defining trait being a bold and persistent commander. Rather, it was his moral character. Unlike many leaders, rather than appearing to want power or relentlessly pursue it, Washington approached leadership with "modesty and humility." He was not consumed by power. He also led by example—commanding from the front line of battles, living simply during the war, and showing his troops that he understood their suffering by using a simple tent for his headquarters.[28]

Self-made and disciplined, Washington was bound by a deep and unwavering commitment to duty and service—in short, civic virtue. There is no better example of such character and virtue than Washington at the zenith of his power. At the crucial moment after winning the Revolutionary War, all eyes were on him, including those of his rival, Britain's King George III. Other great men and military victors from history had seized power or demanded accolades, titles, and wealth—the spoils of war. Accordingly, after the war George III posed to the American painter Benjamin West, who was then working in London, the question of what Washington would now do. Would the general seize control of the military or take over the government, the sovereign asked? "No," the artist responded. "They say he will go back to his farm." In response, the incredulous and still indignant monarch is said to have blurted out, "If he does that, he will be the greatest man in the world."[29]

Such behavior among leaders was not common but had occurred before. In the fifth century the great hero Cincinnatus was called by the Roman Senate to lead the army against foreign invaders. After saving Rome, he could have been emperor, but he chose an unselfish retirement from public life and was consequently celebrated throughout the empire as the embodiment of civic virtue.

Inspired by the story, Washington ordered a bust of Cincinnatus from London, which he displayed prominently in his home. Tellingly, like Cincinnatus before him, Washington refused a salary to lead the Continental Army and, after winning the war, simply exchanged his sword for a plow. He retired. It might be said, in historic context, that two of his greatest accomplishments—and most telling examples of his true nature—were what he did *not* do. Washington would forgo power in 1783 after the war and then resign the presidency in 1797 after just two terms in office.[30]

PART II

THE
QUESTION
OF A
CAPITAL

CHAPTER 6

Swords in Their Hands

A government of laws, and not of men.
John Adams

I t was a battle that would change the course of history and mark the beginning
of the end of the long war. The improbable victory for the upstart Americans
came six and a half years into the war. It happened in the early months of
1781, when Gen. George Washington discovered that a massive force led by
the British commander, Lord Charles Cornwallis, was on the move from South
Carolina to Virginia. Washington seized the opportunity by racing his army
all the way from Rhode Island to intercept his foe. Importantly, Washington's
own command was buttressed by America's ally in the war—a sizable French
force led by the Comte de Rochambeau and Marquis de Lafayette, thus finally
giving Washington numerical advantage over the large British Army. The gamble worked. He caught the redcoats with their backs to the sea at Yorktown on
Virginia's eastern coast.

Simultaneously, Washington coordinated with Adm. François-Joseph-Paul
de Grasse to have his French fleet sail from the West Indies to engage the
Royal Navy, which it did. The French forced the smaller British squadron in
the Chesapeake Bay to withdraw, thereby eliminating any chance for Lord
Cornwallis's army to be reinforced or evacuated. Admiral de Grasse then transported additional troops for Washington and blockaded the Virginia Capes
off the coast of Yorktown. The pieces were falling into place for the American

commander to achieve the decisive victory he sought, one that would finally end the revolutionary struggle.[1]

With his back to the water, Lord Cornwallis ordered his troops to dig in on the low-lying coastal plains of the Chesapeake. He would not go down without a fight. Washington, pressing his advantage, countered by having trenches constructed in a long semicircle around the British line, ensnaring Cornwallis's army against the York River and larger bay. Then, in late September 1781, the siege began. Washington would fire the first cannon.

Day after day for three weeks, deadly artillery fire rained down on the British positions. To make matters worse for Cornwallis's desperate army, a last-ditch effort to escape along the coast was blocked by French units led by Lafayette. The crucial blow was dealt on October 14, when the forward British redoubts, which had secured the perimeter of their southern line, were overrun in a bayonet attack orchestrated by Col. Alexander Hamilton. With the British cannons neutralized and their earthworks breached, the die was cast. Lord Cornwallis had no option but to draft a short note on October 17 to be delivered to his adversary. In it he said simply, "I propose a Cessation of Hostilities for Twenty four hours . . . to settle terms for the surrender." And with those words it was over. Washington had masterfully outmaneuvered Cornwallis at every turn.[2]

Two days later the formal surrender occurred, but with a glitch. Exceedingly bitter and profoundly embarrassed, Cornwallis could not bear to face the man he deemed unworthy of opposing him. Pleading illness, the British general sent his second in command, Gen. Charles O'Hara, for the customary gesture of surrender in the eighteenth century: the vanquished general's sword would be presented to the victor. Instead of offering the honors to Washington, as was protocol, General O'Hara attempted to surrender to Comte de Rochambeau.

The French general promptly declined and directed the British officer to Washington. However, irritated by yet another rebuke by his enemy, the tall colonial general coldly waved his foe away. Washington would not grant Cornwallis's second the satisfaction. Instead, he ordered his own second in command, Benjamin Lincoln, to accept the sword of surrender. Poetically, insult was added to injury, for it was none other than General Lincoln who had been on the receiving end of the British forces—including those commanded by Cornwallis—a year earlier during the Siege of Charleston. The irony was lost on no one.[3]

Cornwallis swallowed enough of his pride to request his army be given a "proper" ceremonial surrender; that is, they would capitulate with flags flying and in a procession of bayonet-bearing muskets. The problem was that Cornwallis had earlier denied the Americans the same courtesies at Charleston and then let loose the full vengeance of war on the local inhabitants of the key southern city. Similarly, he and other British commanders had routinely ignored the conventions of warfare and treated continental forces with contempt or, in the case of those unfortunate enough to be captured as prisoners, far, far worse. It had been total war, and Washington's army and his fellow citizens had more often than not been the recipients of it. Washington thus rejected his opponent's request. There would be no honor in Cornwallis's defeat that day.[4]

Absent the hundreds of men killed or wounded during the siege, the remainder of Cornwallis's army—a long red line of over five thousand soldiers and roughly a thousand sailors—threw down their muskets in disgrace. History records that during the surrender, many British soldiers wept openly, and prophetically, their military band played the popular tavern song "The World Turn'd Upside Down."[5]

Yorktown would mark the last major battle of the Revolutionary War. The decisive victory prompted the commencement of peace talks in Paris. Nevertheless, the end to hostilities did not occur after the surrender, as had been hoped and expected. The negotiations, which were begun six months later by the American contingent of Benjamin Franklin, John Adams, and John Jay, dragged on, slowed by the collapse of Lord North's Tory government back in England and the prime minister's resignation in disgrace. The coming peace was also repeatedly delayed by the rudimentary transportation and communication systems of the day, and for their part the defiantly stubborn British negotiators dragged their feet, postponing the inevitable. The Treaty of Paris, which formally ended the long conflict and recognized the United States as an independent nation, was not officially signed until September 3, 1783, a long two years after the surrender by Cornwallis at Yorktown.

The repeated delays in securing the peace offered little opportunity for Washington and his army to celebrate their triumph at Yorktown. Rather, the period after the grand victory amounted to something of a cold war between the belligerent armies. Washington's troops remained in uniform; British regulars remained in force and in control of New York City. Waiting.

Washington had picked for his final military headquarters the small village of Newburgh, hugging the west bank of the Hudson River in New York. Nestled along the rolling foothills of the Shawangunk Mountains and surrounded by fertile farm fields, it was a scenic location from which to await the end of the war. It was a site well chosen for other reasons. The river offered access to transportation; Newburgh sat near the crossroads connecting New England and the mid-Atlantic colonies. It was also far enough north of the British headquarters in New York City for Washington to avoid a surprise attack but close enough for him to keep an eye on the enemy. This scenic and strategic site ended up being both the general's longest continual headquarters and his final command post.

In the camp were roughly eight thousand soldiers, a comparatively large army for the war. They were housed in a few hundred log cabins and huts built by the soldiers along the bank of the river during the first winter. As was customary for Washington, his headquarters was well organized. "Discipline is the soul of an army," was the general's motto. Not surprisingly, he ordered, "Any hut that will be built irregularly, shall be demolished." Sure enough, cabins not meeting proper standards were torn down and rebuilt. All this was necessary for discipline and morale as the army drilled and waited, and waited. Yet a well-run camp went only so far in bolstering the army's spirits or filling their stomachs— or getting the troops paid.[6]

While the final months of the war proved to be a bitter pill to swallow for the obstinate British, it was an entirely different challenge for the Continental Army. It had been many years since the first shots of the war were fired on April 19, 1775. Farmers needed to return to their unsown fields, and families missed their fathers and sons; but such overdue reunions had to wait. The two winters that followed Yorktown brought only more months of dull inaction and bone-chilling weather. Then, out of the ashes of war, a new threat emerged for Washington. Boredom soon turned to bitter frustration, then to outright rebellion.[7]

Tensions escalated throughout the land as the economy ground to a standstill and currencies were rendered valueless. As a result, soldiers and veterans were unpaid. In an attempt to resolve morale and reenlistment issues three years before the end of the war, Congress had pledged that, after their official discharge, officers in the Continental Army would receive a lifetime pension valued at half the amount of their pay. However, that promise did little in the way of providing regular payments until enlistment periods ended. The situation was so dire that, during the summer of 1781, the French commander Rochambeau had to provide General Washington with several chests of gold coins to entice the Continental Army to fight at Yorktown.

Throughout the final year of the war, the issues of military pay and pensions were debated but ultimately—and shockingly—deferred. The underlying problem preventing cooperation and coordination among the colonies over military pay and other issues was the fragmented system of government under the Articles of Confederation. The problem was exacerbated by the emerging divisions between northern and southern states, large and small states, communities on the East Coast and those along the western borders, and of course, between the pro- and anti-government factions. Fissures also erupted between abolitionists and slavers as well as among shippers, merchants, tradesmen, and farmers. All these fault lines prevented the Continental Congress from acting to resolve the financial crisis facing the army or choosing the site for a capital.

A possible answer to the funding dilemma had presented itself in the final year of the war in the form of an emergency amendment introduced by the federalists. The proposal was designed to grant Congress the power to establish an import tariff known as an "impost" in order to generate funds for the troops. Despite the obvious and mounting crisis, it was defeated in November 1782 by the small-government faction. Blinded by their distrust of any form of centralized government, these politicians even went so far as to pass measures in the states that disallowed lifetime pensions for veterans. Ironically, many of these politicians were the same ones who had beaten their chests hardest for war, then refused to fund the soldiers or the war. (Disturbingly, this same scenario would play out again in the War of 1812 and the Mexican-American War—and from the same region of the country and similar anti-government factions.)[8]

News of the impost's defeat arrived in Washington's headquarters at a time when he could ill afford it. Congress's pledge back in 1780 to provide a pension for the soldiers had also been rescinded when Robert Morris, the superintendent of the treasury, realized there were inadequate funds to make good on the arrangement. Congress lacked the ability to raise money to meet its financial obligations. The result was that the government soon ceased all payments to the army. Most of the men camped at Washington's headquarters in Newburgh that final winter had not been paid in months, some for over a year.

And so, one year after Cornwallis's letter of surrender at Yorktown, General Washington found himself reluctantly writing his own worrisome letter. So alarmingly had the situation in the Continental Army deteriorated in the final winter of the war that Washington worried whether his soldiers would even remain loyal to the revolutionary cause. He shared his concerns with Congress, warning that even though "the patience—the fortitude—the long, & great sufferings of this Army is unexampled in history, there is an end to all things, & I fear we are very near to this."[9]

Soldiers began threatening to leave the army before their enlistments ended. Others refused to fight. They had sacrificed much during the long war. It must be remembered that in a day and age before government social programs, a farmer who went to war with no one to tend the crops or livestock and a clerk who had abandoned his shop to fight were likely to return to complete financial ruin. Moreover, the harsh winters after Yorktown brought hunger, disease, and the tedium of months of inaction. Soldiers were reduced to scavenging for food. They suffered from a lack of medicine and warm clothing.

Despite Washington's pleas to Congress for more funds and supplies, there were shortages of everything, and the colonial economy had long since collapsed, prompting Washington to complain that a "wagon load of money will scarcely purchase a wagon load of provisions." Now, at the end of the war, boredom and a lack of pay had replaced the enemy's muskets and infantry as his chief threats. In short, conditions were ripe for rebellion.[10]

It had happened before. Exhausted and hungry, a group of soldiers mutinied back in January 1781. Mindful that his army was watching, Washington acted swiftly and boldly to disarm and subdue those rebels. He described the brief crisis matter-of-factly and in his typical succinctness, stating, "Two of the principal Actors were immediately executed on the Spot, and the remainder exhibiting genuine signs of contrition, were pardoned." These actions worked, but only for the time being.[11]

Meanwhile, soldiers still waited for their pay, and frustrations simmered.

Sure enough, as Washington struggled in the final months of the war to prop up the sagging morale of his troops, mutiny arrived in camp, yet in a most unexpected way—not from cold, hungry soldiers but from senior officers, including those in the general's own headquarters. The resulting crisis threatened to undo all that the army had accomplished. The larger prizes—ceasing hostilities, forging a peace, and building a new government—were now in serious jeopardy.

It started with a group of officers, tempers frayed, drafting a letter notifying Congress of the sobering situation at Newburgh. It also included the thinly veiled threat that "any further [congressional] experiments on their patience may have fatal effects." There was the suggestion that starving, disaffected soldiers might simply lay down their muskets and go home, leaving the country vulnerable to British attack, or worse—the more radical elements of the officer corps might even march on Philadelphia. One disaffected officer even signed his name "Brutus." Washington could count on the loyalty of such trusted friends as now-congressman Alexander Hamilton, Gen. Nathanael Greene, and Gen. Henry Knox, who even pledged that he would never mutiny or oppose either Washington or "the Enemies of the liberties in America." But a rival faction against Washington was gaining strength.[12]

In December 1782 Washington summed up the situation to a close confidante in Congress, writing, "The temper of the army is much soured and has become more irritable than at any period since the commencement of the war."[13] Soon, whispers of rebellion spread through headquarters, and it appeared that Washington's army would collapse or revolt before the long-delayed peace treaty was signed. Mindful of the threat, a few weeks later Washington wrote to his generals that he needed to keep a close watch on his army "like a careful physician to prevent if possible the disorders getting to an incurable height."[14]

General Knox responded to the mounting crisis with his own letter to Congress. It offered a compromise—in place of the lifetime pension, officers might be open to accepting a lump sum payment. Such a letter would not have been written or sent by Knox, of course, without the express consent of or at the behest of Washington. In late December 1782 a delegation of officers that included Gen. Alexander McDougall, Col. John Brooks, and Col. Mattias Ogden met with Superintendent Robert Morris, Congressman Hamilton—himself a veteran of Washington's headquarters—and other leaders to underscore the seriousness of the situation and negotiate Knox's compromise. Other delegations met for similar purposes.[15]

On January 6, 1783, Congress finally formed a committee to address the ongoing issue of paying the army and the Knox proposal. However, despite Hamilton's support, this too failed. Morris and the decentralists were unmoved; there were simply no funds, they maintained. The officers responded with additional appeals and threats, as indicated by Colonel Brooks, who warned, "a disappointment might throw [the army] into blind extremities." Alarmed, one member of Congress reminded his colleagues, "The army have swords in their hands. . . . You know enough of the history of mankind to know much more than I have said."[16]

Prompted by Hamilton and the federalists who hoped to pressure their colleagues to act, Congress reconvened in an emergency session on January 22. But Morris was unflinching, even threatening to resign as superintendent of the treasury, a problem that Congress tried to keep secret in order not to further escalate tensions and undermine what little remained of the public's confidence in the government. Through January and February, additional emergency measures were introduced by the federalists to deal with the payment and pension crises. Despite the mounting threats, Congress, led by the decentralists, once again failed to act.[17] The talks ultimately collapsed on February 13.

Hamilton, recognizing the warning sign, immediately dispatched a letter to Washington. In it he urged Washington to take the lead, predicting, "The difficulty will be to keep a complaining and suffering army within the bounds of moderation."[18] Amid the impasse more fuel was thrown on the already smoldering fire. With negotiations in Philadelphia stalled, word arrived in Congress and at Newburgh that the other negotiations—the peace talks in Paris—were making progress. The end of the war was imminent. Nevertheless, that good news from Paris also meant that the officers and soldiers would likely never be paid.

Panicked, Hamilton again wrote Washington, begging him to "take the direction" before it was too late. Hamilton believed only Washington could yet save the army from rebellion and in doing so save Congress and the young republic. Washington's former aide-de-camp was not alone in his assessment. Washington had commanded the army since the beginning of the war, outlasting several of his British counterparts, including Thomas Gage, William Howe, Henry Clinton, Jeffrey Amherst, and Henry Seymour Conway. Likewise, the Continental Congress had gone through several temporary capitals during the war and even more presiding officers of that legislative body. Washington, however, had been the *one* constant throughout the long conflict. And he had done the impossible—held a collection of sparsely trained soldiers and hungry militiamen together year after year to defeat the world's most powerful army.

Uncharacteristically, the general hesitated, worried that a heavy hand by him at such a sensitive hour would be misinterpreted as a military cabal, thereby undermining the principle of democratic rule and all they had fought for. Of course, to not act carried the same risk. Moreover, he had yet to discover the men behind the cabal. Washington and the wartime government were in a bind.[19]

CHAPTER 7

Mutiny!

Here, sir, the people govern.
Alexander Hamilton

George Washington is remembered for his stoicism in the face of adversity. Yet during the final winter of the conflict, Washington was dealing with more than the weather and defections; he was wrestling with his own frustrations. Duty had prevented him from enjoying the company of his family. Only during the winter encampments did he see his wife, who faithfully traveled vast distances by carriage to be at his side. Yet the general's mood that final winter of the war was so dark that he contemplated telling his wife *not* to join him at Newburgh.

War had disrupted his family in other ways. Though the general never had children, he embraced his wife's children and grandchildren from her first marriage as his own.[1] Yet the war caused him to miss the birth of a granddaughter in 1779 and grandson—who was his namesake—two years later. The war also claimed Martha Washington's only surviving child, Jacky, in 1781, and the general was still grieving the loss as the war wound down in 1783. So too did he still feel the pain of losing Col. John Laurens. The young officer was more than an aide-de-camp; the general considered him, along with Alexander Hamilton and other young aides, to be part of his "military family." Tragically, in the final months of the war, Laurens, who was only twenty-seven, died bravely in a skirmish that drove the remaining British troops out of his native South Carolina.

Moreover, Washington had not seen his home for years, with the sole exception of a brief visit in 1781 during a lull in the fighting. He desperately missed his beloved Mount Vernon estate. Like many of his officers, Washington had assumed the war would be over soon after Yorktown in 1781. He had planned to celebrate the new year back home in retirement. Instead, he was stuck at his Newburgh headquarters for yet another bitterly cold winter. One gets a sense of the depth of the general's frustration through a rare admission of his true feelings. Usually known for his reticence and restraint, Washington wrote that final winter to his colleague Gen. William Heath of Massachusetts, complaining, "Without amusements or avocations, I am spending another winter (I hope it will be the last that I shall be kept from returning to domestic life) among these rugged and dreary mountains."[2]

To make matters worse for the proud and somewhat vain general, his fifty-first birthday that February brought with it a series of physical aches and pains along with faltering eyesight. For a man who had long loved the saddle, riding now proved difficult and was accompanied by back pain. He had lost his teeth and was forced to wear unsightly, uncomfortable dentures made of bone and hippopotamus ivory and held in place by mesh and wire, such that it was difficult to chew food or even to laugh aloud, lest the set of false teeth fall out.

One account of the once-handsome leader at the end of the war noted, "He was fine-looking until [now]. . . . Those who have been constantly with him since that time say that he seems to have grown old fast."[3] Washington, both feeling and showing the effects of war and age, began worrying about his health. The indomitable leader had begun borrowing spectacles from his officers until he was forced to order glasses from a physician in Philadelphia. Ironically, this minor malady would soon end up helping to prevent mutiny in a most unlikely way.[4]

The frustration of the officers in camp that winter was such that by March rumors swirled that the troops might turn on General Washington. Some officers began aligning with Washington's longtime rival, Gen. Horatio Gates, who was discovered to be the leader of a radical faction that hatched what became known as the "Newburgh conspiracy."[5]

On March 10, 1783, an unsigned letter was circulated at the army's Newburgh headquarters in New York. It threatened the government with an ultimatum: Congress would fulfill the financial obligations owed to the soldiers, demanded the letter, or the officers would either disband or march on Philadelphia. There would be no compromise by the army. Later that same day another anonymous letter appeared in camp calling for all officers to assemble at 11:00 in the morning on the eleventh of the month. It also appealed to officers to abandon General Washington and side with the rival faction in camp led by General Gates.

Washington was livid when he heard the news, calling the letters and the meeting, which was organized without his consent, "irregular" and "disorderly." Even though he had a thorny history with General Gates and did not trust him, Washington wanted to believe that the anonymous letter was not from his own officer corps; rather, he suspected it might have been the work of Superintendent Morris or decentralist members of Congress in Philadelphia.[6] Washington chose not to be present at the traitorous meeting. Nonetheless, as other letters and rumors appeared the same day, the timing suggested the mutiny came from within Washington's headquarters at Newburgh.[7]

The general finally acted, calling for a meeting of the officers on March 15. However, Washington was vague on the details of the meeting. On purpose. The officers gathered at a large building in the camp known as the "Temple" or simply the "New Building." Washington had ordered the structure built during the long, dull months after the Battle of Yorktown to serve as a chapel on Sundays and place for ceremonies and gatherings. Interestingly, it was from the Temple that Washington had earlier awarded commendations for valor in battle, which included bestowing three sergeants with purple, heart-shaped medals—making them the first Americans to receive the hallowed honor. The Temple, therefore, had special meaning for the officers, and from this structure the cause of liberty faced one of its greatest threats.[8]

The time had arrived. One by one the officers nervously filled the hall on the morning of March 15, uncertain as to whether their commander would attend this second gathering. After several tense moments it appeared the everpunctual Washington was not coming. The buzz of anxiety-filled voices and bickering in the crowded building finally quieted as General Gates took the floor and welcomed the officers. At the outset of his comments, however, the disloyal general was interrupted. Amid gasps from the audience, Washington appeared. He had entered the building through a side door.

Initially, several officers protested, failing to show Washington the respect he always commanded and marking one of the first times in his life that he faced a hostile crowd. Washington was undeterred. He flatly ordered Gates to surrender the stage, which the conspirator wisely and immediately did. Washington then began to talk. He was not known as an orator, and his speeches were always short, never given extemporaneously, and usually uttered so quietly that listeners were forced to lean forward, straining to hear his words. However, this day Washington's rage was barely contained as he lectured the mutineers in stern but thoughtful terms.

The commander went straight to the point: "Gentlemen, by an anonymous summons, an attempt has been made to convene you together; how inconsistent with the rules of propriety! How unmilitary! And how subversive of all order and discipline!" Washington did not spare the author of the letter and the leaders of the cabal. Instead, he exploded, "This dreadful alternative, of either deserting our Country in the extremist hour of her distress, or turning our arms against it . . . has something so shocking in it, that humanity revolts at the idea. My God! What can this writer have in view, by recommending such measures! Can he be a friend to the army? Can he be a friend to this country? Rather is he not an insidious foe?"

Washington stated unequivocally that he opposed anyone "who wickedly attempts to open the floodgates of civil discord and deluge our rising empire in blood." The room fell coldly silent. The moment had arrived for the officers to pick their sides—and to do so very carefully. Washington warned, "Let me entreat you, gentlemen, on your part, not to take any measures, which viewed in the calm light of reason, will lessen the dignity, and sully the glory you have hitherto maintained." The general then offered a choice: "Let me request you to rely on the plighted faith of your country, and place a full confidence in the purity of the intentions of Congress."

No one had sacrificed more than Washington had. He had endured every hardship faced by the army. As a commander, he had led from the front, and while soldiers and officers had come and gone, he had fought from the very beginning of the war. He thus reminded the captive audience,

> If my conduct heretofore has not evinced to you that I have been a faithful friend to the army, my declaration of it at this time w[ou]ld be equally unavailing and improper. But as I was among the first who embarked in the cause of our common country; as I have never left your side one moment, but when called from you on public duty; as I have been the constant companion and witness of your distresses and not among the last to feel and acknowledge your merits . . .

With the audience now silent and hanging on his every word, the general drove home his point: "It can scarcely be supposed at this late stage of the war that I am indifferent to [your] interests."[9]

Washington commanded the room. To a man, the officers were overwhelmed by the power of his words and volcanic anger. Then the general sealed the moment. Pausing and collecting his emotions, he reached into his pocket and produced a letter sent to him from Congressman Joseph Jones of Virginia. Struggling to see the small print, the general hesitantly reached into another pocket for his spectacles. The silence only punctuated the point he was about to make. As he donned the small glasses, Washington informed the men that he wanted to read the letter aloud. Most of the officers had never seen their commander wear spectacles before, and the image of the great Washington fumbling to put them on stunned the room.

Washington's tone became solemn: "Gentlemen, you will permit me to put on my spectacles, for I have not only grown gray but almost blind in the service of my country." The general's many sacrifices were on display. The visual reminder of all their commander had endured drained the spirit of rebellion from the audience and wetted the officers' eyes.[10]

The general closed the twenty-minute speech by putting the glasses back in his coat pocket. Speaking from the heart, he asked his comrades to "give one more distinguished proof of unexampled patriotism and patient virtue." He called on them to stand together and on principle demonstrate their "full confidence in the purity of the intentions of Congress." Finished, Washington turned and abruptly walked out of the Temple. It was the eighteenth-century equivalent of a mic drop.[11]

The noted Washington biographer James Thomas Flexner called the Newburgh meeting "probably the most important single gathering ever held in the United States." The Newburgh conspiracy was over, the plot foiled in a most theatrical and poignant way.[12] A master of stagecraft with a flair for the dramatic, Washington understood and frequently relied on his natural charisma and imposing presence. We will never know for sure, but it is likely he planned his appearance and comments down to the last detail—arriving late and even orchestrating the touching moment of reaching for his spectacles. The only voice raised in anger was that of Col. Timothy Pickering, who chastised his fellow officers for the hypocrisy of now condemning the anonymous letter that only days prior they had supported. The evidence pointed to Maj. John Armstrong, an aide to General Gates, as the likely author of the anonymous letters. It no longer mattered. Not a single officer now stood with Gates.[13]

After defusing the attempted cabal at his Newburgh headquarters in the spring of 1783, George Washington exited the Temple, leaving the stage to his trusted friend Gen. Henry Knox, who oversaw the drafting of a resolution to be sent to the Continental Congress affirming the army's "unshaken confidence" in their elected officials. On Washington's direction the letter reiterated the army's "abhorrence" and "disdain" for violence and the threats implicit in the earlier letters. Even though the resolution passed unanimously, the officers also felt the need to add an addendum stating their loyalty to Washington, writing, "The unanimous thanks of the officers . . . the officers reciprocate his affectionate expressions, with the greatest sincerity of which the human heart is capable."[14]

On March 18 Washington wrote to Elias Boudinot, president of the Continental Congress, with news that the threat was under control, stating quite formally, "The result of the proceedings of the grand convention of the officers, which I have the honour of enclosing to your Excellency for the inspection of Congress, will, I flatter myself, be considered as the last glorious proof of patriotism which could have been given by men who aspired to the distinction of a Patriot army." The general then assured Congress that the army "will not only confirm their claim to the justice, but will increase their title to the gratitude of their country." In a masterful political touch Washington also had a copy of the anonymous conspiracy letter sent to Congress in order to put pressure on them to resolve the payment crisis, which still posed a threat to the cause of liberty.

Led by the federalists, a new congressional committee acted with much haste, hammering out a compromise over the issue of pensions and pay. A final agreement was reached and crisis averted; the army would receive five years of full pay rather than a lifetime pension at half pay, and veterans were given government bonds that could be redeemed at full value. A few of the officers, still concerned about Congress's abysmal record on the issue, threatened to remain at the Newburgh camp until the first payment was received, but Washington disallowed it. It was determined that they would receive three months of pay and then, after announcing on April 18 that the war was ending, Washington gradually began the task of furloughing the soldiers.

The general's mood was atypically giddy. Gone was the usual reserve and stony exterior as he waxed poetic to his soldiers, predicting, "Happy, thrice happy shall they be pronounced hereafter, who have contributed any thing . . . in erecting this stupendous fabric of Freedom and Empire on the broad basis of Independence; who have assisted in protecting the rights of human nature and establishing an asylum for the poor and oppressed of all nations and religions." When releasing the first group of officers and soldiers, Washington personally signed countless discharge papers and emotionally shook the hands of each officer.[15] Like the long war, the threat of mutiny finally appeared to be behind them.

However, the celebration was again interrupted. Two more unanticipated threats emerged that nearly undermined the victory.

The first threat involved the patchwork agreement in Congress to pay the army. The deal fell apart at the last minute amid decentralist concerns about who was eligible for the bargain and what role the states would play in contributing payments. Underlying the anti-federal rationale, however, was a growing obstructionism to almost every measure by the most radical members of this political faction.

Hamilton and other federalists countered by offering emergency proposals through the month of May, including payments in land. But they were unsuccessful. Believing that the longer the army remained in uniform the more unruly they would become, Congress foolishly voted to order the army disbanded before all the payments were official.[16] Washington was outraged. His influence and orders had been usurped, and he worried that the army would surely now mutiny. He wrote to one member of Congress, "I fix it as an indispensable Measure, that previous to Disbanding of the Army, all their accounts should be completely liquidated and settled."[17] The general was right to be concerned. Many officers and soldiers recognized that the furlough might be an excuse for Congress to avoid paying them.

With the army again on the cusp of rebellion, Washington was forced to find an emergency solution. He averted another crisis by notifying Congress that he intended to allow each soldier to decide for himself whether to stay in uniform or accept the furlough. Congress met in June to debate their commander's recommendation. Fortunately, on June 19 they acquiesced to his considerable political influence and approved the action. Rebellion was again avoided.

However, a second situation was brewing in Lancaster and Philadelphia. A group of soldiers in Pennsylvania never received the news of Washington's arrangement to provide terms that were more favorable. They decided to take the matter into their own hands and march on Congress with arms.[18]

While meeting in Philadelphia, Congress received an urgent message on June 17 that a group of unpaid soldiers was threatening action if their demands were not met. Despite the earlier situation at Newburgh, the legislators again ignored the warning. Just two days later they received word that the threat was real. Eighty soldiers were seen marching from a base in Lancaster, just west of Philadelphia, to the city. Along the way, the disgruntled soldiers commandeered a munitions depot and met with others stationed in and around the city. Soon their numbers swelled to four hundred to five hundred armed soldiers and veterans. Their target: the State House (a.k.a. Independence Hall), the site where both Congress and the Pennsylvania Executive Council had been convening for several years—and the exact spot where the Declaration of Independence had been read and adopted nearly seven years earlier.[19]

On June 21, 1783, the soldiers arrived at the State House. In Philadelphia the mutineers were greeted by rowdy, drunk civilians who poured into the streets in solidarity with the unpaid veterans. Proclamations notifying citizens and soldiers of congressional orders against public protests had been posted around the city, but drunken revelers simply tore them down. Crowds soon blocked the doors of the historic building. The situation continued to deteriorate.

Not long before the incident, Congressman James Madison had predicted that, over the next six months, the future of the nation would be decided. He was correct. The tensions in Newburgh and Philadelphia, like the political struggles over paying the army and situating the capital, would determine whether the new nation would, in his words, be one of "prosperity and tranquility" or one of "confusion and disunion."[20] It appeared to be the latter.

With the State House surrounded, the president of Congress, Elias Boudinot, called for an emergency meeting, prompted by an urgent request from Alexander Hamilton. However, too few members were willing to brave the hostile crowd to achieve a quorum.[21] The Pennsylvania Executive Council, the state's governing body, did the same, but in a different room inside the building. The state government declined to take action against the demonstrators, and Congress only had the authority to authorize force in times of war. Philadelphia became both a powerful symbol and an early testing ground not just for the debate over whether the national government or the states had power to intervene in military affairs but whether the new government would be respected as legitimate. The quandary of authority raised by the mutiny later inspired the idea of "exclusive jurisdiction"—that is, Congress and the federal government would retain authority in any federal "district," not the state or municipality in which the district lay.

Congress proposed a misguided and ruinous plan. They asked the leaders of Pennsylvania, including John Dickinson, a member of the Continental Congress and the new "president" of Pennsylvania, to use the state militia to put down the demonstration and disperse the hostile crowd. This meant that, shockingly, as the war was ending, one of the first acts of Congress nearly involved marching a state militia against veterans of the Continental Army. Others considered whether General Washington should intervene militarily in the matter. Furthermore, Congress threatened that it would have to abandon Philadelphia if it were not guaranteed protection. It was a tense standoff.

Thankfully, Dickinson refused to call out Pennsylvania's militia to engage the mutineers. Cooler heads prevailed. General Washington likewise judiciously declined to march his army to Philadelphia. Bloodshed was avoided, and the mutineers later allowed members of Congress to leave the building. With the crisis averted, but far from resolved, that evening Congress achieved a quorum and ingloriously departed Philadelphia for Princeton to complete the legislative session. Washington sent his aides to take depositions, make inquiries, and restore order, but again wisely refrained from a show of force.

The mutineers worried about reprisals, but negotiators, including the noted physician Dr. Benjamin Rush, were able to convince them to lay down their arms.[22] At the same time, the Pennsylvania Executive Council and several prominent citizens, such as the wives of both Dickinson and Superintendent of Finance Morris, successfully petitioned Congress and General Washington on the soldiers' behalf. A few of the ringleaders were later arrested and faced court-martial; two were sentenced to hang. Ultimately, however, all the mutineers were pardoned, likely on the advice of Washington. Another crisis was avoided in just four tumultuous months, but just barely.[23]

CHAPTER 8

The Day the War Ended

You will never know how much it has cost my
generation to preserve your freedom.
John Adams

British forces ultimately had to abandon occupied communities up and down the Eastern Seaboard. As the Union Jack came down, flags of the new country went up everywhere, one of which in New York City was even nailed to a greased pole in order to make it difficult for royalists to remove. In that same city, which the British had held since 1776, the last remnants of the king's troops finally departed their military headquarters on what came to be known as "Evacuation Day"—November 25, 1783. They were not the only ones. Thousands of bitter and fearful loyalists also set sail, some for the nearby British West Indies or Canada, others for England. Most took their earthly possessions with them. However, they also took their money, skills, trades, and governing experience. Who would now build the ships, maintain the ports, or manufacture plows and armaments? Independence brought freedom but also turmoil, chaos, and threats to the very foundations of civil society.

Of course, the usual affairs that mark the end of any long war played themselves out in both patriotic festivities and lawless releases of pent-up frustrations. Amid the celebrations of independence, families were still grieving the loss of loved ones. Elsewhere, rowdy mobs took to the streets to attack neighbors who happened to have been on the "wrong side" of the war's outcome.

Domestic life in America had been interrupted by eight long years of conflict. Villages showed the signs of fighting and destruction, and many farm fields lay fallow. Britain's naval blockade of ports along the Eastern Seaboard had left communities in ruin and people wanting. As a result, merchants had been forced to close their doors, and essential commodities remained scarce even after the fighting. Britain's mercantile practices had kept the former colonists completely reliant on English goods.

The newly independent nation now faced the prospect of a lengthy and expensive reconstruction. Lacking funds and skilled professionals, the experiment seemed doomed to fail. The promise of liberty had served as the glue that held the outmatched continentals together during the war, but lacking a common enemy in the tumultuous postwar years, the absence of national unity hindered cooperation and undermined consensus on the critical postwar debates. To be sure, the loose confederation of states was divided, in debt, and distrusted even the idea of a central or national government. Almost as leery of one another as they were of foreign powers, the states were unable to agree on the terms of trade among themselves, let alone with foreign powers. Something needed to be done. Immediately.

Americans soon began to question whether the experiment in self government would survive or whether another system of government was needed. One influential voice was John Jay, who would go on to serve as the first Chief Justice of the United States. Jay shared his concern with his friend George Washington, writing, "Our government should in some degree be suited to our manners and circumstances, and they, you know, are not strictly democratical."[1] For his part, Washington maintained his confidence in the cause of self-government and in his compatriots but understood the gravity of the situation, admitting to Jay, "We have errors to correct."[2]

The upstart republic, it appeared, was in danger of unraveling in part over the debate about a capital city. Americans were divided over whether they even wanted a capital for their new government, and their leaders, who had fought alongside one another in the war, were now on opposite sides of these debates. The sheer importance of establishing a capital made it even more problematic. At one point Congress was so desperate that a few members even considered an absurd compromise to have two seats of government. As Congressman Hugh Williamson of North Carolina observed, "Attempts to fix the seat of government, in every county where the people have the right of suffrage, are marked by the effects of passion and private interest."[3]

Unable to agree on a single site for a capital, the practice of using a revolving seat of government continued "unsettled" through the postwar reconstruction, and any effort to reconcile the problem was further exacerbated by the "financial confusion and social flux" in the postwar years. The *Pennsylvania Packet*, a prominent newspaper, was far less diplomatic than others in its assessment: "Was it with these expectations that we launched into a sea of trouble, and have bravely struggled through the most threatening dangers?"[4] Indeed, the *Packet* shared the views of many of its frustrated readers when it opined, "Have we fought for this?"[5]

It was also becoming clear that the new republic still needed the man who had led them through the war.

It was with words, not muskets, that Washington had won the final "battles" of the war at his Newburgh headquarters and in Philadelphia. His speech at Newburgh, his judiciousness in not overreacting in Philadelphia, and his presence throughout the critical year of 1783—as had been the case throughout the revolution—ensured that the new nation would not only win the war but also claim the peace. There was a lesson to be learned from the near catastrophes. To Washington's mind, the Newburgh conspiracy and Philadelphia mutiny demonstrated quite clearly the need for a permanent capital as a crucial symbol of and impetus for a stronger government and national unity.

Washington traveled to Princeton after the crises to advise Congress and begin promoting his vision for the direction of the new nation. He was pleased to find a rather receptive audience. That October, on Washington's urging, Congress finally agreed to consider a permanent seat of government. Although the body was again unable to agree on a suitable location, the matter was at least being seriously debated.

Congress, never again wanting to be held at the mercy of a state or city, was also motivated to act because of the need for "exclusive jurisdiction"—that is, Congress, *not* a state or municipality, would control whatever capital city or federal district might be established. Indeed, the memory of the mutiny at Philadelphia was fresh in the framers' minds four years later when they created in Article 1, Section 8 of the Constitution a federal district apart and distinct from the states. The measure stated that Congress had the power "to exercise exclusive legislation in all cases whatsoever, over such District."

After advising Congress on these and other matters, Washington reached out to the states, knowing he needed to inform them of the state of affairs and rally them to embrace the spirit of union. However, he also used the moment as an opportunity to speak directly to the people and lay out his vision for the nation. It was a wise decision. The war was over, and his countrymen had questions and anxieties. They needed leadership and reassuring.

And so the commander formally addressed the citizens of the new nation through a series of announcements beginning on June 8, 1783, known as the "Circular Letter to the States" or simply as the "Letter of Farewell."

Through the month of June all the chief executives of the states received letters from Washington that were then widely reprinted by newspapers throughout the country.[6] In the Letter of Farewell, the general reminded the public of the exciting drama of self governance on which they had embarked. They were joining him, he observed, in ushering in a new age, one blessed by the promise of enlightenment and dedicated to liberty.

Nevertheless, he warned, "At this auspicious period, the United States came into existence as a Nation, and if their Citizens should not be completely free and happy, the fault will be intirely their own."[7] To that end, he noted that the struggle was not yet over. Washington identified several actions necessary for the young republic to survive and prosper, including the need for a national governing body to regulate their actions and engage in trade and relations with Europe. It was also of vital importance for the new nation to repay debts accrued during the war, to both European allies and its own veterans, who, according to Washington, were also owed a "debt of honor" for their patriotic sacrifices.[8] These issues went hand in hand and were priorities for the general.

Furthermore, he reminded the public and state leaders of the need to maintain a federal army and state militias that were properly trained and equipped. Once again, he noted, this would require a robust national government and financial solvency. The general closed by urging his fellow citizens to pursue peaceful and positive relations with foreign powers and among one another. However, the main thrust of Washington's advice to the new nation was that it be united.

Cognizant of the near-disastrous uprisings in the final months of the long conflict, Washington encouraged the people and their leaders to "forget their local prejudices and policies" and "sacrifice their individual advantages to the interest of the Community"—community being, of course, the nation. This was, warned the commander, "the moment to establish or ruin [America's] national Character forever."[9] He was correct.

The Letter of Farewell was well received. Several leaders of Congress, including Elias Boudinot, who was serving as the body's president, heeded Washington's warning that "the Honor and dignity of the United States are at stake."[10] More important, Washington had, for the first time, made public his dream of a unified nation, a stable and strong national government, and a collective and national spirit among the people. In the crucial moment after the war and amid great uncertainty, Washington offered a vision for the future. He was the one constant in the tumult and uncertainty of the cessation of war, the one variable that captured the public's confidence and imagination.

After visiting Congress and touring several cities at the close of the war, General Washington rode to Philadelphia, arriving a few days before Christmas in 1783. At a public ceremony he surrendered his military commission, one he had received so long ago on June 15, 1775, and delivered a brief farewell address. Washington's words and actions held great symbolic power for the people of the new nation. In his farewell the great commander eloquently reminded his fellow citizens, "With our fate will the destiny of unborn Millions be involved."

By winning the war and handling the final, fitful months of it in the manner he did, Washington had shown his fellow Americans and the world that a new way of governing was possible, one in which the people were not beholden to a monarch and in which the rule of law, not the military, an individual, or a mob, would lead.[11]

After meeting Congress in Philadelphia, Washington mounted his horse and traveled home to his Mount Vernon estate. He arrived on Christmas Eve. However, this, contrary to the nickname given to his famed circular letter, would not be his farewell.

CHAPTER 9

A Singular Destiny

*I have no lust after power but wish with as much fervency
as any Man upon this wide extended Continent, for an
opportunity of turning the Sword into a plow share.*

George Washington

Washington yearned for retirement after the long war. He was tired, his health was not what it once was, and he missed his home and family. The revolution had taken a toll on him both physically and emotionally. The tall, strong general was exhausted and feeling his age when he finally arrived home on Christmas Day 1783. Yet it was with fervor and fidelity that Washington devoted himself to the mundane affairs of domestic life.

Mount Vernon had been neglected during the war and was badly in need of repair and his presence. The roof leaked and production on his farms was down because of mismanagement and the escape of some of his slaves during the war. Because Washington had declined a salary as the commander of the Continental Army, and with unpaid debts mounting, his finances also demanded his attention. Nevertheless, when struggling members of his extended family and hungry veterans came to him with hands out, he routinely obliged them. The result was that the general was soon forced to submit his expenses to Congress for reimbursement, but the nation was in such debt that Congress could pay him only in severely devalued certificates. Washington eventually sold them at a fraction of their worth.

This long-awaited retirement was not to be; duty would again call. The nation was, after all, also being mismanaged, and its financial situation was bleak. Just as James Madison would later urge Washington to attend the Constitutional Convention in order to give it legitimacy, the Founders recognized that the general—the most celebrated man in the nation, who was likely even more popular than the ideals of the new republic and far more trusted than the fledgling government—was the one person who could bring the factions together and resolve the new challenges facing them. Washington was pulled back into the turmoil of public life from, as he stated, "under vine and fig tree."[1]

Wading into the fray, Washington recognized the opportunity to pursue his vision for the nation and, in the process, further sharpened the details of his plan, one rooted in a lifetime of beliefs, experiences, and ambitions. "We are either a *United* people under one head, & for Federal purposes," he wrote, "or, we are thirteen independent Sovereignties, eternally counteracting each other." In that sense he recognized that, left unattended, the festering problems after the war would destroy the grand experiment and that the young republic "never shall establish a National character, or be considered on a respectable footing by the Powers of Europe."[2]

With the mutinies at Newburgh and Philadelphia fresh on his mind, Washington warned, "I see no greater evil, than disunion." Unity among the states and people, he argued, were "essential to the well being, I may even venture to say, to the existence of the United States as an Independent Power."[3]

Despite the clarity of his vision, there were more questions than answers. As to the details of "how" to develop a capital city and new nation, they had yet to be worked out, of course. As he warned, "To form a new Government requires infinite care and unbounded attention, for if the foundation is badly laid, the superstructure must be bad. . . . A matter of such moment cannot be the Work of a day."[4] The general would again be called on to lead, only this time with more ambiguities than during the war. The drama of forging a capital and a nation threatened to unravel his reputation, one he had long nurtured and deeply valued.

The solution was a strong national government nurtured by a budding American identity that would unite the fractious country. The first of many steps, each fraught with challenges, would therefore be to convince his fellow citizens to establish a permanent capital. And he set about to make that happen.

Of the task and the man behind it, Abbé Correa, Portugal's foreign minister, aptly remarked, "Every man is born with a bag of folly which attends him through life. George Washington was born with a very small bag, which he kept to himself, and never imparted any of it on the world until the metropolis of the nation was founded, when he emptied the whole of it in this city."[5]

Washington was at the center of these momentous debates, and it would be his vision, strength of character, and surprising political acumen that would help establish a capital city. To be sure, Washington has been rightly credited by history with possessing several worthy attributes—much has been written about his integrity, charisma, and physical stature, for instance. However, a case can be made that the former surveyor was also a visionary and a crafty politician.

Through the long war Washington developed a nuanced view of foreign affairs, honed his political savvy, and demonstrated a penchant for self-restraint and judiciousness. His leadership skills came not from what he had done on the battlefield per se, but rather came courtesy of what he achieved in between battles. The general held together an army that shivered and starved in winters and dealt with a shortage of blankets, shoes, and gunpowder during combat. He managed the egos of generals, the whims of public opinion, turmoil within his own ranks, dissent and dysfunction in the Continental Congress, and bickering among thirteen former colonies that distrusted one another almost as much as they disliked the British. Indeed, far from the figurehead caricature in which he is sometimes portrayed, through the war he proved himself a canny politician whose refusal to be corrupted by power would soon help forge and then solidify the bonds of a shaky union.

Washington, more than any other Founder, would develop the idea of a strong, unified nation and a stable federal government. It was his vision that would ultimately carry the debate. This aspect of his legacy is, however, generally underappreciated. Three of the earliest biographies of Washington, for instance—those by Parson Mason Weems, John Marshall, and Washington Irving—and many of the later works on his life fail to discuss his pivotal role in building the capital city, his deep passion for the enterprise, or his visionary leadership in uniting the fractious states.[6]

Where some saw meadows, farms, and woods on the Maryland-Virginia border, Washington saw a new Rome; while many bemoaned navigation challenges on the Potomac, Washington saw a river to rival the Danube, Seine, and Thames; while others decried the bickering and sectional interests as irreconcilable, Washington saw and advocated union; while some fretted whether the struggling experiment in popular government would succeed, Washington saw the makings of a great power. There was another facet to his vision. The noted Washington biographer Ron Chernow adds, "He was somebody who had a real vision of the country. Not just a vision of American power and riches, but a real vision of American morality—what we stood for, what the character of the country was."[7]

The former colonists lacked a sense of nationhood and a unifying American identity, two of the many elements necessary for any nation to thrive and endure. It was Washington who understood the connection, recognizing that a grand and vibrant capital could address these shortcomings and help legitimize both the nation and its government.

In a larger sense it is hard to imagine the American Revolution happening without Washington; his leadership of the war and reassuring presence at the Constitutional Convention were inestimable. He molded the very institutions of government through every action and inaction during the inaugural presidency. Even his nearly unprecedented act of voluntarily relinquishing power— military and political—allowed the nation to outlive him. Washington's friend and general Henry Knox even observed that it was not the Constitution but Washington's great character that made the nation and held it together through the early years of the republic. He was right.

Similarly, Thomas Jefferson eloquently described Washington's legacy in this way: "The singular destiny and merit, of leading the armies of his country successfully through an arduous war for the establishment of its independence; of conducting its councils through the birth of a government, new in forms and principles, until it settled down into a quiet and orderly train; and of scrupulously obeying the laws through the whole of his career, civil and military, of which the history of the world furnishes no other example."[8] Recognizing what Jefferson saw, William Smith, a member of Congress from South Carolina, said simply that any new capital city be named "Washingtonopolis!"[9]

Washington was born in 1732, a time when Britain's North American colonies were a major part of the empire. It was a time when "rule by birth" was still common. Monarchs ruled based on heredity and by the grace of the Almighty. However, as the colonies grew in importance over the next few decades, radical ideas began to form and the spark of revolution was lit. Inspired by the Greeks and Romans, Washington and his fellow Founders sought to create something unique in the annals of history. The vision of a grand, Roman-inspired capital and unified nation was distinctly Washington's.

It was certainly a heady time for the former colonials. The promise of the revolution was felt everywhere, and nothing less than the basic character of the new nation would be shaped in the postwar years. Writing to his friend and fellow revolutionary John Jay, Washington gushed, "What astonishing changes a few years are capable of producing."[10] Indeed, it was, according to Gordon Wood, the "dean" of Revolutionary era historians, a period of "very high expectations."[11]

CHAPTER 10

Fixing the Seat of Government

This government, the offspring of our own choice, uninfluenced and unawed, has a just claim to your confidence and support.
George Washington

The debate over a seat of government that raged in the years immediately after the Revolutionary War was not new. As early as 1751 a group of colonial leaders proposed that each colony send commissioners to an annual political meeting. The site suggested for the event was Albany, New York. Three years later the plan was finally enacted, and several commissioners gathered in the city, inspiring Benjamin Franklin to develop what was referred to informally as the "Albany Plan of Union." Franklin's Plan of Union contained a proposal for a "permanent council" that would meet in his adopted hometown of Philadelphia. The Permanent Council could then recommend whether to continue to meet there or move to another city. However, there was little agreement among colonial leaders, and the Plan of Union fell apart.[1]

A decade later opposition to the Stamp Act of 1765 compelled colonial leaders to again meet, this time to protest the measure and determine a course of action. Delegates gathered in New York City and, hoping to achieve a degree of unity among the colonies, once again proposed the establishment of a permanent council that would convene on a regular basis in a single location. This effort also failed.

It would be the same story in subsequent years when, despite a bevy of new taxes and intolerable actions imposed by the Crown and events as momentous as the Boston Massacre in 1770 and Tea Party in 1773, colonial leaders remained unable to organize a council of the colonies, much less a permanent seat for such meetings. One of the sticking points throughout the 1750s, 1760s, and 1770s was where to locate the seat for such a council.

The early disagreements foreshadowed the later gridlock over whether there should be a fixed or permanent seat or whether there should be multiple, rotating sites. Representing the former position, Joseph Galloway of Philadelphia advocated a single, fixed location, while his fellow Philadelphian, Benjamin Franklin, proposed using multiple sites as a way to "spread the wealth," so to speak, and thereby engender goodwill and unity throughout the colonies. Ultimately, very little was settled regarding the establishment of a colonial council or location for such meetings. Until 1774.

One of the earliest Revolutionary meetings occurred in 1774, when Virginia's leaders issued a call for a congress comprising delegates from the colonies. As to the location they suggested only that it be at a "place annually as shall be thought most convenient."[2] The sites colonial leaders considered included, initially, New York City and Annapolis, but they eventually settled on Philadelphia. Pennsylvania's Assembly offered the State House as a site, but Congress selected Carpenter's Hall as the temporary meeting place. The delegates at the First Continental Congress finally convened from September 5 to October 26, 1774, but the site of the gathering was not without its detractors. Virginians, as the most influential of the southern delegations, led the opposition to a meeting in a northern colony, offering fodder for the old colonial-era joke "Virginia, where all geese are swans."[3]

The rationale for selecting Philadelphia would guide the debate over a capital for the next few years. For instance, the delegates generally wanted a central location between the South and New England, which Pennsylvania offered. They preferred a major city like Philadelphia, which happened to be religiously diverse, had sufficient lodging, and boasted decent transportation in the form of roads, bridges, and rivers. It was therefore reasonably accessible for delegates from Delaware, Maryland, New Jersey, Virginia, and the interior portions of Pennsylvania. The city was also accessible to the Atlantic Ocean. Location mattered.[4]

Residents of Philadelphia vigorously promoted their city and celebrated when it was selected—perhaps Philadelphian geese were also swans! They had good reason to celebrate. Having influential leaders gather in their city brought important commercial and trade advantages along with lucrative political connections. Even though Philadelphia now seemed to have a leg up on other cities in the competition to be the capital, the debate over a permanent seat continued. Indeed, the appearance of unity was a facade.

Philadelphia's preeminence engendered jealousies and opposition among the other states and their provincial leaders. One such legitimate concern about Philadelphia was the periodic episodes of smallpox and yellow fever that plagued the city in summers. Another was the cost of living, which would increase over the ensuing years because of the growing population and its political importance. There were also political sensitivities; other cities and states did not want Philadelphia or Pennsylvania becoming too important.[5]

In 1775 a few members of the Continental Congress therefore raised the possibility of moving to Massachusetts. Such a move would, they reasoned, also allow them to be closer to the bulk of the initial resistance to British rule and early fighting. Whether southern states would go along with a move farther north, however, was doubtful. Connecticut's delegation seized the opportunity by offering Hartford or New Haven as an interim meeting site and one not as far north as Boston. New York again offered Albany, the location where the first council had gathered two decades earlier.

That next year, even Thomas Paine, in his influential pamphlet *Common Sense*, called for unity and a representative political body that would convene to debate and address grievances. However, the issue was so contentious that he too, perhaps wisely, did not weigh in on a specific location. Southern delegates ended up opposing all of them, and squabbling among the Founders ensued. Quite farcically, colonial leaders were unable even to agree on where to meet to discuss the location of the council seat.[6]

The Second Continental Congress returned to Philadelphia in the summer of 1775, soon after the fighting had begun, and again the following summer to draft the Declaration of Independence. Yet just as Philadelphia seemed to be emerging as the ad hoc capital after the historic summer of 1776, British forces threatened the city. In December and with the redcoats on the march, Congress boldly claimed it would not leave, but within one day of the announcement, the congressmen learned that Gen. William Howe's massive army could not be stopped. They promptly abandoned the city for Baltimore. The embarrassment proved problematic in other ways.

Baltimore was, at the time, a town of only a few thousand people and was plagued by poorly maintained dirt roads, an unsafe water supply, disease, and few public buildings. Predictably, many congressmen complained about the new capital. Samuel Adams and Elbridge Gerry of Massachusetts, however, recommended they remain in the city. With so few distractions, they noted in jest, Congress managed to accomplish more in a few weeks in Baltimore than in several months in Philadelphia.

However, several members of Congress, led by Robert Morris and Dr. Benjamin Rush of Pennsylvania, reminded their colleagues of Pennsylvania's preferred central location within the former colonies. They built support to move back to Philadelphia if the situation presented itself. In late February 1777 a committee voted and, by a single vote, recommended moving back to Philadelphia when it was safe to do so. Foreshadowing future problems with a North-South divide, the vote came down on sectional lines. And so, after a winter in Baltimore, Congress returned to Philadelphia that March after the British had abandoned the city.

Yet the situation was far from resolved. In 1777 some members maintained that the continued military threat to Philadelphia, compounded by the discovery of a growing royalist population in the city, required that they consider another location. However, others worried that abandoning the city again would be seen as an act of cowardice and could encourage the loyalist movement. A compromise proposal emerged to remain in Pennsylvania but move to a safer city, leading John Adams to suggest Lancaster or Reading. Other cities considered included Bethlehem, Easton, and York. The issue remained contentious.[7]

The issue returned that following fall when General Howe resumed his campaign to capture Philadelphia. Fighting erupted at nearby Brandywine in September, leading Alexander Hamilton to warn General Washington and Congress that a British attack on the city was imminent. The British clashed with Washington's army again in October just west of the city at Germantown. General Howe ultimately did take the city, forcing Congress to again flee, this time to Lancaster, then one day later to nearby York, where they would remain for several months. Washington's army established a camp at Valley Forge outside Philadelphia.

Congress survived the embarrassment of so many moves, and Washington's army survived a brutally cold winter at Valley Forge.[8] Howe was not as fortunate. With few decisive victories on the battlefield and a reputation for caution, the British general was pressured to resign his command. The city of Philadelphia was spared when the Crown ordered Sir Henry Clinton, the new commander, to prioritize the defense of Britain's military headquarters in New York City, which now faced threats from France's entry into the war. General

Clinton evacuated Philadelphia in June 1778, thus allowing Congress to once again return to Philadelphia, where they reconvened on June 27.[9]

With the war raging, in 1779 Congress formally debated the idea of establishing a federal capital once independence was achieved, likely the first official instance of this happening. The debate was brief and included a discussion about purchasing land and the types of buildings the permanent seat would require. In terms of a location there was, not surprisingly, little consensus and even less progress. Princeton, New Jersey, however, had the honor of being the first known mention of a possible capital.

Nonetheless, Congress remained in Philadelphia from 1778 through mid-1783, meeting initially at College Hall and then at the State House. The city, of course, had played a vital role in building support for the revolution, hosted the First Continental Congress, witnessed the writing of the Declaration of Independence, served as an interim capital during much of the war, and was one of the largest cities in the former colonies. Philadelphia proved to be such an effective and popular location that it would later welcome the Constitutional Convention and serve as the temporary capital during most of Washington's inaugural presidency.[10] Yet the issue of a seat of government was so fluid and created such tensions that, when Congress concluded its session and departed Philadelphia on June 21, 1783, many people read the departure as perhaps signaling that Philadelphia would never be the capital. Likewise, when Congress reconvened in Princeton at the end of June, it appeared to some that the city might become the capital.[11]

While Congress was in Princeton, word arrived that the Treaty of Paris, the agreement that finally ended the long war, had been signed on September 3, 1783. Given the difficulties of travel in the eighteenth century, news of the long-awaited end to the hostilities took weeks to reach Congress and longer to reach the public. However, it brought with it new urgency to resolve the matter of finding a suitable location for the government.

During the preceding spring and summer, Congress anticipated the end of fighting by establishing a committee to address the issue. Several states responded by making generous offers of land for a capital. A second committee was established to address the dilemma of jurisdiction, that is, whether Congress should control the capital. Elias Boudinot, native Philadelphian and friend of both Benjamin Franklin and George Washington, represented New Jersey in Congress and served as president of the Continental Congress in 1782 and 1783. He helped organize an offer of land from his adopted hometown of Elizabeth (also known as Elizabethtown). It would, he proposed, stand as a possible site for the capital.

While many members realized the need for what became known as "exclusive jurisdiction," they also worried that it smacked of monarchy and central power. There were also questions about the status of the residents living in such a federal district. Would they be residents of a state? Would they have full rights, including voting rights? To that end, James Madison proposed a compromise of exclusive "legislation" (politics) rather than "jurisdiction" (place), and soon many of the offers of land for a permanent capital were contingent on the contentious question of jurisdiction.[12]

In the waning days of the war in September 1783, the Jurisdiction Committee made another attempt to resolve the situation when they reported that Congress should assume jurisdiction over any capital city and recommended a federal district not exceeding six miles (or thirty-six square miles) but not to be less than three miles (or nine square miles) in size. Yet despite the progress toward resolving the location of the capital, a few states and leaders remained unconvinced there should even be a permanent capital.

Philadelphia was still the frontrunner to be the capital. The fact that the city was located in the "Keystone State" of Pennsylvania—one of the largest states and one centrally located geographically—only reinforced its advantages. Nevertheless, opponents of a Philadelphia capital emerged even within other towns in Pennsylvania and among influential Founders.

Other leaders were emboldened by the memory that none other than George Washington had been against the city as the site for the First Continental Congress back in 1774. And so, as debate over a capital intensified at the end of the war, about the only two points of consensus among representatives was their opposition to Philadelphia and opposition to any city or state other than their own as the capital. The debate was back to where it started.[13] Both issues—a permanent capital and congressional jurisdiction—proved to be too controversial among the states.

With the war winding down in June of 1783, Elbridge Gerry of Massachusetts proposed that Congress reopen debate about a permanent capital. He suggested a capital by the Delaware River near Trenton, New Jersey, or along the banks of the Potomac next to Georgetown. Gerry's position reflected the popular belief that any capital needed to be situated along a major river. Contemporaneously, all the states sent delegates to discuss a course of action for governing the new nation, including what to do about a capital.

General Washington visited Congress at Princeton and discovered the extent of tensions and divisions over a permanent capital and its location. Because of the near mutiny in Newburgh and brush with an armed coup in Philadelphia a few months earlier, Washington well understood the precarious nature of the new experiment. Yet Washington had to tread lightly. His reputation had become so formidable that he played into the debate when his mere presence in Princeton unintentionally contributed to speculation as to whether the city was in the running to be the seat of government.

The debate picked up in earnest that fall but became cluttered with many proposed locations. For example, representatives from New York proposed locations north of New York City along the Hudson River. Such a site, they maintained, would be less prone to foreign attack than those near other coastal rivers would. One of the proponents for a Hudson River site was Robert Livingston, the noted lawyer and diplomat. Livingston began advocating on behalf of the town of Kingston, just north of Newburgh and Poughkeepsie on the Hudson. Simultaneously, another New Yorker, Alexander Hamilton, unsuccessfully pushed New York to cede land or offer a town in the state for the new capital. The Hudson location and other New York proposals failed to gain adequate support.[14]

Representatives from Delaware offered Wilmington, nestled next to the Delaware River and its smaller tributary, the Christina River. The location afforded convenient access to the Delaware Bay and Atlantic and was centrally located between northern and southern states. The Maryland delegation tried to block any further discussion altogether, however, lest a site other than one along the Potomac or Chesapeake emerge. The chess match continued when northern states failed to back Delaware's bid, prompting the state's representatives to threaten to support a capital in nearby Maryland.

One Marylander had written a widely read letter promoting Annapolis as the site for a capital. It was published anonymously under the pseudonym "Aratus," the ancient Greek poet known for writing about heaven and celestial bodies as well as for promoting the public good over private interests. Annapolis, "Aratus" argued, was centrally located and had a sound economy yet an affordable cost of living. Moreover, Annapolis was free from political turmoil and had good seafood, which the author believed was an important criterion for a capital. The letter went so far as to identify a specific plot of land amounting to twenty square miles by the Severn and South Rivers.[15]

City and state leaders responded to the letter by donating three hundred acres and a few public buildings toward a capital city and pledged funds to build lodging accommodations for each state's congressional delegation. This marked one of the earliest comprehensive "bids" to be the capital. The letter ended up influencing the national debate and prompting a flurry of other "marketing" efforts on behalf of cities across the country.[16]

Over the summer offers of land for a capital poured in from Maryland, New York, Pennsylvania, Virginia, and New Jersey, the latter proposing locations in New Brunswick, Newark, and Elizabeth.[17] Wealthy individuals even offered their own land and funds. One such person was a prominent physician in Philadelphia. Even after the debate, offers were made. For example, the residents of Germantown just outside Philadelphia banded together to promote their community in what was fast becoming a bidding war.[18]

During the debate over the aforementioned proposals, one could count on opposition from Virginia and other southern states to any capital in the north. Virginia's leaders presented a largely unified front in both organizing opposition to northern cities and uniting other southern states to the causes of slavery and a southern capital. In fact, the geopolitical fight over a northern versus southern capital that simmered throughout the war years ended up lasting from 1783 to 1790. Along with slavery, it constituted the primary focus of the South's postwar agenda.[19]

Both the plethora of proposals from the North and the growing support for Annapolis or a site in Maryland prompted Thomas Jefferson and James Madison to organize plans for a capital in the Old Dominion. As early as June 1783 Virginia had offered Congress land in Williamsburg, the former colonial capital, along with the promise of public buildings such as the Governor's Palace. The ensuing proposals from Virginia were attractive and included much more in funds and acreage than was typically offered by other states.

Virginia's leaders then hatched another plan. As a backup strategy in the event a location on the Maryland side of the Potomac was chosen, Virginia countered with its own proposal for a capital on its side of the important river. Advocating two locations within their state, however, ended up being shortsighted. It only served to divide Virginians—advocates for Williamsburg opposed the Potomac site, and vice versa—and ultimately weakened their voice.

However, as the political dynamics of the capital debate shifted in Congress, Jefferson and Madison again adjusted their approach. The two neighbors covered all their bases by lobbying for a joint offer from Maryland and Virginia for a site on the Potomac by the borders of both states. The two friends had become concerned that a similar proposal might arise in the north—that New Jersey and Pennsylvania would align to select the Delaware, a river that flowed along the border between the two neighbors. A shared capital, they reasoned, would be preferable to no capital at all or, worse yet, one in the north.

Jefferson and Madison were joined by Maryland representatives Daniel Carroll and Thomas Sim Lee, both of whom happened to live by the Potomac and owned vast tracts of land in the region. Perhaps most important, however, through the process of promoting the compromise site, the two influential Founders joined Washington in becoming staunch advocates for a Potomac capital.[20]

Virginia offered Congress the sum of 40,000 pounds for the site but expected Maryland to pony up 60,000 pounds. This slight to their alleged ally threatened to unravel the plan and alliance. Maryland countered with a proposal for a capital at Georgetown, which was on its side of the Potomac. Because Maryland was also considering sites along the upper part of the river and Chesapeake Bay—farther from Virginia's population base—Virginians were forced to support Georgetown for practical reasons: it was closer to Virginia. The alliance between the two Potomac states remained precarious. Despite Virginia's influence, Congress would never actually meet south of Maryland.[21]

After the voting began on October 7, it quickly became apparent that a tie existed. It was resolved by a majority for a site on the Delaware River near Trenton. This angered the southern delegates. Elbridge Gerry proposed a bold solution: a resolution for a second seat of government on the Potomac near Georgetown. This united the New England and southern states in an unlikely alliance, and Congress passed the so-called dual-residence agreement on October 21.[22]

Congress came to no decision about federal jurisdiction. Soon after arriving at Princeton, it appointed a committee to consider the subject. Emboldened by the offers received by Congress over the summer and the public discussion that ensued in the wake of the Philadelphia mutiny, the committee reported that Congress should have exclusive jurisdiction over a federal district. Such a proposal was opposed by many state delegates who believed it would threaten states' rights, so Congress did not act—that is, not until 1787 when James Madison proposed it be added to the Constitution.[23]

Early in November Congress adjourned to Annapolis, where it remained until August of 1784. Three months later, it reconvened at Trenton and took several actions to stabilize the federal government. Among these was the decision on December 20 to abandon the dual-residence agreement. Three days later, it adopted a measure to locate the seat of government on the Delaware River near Trenton and move Congress to New York City.[24]

Regarding his reservations about the Delaware River location of the capital, Washington added, "If the union continues . . . I will agree to be classed among the false prophets." He then encouraged his former military aide and friend, Richard Henry Lee—now a Virginia delegate to Congress—to block appropriations to implement the measure. "Fixing the Seat of Empire at any spot on the Delaware," noted Washington, "is in my humble opinion, demonstrably wrong." He showed both his hand and his political insights, noting, "To incur an expense for what may be called the permanent seat of Congress at this time, is I conceive evidently impolitic; for without the gift of prophecy, I will venture to predict that under any circumstances of confederation, it will not remain so far to the Eastward long; and until the public is in better circumstances, it ought not to be built at all."[25]

Washington was dismayed by the vicious nature of the debates in Congress, the parochial self-interest, and the lack of progress on the vital issue, predicting that the Delaware River site would not work and that a new one would have to be chosen. A few years later he recalled, "The two great questions of funding the debt and fixing the seat of government have been agitated, as was natural, with a good deal of warmth." He understood the impact of the debate on his vision of a unified nation and the consequences of continuing to do nothing, noting, "These were always considered by me as questions of the most delicate and interesting nature. . . . They were more in danger of having convulsed the government itself than any other perils."[26]

As for a solution on the site of the capital, that would have to wait for a few more years.

CHAPTER 11

Political Architecture

*The city will express in the stile of our Architecture the sublime
Sentiment of Liberty, the grandeur of conception, a Republican
simplicity, and that true Elegance of proportion.*

Commissioners of the Capital City, 1793

A s was noted earlier, the Philadelphia mutiny of 1783 had soured many
citizens on the city serving as a possible site for the new nation's capital. However, the crisis had other potentially more damaging effects; it had
tarnished the image of Congress and the nascent government.[1] Congress was
desperate to find a path forward, yet it remained plagued by internal bickering
among political and sectional factions. The only answer appeared to be George
Washington.

Unlike Congress, the general came through the war with his reputation en-
larged. During the war, for example, protesters jeering, "God damn the King!"
often added chants of "God bless George Washington!" Likewise, at one riot
in New York City in 1776, residents tore down a large statue of King George
III on horseback and then melted it down to make musket balls to fire at the
British. In the statue's place would later stand a monument of Washington. By
the close of the war, swelling crowds, filled with patriotic fervor, would clamor
to get a glimpse of the great Washington. Cheers greeted him wherever he went.
The victor of the Revolutionary War captured the hearts and minds of his countrymen perhaps as much as, if not more than, the abstract principles of self
government and liberty, and certainly far more than Congress or the promise of

a capital city and its attendant buildings and institutions. Washington, it turned out, was perhaps the closest person or symbol to the embodiment of the elusive notions of Americanism and national identity that he sought to promote among the people.

Congress was well aware of the general's commanding presence and the adulation afforded him by the public. So with the war over and facing the prospect of having to again move to another temporary meeting site, Congress did what politicians tend to do: they linked themselves to someone or something popular. In this case, they hatched a plan to erect a memorial to Washington. As one writer described, "For the badly maligned Congress, association with the man widely regarded as the American Cincinnatus was an opportunity to bask in reflected glory of the pre-eminent symbol of national unity."[2]

To be sure, no honor appeared to be too great for the man who won the War for Independence. Reminding the people of Washington would, Congress hoped, help them to govern, lend legitimacy to the struggling government, and avoid another uprising by unpaid veterans. The plan was unveiled: it would be an enormous bronze statue of the general on horseback, one that would sit atop a marble pedestal. Washington's triumphs—driving the British out of Boston, crossing the Delaware River to defeat the Hessians at Trenton, and of course, achieving the decisive victory at Yorktown—would be engraved into the base. The monument would be the architectural embodiment of the new republic.

However, because the new nation lacked a permanent capital, the joke became that Congress would be forced to haul the massive memorial from city to city. The twin dilemmas of one statue and two seats of government prompted Francis Hopkinson, one of the signers of the Declaration of Independence, to suggest jokingly that they build a statue the size of history's infamous Trojan horse; this way Congress could simply get inside the memorial before each move. Given Congress's raucous nature, there was another joke inherent in the wisecrack: a host city had to agree to accept them![3]

Congress was eager to commission one of the world's foremost artists for the symbol of the nation. Benjamin Franklin suggested Jean-Antoine Houdon, who had already produced a famous bust of Washington.[4] The problem was that Congress had yet to resolve the financial crisis and therefore lacked the funds to bring Houdon from France and cover his exorbitant fee. With anti-federalists and southern members unwilling to negotiate over finances, the great statue was postponed.

When Washington later became president in 1789, he nixed the planned statue over concerns about the cost and the possible appearance of monarchical ambitions. French-born architect and Revolutionary veteran Pierre Charles L'Enfant later included an equestrian statue of Washington in his plan for the capital city.[5] A decade later, after Washington's death, Congress again debated the idea of a suitable memorial to the Founder, including a plan for a pyramid-shaped mausoleum in the Capitol rotunda. Both those projects were abandoned. A fitting memorial would have to wait but would eventually find a home on the National Mall.

Despite Congress's inability to complete the great statue, the debate underscored the importance of what might be called "political architecture," symbols of national identity and, on a far more practical level, the implausibility of moving the government from city to city every few months. Momentum was building to resolve the debate over a capital city, but this was easier said than done.

The lack of a monarch, a head of state, and a seat of government presented the Founders with both challenges and opportunities. Whereas most capitals around the world and throughout antiquity grew out of existing cities of importance and were also capitals of commerce and culture (St. Petersburg and Madrid are notable exceptions), the new city Washington would help establish would be built near only a few small commercial centers. Described as "a plan wholly new," the capital would be carved out of agricultural land and woods and filled with entirely new possibilities limited only by politics, funding, and imagination.[6]

Yet the process of building a new city was not entirely, well, *new*. All across America this had been happening throughout the seventeenth and eighteenth centuries on a smaller level, as newly arrived immigrants bought and sold land, developed lots, and built new towns and villages out of nothing. Discoveries of vast, rich lands to the west sent waves of settlers and adventurers chasing opportunity and freedom, and soon new communities sprung up out of the wilderness.

Yet in practicality, the new would be blended with the old. Even though a war had just been fought to break free of the customs of Europe, that continent continued to be a major influence on the debate about a new capital and nation. Washington and other revolutionaries naturally looked to Europe for their inspiration. Many of them, after all, had English ancestry and European sensibilities, which explains why the framers of the Constitution who sought to break with "old Europe" would nevertheless end up drawing on the philosophical works of classical Greek thinkers and European intellectuals such as Locke, Rousseau, and Montesquieu. So too would the political architecture of Europe influence the capital city. Accordingly, Washington and the Founders did not thoroughly reject their English heritage; they embraced much of what it was to be English, revolting, in the words of Professor Gordon Wood, "not against the English constitution but on behalf of it."[7]

Americans of English descent were not a racial group long oppressed, denied the free practice of their culture or language, and therefore left with no other recourse than to fight for their lives and liberties. Many lived as comfortably and freely as their counterparts back in England, some perhaps more so. In addition, many Americans were undeniably English in terms of their language and heritage. Their political allegiance was to the Crown, but something had been happening in the North American colonies. Noticeable differences were occurring in the foods they ate, the way they practiced religion, and a variety of unique social customs. Separated from their motherland by a vast ocean, Americans had grown apart and had developed their own culture. Such was the case with George Washington, whose lineage was traced to England and who had been a loyal subject of His Majesty all his life. However, Washington and his neighbors were now becoming less and less English in character.[8]

It was also the age of reason, and a transformation was occurring. A new way of thinking about liberty and equality had emerged. The Founders were, according to Professor Wood, students of the Enlightenment, steeped in "classical antiquity, Christian theology, English empiricism, and European rationalism." As John Adams proudly boasted, "Let us study the law of nature, search into the spirit of the British constitution; read the histories of ancient ages; contemplate the great examples of Greece and Rome; set before us the conduct of our own British ancestors, who have defended for us the inherent rights of mankind against foreign and domestic tyrants and usurpers."[9]

Washington, a man who had never visited Europe, would soon turn to such architects as James Hoban, who had been born in Ireland, to design the presidential home and L'Enfant to develop a plan for the capital city. Later, architects such as Benjamin Henry Latrobe, an Englishman of French ancestry, would finish their work. Washington and Thomas Jefferson, though political opposites, both actively recruited skilled immigrant labor from Europe—from German stonemasons to Scottish craftsmen—to build the new capital. Fittingly for a new experiment in self-government peopled by diverse groups from around the world, noncitizens and immigrants helped win the war and then build its capital.

These workers would ultimately help to forge the character of the nation. And in so doing, a hybrid approach of old and new was emerging, one that was also both idealistic at times and pragmatic at times. In this sense the budding political system and capital were therefore uniquely American.

To be sure, while the founding was unique in world history, it was not rooted in a grand, new political theory of independence, governance, or revolution. Rather, it was inspired by an amalgamation of existing political philosophies. Likewise, independence came courtesy of colonial *rebellion* rather than *revolution* in the truest sense of the term. As Daniel Leonard, an attorney and loyalist living in Massachusetts during the revolution observed in 1775, never before in history had a revolution occurred "with so little real cause."[10] American colonists, after all, had a degree of home rule and were the beneficiaries of British trade, protection, and citizenship.

Thus, the revolution was in some ways "without an immediate oppression, without a cause depending much on hasty feelings as theoretical reasoning," admitted the Founder Edmund Randolph.[11] From the perspectives of royalists and loyalists, it was the most "unnatural rebellion that ever existed."[12] Those who rose up in the North American colonies rebelled not because there was insufficient home rule but, in the words of Gordon Wood, perhaps because "they had had so much" of it. America's national birth certificate, then, can be said to have been a declaration of independence rather than a grandiose treatise on the rights of humankind.[13]

Furthermore, in most nations, government was the dominant institution, and it predated large-scale private commerce and other institutions. However, it was the other way around for Americans, who often neither valued nor trusted government. Removed from urban areas and living in a sparsely populated landmass, many Americans did not feel the effect or benefits of government in their everyday lives but vividly recalled the mistreatment by a powerful, central government in London, which left a bad taste in their mouths. As one scholar noted, the public felt its government was "an institution of too little significance to attract population and wealth to its residence."[14]

Long after the war had ended, for instance, the idea of these (plural) "united" (adjective) States rather than the (singular) "United" (noun) States was as common as Thomas Jefferson's reference to "my country" as meaning Virginia. Accordingly, public institutions developed slowly and under suspicion, all of which limited the selection of a capital city and development of the sense of nationhood. Such mindsets would end up presenting Washington with yet another challenge in his effort to build a capital city and forge a united nation and American character.[15]

Yet in America a hatred of tyranny, complete rejection of Old World institutions—such as the monarchy, a state church, a military officer corps, and aristocratic privilege—and radical ways of thinking about liberty replaced the age-old mindsets of the privileged class and the unquestioning obedience to the monarch that existed in Britain and much of Europe. In a larger sense, however, the belief that "all men are equal," along with a "set of common assumptions" about popular sovereignty, self-government, and the free market, was forging a nascent American creed and political culture among the Founders and their fellow citizens.[16]

The Founders were well-read men and therefore knew that some European political philosophers pondered whether a republic based on popular sovereignty, representative government, and individual rights was realistic, much less in such a geographically large, unexplored, and untamed land. Would diverse peoples without a sense of shared purpose, identity, or common values unite? Founding a nation and establishing a political and legal system, after all, are just part of the process of physically building a nation. Moreover, that architectural embodiment of the nation was only part of the process of establishing a sense of nationhood. There was much more work to be done, not just to build a capital city but to develop an American character and national identity among the new states and independent-minded, often geographically isolated former colonists.

The 1770s and 1780s were also a time for determining the status of race relations and the role of "the peculiar institution" of slavery in the new nation. It would be but one phase of the long sectional struggle between northerners, with one view of the new nation, and southerners, with quite another perspective. Whether it was slavery, the debt question, paying veterans, or the location and composition of the capital city, sectional divides formed and undermined the spirit of national unity Washington so desired for his countrymen. Seemingly, two somewhat separate American cultures and characters were forming.

These disagreements went beyond simply a North-South geographical tug-of-war and the fate of countless enslaved persons. A new front emerged when northerners generally favored a capital nearer to bigger cities, commercial sites, ports, and centers of trade, which yet again reflected the European tradition and a developing political culture in the northern half of the country. Some southerners, however, wanted aristocratic plantation owners and slavery to dominate the new nation and therefore advocated a small capital away from banks, merchants, foreign influences, and big cities. These elements, they believed, would corrupt their agrarian, landed ideal and southern "way of life."

What emerged were two distinct architectural and geographical visions for the capital city and its buildings, one embracing grand Greco-Roman palaces near urban centers, the other preferring simple brick structures in rural areas.

Both perspectives reflected not only the political culture of the regions but the competing views about the role of government and the very future of the republic. It all would be inextricably linked to the capital city.

Paraphrasing Carl von Clausewitz's famous line that "war is diplomacy by other means," one might say that architecture was politics by other means.[17] Washington and his fellow Founders understood that the new capital city's location and composition would be symbolically important. More than a city or collection of buildings, it would be the embodiment of new ideals and a new order. From its location to the composition of its buildings, the city would help determine what kind of nation the United States would become. A nation of commerce and urban centers or an agrarian land of small villages? A nation with a strong federal government or a confederacy of loosely aligned states? A country with slave labor? One resembling the powers of Europe? A democracy or a republic?

In the words of Congressman James Jackson of Georgia, the new city "might be compared to the heart in the human body. It was a center from which the principles of life were carried to the extremities."[18] As such, the capital city would both forge and reflect a "political culture" of democracy and, Washington hoped, imbue the public with an American spirit and identity.

The famous British architect, Sir Christopher Wren, writing in the seventeenth and eighteenth centuries, echoed such views, noting, "Architecture has its political Use; public buildings being the Ornament of a Country. . . . It establishes a Nation, draws People and Commerce, makes the People love their native Country, which Passion is the Origin of all great Actions in a Commonwealth."[19] Others throughout history understood this linkage, including, tragically, Adolf Hitler and his architect Albert Speer, who once boasted, "I, too, was intoxicated by the idea of using drawings, money and construction firms to create stone witnesses to history, and thus affirm our claim that our works would survive for a thousand years." At least that was his führer's mad idea.[20]

Thomas Paine long ago observed that government "is only the creature of a constitution." Such a governing document is an antecedent to government, but the philosophical and legal foundations of governance need a home, buildings, a citizenry, and much more to function as a guidepost for the ideals enshrined in a constitution. The city of Washington is presently filled with lasting memorials and iconic backdrops for democracy, from the Washington Monument and Lincoln Memorial to the Martin Luther King Jr. Memorial and Vietnam Veterans Memorial Wall. Such physical or architectural representations of the nation have been featured on postage stamps and currency, in song, and in countless books and films. Even by the end of the nineteenth century, such symbols had become indelibly connected with the nation and patriotism. In modern times, for better or worse, commercial advertisers have used them to sell everything from cars to insurance.[21]

Undeniably, any capital city and the public buildings housed in it are much more than brick and mortar. A capital city instills a sense of nationhood in the hearts and minds of citizens and establishes an identity both internally and beyond a country's borders. It functions like other important symbols of a nation, such as a flag or national anthem, the Great Seal, and even an identifiable landmark or a military victory. Accordingly, many Americans would today point to the Stars and Stripes, the bald eagle, or the White House and Capitol as enduring symbols of Americanism as readily as they would cite the principles of judicial review, popular sovereignty, or bicameralism.

Impressively, Washington appreciated well beyond most of his compatriots and fellow Founders that, as the joining of architecture with the political agenda, the capital and its buildings are visible manifestations of political philosophy. Their design also reflects the classical Greek and Roman philosophical origins of democracy and republicanism.

Likewise, the design for the presidential home by the architect James Hoban was that of a country house rather than a palace, thus reflecting the republican values of the new nation. Even the physical separation of the president's house and the capitol—sitting on opposite ends of Pennsylvania Avenue in the city—reinforces the doctrine of "separation of powers." While it is logistically impossible today, once upon a time, the White House used to be open for public receptions on New Year's Day; the public simply walked through the front doors for refreshments. Only in such a republican experiment could "people of all ages, rank, conditions, and color have rubbed shoulders on an equal footing to shake hands with the first citizen in the land." Indeed, much about the capital city both projects and reflects the young republic's ideals and principles.[22]

Architecturally and politically, the White House is quintessentially American in other ways, including its common name. The term "White House," for instance, was not officially used until President Theodore Roosevelt had it placed on his letterhead on October 12, 1901.[23] As the noted writer James Fennimore Cooper quipped after visiting the building in 1828, "The Americans familiarly call the exceedingly pretty little palace in which their chief magistrate resides the 'White House'; but the true appellation is the President's House."[24] Initially, the building was known as the "President's Palace" and "Executive Mansion," or simply the "President's House," an unpretentious custom befitting republican simplicity and reflecting the ideals of the nation.

Accordingly, as the manifestation of both politics and architecture, the Executive Mansion remains a place of pilgrimage for countless people from around the world. While the same might be said for homes such as George Washington's Mount Vernon, Thomas Jefferson's Monticello, and James Madison's Montpelier, all of which attract tourists, visitors are drawn to them for quite different reasons. In large measure they are popular sites because of the personalities of the former occupants and grand architecture. The White House is something more and altogether different.

The people in office, after all, may come and go with elections, but the buildings and capital city remain as steadfast symbols of a people or nation. They are a part of every American's national inheritance. "I never forget," said Franklin Roosevelt in one of his popular fireside chats on the radio, "that I live in a house owned by all the American people and that I have been given their trust."[25]

PART III

THE
GREAT
DEBATE

CHAPTER 12

Convention

Annuit coeptis. (Favors our undertakings.)
US Senate Chamber

Republicanism and revolution were ideas that had been contemplated and nurtured for centuries, if not millennia. The Founders devoted much time and energy to debating these topics, finding inspiration in the words of great philosophers from history and using them to justify the Declaration of Independence. Yet the shadow hanging over their work was the knowledge that many philosophers had long speculated that a republic would not work, especially in such a large, untamed, and diverse country; republicanism, it was believed, would likely devolve into tyranny.

The government remained weak, the people remained divided, and Washington's longed-for sense of American identity and nationalism had yet to take hold. The bitter conflicts and factions in the postwar years were proving the naysayers true. Then it happened. On the heels of the Newburgh conspiracy and Philadelphia mutiny of 1783, the incipient experiment in self-government nearly came unhinged for a third time—and it was again from internal violence and revolt rather than a foreign threat.

In 1786 a disgruntled Revolutionary War veteran named Daniel Shays led an armed rebellion against the government of Massachusetts. Like his predecessors at Newburgh and Philadelphia, Shays was a veteran of the war. He had enlisted at the beginning of the revolution and fought in such iconic battles as Lexington,

Concord, Bunker Hill, Ticonderoga, and Saratoga, rising to the rank of captain. Wounded, he resigned and went home. Unpaid.[1]

In the years after the war Shays emerged as a spokesperson for and leader of fellow veterans and struggling farmers in rural western Massachusetts who were angry at perceived economic injustices. It appeared to them that the state's government was working only on behalf of the more powerful, populous, and prosperous communities along the Eastern Seaboard, not for rural western farmers. The situation was rife with discontent and uncertainty, made all the worse when numerous petitions by the public went unaddressed by the state legislature. Moreover, the situation in western Massachusetts was indicative of the situation across much of rural America at the time.

When the state legislature adjourned in August, angry demonstrations began to form throughout the western communities. Protests broke out at courthouses. Soon anger prevailed over civility, and farmers began destroying public property. Threats were made on both sides. Led by Shays, mobs of desperate farmers armed themselves, and the state legislature responded by suspending habeas corpus. Chaos and an armed insurrection threatened not just Massachusetts but areas across the fledgling republic. Samuel Adams, the former firebrand leader of the Sons of Liberty and Boston Tea Party, did not help matters when he suggested that foreign agents might be behind the rebellion. Labeling the mob's actions treason, he called for putting the insurrectionists to death. In September the state supreme court ordered the arrest of several rebellious citizens. No one stepped forward to de-escalate the mounting crisis.[2]

Tensions escalated, prompting a deeply disturbed George Washington to label the actions of Shays and the Massachusetts farmers a "formidable rebellion against the laws & constitutions of our own making." To get to the source of the problem, the former general dispatched letters to his former officers in Massachusetts, asking, "Are your people getting mad?—Are we to have the goodly fabric that eight years were spent in rearing pulled over our heads?" He warned, "Commotions of this sort, like snow-balls, gather strength as they roll." Washington worried that the nation was unraveling, writing, "Our Affairs, generally seem really, to be approaching to some awful crisis." They were.[3]

Shays and his followers seized courthouses in the western part of the state to halt foreclosures. Governor James Bowdoin countered by calling up a force of twelve hundred state militiamen to be led by Benjamin Lincoln, a former general of the Continental Army and Washington's trusted friend. By January 1787 armed insurgents comprising hundreds of disaffected, poor farmers were on the march. Their plans now included commandeering the federal armory at

Springfield. If successful, they would be in possession of an arsenal of weapons and powder sufficient to launch a small war. Washington rallied support to oppose the insurrection while General Lincoln was allotted additional troops by the state.

The escalating crisis came to a head on January 25, 1787, when Shays approached the armory with roughly fifteen hundred men. There General Lincoln met him with a force of over three thousand blocking their path. Lincoln ordered the insurgents to disperse. When they did not, he fired warning shots. Shays and his men held their ground, so Lincoln launched a barrage of artillery fire that killed four of the insurgents and wounded approximately twenty. Fortunately, most of the farmers fled rather than fought. The rebellion lasted just six months and resulted in only a handful of deaths and injuries.

Several rebel leaders were captured. Shays initially fled to Vermont, then to New York. He and his ringleaders were sentenced to death in absentia. Although he was deeply unsettled by the incident, a magnanimous Washington fully supported the pardons in 1788 that eased the tensions. Later in life, Shays even received his federal pension for service in the war.

However, the uprising alarmed politicians and threatened peace and stability throughout the country. Civil discontent remained very real after the affair, and the wounds would linger for years, in part because most of the militiamen who opposed Shays were from eastern Massachusetts, whereas most of the rioters were from the rural, western part of the state, reflecting the Eastern Seaboard–western split throughout the country. Nor was this the first or only unruly situation. Elsewhere in the country, people were refusing to pay their taxes, and both peaceful protests and violent confrontations and seizures of property were occurring.[4]

The insurrection highlighted the weakness of the Articles of Confederation, the nation's meager finances, and the desperate need for a standing army and political reform. The incident also reaffirmed Washington's concerns about the weakness of the government and lack of national unity. Of the uprising, the general wrote to his friend Gen. Henry Knox expressing his desire "that good may result from the cloud of evils which threatened, not only the hemisphere of Massachusetts but by spreading its baneful influence, the tranquility of the Union."[5]

In 1786, Madison and Hamilton called for a convention in Annapolis, Maryland, to address the governing crisis and shortcomings of the Articles. The effort accomplished little. The budding sense of promise and effort to build a nation had given way to a sectional divide. In hushed tones, members of Congress were speculating in 1786 and 1787 whether the country would long endure. Would it end at the hands of a North-South split or an East-West divide, or perhaps the states would become separate countries or join regional confederacies?[6]

Shays's Rebellion ended up being a needed catalyst for reform, which occurred at the Constitutional Convention in Philadelphia, where a few dozen delegates finally gathered in May 1787 to amend the Articles. The incident also contributed to Washington's return to public life.[7] The stakes were high, and given the failures of the Annapolis Convention and rampant civil unrest in 1786, the odds of success were not promising.

Washington initially declined the offer to participate; he had, after all, famously announced at the end of the war that he would "take leave of all the employments of public life." Moreover, Washington risked all he had accomplished by attending. Like Cincinnatus, however, the man who had once relinquished power was needed again. Washington understood the uniqueness of his position, as did the other framers. His image and reputation were among the few assets of the new country. With a nod to civic duty, he joined Virginia's other delegates in Philadelphia.

The best minds in the country gathered and, in the ensuing weeks, devoted considerable time and energy pondering the nature and scope of government and debating such contentious issues as slavery, rights, representation in Congress, the powers of the federal government, and the election of a president, each of which proved enormously challenging. Most important, they completely abandoned the Articles and opted to create something new.

After several contentious weeks during that hot, humid summer, the delegates with federalist leanings were able to cobble together enough support to establish a constitutional system of government. Washington was enormously pleased that the convention addressed the looming problems by proposing measures to strengthen the government. The popular version of events often suggests that Washington played little role at the gathering. This narrative records only that he participated in few debates and was unfamiliar with most of the philosophical readings that engaged the other Founders. However, this interpretation neglects the fact that Washington was selected as the presiding officer, a role no one else could have filled. It must be remembered that the Convention took place behind closed doors, and support for the ambitious undertaking was dubious. Elected by his peers in the same building where he had been selected as commander in chief twelve years earlier, however, Washington's presence added a reassuring calm and confidence to the gathering both among the framers inside the meeting and for the public outside the building.

It has been properly suggested by some historians that it is unlikely the Constitution would ever have been ratified had he not endorsed it. Or as one of Washington's opponents admitted, "His influence carried this government."[8]

One of the many issues of contention at the Convention was once again the matter of a permanent seat of government, although, amidst the more pressing matters of how to create a government, it received little attention. After so much squabbling for so many years, the same questions remained: Should a new capital be built or an existing seat of state government used? What was the proper scope and scale of such a city? Would Congress have exclusive jurisdiction over the city? What type of buildings would fill it? How would the financially strapped nation pay for it? These would soon become among the most divisive questions facing the new republic—and they, once again, went largely unanswered.

The issue of a permanent capital came to the floor of the Convention twice. The first instance was courtesy of George Mason, who suggested that the Constitution on which the framers were working did not permit the selection of any *state* capital, so perhaps it also precluded naming a *national* capital. The topic had been fraught with sensitivities and self-interest for years, so Mason's point gained some support. Elbridge Gerry of Massachusetts agreed but also offered advice should they end up deciding to select a site for the capital: he warned against selecting a large commercial center. Several southerners concurred, including Hugh Williamson of North Carolina, who also correctly predicted that the public would be emotionally vested in the location of a capital and that commercial interests would only make the decision more politically precarious. The issue remained contentious.[9]

Others wanted to avoid having to make the decision at the Convention altogether. One of them was Gouverneur Morris, who rightly worried that any choice or location would divide the delegates—a location in the North would alienate southerners and vice versa—and therefore ultimately undermine any agreement that came out of the gathering. To be sure, the question of having, much less identifying a location for, a capital city was so sensitive that it threatened to unravel the entire summer's work. Support for the document the framers produced that summer was precarious enough without the added controversy of determining the location of a capital. The consensus that emerged among the delegates was that they should leave the thorny issue of a capital alone—again.

Nonetheless, the idea of selecting a location for the capital was too irresistible. Some of the delegates were enticed to weigh in on the matter, including Robert Morris, who suggested Newburgh, which was around sixty miles north of New York City by the Hudson River and had hosted General Washington's final wartime headquarters. The site was defensible, well-known by the framers and military commanders, sat beside an important river, and yet was located far enough away from the coast to prevent an easy attack by a foreign naval power. Virginia senator William Grayson suggested Georgetown as a possible location. The debate continued as it had for years along sectional lines and with parochial interests in the fore.[10]

There was ample pushback against any named location, but there were also pressing concerns about the ability to govern the newly independent states with the country still lacking a permanent capital. Rufus King of Massachusetts warned of the problems stemming from transient capitals, which had been the experience of the past few years and would continue to plague the government. In total, roughly thirty sites would ultimately be proposed for the capital. The idea of transient capitals was so noxious that George Mason changed his mind and withdrew his proposal to prohibit naming a location for the capital. The *New York Daily Gazette* would later opine one year into Washington's inaugural presidency about members of Congress "who talk of moving from place to place with as much indifference as a set of strolling players."[11]

The second context for debating the issue of a capital was legalistic hairsplitting. For instance, Rufus King and James Madison introduced their own measure that required a law—rather than the convention—to determine or change the residence of Congress. This would empower Congress and delay any decision. The debate raised additional questions: Would Congress necessarily have to convene in the capital? Could the Constitution dictate residence? Did Congress have the power to adjourn to a different location without having to pass a law? If the answer was yes, then the legislature might not need executive approval for the location.

Madison changed his position and argued that, if a capital had to be selected, then a central location rather than one that favored the North or South, or East or West, was preferable. This proposal marked an important advent in the contentious debate (and echoed Washington's preference). However, he still felt the First Congress should have the power to pick the location through legislation. Madison admitted, though, that the new executive office they were discussing might be required to sign off on the law.[12] The ensuing debate over Congress selecting the location of a capital ended up being the first public debate on the constitutionality of an act of Congress.[13]

CHAPTER 13

Ten Miles Square

Laus Deo. (Praise be to God.)
Inscription atop the Washington Monument

The delegates ultimately agreed in Article 1, Section 8 of the Constitution to grant power to Congress to deal with the matter of a capital city. This section of the Constitution set out the various powers of the legislative branch, the last of which was listed in paragraph 17. It read,

> The Congress shall have Power . . . To exercise exclusive Legislation in all Cases whatsoever, over such District (not exceeding ten Miles square) as may, by Cession of Particular States, and the Acceptance of Congress, become the Seat of Government of the United States, and to exercise like Authority over all Places purchased by the Consent of the Legislature of the State in which the Same shall be, for the Erection of Forts, Magazines, Arsenals, Dock-Yards, and other needful Buildings.

Thus, paragraph 17 addressed four important issues, one being that the eventual district containing the capital could function under the exclusive jurisdiction of Congress. Another was the capital's size. It also allowed Congress to accept any land ceded by the states for a capital city, discussed federal jurisdictions, and empowered Congress to erect buildings, forts, and other necessary public infrastructure—in other words, to build the capital.

Mostly, however, at long last, the new Constitution provided for the establishment of a national capital, but the issue of its location was far from resolved
and the wording was lacking details except that the "seat of government" could
not exceed "ten Miles square" (100 square miles). Madison later defended the
selection of "ten Miles square" for the capital city in Federalist No. 43, saying
a city of that size would be too large for any one state to host. Therefore, being
"too great a pledge," as he put it, the capital would require cooperation by numerous cities and states, working together to create public buildings. Article 1,
Section 8, paragraph 17 was designed to help unite the nation. In this respect,
Madison echoed Washington's long-held sentiments.[1]

The consensus was forming that Congress and the states would play a joint
role in selecting the location, yet Congress would retain "exclusive jurisdiction"
in the new federal district. That is, the federal government through Congress
would have power to govern whatever location was chosen for the new capital
city. Congressmen had learned a lesson from the Philadelphia mutiny of 1783
when they were nearly held hostage.

Still, some worried about their city—or any city—being selected as the permanent capital. Would they have rights as a resident of that state or would all
decisions in the city be determined by Congress? This concern led some residents of locations under consideration to oppose their own city's bid.

One such perspective came from Pelatiah Webster, a minister, statesman,
economist, and influential pamphleteer who was born in Connecticut but lived
in Philadelphia. Webster wrote a widely read essay that not only opposed his
adopted city as a potential site but also argued that, while Congress needed jurisdiction over a capital city, it should not have exclusive jurisdiction. The argument resonated for obvious reasons but also because Americans had an aversion
to big cities and many anti-federalists and southerners shared the Jeffersonian
perspective that the urban experience tended to corrupt and distract people
from the nation's business.[2]

Others, including many federalists and northerners, wanted a grand capital in the European tradition, complete with a scientific society, botanical
garden, and array of cultural organizations. Charles Willson Peale, the noted
Philadelphia-based artist, eagerly announced he would move his art gallery to
this new city. A few influential voices, such as the Reverend Jeremy Belknap
of Boston, even favored a national museum of sorts, one that displayed items
confiscated from the British during the war in order to help "fan the flame of
liberty and independence."[3]

The Founders were faced with the dilemma that the main cities in the country were hardly cities in the European sense. Most lacked the necessary public buildings and infrastructure to host the new government. At the same time, it seemed doubtful that a grand new capital would be possible. The country had too few skilled architects and master builders for such an ambitious undertaking, and the construction of a new capital city required significant financial resources—something the nation did not have. Moreover, Washington's beloved Potomac was particularly rural at the time. Although not a region of swamps, as is sometimes incorrectly suggested by books today, it was defined by rolling hills, forests, and lowlands containing rivers and creeks that at times overflowed their banks and flooded the area. It was also a location lacking adequate materials, transportation, workers, and such necessities as sawmills, lumberyards, and brick kilns and brickyards for a project on the scale of a capital.

The leading voice on all things regarding the capital city, of course, was Washington, who wanted the city to be filled with cultural institutions and the necessary public accommodations, such as meeting spaces for Congress and a home for the president. Additionally, he hoped to see a national university established there, one that would attract the most talented Americans from across the country to both help unite the nation and nurture its future.[4] In short, Washington dreamed of a grand "metropolis." It would be built on a scale unimaginable to most of the Founders and on an absurdly rushed schedule of only ten years. It was Washington's vision, and he alone had the "moral authority" to implement such an outrageous plan.[5]

The many questions surrounding how the new nation would function and what to do about a capital city were only partially answered in Philadelphia that hot, humid summer. The meetings had taken place away from the eyes and ears of the public and press, contributing to the uncertainty and anxiety about what would happen to the new, struggling nation. One of those curious about the drama in Philadelphia was Elizabeth Willing Powel, the opinionated prominent socialite, wife of the city's mayor, and a close confidante of George Washington. The premiere *saloniste* of the era was on hand when the framers concluded their work on the Constitution. It has been recorded that she approached the great Benjamin Franklin and allegedly asked, "Well, Doctor, what have we got? A republic or a monarchy?" The elder statesman of the convention is said to have responded, "A republic, Madam," then quipped, "if you can keep it." Indeed.[6]

The framers who gathered at the convention accomplished much, and given that republicanism and self-government were radical concepts, they likely achieved as much as was possible. They had drawn on two thousand years of political thought and blended it with a few original ideas. Apropos to the capital, they wisely focused on how government should function rather than where it should be because, in the words of one prominent historian, "Had the delegates somehow been able to agree on a site, they would thereby have threatened the possibilities for ratification of the Constitution." They also wisely produced a document that could be interpreted, was flexible enough to adapt to changes and varying interpretations, and would thus always be a living document. Alexander Hamilton would, at the behest of Washington, later develop the doctrine of "implied" powers, which further enabled the inaugural president to govern and the document to remain relevant.[7]

Despite Washington's hope that the prospects of a national capital would unite Americans, the agreement in paragraph 17 reopened old divisions. As they had done during the early debates over a capital and the process of framing a constitution, the anti-federalists put up a fight during the ratification process such that it was uncertain as to whether the requisite number of states would ratify in order that the Constitution be put into effect. Such influential voices as George Mason and even some northerners like Mercy Warren of Massachusetts led the charge.

Patrick Henry, who had declined to attend the Constitutional Convention, saying he "smelled a rat," led the effort against his native Virginia ratifying the Constitution, warning his fellow delegates, "I conceive the Republic to be in extreme danger." Henry was so staunch in his opposition to ratification that he thundered against the Constitution's famous opening line, asking, "What right had they to say, 'We, the People'?" He said of the Philadelphia delegates, "Who asked them to speak the language of, 'We, the People,' instead of 'We, the States'?" When northern states ratified the document rather quickly, the famous orator even accused Delaware of having done so without even reading it because the state wanted to be the site of the capital.[8]

Another anti-federalist at the ratification convention in New York chimed in, "How dangerous this city may be, and what its operation on the general liberties of this country, time alone must discover." He likened the proposed new capital to Rome, while other anti-federalists said it would grow larger than Rome and London, and become even more corrupt.[9] In the words of the noted historian Kenneth Bowling, "To those Americans who worried about the survival of republicanism, the dangers of the magnificent capital were immense, particularly if it became a commercial as well as a political city."[10]

Article I, Section 8, paragraph 17 soon became a rallying point for all that was wrong with the Constitution, even though the critics did not yet know the location of the proposed city. A federal city of a hundred square miles smacked of overreach and monarchy, claimed critics, who worked to derail the entire debate.

Concerns over the location and size of the future capital city continued to be raised with anti-federalists, who even speculated that the grand buildings and large city would result in the citizens being oppressed. The anti-federalist and southern alliance also opposed the ideas of establishing cultural institutions, Washington's dream of a national university, and a capital that would be a commercial center, which they saw as mere symbols of wealth and power. Such a city, they cautioned, would also invite corruption as exemplified by such frivolities as museums, universities, and presumably even the proposed statue of George Washington.

All the while, their true motives seemed to be self-interest and protecting slavery. This was not new, nor would it, of course, be the end of the argument over slavery. Some proposed that states pay a tax based on their population and that representation be linked to population. Southern states favored counting enslaved people toward approving political representation but not toward tax burdens. Of course, this bitter issue would influence both the infamous three-fifths clause and later debates that led to secession.[11]

Another similar argument over the location of the capital city involved control of the lands to the west, from the Mississippi River down to the Gulf of Mexico. State charters typically limited their lands to the Eastern Seaboard, and therefore legislatures and landowners worried that, because some states were seeking land claims all the way to the Mississippi, Virginia would try to claim the West. Landowners stood to benefit from the westward expansion, so it finally took a deal brokered by Thomas Jefferson, whereby the Old Dominion agreed to abandon its western claims. The western territories would come into the union as new states on an equal basis with the original thirteen colonies, yet it was also anticipated that the population base might move westward or into Canada, thus changing the complexion of the nation and notions of the geographic center of power.

Alexander Hamilton of New York, James Wilson of Pennsylvania, and other federalists advocating for both the capital city and ratification of the Constitution took to the press to promote the benefits of both. Hamilton extended conciliatory proposals at the ratification convention in New York in hopes of building support. One important measure allowed residents of the federal district to vote for representatives in the US House. Wrote Hamilton, "A provision shall be made by Congress for their having a District Representation in the Body."[12] He further suggested that residents of the state who ceded land for the new capital be permitted to remain residents of that state.

Hamilton also famously asked James Madison and John Jay to join him in writing a series of essays arguing the merits of the Constitution. The resulting *Federalist Papers* would help to ensure its passage. Other federalists offered compromises such as limiting the federal district to three square miles; still others proposed denying the new federal government the right to any land or building in the city not functioning directly for the new government.[13]

The ruckus over the capital during ratification was so toxic that it spilled over into other constitutional debates, most notably the presidency. The large federal city seemed to stoke fears of a monarchical chief executive with a large military under his control, even though most everyone gathered knew that the trustworthy Washington would likely become that executive. The concern was who would lead after Washington.

Similarly, there was disagreement as to the name for the new capital, whether it be "Columbia" or the generic "Federal City." The latter term conjured images of a large government sequestered away, unresponsive and unaccountable to the public. The Founders were classicists and knew their Roman history; they therefore worried about the imperial nature of any grand city. The name would be symbolically important.

The debate over exclusive jurisdiction came back with a vengeance during the fight to ratify, leading Samuel Osgood, a member of the Board of the Treasury, to report that the capital city "has cost me many a sleepless night to find out the most obnoxious part of the proposed plan . . . and I have finally fixed upon the exclusive legislation in the Ten Mile Square . . . What an inexhaustible fountain of corruption are we opening?"[14]

The capital debate figured into the ratification of the Constitution in another way. The states that ratified it quickly—Delaware, the first state to do so on December 7, 1787, followed by Pennsylvania and New Jersey a few days later—did so in part because they hoped to lure the new capital city within their borders. Delaware was also the first state to offer a "ten Miles square" plot of land for a new capital. New Jersey, which ratified the document on December 18, offered its own land by Bordentown and Washington Crossing; the state also worked in conjunction with Pennsylvania to designate available lands straddling the Delaware River, which separated both states. Robert Morris championed this site, situated roughly thirty miles north of Philadelphia by the falls of the Delaware. It so happened that the site included land he owned.[15] The Pennsylvania Ratification Convention offered Congress ten miles square anywhere in the state excepting Philadelphia and two adjacent suburbs. This left the possibility of Congress choosing nearby Germantown, which became a contender.

After months of ratification debate, New Hampshire ratified the document on June 21, 1788. With the Granite State becoming the ninth state to ratify, the nation had reached the required number of states to adopt the Constitution. Washington was delighted by the news but also pleased that Alexandria was the first community in the new country to have a public celebration in honor of ratification. He was also pleased that Virginia ratified it just days later, on June 25, the tenth state to do so.

That July there were grand parades in New York City marking the anniversary of the day Congress declared independence from Britain. Cannon salutes woke people from their slumber just before dawn, church bells rang, and people congregated in the streets. The city of Philadelphia also hosted a grand parade to mark the occasion. One of the parade organizers, Francis Hopkinson, a signer of the Declaration of Independence, promoted a new federal city he hoped would be named "Columbia" by printing pamphlets that read "Behold! Behold! An empire rise! . . . Wisdom and valour shall my rights defend, And o'er my vast domain those rights extend."[16]

Even though Washington celebrated the affirmation of the Constitution, he remained deeply concerned because New York, North Carolina, and Rhode Island had yet to ratify the document. There was still the possibility that they would vote down the measure, raising the question of how the nation would move forward without some of its states. Equally pressing was the matter that the government needed New York to join the union because Congress was scheduled to convene in New York City. Washington was also to be sworn in as the new nation's first president—in a state that might not be a part of the new government.

So much time and energy had gone into selecting New York City as the interim capital that if New York voted no, Congress might have to abandon the city. The First Congress and Washington's inauguration would need to be rescheduled. The question of a capital city would be back to square one, to say nothing of the specter of the nation potentially unraveling.

Washington waited anxiously, requesting that Madison and Hamilton provide him with regular updates regarding the state's ratifying convention. In a rare gesture he also let his preference be known, seemingly to balance the influence of George Clinton, New York's anti-federalist governor. Finally, on July 26, 1788, New York voted to ratify the Constitution, thus alleviating the immediate problem. Bells, cannons, and public revelry marked the occasion.

It might be said, however, that there was drinking on both sides. Some politicians and newspapers attributed New York's decision to finally ratify solely to the state's wanting to retain the seat of government. Others wondered if Washington's endorsement tipped the balance.[17]

Either way New York was finally a part of the new nation, but in name only, as anti-federalists remained staunchly opposed to the Constitution and threatened to continue the fight even after its ratification. Around the country, fights broke out, and some anti-federalists as well as residents of Virginia, Georgia, and the Carolinas burned copies of the Constitution at public ceremonies.

March 4, 1789, the day designated for the Constitution to take effect—and thereby the new government that Washington had fought so hard to create—came and went without North Carolina or Rhode Island formally joining the union. Thus, the new government began operating with just eleven "member" states and uncertainty as to where the permanent capital would be located.

Washington knew there was work to be done to realize his dream of "an indissoluble Union of the States under one Federal Head." It was getting closer, but not yet there.[18]

CHAPTER 14

An Inauguration

Novus ordo seclorum. (A new order of the ages [is born].)
US Senate Chamber

Although the Constitutional Convention affirmed that there would be a capital city and it would be no more than "ten Miles square," the pressing matter of whether to keep New York City as the interim seat for the government while Congress debated where to locate the permanent capital had proved contentious throughout the summer of 1788. Several sites had been considered to host the temporary new government. New York City and Philadelphia had their advocates. These cities were two of the few with the necessary infrastructure to accomplish the task and were two of the largest and wealthiest cities in the country. The selection of a *temporary* capital had other implications. In the words of historian Thomas Flexner, the two cities still hoped to be "principal contenders" in the fight to become the *permanent* capital.

Both cities had lobbied Congress and undertook an array of civic improvements throughout 1787 and 1788, such as constructing new streets, lighting, and public buildings. New York raised $65,000 and hired L'Enfant to renovate the venerable City Hall, originally constructed in 1703 and now rechristened Federal Hall.[1] Meanwhile, newspapers in both cities lauded their virtues and heaped criticism on the other's alleged lack thereof. This competition over the temporary residence of Congress continued until July 1790 when the matter was finally decided in favor of Philadelphia.[2]

The South Carolina delegation and some other southerners had been vocal in their opposition to Philadelphia as the temporary site, even though it was not as far north as New York City. Their concern was that Pennsylvania had a law that any slave who resided in the state for a period of six months would be declared free. Pennsylvania also had an influential Quaker population and numerous abolitionist societies. A capital in the state would potentially threaten the South's "peculiar institution."

A deal of sorts was worked out that, if Philadelphia were chosen as the interim capital, the state would not enforce its antislavery laws on federal officials and that they would pertain only to inhabitants residing there for a certain period.[3] However, southerners still worried that slaves might find out about the law. They therefore supported New York City's bid while masking their racism with a variety of excuses—one being that it was possible to sail from Charleston to New York City, but it would require traveling up a river to reach Philadelphia. Later, when Washington was serving as president in Philadelphia, even he found a way to mitigate the law by having his own slaves periodically leave the state and return to Virginia.[4]

As support for Philadelphia to be the temporary capital waned, Connecticut and New Hampshire began supporting New York City. Pennsylvanians offered a hastily conceived measure to switch the site to Lancaster, but it failed. More interested in denying New York City than anything else, they even attempted to insert Baltimore into the debate.

Sectional rivalries were again unleashed. Hamilton, a New Yorker, countered by informing southerners that Baltimore was simply a ruse to make Philadelphia the permanent capital. Hamilton was able to entice Connecticut, Massachusetts, New Hampshire, New Jersey, New York, and South Carolina to support his city, whereas Delaware, Maryland, Pennsylvania, and Virginia supported Philadelphia—at least initially. Rhode Island switched back and forth, earning it, at the time, the derogatory nickname "The Little Whore." Thus was the bitter nature of the debate.[5]

In addition to the North-South and East-West factions, the geographic divisions also included rifts between New England and the mid-Atlantic states of Delaware, Maryland, New Jersey, and Pennsylvania and, of course, the ongoing animosities over the issue of slavery. Southern states saw the institution as central to agriculture and shaping the future balance of power. The population, they reasoned, would move southward and westward and eventually align politically with the South. If they could therefore delay any decision on a capital long enough, the base of power in the nation might favor them. There were even international tensions and implications regarding the location of the capital city. France, for instance, believed a southern location would weaken the United States as a potential rival and therefore be in its best interest.[6]

It is no wonder Washington wrote to his fellow Virginian Henry Lee bemoaning the tumultuous nature of the debate and describing the question of selecting the site for the seat of government as "pregnant with difficulty and danger."[7] During these heated debates Washington initially worried that the bickering and gridlock over the capital city might undermine implementation of the recently ratified Constitution, and then later he worried that it would weaken the document's legitimacy. He told allies, "A respectable Neighbour of mine has said, the Constitution cannot be carried into execution, without great amendment." He was likely speaking of George Mason, who was a very influential anti-federalist.

So too was Washington disgusted by the lack of civility in the debate. Members of Congress had resorted to vilifying one another, and tensions were harming personal friendships.[8] This included Washington's own relationships, such as when fellow Virginian Patrick Henry later alleged that "in every mouth" around the country people believed Washington was making himself a dictator or monarch.[9]

The vote for a site for the temporary capital finally occurred on September 13, 1788, with Congress selecting New York City. It had proved to be a disagreeable process, prefiguring the combativeness of the looming debate in the First Federal Congress over a permanent capital. Soon after the new members of Congress arrived in New York City, and sensing the ongoing tensions over a location for the capital city, the widely read *Federal Gazette* opined on the debate over a permanent capital, "It is evident that the sooner that great question is determined the better—otherwise it will prove the cause not only of disputes, but of such jealousies, as many lay the foundation of dissentions that may prove fatal to the union."[10]

The first Electoral College had been organized on January 10, 1789. The vote among each state's electors was unanimous—George Washington. Washington had gained important skills commanding a large army spread across a vast country and had essentially functioned as a virtual head of state since 1776. He had also emerged as the most influential man in America. It would be George Washington, more than Congress, which since the outset of the war had showed itself to be weak and largely ineffectual, who would now be a symbol of the new government in 1789.

Although a burning ambition was a part of his disposition, it must be remembered that Washington claimed hesitancy to reenter public life after his retirement. Moreover, *President* Washington was not the same man as *General* Washington. He was now fifty-seven. His arthritis caused him great discomfort, and he was ever mindful of his faulty hearing and fading memory. Groaned the new president, "My life has been a very busy one, I have had but little leisure to read of late years, and even if I had been favored with more leisure, my memory is so bad I can get little advantage from reading."[11]

Washington was always quite self-conscious about many things but especially about the loss of his teeth. By the time he was president, he had but one tooth remaining and had, for years, been forced to rely on large, ill-fitting dentures that forced his lips forward as if he were wearing a modern athlete's mouth guard. At one point the president complained that a particularly uncomfortable set of dentures would "bulge my lips out in such a manner as to make them appear considerably swelled." He requested the dentist provide a new set that did not "in the least degree force the lips out more than [they] now do, as it does this too much already." Mrs. Washington suffered the same discomforts and embarrassments with her own dentures.[12]

A dentist named John Greenwood, who had fought in the war with Washington, made several sets of dentures for his former general. Some used human teeth, others were made of hippopotamus ivory and held together by an unwieldy contraption of metal springs (contrary to the old wives' tale, they were not made of wood). The ivory often stained, however, to resemble wood, and Washington's dentures were further discolored, likely because of all the wine he consumed. In fact, his dentures were nearly black. Accordingly, Dr. Greenwood wrote to President Washington with advice: "I advise you to either take them out after dinner and put them in clean water and put in another set or clean them with a brush and some chalk scraped fine."[13]

The situation affected the president's ability to eat, speak, and even laugh. Wires and springs continually rubbed against and irritated his gums and lips, forcing Washington to use ointments that appeared to have included laudanum (an opiate) to relieve his sore gums. So sensitive was Washington to his image that he and his dentist communicated in secret. Private messengers were dispatched with letters and dentures. His teeth would, of course, be but one of the new president's many concerns, and he would, in the end, give Dr. Greenwood his final tooth when it fell out as a memento of appreciation for his service.[14]

Because of the rudimentary transportation system and uncertainties about conducting a vote, an anxious Washington did not receive news of the Electoral

College result until April 14. Two days later the newly elected president bor-
rowed money for the trip and then set off for the temporary capital, accompanied by Charles Thomson, the secretary of both the Continental Congress and
Confederation Congress, and Col. David Humphreys, his former aide during
the war. Just before leaving on April 16, he shared his concerns with a friend:
"My movements to the chair of Government will be accompanied by feelings
not unlike those of a culprit who is going to the place of his execution; so unwilling am I, in the evening of a life nearly consumed in public cares, to quit a
peaceful abode for an Ocean of difficulties, without that competency of political
skill—abilities & inclination which is necessary to manage the helm."[15]

The man known for his stoicism was confronted by a bit of self-doubt. What
if the government failed? Could he strengthen the precariously fragile republic? Ever conscious of his image, Washington's reputation was at its zenith and
would likely be tarnished in office.[16]

Washington was right to be worried; expectations were very high and the
ex-general was one who always fretted the prospects of failing. He shared these
views with his close friend and soon-to-be secretary of war Henry Knox, writing, "I am sensible, that I am embarking the voice of my Countrymen and
a good name of my own, on this voyage, but what returns will be made for
them—Heaven alone can foretell." It was one of the few times Washington let
down his guard and expressed his feelings.[17]

However, another side of him wanted the prestige, and he was better posi-
tioned to lead than perhaps anyone else in the country. Duty called, and much
work remained in order to fulfill Washington's vision of a strong government,
national spirit, and sense of unity among the former colonies as well as his hope
for a grand, permanent capital to help cement these goals. As he mentioned to
his revolutionary friend and mentee, the Marquis de Lafayette, the new country
still had "character to develop."[18]

Washington recorded his feelings about the trip and challenge before him
in his diary: "I bade adieu to Mount Vernon, to private life, and to domestic
felicity; and with a mind oppressed by more anxious and painful sensations
than I have words to express, set out to New York . . . with the best dispositions
to render service to my country in obedience to its call, but with less hope of
answering its expectations."[19]

The president-elect's path to New York City took him through Alexandria,
Georgetown, Baltimore, Philadelphia, Trenton, and other cities. At each stop
he was met by large adoring crowds and elaborate celebrations. Thousands

showed up in Philadelphia to see him when he passed through the city. Balls and banquets were held in his honor and military escorts and parades marked his travels.

Finally, on April 23 Washington sailed on a small barge across the water to New York City, accompanied by a crew of thirteen sailors and escorted by scores of private boats. Cannonade salutes rang out across the harbor, clanging church bells welcomed him to the city, and thousands of spectators gathered along the waterfront and throughout the city.[20] The new president landed at a wharf near the foot of Wall Street, where Governor George Clinton welcomed him along with an ensemble of congressmen and dignitaries. Washington made his residence at Samuel Osgood's large square brick home on Cherry Street at the corner of Pearl Street. Osgood, who had built the lavish and spatial house in 1770, rented it to Congress for Washington, who staffed it with roughly twenty aides as well as slaves and nonslave servants he brought from Mount Vernon.

Despite the delays in the ceremony, which the Confederation Congress had set for the first Wednesday in March, the large public reception for the new president was encouraging. By dawn on Thursday, April 30, a crowd of people had already gathered out front of the presidential home, eagerly awaiting history and the man who would make it. At noon the throng of curious onlookers and eager citizens followed Washington to Federal Hall, along Queen Street and the present site of Pearl and Broad Streets. The new president looked the part, attired in a dark suit, white silk stockings, shiny silver shoe buckles, and a royal, dark red overcoat. At his hip hung a steel-hilted sword. He stood a full head taller than those around him.

At Federal Hall Washington was greeted by members of the House and Senate. Vice President John Adams announced that the inaugural ceremonies would begin. The chancellor of New York, Robert Livingston, administered the oath to Washington from the second-floor balcony overlooking the enthusiastic crowd below. Nervous, the president's words were barely audible; his voice wavered and his hands shook. At the conclusion of the brief oath, Livingston bellowed, "Long live George Washington, President of the United States!" Crowds roared the refrain, and a thirteen-gun salute was signaled.[21]

The new president retired to the Senate chambers, whereupon he delivered in a hushed and solemn voice the very first inaugural address. It was only 1,419 words in length and would become but the first of many precedents set by Washington. Most presidents serving since Washington have followed his lead in both content, format, and length of their inaugural orations.[22]

Another immediate and ceremonial item of business was the title by which he was to be addressed. With characteristic humility and befitting the new republic, Washington rejected the laudatory epithet proposed by John Adams and Congress—"His Exalted Highness the President of the United States of America and Protector of Their Liberties." It was too monarchical. He would be called simply "Mr. President."[23]

CHAPTER 15

New York City

They had no government left, the constitution was detestable; there was no confidence to be placed in the Americans, the public debt would never be paid; and there was no faith, no justice among them.

J. P. Brissot de Warville of France, describing the new nation

Mrs. Washington, delayed by the perils of travel in the eighteenth century, arrived in New York City a few days after her husband's inauguration with her grandchildren in tow. She too had encountered crowds of well-wishers and was unprepared for the level of outpouring of public adulation.

Irrespective of the spontaneous celebrations that broke out by the steps of Federal Hall and throughout the city, and the arrival of his family, President Washington understood the gravity of the situation and agonized over it.

Indeed, when inaugurated, Washington was in a "dark" mood, one rivaling the "blackest hours of the Revolution." Not only had the delays in confirming the official results of the Electoral College and his declining health caused him great anxiety, but much of the country, including eastern Virginia, was in the grips of a drought. His crops were failing, his finances had yet to recover from the war, and seeds and other important provisions he had ordered from Europe had yet to arrive, thus putting the important spring planting in jeopardy.[1] Moreover, the new nation still lacked a permanent capital and consensus as to its location, while the executive branch of government lacked organization, protocols, staff, and frankly, the ability to function at all.

The Constitution and convention that framed it offered little in the way of detail about the nature and functions of the office of the president. Article II, which governs the executive branch, was vague. Questions remained: How was he to hire staff? How many staffers should he hire? What were their roles and responsibilities? Did he have the power to remove them from office? Even the advice and consent provision was unclear about the extent to which the president was to interact with the Senate.

Washington correctly observed, "I walk on untrodden ground. . . . There is scarcely any part of my conduct which may not hereafter be drawn into precedent."[2] He would be forging the office through his every action and inaction, setting long-lasting and important precedents, including the historic burden of being the first to seek balance between kingly customs and republican values, yet all the while without a permanent seat for the new government.[3]

Moreover, according to an arrangement made under the Congress during the Articles of Confederation, the presidential term had been scheduled to commence on March 4. When both the Senate and House of Representatives convened for the first time, they had been forced to adjourn owing to a lack of a quorum. Because of primitive communications, a few pending elections, and a mix of illnesses and bad weather, only eight senators and thirteen representatives showed up at Federal Hall that day. Robert Morris, who was staying across the Hudson River from the city, did not dare cross the river until the morning. Writing back home to his wife, he complained, "The wind blew so hard, the Evening so dark & Fogg so Thick." Therefore, ten days later, when James Madison finally arrived in New York City, the government had yet to meet. Admitted Madison, "When a Quorum will be made up in either House, rests on vague conjecture." It was another embarrassing start for the new republic.[4]

The delays also meant that the results of the presidential election could be neither officially counted nor confirmed. That would have to wait until April 1, when the House finally had enough members present to convene. Yet their only item of business that day was to select Frederick Muhlenberg as Speaker and John Beckley as clerk. Five days later the Senate managed to achieve quorum, select John Langdon of New Hampshire as president pro tempore, and in a joint session finally confirm the results of the electoral vote.[5] It was certainly an inauspicious start for the nation and its new president, and in a city with a history.

Gen. William Howe, after all, had ingloriously kicked Washington out of New York City in 1776. During the remainder of the war, Washington had longed to retake the important city but was unable to mount a campaign to dislodge the British from their North American headquarters. It was therefore bittersweet when Washington reentered the city at the head of a grand parade after the British abandoned both the war and city on November 25, 1783, a date thereafter celebrated as "Evacuation Day."

However, more recently, the city had functioned as the interim capital for Congress from January 1785 until the fall of 1788. It would go on to serve as the temporary capital for the new nation from March 1789, when a few members of the First Congress trickled into the city, through the summer of 1790, when Congress adjourned.

As for Mrs. Washington, she was reluctant to be in such a public position and was similarly hesitant about both her public role as host and the new city. Writing to her niece, she expressed her concerns and unhappiness quite vividly. "I live a very dull life and know nothing that passes in the town. I never go to any public place." Of the demands of public life, she scowled, "I think I am more like a state prisoner than anything else; there are certain bounds set for me which I must not depart from, and I cannot do as I like, I am obstinate and stay at home a great deal."[6]

Yet Mrs. Washington did function as host and, like her husband, fashioned customs and formed the role of presidential spouse. She was also enormously popular. The couple organized official receptions as part of the presidency, determining who would be invited, how many guests would be on the list, and even how they should greet these guests. Washington opted for a dignified presence but informal receptions. In doing so, the first couple managed to find the elusive balance between European monarchical airs and the casual simplicity the new republic demanded. If anything, Washington erred a bit on the side of being reserved and aloof in his interactions with the citizenry. Yet he clearly understood the vital role of both stagecraft and statecraft.[7]

The Washingtons were, however, criticized by some for their choice in transportation. The first couple's cream-colored coach was festooned with elaborately decorated panels of floral scenes, seemingly inspired by Louis XVI himself. It was drawn by a half-dozen horses, attended by coachmen and footmen decked in bright-colored livery, and sometimes joined by a cavalry escort. Interestingly, Washington had never traveled to Europe and had certainly not enjoyed such a privileged upbringing. However, his generals and advisers during the war had included aristocrats from Europe, and the president understood that such customs had a prominent place in governance across the ocean. Such trappings of power were, to a degree, necessary to establish a sense of legitimacy for the new government in the eyes of the world. Yet all this was contrary to Jefferson's self-professed simplicity and soon became a part of the southern and anti-federalist barrages leveled against the president and his supporters.[8]

The city boasted a population of roughly thirty-three thousand people with twenty-two churches, six markets, a post office, banks, and numerous publishers and newspapers. Although but a "town" by European standards, it was a bustling port city filled with traders, shippers, merchants, and financial speculators.[9] New York City had an energy and the promise of opportunity but also an untamed and unruly character to it. A bewildering array of currencies— Spanish doubloons, half guineas, English pounds, and so on—were still used. Indeed, the city that welcomed George Washington boasted an eclectic blend of West Indians; runaway slaves; southerners selling cotton and agricultural produce; a smattering of former loyalists to the Crown; French aristocrats who had lost their money, lands, and titles in the revolution of 1789; and new immigrants.

Congressman John Page of Virginia was unimpressed, writing, "The town is not half so large as Philadelphia, nor in any way to be compared to it for beauty and elegance. . . . The streets are badly paved, dirty and narrow, as well as crooked." He and others noted that the city also lacked shade trees and sidewalks, and most of the population was without an adequate water supply. Thomas Jefferson later complained of the city's climate, writing, "Spring and fall they never have; as far as I can learn, they have ten months of winter, two of summer with some winter days interspersed."[10]

Congressman Fisher Ames of Massachusetts was less charitable. "While I am shut up here in this pigsty, smelling perfumes from wharves and the rakings of gutters," he complained, "I long for the air and company of Springfield." Others pointed out that the new capital city was "overrun" by hogs, dogs, and garbage. Quite an indictment![11] So too were the signs of distress and destruction from the war and long British occupation still quite visible throughout the city.

In a critique that might find traction in the present day, many Americans seemed to also oppose New York City, as it did not "feel" like the rest of the nation. While the new Federal Hall was certainly a majestic site, described in newspapers as "an edifice that would grace any metropolis in Europe," others condemned its opulence and stateliness as "a fool's trap."[12]

What may have been assets for the city were, however, liabilities in the eyes of many southerners, including such influential voices as Thomas Jefferson, who particularly loathed financiers and banks and preferred a genteel southern village as the site for a capital.

Likewise, the selection of New York City as the temporary capital did nothing to relieve tensions about a permanent site. No sooner had the government arrived in New York than debate began in earnest about whether to shift the temporary capital to Philadelphia. The effort was not surprising to people living in the 1780s and 1790s. State capitals, after all, had often been moved as populations shifted. North Carolina, South Carolina, and Virginia all moved their capital cities away from the coasts and, in accordance with growing populations, westward. A few years later New York and Pennsylvania would also move their capitals. Therefore, in the minds of many citizens of the eighteenth century, the site of a capital city was subject to change. New Yorkers, of course, wanted their city to remain as the temporary capital.

Throughout New York City's time as the seat of government, the public and press wondered if and when the capital would be moved. All the while New York City did all it could to accommodate and please the First Congress. Some New Yorkers even suggested parts of Brooklyn and King's County in a last-ditch effort to offer Brooklyn Heights as the capital. However, momentum was building to move the temporary capital to Philadelphia.[13]

Members of the Pennsylvania congressional delegation had been proposing adjournment to Philadelphia since the day New York City had been selected to host the temporary capital. Of course, questions arose as to whether Philadelphia was the best site in Pennsylvania. This again split the Pennsylvania congressional delegation, some of whom preferred any place but Philadelphia. Suddenly, nearly every conceivable location in the Keystone State made its case. Merchants, residents, and land speculators were eager to share their views.[14]

Some Pennsylvanians favored a site by the Susquehanna River, west of Philadelphia. Senator Robert Morris, a Pennsylvanian, preferred either Philadelphia or a site just north of Philadelphia along the Delaware River bordering New Jersey (he owned land in the area).[15] Senator William Maclay, who owned land in Harrisburg, proposed it as a possible site, while Representative Fisher Ames sarcastically suggested Pittsburgh. Still others proposed Carlisle, Lancaster, Reading, and York.[16]

Only one year after George Washington was sworn in at Federal Hall and the new government had moved to New York, it prepared for another difficult and costly move—to Philadelphia.

CHAPTER 16

The Great Debate

Without Freedom of Thought, there can be no such Thing as Wisdom;
and no such Thing as publick Liberty, without Freedom of Speech.

Benjamin Franklin

By 1790 the nation finally had a constitution, an interim seat for government in New York City, and a fledgling government, but not a capital city. The noted historian of the First Congress and capital city, Kenneth Bowling, referred to the ensuing discussions over the capital city as the "great debates." The debate began in August 1789 and lasted through the end of the session in September; it began anew off the floor in January of 1790, came to the floor in June, and was finally resolved the next month. They were, by far, "the most intense and explosive of the first session." The issue, after all, went to the core of what kind of nation America would be and also involved the debates that had been swirling for years over the power of the executive, the future expansion of the nation, sectional divides, the rift between large and small states, and, of course, slavery. It was the mother lode of all political debates, even overshadowing such pressing matters as the creation of the judiciary and the mounting debt.[1]

On August 27, 1789, only months after Washington's inauguration, Congressman Thomas Scott of Pennsylvania rose in the House chamber to propose that "a permanent seat for the government of the United States ought to be fixed as near the centre of wealth, population and extent of territory, as shall be consistent with the convenience of the Atlantic navigation, having also a due regard to the circumstances of the Western country." This position, while not so subtly advocating a capital in his home state, would influence the ensuing debate about the permanent site.[2]

Even though the debate continued to border on the absurd and was plagued by self-interest, economics, politics, and geographic sectionalism, Philadelphia remained as the front-runner for the temporary capital.[3] The city's residents were widely seen as more politically astute than the New Yorkers, and their social affairs were far more formal and elaborate than nearly anywhere else in the country.[4]

On May 24, 1790, Robert Morris proposed the capital be moved to Philadelphia, but the measure was postponed by a close 13–11 vote in the Senate. Yet momentum for relocating the capital had swelled. It soon became a matter of when, not if, the capital would be moved, and Congress began debating the date. Some proposals suggested a date in August, when Congress recessed. It was finally agreed that when the First Congress's term ended in March 1791, the Second Congress would govern from another city.[5]

When it was time to vote to move the temporary capital, Representative Benjamin Goodhue of Massachusetts, a Harvard-educated federalist, threw another monkey wrench into the mix. He proposed that the temporary capital remain in New York City until a permanent capital was selected and built. Of course, this made sense.

In response to Goodhue's comments, an "inflamed South rose to its defense with passion." Richard Bland Lee (brother of former Congressman Henry Lee) and Daniel Carroll of Maryland responded by proposing a new resolution: the key criterion for a future capital city—be it temporary or permanent—should be proximity to the Atlantic Ocean. This requirement would advantage a few of the proposed sites, including the Potomac. But Goodhue also claimed manufacturing states would grow faster than agricultural states, so moving the capital—be it temporary or permanent—to the Potomac would place it too far south of the population base.[6] Congress was, yet again, back on familiar battle lines in the struggle to site the capital.

To orchestrate the move to Philadelphia, some Pennsylvania delegates courted their colleagues from New Jersey, who realized that a capital in or near Philadelphia and by the Delaware River advantaged them as well; others allied with the South in opposition to New York and other sites deemed to be too far to the north. They hoped to bring the capital farther south. In the deal making surrounding the move, some Pennsylvanians proposed keeping the temporary capital in New York in exchange for placing the permanent site in their state.[7]

Of course, Philadelphia had the advantage of history. The city had played such a prominent role in independence. Pennsylvania's delegates soon abandoned other sites in their state and rallied around Philadelphia as the temporary capital.

Ultimately, the deal would be made to move the temporary capital to Philadelphia, believing that site was better suited to host the government than New York City. This move excited the residents of Philadelphia. That did not end the debate, however. One of the remaining impediments to the hopes of New York City and Philadelphia to host the temporary capital was Washington's lack of enthusiasm for both cities. Lest New Yorkers find hope in this reality, Washington was slightly less opposed to Philadelphia.[8]

Debate over the location continued through all of 1789 and 1790, much of it over the issue of "centrality." Congress, it was reasoned, could best govern the new republic if no single place was too distant from the physical capital. However, the factions then turned to a bitter argument over how to define "centrality." Should centrality be defined by geography? Based on population? How would it be measured? Large areas of land were as of yet unexplored, much less settled, and no one knew how the population of the new nation would grow or shift. Moreover, when Scott introduced his call for a capital, a census had yet to be taken.

Therefore, ironically, the argument put forward by Scott and others such as George Washington that a central location would help to unify the nation threatened to tear it apart. Some newspapers and members of Congress even predicted the republic would crumble by the end of 1789. The same predictions were heard the next year. The issue, grumbled Washington, was now causing "more bitterness, more sectional divisiveness and more commentary by participants" than any other issue, including slavery.[9] Of course, the failure to settle the matter one way or the other and designate a capital "will lay foundation for animosities that no government can prevent or heal," wrote the *Pennsylvania Gazette* in 1789.[10]

Many northerners viewed centrality as being based on population, and it seemed that the center of the country—as it then existed—was along the Susquehanna River, which coursed through Pennsylvania and emptied into the Chesapeake Bay in Maryland. Accordingly, the Susquehanna River became a possible site. However, Congressman Richard Bland Lee of Virginia, a rare federalist among the southern members, introduced a proposal for "the banks of the Potomac" to replace the Susquehanna and other northern sites. Sites north of Virginia and Maryland, he maintained, would be unfair to people living in the South and the growing population in the West. Southern states, he reminded

Congress, had struggled mightily to ratify the Constitution in part over concerns about political power being vested in the North.[11]

Lee was not alone. Many other southern delegates, including most of Virginia's representatives, wanted to consider population as well as geography.[12] As expected, northern representatives objected. One of them, John Laurence, a member of congress from New York, reminded Congress that the South had been the source of problems regarding an array of issues, including the nation's inability to raise revenues, finance the debt, and end slavery. Southern obstructionism had affected and was continuing to harm the whole country.

Madison objected to the criticism, echoing Lee's point about the dissatisfaction and division in the South over the Constitution, claiming rather imaginatively, "If a prophet had risen in that body, and brought the declarations and proceedings of this day into their view, that as I firmly believe, Virginia might not have been a part of the union at this moment."[13]

Throughout the debate the idea of centrality was defined in ways that were creative and benefited those making the point. Some in the South went so far as to consider territories in the West Indies (where trade and slavery existed) in their equation of centrality. The capital, they maintained, could not be too far from the lucrative trade with the islands—which meant it belonged in the South. Some in the North countered with suggestions that Congress should consider whether Canada would eventually become part of the nation, which would shift the central location markedly northward.

Southerners also focused their arguments on the possible future westward expansion of the population and the way it would shape the geographic and political nature of the nation, including the issue of slavery. After all, Congress was paying veterans of the war via land in Ohio, and the Northwest Ordinance had been passed during the Constitutional Convention of 1787. Some Americans were already beginning to travel westward in search of cheap land, and thousands had already flocked to the Ohio River region, leading Congressman Elias Boudinot of New Jersey to write, "The western country blossoms like a rose and affords happy asylum for all the oppressed of the Earth. Plenty of the finest land in the Universe may be bought here."[14]

Indeed, it appeared that other settlements would soon be popping up beyond the Appalachian chain and farther south. Moreover, on November 21, 1789, North Carolina had entered the union, and statehood for both Kentucky and Tennessee was pending (they would enter the union in 1792 and 1796, respectively). The lure of new, fertile agricultural lands would entice more settlers and with them the promotion of slavery, which would enhance the South's political power. With this in mind some southern members of Congress attempted to put off the debate on the permanent capital until additional western states came into the union and the population base shifted westward. Jefferson, for instance, saw Virginia as the beneficiary of the western expansion, claiming the Potomac was "the only point of union which can cement us to our western friends when they shall be formed into separate states."[15]

Manasseh Cutler, a developer and political opportunist, even went as far as to suggest a capital on the banks of the Scioto River in southern Ohio, conveniently at the exact spot where he hoped to develop a population center.[16] Former delegate David Howell of Rhode Island even raised the thought of building it in Pittsburgh or the West. The land was cheap, and it would have the added benefit of establishing a new population center. So too would the sale of the new lands help to pay off the debt.[17]

On the other hand, the potential impact on the balance of political power of the westward expansion was so alarming for the eastern elite that Elbridge Gerry of Massachusetts and Gouverneur Morris of New York, two of the most influential leaders at the Constitutional Convention, had even tried to pass a clause specifying that the founding Atlantic Seaboard states would always have special power in Congress.[18]

The idea that any settlement in the West would be to the political detriment of the East only exacerbated the regional rift. Soon, satirical pieces appeared in newspapers lampooning these western advocates. For instance, one anonymous writer from Connecticut wrote in a New York newspaper that the country might need a constitutional amendment so that "the residence of Congress shall not be in . . . the howling wilderness!"[19]

It was apparent that, despite the debate, the capital had to be centrally located, be it geographically or population-wise or both. The formidable Richard Bland Lee, a member of the influential Lee dynasty of Virginia and close associate of Washington, added another wrinkle to the centrality debate. He recommended that "a place as nearly central as a convenient water communication with the Atlantic Ocean, and an easy access to the Western Territory will permit, ought to be selected and established as the permanent seat of the Government of the United States." London had the Thames and Paris the Seine. Peter the Great had even relocated the Russian capital to St. Petersburg on the Baltic Sea. Lee's recommendation made sense because of the importance of waterways, including both the Atlantic and key rivers, to the success of the new nation in terms of trade, communications, and defense. The proposal also reflected Washington's long-held beliefs and preference for the Potomac.[20]

The new capital city would need to link the East with the West, the North with the South; have a navigable river and access to the sea; and be centrally located. Given the criteria, several communities along the Delaware, Susquehanna, Hudson, Potomac, and other rivers were considered. By 1790 at least sixteen different sites had submitted proposals or petitions to the First Congress hoping to host the capital, including communities along the Chesapeake Bay and the Delaware, Potomac, Schuylkill, and Susquehanna Rivers. Other towns had not submitted proposals but were a part of the conversation, including Annapolis, Charlestown, Cumberland, Frederick, and Havre de Grace in Maryland, to name a few. There was also some support for Georgetown in Maryland, Germantown in Pennsylvania, and Trenton in New Jersey.

Even the village of Hancock, sitting by the borders of Maryland, Pennsylvania, and Virginia entered the fray, with town leaders suggesting its proximity to all three states made for an ideal capital. Moreover, roads leading to all three states—which were part of the Tuscarora Trail, the old path used by generations of Indians and explorers—converged not too far from the village. Sounding like a modern chamber of commerce or tourism board, town elders even reminded Congress that its warm springs were a popular and delightful spot.[21]

To address these questions, George Washington signed the Census Act on March 1, 1790, declaring that a census be administered by the marshals of the US judicial districts. On August 2, 1790, the results were made available and gave context to the debate over centrality and the location of the capital.[22] The census affirmed the geographic midpoint of the country to be Chestertown, Maryland, which was only a few dozen miles from the towns of Georgetown and Alexandria. This reinforced Washington's position.[23]

The debate over centrality ultimately came down to sites along two rivers—the Susquehanna and Potomac. Advocates of the Susquehanna River proposed that Congress appropriate money to purchase land and start erecting public buildings at an appropriate (and central) site along the Susquehanna's banks in Pennsylvania. The Pennsylvanian Robert Morris summed it up in a letter in September to his wife, saying, "The Grand question for the permanent Residence seems to the Public Eye as if it were fixed on the Susquehanna." However, he also added that he spoke with Washington about the location and the President was "much dissatisfied" with him and the Susquehanna.[24]

During the fiery debate over the permanent capital, Representative Lee of Virginia tried to remove any mention of the "Susquehanna," but it was narrowly defeated. In an effort to compromise, Robert Morris then foolishly pushed for the Delaware River instead of Susquehanna, which weakened and ultimately split the northern coalition. Nonetheless, parochial interests reigned, and he was joined by representatives from New Jersey, a state that bordered the Delaware, including Elias Boudinot, who claimed the Susquehanna was prone to flooding. Therefore, Boudinot proposed that the bill be rewritten to say "Potomac, Susquehanna, or Delaware" instead of "Susquehanna," but it too failed.[25]

Some Marylanders proposed that the language in the bill not include any mention of the "East Bank" of the Susquehanna but rather use the word "Banks." The Marylanders were concerned about whether Philadelphia (which is east of the river) or Baltimore (which lies southwest of the river) would be the most influential city. This effort further weakened the northern coalition, which was fraying under so many different interests and locations. At the same time and perhaps most important, the Susquehanna location was not to Washington's liking.

Representative George Gale of Maryland, who shared Washington's enthusiasm for the Potomac, promoted a tactic that further derailed plans for a site along the Susquehanna. His proviso declared that any site along the Susquehanna must first ensure that measures were taken to remove boulders and natural barriers in the river in order to improve navigability.[26] Compliance with the Gale Proviso was logistically, financially, and politically difficult. Members of Congress today would recognize it as a "poison pill," a legislative trick to defeat a measure by inserting an unpopular provision into it.

Then, with support for the Susquehanna eroding, Virginians Madison and Lee proposed that the bill either remove the word "Susquehanna" and replace it with "Potomac" or insert the words "or Maryland" after the "banks of the Susquehanna in Pennsylvania." It was another clever poison pill inserted into the debate, as it pitted northerners against one another. The measure narrowly failed, but support for the Susquehanna dissipated.[27] Madison even melodramatically wondered aloud whether the South would long exist in the new nation if the Susquehanna hosted the capital.[28] Other southern legislators proposed a site by the confluence of the Potomac and Conococheague in the Maryland-Virginia area.[29]

While the debate continued, another concern was raised: Should the seat of government be in an urban or rural setting? An urban and commercial center would give the new capital legitimacy and credibility, reasoned many northerners. For instance, Vice President John Adams favored an urban center and was supported by Senator Tristram Dalton of Massachusetts, who predicted the country would struggle for years if it had an undeveloped, rural capital. Few proponents of a small, rural, or entirely new capital city, after all, were considering the immense costs for the debt-ridden nation to build an entirely new city. Of course, these rural advocates also failed to consider that any new rural capital would likely eventually develop into a city.[30]

Other leaders proposed the idea of the capital being in a "center of wealth," but James Madison and other southerners countered that people of all classes and wealth lived in the country and should have equal access to the capital city. The argument resonated not so much because of the obvious self-interest behind it but because "equal access" was important to most everyone, as it reflected the republican aspirations of the new nation. Madison even proposed the opposite definition of centrality of wealth—that the capital be established in the South because the region was poorer and possibly stood to benefit the most economically. Predictably, the South backed the proposal and the North opposed it. The proposal failed.

Many proponents of a rural capital were inspired by self-interest and perpetuating slavery, but there was also a prevailing utopian ideal. Thomas Jefferson had long noted what he believed to be the corrupting influence of the urban experience, which he felt defined parts of Europe. He embraced a utopian agrarian ideal, whereby men owned the land they farmed. Such an arrangement would promote equality, hard work, thrift, and godliness, reasoned Jefferson. A little dirt under the fingernails was good for citizenship, it seemed. As a result, some of his supporters feared that cities such as New York and Philadelphia would corrupt the entire country and Americans would be repeating the mistakes of Europe. Rather, Jefferson and Madison advocated bucking history by establishing a new capital in a brand new town. The radical notion appealed to Washington.

Yet an existing city offered the benefits of commerce and trade, financial resources, culture, talented craftsmen, a population for armies, and more. All the existing population centers were on the Eastern Seaboard, which had the added benefit of the Atlantic Ocean. However, that raised related concerns that the site, if by a major waterway on the Eastern Seaboard, should be an ice-free port, safe from a naval attack, and sheltered. Any logic behind the capital being placed in an existing population center—or any location, for that matter—was lost in the political tug-of-war.

Every step forward on the question of the capital seemed to be accompanied by a step backward—and a costly and contentious step at that. Even if Washington shared the preference of his fellow Virginians and southerners for a capital on the Potomac, he worried that their methods were splintering the nation. Of the continued obstructionism by his fellow Virginians and southerners to any resolution about the location of the capital, Washington warned that if it "were so dangerous to live in a nation with a capital not in the exact spot you want," what about "living in separation?"[31]

In private Washington fumed. To his trusted treasury secretary, Alexander Hamilton, he vented about "narrowminded politicians . . . under the influence of local views."[32] Writing to his favorite relative, Bushrod Washington, the president complained of the opposition, saying of these detractors' alleged arguments, "The real ones are concealed behind the Curtains, because they are not of a nature to appear in open day."[33] Even Madison admitted that "the real object of all their zeal in opposing the system" during the debate over the capital came down to "the supremacy of the State Legislatures."[34] Said Madison, "The business of the seat of government is become a labyrinth for which the votes printed furnish no clue."[35]

Hamilton observed with dismay to John Jay that "by Spring of 1790 [Washington] was under pressure by the South and Virginia." Echoing the president, Hamilton described the situation as "a spirit which must either be killed or will kill the Constitution of the United States."[36] Washington began worrying whether the capital debate would ever be settled or if it would end up unraveling the new government. He warned, "The establishment of our new Government seemed to be the last great experiment for promoting human happiness."

The "great debate" over the location of the capital city had less to do with centrality, population, wealth, or even the census than with politics.

An opponent to an urban capital as well as the Susquehanna and other northern sites, James Madison used his considerable legislative talents to point out small constitutional discrepancies in each bill as a way to delay or kill such efforts. He no longer seemed the great architect of the Constitution but rather a partisan politician and obstructionist. From the fall of 1789 on, Madison had been a primary obstacle in the capital debate, using such spurious claims against a northern capital as the "primacy" of "local governments" that "will ever possess a keener sense and capacity, to take advantage of those powers, on which the protection of local rights depend." Warned Madison to Congress, "There is no one right of which the people can judge with more ease and certainty, and of which they will judge with more jealousy, than of the establishment of the permanent seat of government."[37]

As an insurance policy in the event Madison's negotiations and tactics did not work, Henry Lee introduced a bill in the Virginia legislature on November 6, 1789, for the Old Dominion to host the capital. In only one day the state organized an offer of lands for a new federal district. Meanwhile, the state's two senators hoped to delay efforts in other states until the next session, even occasioning the first threatened filibuster in the Senate's history.[38]

Likewise, and on advice from Washington, Virginia's political leaders had also sought funding from European investors to develop a grand city by the Potomac. However, Jefferson arrived back in Virginia from Europe in November with news that he could not find interested investors, not even with Washington's endorsement. This prompted the Virginia House of Delegates to pledge funds for improvements along the river and buildings in the new capital. They encouraged their Potomac neighbor, Maryland, to do the same "without delay." Leaders from the two states and representatives from Alexandria and Georgetown met with the Potomac Navigation Company. In a joint effort to boost the Potomac as the best site for the capital, they stressed the good navigation, fertile soil, and abundance of fish and wood along the river, as well as its ability to connect the western territories and bind the nation together.[39]

The three main players in the capital debate at this time were Washington, Jefferson, and Madison, all three Virginians who opposed various locations in the North. Importantly, however, the three men were *Virginians*, not *southerners* in the truest sense. While they were slave owners and believed the South represented their interests, unlike other southerners, they did not object to commercial capitalism, and their livelihoods were in many ways more tied to the mid-Atlantic states than to the southern states.

With several proposed sites in Pennsylvania and the importance of Philadelphia, the Virginians understood that they needed an alliance with the leaders of the Keystone State if they were to get the capital. They also knew that Robert Morris was attempting to enlist the support of New Englanders to undermine the southern effort and secure a northern capital. Indeed, he ended up proposing Trenton, near the Delaware River and Pennsylvania border in New Jersey, as a more attractive alternative than Philadelphia.

It was not the first overture from Virginia's leaders to Pennsylvania. Most likely at the urging of Washington and Jefferson, in 1789 Madison had proposed Virginia's immediate support for moving the temporary capital from New York to Philadelphia in exchange for a permanent site by the Potomac. Most Pennsylvania delegates, in the words of Representative Fisher Ames, "abhorred the bargain," a view likely shared by the Virginians. Yet because members of Congress were switching their votes and alliances almost daily and because the capital debate had been sputtering for years, they also knew that this was one of the few deals that had the potential of passing. Both states would get a capital.[40]

Over the next two years Madison and his fellow Virginians worked to wrangle votes to prevent any further talk of a permanent site in the North. After delaying the decision for years, they suddenly seemed to realize that timing was important—they needed to act while Washington was president and before a possible John Adams presidency. A native of Massachusetts, Adams might be expected to advocate a northern capital in Boston, New York City, or Philadelphia. Thus, Madison continued lobbying his native Virginia and reaching out to enlist the support of Maryland. It worked. Senators William Grayson of Virginia and Charles Carroll of Maryland joined his publicity campaign for the Potomac.[41]

Newspaper articles, pamphlets, and broadsides poured forth celebrating the river, several of them quite over the top. One outrageous attempt to promote the Potomac was the publication of a pamphlet back in October 1789 titled *Political Opinions Particularly Respecting the Seat of the Federal Empire*. It came courtesy of John O'Connor, a Potomac-area publisher from Ireland who printed the *Potomac Magazine*. O'Connor likened the river to the Thames, Seine, and Rhine but said they were mere creeks or tributaries compared to the Potomac, which, he boasted, was capable of harboring ten thousand ships the size of Noah's ark, housed countless intellectuals along its shores, and could "clothe and cherish the perishing sufferers in the wilds of Siberia, as well as the pampered Alderman on the English Exchange." His beloved river, he believed, like George Washington, had been placed there by "Providence." Together, the general and river would bestow "every blessing to the human race." Now that is a river and a leader![42]

Baltimore's *Maryland Journal* joined the effort, publishing a satirical conversation between the Potomac and Patapsco Rivers titled "A Conference between the Patapsco and Potomac Rivers." In it the rivers debated their merits for hosting a capital city, with the Potomac reminding its foe of its unparalleled importance. After all, it reasoned, it was George Washington's home! Said the river, "I am become so exceedingly vain, that I almost conceit myself no longer common element, but the most refined nectar." Echoing the congressional debate, both rivers dismissed the feasibility of an inland or western capital, while extolling the virtues of their navigability, trade, and centrality. The Potomac finally rested its case by reminding all other rivers, "It has been the invariable practice of all wise founders of Empires, Kingdoms and States . . . to cement and support their dominions by one great Metropolis."[43]

Other satirical essays appeared, such as one from Oliver Goldsmith, penned in the *Maryland Journal* under the pseudonym "Citizen of the World." In it the author makes a case for putting the capital in Georgetown. George Walker, writing as "Civis," published similar essays advocating the natural and commercial benefits of Georgetown and the Potomac.[44]

Yet another pamphlet, this one titled "The Expostulations of Potomac," written by Gen. Adam Stephen of Virginia, claimed that the power of Philadelphia—if it became the capital—would compromise and eclipse all other cities and states. The best alternative for New Englanders, Pennsylvanians, and all Americans, argued Stephen, was to build the capital on the banks of his river. This pamphlet was reprinted throughout the country.

Another important article appeared on January 22, 1790, in the *Maryland Journal*. This essay weighed in on the main debate of centrality. Published anonymously under the title "The Federal City Ought to Be on the Potomac," it maintained that only the Potomac could satisfy the North-South and East-West rifts because it held the promise of connecting them.[45] Additional articles poured forth through 1789 and 1790.

Given the nature and extent of the publications supporting the Potomac, the joke outside Virginia became that residents of the Old Dominion believed the Potomac was "Euphrates flowing through paradise!"[46] Pressing their advantage, Virginians initiated a four-hour-long debate in Congress to secure a vote for their river, which newspapers described as "ingenious and animated." However, the measure narrowly failed. Representative Fisher Ames of Massachusetts, in reference to seemingly underhanded efforts by the Virginians, crowed that one bill "was a hair breadth business." Taking a swipe at Washington, Ames added, "For a vote in five minutes would probably have made it a law, except the King's signature."[47] Growled Representative George Clymer of Philadelphia, "The Virginia pride is at present much hurt and heaven and earth will be moved, but they will never be able to bring us to the Potomac."[48] Or so he thought.

Virginia's stonewalling and lobbying paid off; momentum had shifted in favor of the Potomac, which appeared to be the "last site still standing" from the vicious debate. Moreover, continued postponement of the decision on a capital was not acceptable and was producing further bad blood. Congress was feeling the heat, newspapers reflected the bitter and varied disagreements on the matter, and it had become apparent that the best course of action might be to grant Washington the power to name the site.

Therefore, the debate eventually shifted to authorizing the president to appoint a body of commissioners. Together, they would be charged with selecting the site of the capital city, then overseeing its planning and construction. Of course, any such provision would benefit Virginia because Washington had long advocated a Potomac site for the capital.

Ironically, southerners and anti-federalist lawmakers, however, expressed concerns that the power to select commissioners should not be vested with the president but with Congress, even though they stood to benefit from the very position they opposed. This time their opposition was ideological and was led by Thomas Tudor Tucker and Thomas Sumter of South Carolina, who believed the very first presidential commission to be an abuse of executive power. The establishment of a presidential commission to pick the site of the capital would put the hot spotlight squarely on Washington.[49]

Pressure built for him to act—both for and against a commission. Robert Morris, for instance, encouraged Washington to weigh in on the developing issue, but the president was hesitant to stumble into a political minefield, especially as momentum had shifted in his favor. Washington's friend and fellow Virginian Richard Bland Lee asked the president to veto the measure, but he declined. Dr. David Stuart, another of the president's close friends, wrote to him about the new twist in the capital debate: "The people here [Alexandria] say that their expectations of its being on the Potomac were always centered in you, and hope that as your opinion has been long known on the subject, it will never pass with your concurrence."[50]

Washington was damned if he did and damned if he did not.

Despite the pressure, Washington was keen to not show his hand in the debate in too obvious and too public a manner. It was a wise decision. As the noted historian Richard Norton Smith reminds us, Washington typically "kept his distance from this debate and all others."[51] The president, according to Smith, knew that the debate was less about what was best for the nation; it was a matter of "local pride, individual greed, and sectional advantage."[52] He would thus give the appearance of remaining above the fray but would have others work to advocate his strong interest in appointing commissioners and selecting the site for the capital.

A last-minute amendment, which mandated that the presidential commission be charged with selecting a capital "in Maryland or Pennsylvania," failed—by a single vote! Despite opposition from the South and Delaware, another bill narrowly passed that authorized the government to borrow up to $100,000 to purchase land and erect public buildings for a capital. After considerable debate the proviso passed: the president was empowered to appoint commissioners for the task of selecting and building a capital.

The First Federal Congress had some noteworthy achievements in 1789 and 1790 despite the gridlock over the capital. It created a revenue system, organized the judiciary, confirmed justices to the Supreme Court, and began work on Madison's initial amendments to the Constitution, which would famously become the Bill of Rights. Nevertheless, the debate over the location of the capital city had hindered progress on other important business. At the close of Congress's session, Senator William Grayson, an anti-federalist from Virginia, wrote to Patrick Henry, "The members would have parted [in a] tolerable temper if the disagreeable altercations on the score of the seat of government had not left very sharp impressions on the minds of the Southern gentlemen."[53] Exasperated from the debate, Fisher Ames of Pennsylvania wondered, "The Lord knows what the next session will produce in regard to that subject!"[54]

The one certainty was that Washington, the former surveyor and land speculator, would make one of the most important land acquisitions in history.[55]

CHAPTER 17

The (Second) Most Famous Dinner in History

It was observed . . . that as the pill would be a bitter one to the
Southern states, something should be done to soothe them.

Thomas Jefferson

The winter and spring of 1790 saw a continuation of raucous debates over determining a location for the permanent capital, moving the temporary capital, and having the president name the commissioners for the capital city. However, there was another issue pertaining to the capital city that proved just as troublesome.

Several states were deeply in debt from the war to the extent that it was affecting the government's ability to function.[1] The government lacked the ability to raise funds to pay veterans, sustain a standing army, pay off its debts and establish credit, finance badly needed internal improvements, and build a capital city. The question again arose of what to do about the debt.

As had been the case during earlier financial shortcomings during the war and immediately afterward, northerners and federalists generally favored having the national government assume the states' debt and then pay interest on it. Southerners and small government advocates generally opposed the plan but forwarded no alternative in its place. The result was that Congress was somewhat evenly split on the matter of federal "debt assumption," and a bitter debate ensued. In the words of Pulitzer Prize–winning author Ron Chernow, "The twin debates over assumption and the capital grew so venomous that it seemed the Union might dissolve in acrimony."[2] Nevertheless, the two seemingly intractable issues would end up as part of one unusual bargain.

Several members of the New York and New England congressional delegations grew weary of the emphasis on Philadelphia, the influence of Pennsylvania, and what they perceived to be the constant obstruction by Virginia and other southern states on the two critical issues of the debt and capital. Senator William Maclay of Pennsylvania boasted that he voted "dead against the [Potomac] measure from the beginning," prompting Washington to invite the senator to dinner on January 20. During dinner the president cornered the senator in the drawing room in order to press his case for the Potomac. Remembered Maclay, the president "asked me to drink a glass of wine with him. . . . I did not observe him drink with any other person during the dinner." However, the Pennsylvanian was unflinching, despite appeals from both Washington and Jefferson. "I have drowned Jefferson's regards in the Potomac," he later boasted. It was one of the few times the president's personal lobbying failed to bear fruit.[3]

While Washington privately pressed for a Potomac capital, the key leader on addressing the nation's meager finances and formidable debt was his trusted aide from the revolution and secretary of the treasury Alexander Hamilton. Back in September 1789, Hamilton had negotiated with the Bank of North America and the Bank of New York, the only two banks in the new country, for a loan of nearly $20,000 for the new government. It was the start of his debt plan, which helped the fledgling government meet some of its obligations and establish credit. The Continental Congress had borrowed massively from Dutch and French bankers during the revolution. The new government now needed to repay its loans, but the country had no credit, its currency (continentals) was nearly worthless, and some states were threatening to default on their debt obligations.

On behalf of the president, in January 1790 Hamilton submitted to Congress a report on the nation's financial health. The treasury secretary painted an alarming picture—the federal government was $54 million in debt and the states collectively owed an additional $25 million. The size of the debt prohibited the federal government and some state governments from functioning as needed. Therefore, Secretary Hamilton advocated tax revenue and federal assumption of states' debt as a way to retire debt in an orderly, honorable, and gradual manner. However, his plan required a bank and strong Treasury. In typical Hamilton fashion, the plan was a staggering 140,000 words long and included proposals not only to increase revenues, assume states' war debts, and organize a long-term funding system but also to establish a national bank, organize public credit, pay veterans, promote trade with Europe, issue paper money backed by gold, and increase currency issued to stimulate commerce.[4]

However, Hamilton's assumption plan encountered bitter opposition from small government advocates, particularly in the south, who were leery of banks, investors, certificates, and both the federal government and Hamilton. Versions of Hamilton's financial reforms had been voted down in the House a whopping five times, with the opposition being led by Representative Madison. So contentious was the ensuing fight that the sectional split and political schism were threatening to unravel the new government in 1790.[5]

Jefferson and his allies maintained that, because they (Virginia, Maryland, and Georgia, in particular) had either paid off all or most of their war debts, they should not be asked to bear the burden of helping to subsidize the northern states, plus South Carolina, that had amassed large debts fighting the war. Hamilton countered that investors and public creditors might simply sell everything and walk away from any deal. He also suspected that South Carolina and maybe even New England, which had made great sacrifices during the war both in terms of men lost and finances, would threaten to leave the union over the issue, for opposite reasons. "The new government," he warned, "would crash, perhaps bringing the Federal Union down with it."[6]

On a personal level Hamilton bristled that he and Washington had served during the revolution and sacrificed much, while Jefferson, Madison, and some of his other critics had never worn the uniform. Moreover, while serving as governor of Virginia during the war, Jefferson had ingloriously vacated the capital when the British threatened. There was a chasm between Hamilton and Jefferson on the hot-button issues of the day—federal debt assumption, the role of government, the size and location of the capital, and slavery. Whereas Jefferson was a prominent slave owner, Hamilton was against slavery, even going so far as to advocate, with his friend and fellow aide-de-camp, John Laurens, for a black regiment during the Revolutionary War, whose soldiers would be given freedom in exchange for their military service.[7]

Hamilton further alienated himself from southerners in Congress when he wrote of Africans, "Their natural faculties are probably as good as ours." Hamilton and his friend and fellow Founder John Jay collaborated on a proposal in 1785 to create a New York manumission society, one of the nation's first antislavery organizations. Two years later, when the framers were meeting in

Philadelphia, the Society opened an African Free School, one of the first schools for blacks. In 1791 they petitioned Congress to limit the slave trade but again failed because of southern opposition.[8]

Damaging writings from both Hamilton and Jefferson about one another soon found their way into the newspapers and were printed as partisan pamphlets. This was a new and regrettable occurrence. Administrations, believed Washington, should have a plurality of viewpoints but not have internal public quarrels. One ironic glimmer of hope came by way of James Madison. Even though he was a Virginian, Jefferson's closest confidante, and ideologically opposed Hamilton's strong national government, Madison understood Hamilton's detailed financial report and realized the gravity of the nation's economic health. Although he regularly opposed Hamilton, in the end Madison would put practicality over ideology. However, that would have to wait a few more months.[9]

In the meantime, appeals were raised that Washington should veto Hamilton's bill, as it might be unconstitutional. However, Washington took more of an "implied" reading of the Constitution and sided with Hamilton, favoring his secretary's financial plan and the proposal that the national government assume the war debts from the states in order to ensure a more "energetic" government and the ability to maintain a standing army. (It should be noted that Hamilton had, in one night, prepared a 15,000-word essay for the president advocating the now-famous legal doctrine of "implied powers" in the Constitution.) Washington's fellow Virginians would later accuse him of being co-opted by the devilish Hamilton.[10]

However, the president explained his position, saying, "The cause in which the expenses of the war was incurred was a common cause. . . . If then some states were harder pressed than others, or from particular or local circumstances contracted heavier debts, it is but reasonable."[11] Washington further reminded opponents to the plan that, "had the invaded and hard-pressed states believed the case would have been otherwise," and the southern states would later fail to come to their support, "opposition in them would very soon, I believe, have changed to submission, and given a diferent [sic] termination to the war."[12]

Some members of Congress and the public were upset with Hamilton; others were upset with Jefferson; still others were upset with both men. The two bitter issues, like congressional relations, were at an impasse. It was apparent Washington would need to act. The president had not been publicly involved in the assumption debate, but even a word from him "had a way of reverberating" such that it might sway the debate.[13]

George Washington had hoped to resign the presidency after his first term in office ended in early 1793. In 1792 he even asked James Madison to help him draft a farewell address. However, as early as 1790 it was apparent to his supporters, such as Alexander Hamilton, that Washington was needed for a second term. Similar sentiment existed in Congress. Only Washington seemed able to quell the bitter debates and deep divisions that had formed, and in hindsight it is hard to imagine how things would have played out without him at the helm during such a sensitive period in the nation's history.

Washington was the one constant—unwavering, nonpartisan, and dedicated to the principles of republicanism—throughout the fight to fix the nation's finances, build a capital city, and forge the institutions of a brand new government. Yet in the midst of the capital debate in spring of 1790, the president suffered a serious health ordeal.[14]

On May 5, 1790, Washington came down with a severe case of pneumonia. His illness worried everyone. Members of Congress visited Washington with "every eye . . . full of tears." William Maclay, the witty senator from Pennsylvania whose papers provide history with a provocative and contemptuous, and at other times amusing, account of the Founding era, also visited Washington and learned that the physicians were pessimistic. He observed that an extraordinary number of people were rushing to visit the president and a great emotional outpouring was felt throughout the city.[15]

Foremost among those who worried was Thomas Jefferson, who wrote that, with Washington "pronounced by two of the three physicians present to be in the act of death . . . you cannot conceive of the public alarm on this occasion. It proves how much depends on his life." Jefferson admitted feeling "total despair" at the prospect of losing the general.[16]

Washington was stoic about his illness. To his close friends, he was truthful about his physicians' prognosis that he might die, noting that he shared their views. To one associate he admitted, "I have already had within less than a year two severe attacks, the last worse than the first. A third more than probable will put me to sleep with my fathers." But he also announced that the government was in good hands with Alexander Hamilton at Treasury, Thomas Jefferson at State, Henry Knox at War, and John Jay as chief justice. He therefore said his doctors should let the illness run its course.[17]

It must be remembered that Washington came from a line of short-lived men, life expectancies were comparatively brief in the eighteenth century, and medicine was still appallingly primitive at the time. The president had lost his mother less than a year prior and had recently lost his pregnant niece and her unborn

child, deaths that were likely still fresh in his mind. Mrs. Washington was another matter entirely. The First Lady was naturally prone to hypochondria, and
for good reason: Martha had lost two of her four children in infancy at around
the same time she lost her father, father-in-law, and first husband. Of her surviving children, a daughter passed in her teenage years and a son in his twenties.

Terrified, Mrs. Washington summoned John Jones, a surgeon from Philadelphia who had famously cared for Benjamin Franklin, and three other physicians
to attend to her husband. With Washington's situation precarious, Jones and his
colleagues provided continual care. A few days later the fever broke, and charac-
teristically, Washington was up and working the next day.[18]

The nation exhaled. To his close associate the Marquis de Lafayette, the president wrote that his physicians recommended "more exercise and less application
to business," but he grumbled, "I cannot, however, avoid persuading myself that
it is essential to accomplish whatever I have undertaken (though reluctantly) to
the best of my abilities." Jones, however, died a few months later of an accidental
overdose at the hands of his own physician.[19]

Washington's frightening health ordeal was not lost on Congress, which had
been in the grip of its own "capital fever."

No sooner had Washington recovered than Congress was back at it. In June
the debates over debt assumption and the location of the capital continued
with little progress, leading Representative William Loughton Smith of South
Carolina to write in frustration, "Negotiations, cabals, meetings, plots and
counterplots have prevailed for months past without yet ripening to any decision." That same month the Senate again voted 31–11 to postpone a decision.
The sectional rifts were now worse than they had ever been, even threatening
the alliance favoring a relocation of the temporary capital to Philadelphia.[20]

Hope again came from Washington and Hamilton. Both men understood
that they had a card to play in resolving the assumption debate; they would
use the capital city. Likewise, the debate over the capital city might be settled
by using the debt assumption. Hamilton and Madison would conjoin the issues in a brilliant way. It happened that Senator Robert Morris, who had been
the superintendent of finance during the latter part of the Revolutionary War,
favored Hamilton's plan for state debt assumption and wanted the capital city
in Pennsylvania. Morris had grown disillusioned by the vicious quarreling in
Congress and obstruction from the South over the matters, so he invited four
like-minded colleagues—Tench Coxe, a Pennsylvanian serving as the assistant
secretary of the treasury; William Jackson, an aide to Washington who had

been born in England and lived in both South Carolina and Pennsylvania; and Representatives George Clymer and Thomas Fitzsimons, both of Pennsylvania— to join him socially on Friday evening, June 11. They hatched a plan to "accidentally" bump into Hamilton the next morning near the presidential mansion in New York City.

The plan was to promise Hamilton that they would somehow deliver the remaining votes needed to pass his debt assumption proposal in return for the treasury secretary getting President Washington and his federalist allies to support Philadelphia, Germantown (outside Philadelphia), or another location near the Delaware River as the capital. This would require them to swing one vote in the Senate and five votes in the House. They also wanted Philadelphia to immediately be announced as the temporary capital. Hamilton's assumption plan had a lot of support in the North, but Morris and his colleagues needed Hamilton's influence to swing the New York and New England congressional delegations, who opposed moving the temporary capital from New York City and distrusted other capital proposals.[21]

After "running into one another," Hamilton and Morris strolled along the Battery in Lower Manhattan and discussed the deal. Morris got to the point: "We must remove [President Washington] to Philadelphia where he will have room enough to ride as far as he pleased." Hamilton preferred keeping the temporary capital city in New York but was open to locating the permanent capital in Pennsylvania or along the Delaware River (he would later be accused of selling out his fellow New Yorkers) in order to pass his financial reforms and at least move the thorny issue of a location for the permanent capital forward. The men worked out the details of their arrangement. Philadelphia would serve as the temporary capital in exchange for the necessary votes in Congress to pass Hamilton's assumption bill. However, Hamilton knew something that few other leaders knew.[22]

Like Morris, Jefferson had been attempting to arrange his own deals. The secretary of state had hosted Madison and Coxe, the brand new assistant secretary of the treasury and close Hamilton associate, at his home a few days earlier on June 6. He too was trying to arrange a quid pro quo. Hearing rumors of a pending deal involving Hamilton over the debt assumption and capital city and not wanting to be outdone by his nemesis, Jefferson met with Morris on June 15.

The secretary of state suggested a rekindling of the Pennsylvania-Virginia alliance, this time pledging Virginia's support for moving the temporary capital to Philadelphia—immediately and for fifteen years—in return for Pennsylvania agreeing to a permanent capital in Georgetown by the Potomac. Jefferson did not include debt assumption in his proposal, an issue he adamantly opposed. Morris, in turn, shared the arrangements discussed with both Jefferson and Hamilton with Pennsylvania's leaders. They were not excited by either plan but preferred Jefferson's proposal and were enticed by finally resolving the matter of getting the temporary capital. Besides, they assumed that, once they secured the temporary seat of government, it would be easier to secure the permanent site.[23]

Sensing another change in momentum in the debate—this time in his favor—Jefferson dispatched Madison to meet with the congressional delegations from New England. Having shouldered the brunt of the costs and casualties during the revolution, northern states remained deeply in debt and were eager to see Hamilton's debt assumption bill passed. This was the leverage Jefferson and Madison intended to exploit in order to obtain a capital in Virginia. Accordingly, on instructions from Jefferson, Madison proposed that Virginia would stop blocking the assumption bill but in return wanted the capital to be by the Potomac. Members of Congress from Pennsylvania and Virginia met over the weekend of June 19 and 20 to discuss the deal.[24] Nevertheless, there was another, even more important meeting that weekend.

On Friday, June 18, Hamilton met with President Washington at his residence. The president and his secretary had a special relationship. Washington had plucked the orphaned immigrant out of obscurity to make him chief aide-de-camp with the rank of colonel during the Revolutionary War. The loyal, brilliant Hamilton proved to be a gifted wordsmith for the general's letters and speeches, an invaluable translator and interpreter, and an imaginative military and political strategist during the war. Washington, who had longed for but never enjoyed the company of a son, likely saw a bit of himself in the headstrong, ambitious young man who, in turn, likely also found in the general the father figure he never had.[25] Hamilton, more than Jefferson or Madison, had Washington's ear during the inaugural presidency, a reality deeply bothersome to the secretary of state.

The two cabinet members were becoming locked in an intense rivalry, not just for Washington's favor but also over their visions for the country. In that respect the two were polar opposites both personally and politically. Jefferson, forty-nine, a reserved, cerebral, moneyed aristocrat and slave owner from the South, favored a weak and decentralized government, and Hamilton, boyish in his early thirties, a brash, upstart, intense immigrant and abolitionist who relocated to the North, favored a stronger, centralized government. They were two of the chief architects of the new nation and visionaries competing for its future direction. They were also on opposite sides of the debt assumption debate.[26]

Therefore, it was Jefferson, while waiting to see the president that day in June, who observed Hamilton coming out of Washington's residence. Jefferson described his foe: "Hamilton was in despair. As I was going to the President's [residence] one day, I met him in the street. He walked me backwards and forwards before the President's door for half an hour. He painted pathetically the temper into which the legislature had been wrought, the disgust of those who were called the creditor States, the danger of the secession of their members, and the separation of the States." Hamilton usually enjoyed Washington's complete trust and support, but he appeared to Jefferson that day to have been upset over the meeting. The secretary of state further noted of his opponent, "His look was somber, haggard, and dejected beyond comparison . . . even his dress [was] uncouth and neglected."[27]

Jefferson knew Hamilton's dejection was over the ongoing failures to pass his financial plan, particularly debt assumption. The secretary of the treasury had spent months trying to promote his plan. All the while, the currency remained nearly worthless, property was devalued, and the nation still could not pay its veterans or the debts owed the Dutch and French. After small talk Jefferson, who was suffering from a severe migraine headache that day, nonetheless invited Hamilton to join him and Madison for dinner on Sunday, June 20, at his residence on 57 Maiden Lane.

The secretary of state, who had just moved into the rented home, immediately set about altering it to fit his elaborate tastes by hiring carpenters to renovate the home and build bookshelves. He also purchased great stocks of wine. Taking stock of Hamilton, he seemed to feel his foe was vulnerable. Therefore, Jefferson and Madison likely believed they could exploit their earlier deal making on the two issues and bend Hamilton to their liking at dinner. Regarding the dinner invitation, the secretary of state later recorded his thoughts, writing understatedly, "On considering the situation of things, I thought the first step towards some conciliation of views would be to bring Mr. Madison and Colo. Hamilton to a friendly discussion of the subject."[28]

Rather, the party would change history. Much more than debt assumption and the location of the capital were at stake. State pride and the reputations of the leaders squaring off on the issues were also at stake, as was the very future of the republic, which would be shaped in profound ways by the decision that evening.[29]

PART IV

CONFLICT
AND
COMPROMISE

CHAPTER 18

The Grand Compromise

*The ground of liberty is to be gained by inches. We must be
contented to secure what we can get from time to time and
eternally press forward what is yet to get. It takes time to
persuade men to do even what is for their own good.*

Thomas Jefferson to Rev. Charles King, January 27, 1790

A number of controversial issues were brought to the dinner on June 20.
Foremost were state debt assumption and location of the capital city.
Although Hamilton's financial plan and the assumption provision were close to
passing, the three men seated around the dinner table knew that Rhode Island
had finally ratified the Constitution on May 29, 1790—the thirteenth and final
state to do so. Thus, their delegation would soon be seated in Congress. The
problem for Hamilton was that it appeared that Rhode Islanders, unlike their
northern neighbors, opposed assumption. At the same time the Pennsylvania
delegation was supportive of assumption, but only as long as the temporary capital was moved to Philadelphia. It was unavoidable, then, that the two querulous
issues were, for better or worse, conjoined.

All three men seated around the dinner table seemed to realize the stakes
that evening. It was obvious to them that the congressional debate on the two
great issues had caused "total legislative paralysis."[1] Jefferson even warned, "If
this plan of compromise does not take place, I fear one infinitely worse." The
government, Jefferson predicted, would "burst and vanish, and the states separate to take care of everyone of itself."[2]

Hamilton seems to have already hatched a plan based on privileged informa-tion from Washington. Therefore, at dinner Hamilton proposed a four-point deal: First, he agreed to convince northern members of Congress to accept a location for the permanent capital city by the Potomac River on the Maryland-Virginia border. Second, the temporary capital city would be moved to Phila-delphia for the start of the next congressional session in late fall of 1790. Third, Jefferson and Madison would stop opposing the debt assumption and, instead, would help him obtain the needed votes from the South to ensure its passage. Fourth, Hamilton agreed that Virginia (and other southern states) would get favorable treatments in the settlement of state war debts.

Consequently, they all seemed willing to give up something, including strongly held positions. For Jefferson and Madison, it was their opposition to debt assumption. For Hamilton, it was abandoning New York City as a site for the temporary capital. As Jefferson noted in a letter to James Monroe, "In the present instance I see the necessity of yielding for this time . . . for the sake of the union, and to save us from the greatest of all Calamities." Yet not all of Jefferson's supporters would be pleased. For instance, Monroe wrote to his mentor, reflect-ing the predominant view among Virginians, that any deal was "fatal poison."[3]

Jefferson was willing to take the deal and assumed he was getting the better of Hamilton. Nevertheless, both Virginians played into Hamilton's hands. Hamil-ton apparently only feigned defeat. Perhaps he knew more about Washington's passion to build the capital next to the Potomac, his lack of fondness for New York City, and his support for the debt assumption plan. In fact, Washington was preparing to employ his considerable political influence to resolve those very matters.

Jefferson understood Hamilton's special relationship with Washington; he would come to be on the receiving end of it when the president frequently sided with his treasury secretary rather than his secretary of state. Even though his actions indicated otherwise, Jefferson commented at dinner that evening, "The President was the center on which all administrative questions ultimately rested, and that all of us should rally around him and support with joint efforts measures approved by him." However, Jefferson and Madison were perhaps un-aware of the full extent of Washington's desires and intentions. Their zeal and eagerness to dupe Hamilton ended up backfiring.[4]

In short, Hamilton "gave away" that which was already decided. Philadelphia would get the temporary capital and the move would be immediate, but it would host the government for only ten years, as Washington preferred, not fifteen years, per Jefferson's earlier deal. Furthermore, the most important issue in Hamilton's mind was debt assumption. Not only would it convert state debts into federal debts, thereby helping to unite the nation as Washington wished, but it would require a strong Treasury—which Hamilton headed—and a bank, which he was then proposing. Hamilton got nearly all he wanted and everything Washington wanted.

Of course, any deal the three Founders brokered over dinner was conditional on whether the combative members of Congress would trust one another after such a contentious history surrounding the issues. In terms of wrangling votes for their deal, Madison targeted four representatives, including Daniel Carroll, a wealthy landowner who lived along Rock Creek near the Potomac, as a likely convert. Although Carroll was against assumption, like Washington, he loved the Potomac and stood to gain both financially and in terms of political influence by having the capital in his backyard. Perhaps most important, Carroll was a friend of Washington's. Madison visited him and shared Washington's wishes. Carroll went along with the plan.

Another target was Representative Richard Bland Lee of the powerful Lee dynasty of Virginia, who wanted the capital near his beloved state. Madison likely told Lee that the "ten Miles square" site would encompass Alexandria, which was part of his congressional district and on land where he had invested. Madison also flipped George Gale, another Maryland landowner who preferred a Potomac site for the capital, and Alexander White, whose Potomac River district stretched westward toward the Ohio River.

Madison displayed an impressive ability to cut deals.[5] Though lacking in charisma and not known for his oratory, Madison had a "capacity to convince" that was nearly without equal. He put it to good use. The diminutive legislator, who stood just over five foot in height and weighed not much over a hundred pounds—causing colleagues to quip, "so much mind in so little matter"— worked tirelessly on these deals as Jefferson's "loyal lieutenant."[6]

Madison was, however, unable to flip Michael Jenifer Stone of Maryland, who was highly critical of Hamilton's proposals and known for his disinterest in compromising. Yet when Representative Stone learned of the deal, he quickly and opportunistically purchased property by the Potomac in order to cash in on the privileged information Madison shared with him. Thus were the pitfalls of trying to keep the deals on the capital city secret and the questionable integrity and loyalty of more than a few individuals in Congress.

Self-interest, which had long been an impediment to any deal, was now a tool to its success and the basis of Madison's legislative logrolling that followed the dinner.[7] The chips were falling into place; Washington's vision for the capital was unfolding.

Hamilton spoke to the Pennsylvania delegation, assuring them that Philadelphia would be the interim capital and the move from New York City would occur that fall. He picked up some support in the Keystone State. On June 23 Hamilton asked Robert Morris to get Pennsylvania to support both bills in exchange for Philadelphia becoming the temporary capital. The day after that, Morris convened a meeting of leaders from Pennsylvania and New Jersey, who reluctantly agreed to the deal and Hamilton's terms that Philadelphia would be the capital for ten, not fifteen, years. The source for changing Jefferson's preferred fifteen years to just ten years for the interim capital was likely Washington, who was eager to fix the seat of government by the Potomac.[8]

On June 22 Hamilton had also begun meeting with members of Congress from New England to share with them the good news that the federal government would assume their state's debts. He received assurances that they would not block a bill on the capital city's location.

Madison continued to lobby senators and representatives about the merits of the deal. Yet Madison came to loath the wheeling and dealing, admitting, "The business of the seat of Government is become a labyrinth . . . for which the votes printed furnish no clue, and which it is impossible in a letter to explain. . . ."[9] It was particularly frustrating for him that fellow Virginians, including Henry Lee, who thundered against any deal with the federal government and northern states, criticized him. Likening the situation to British taxation of tea, Lee fumed, "It seems to me, that we southern people must be slaves in effect, or cut the Gordian knot at once." Chiding Madison, he continued, "How do you feel. . . . Is your love for the constitution so ardent . . . that it should produce ruin to your native country [Virginia]?"[10]

News of the dinner bargain spread rapidly. Members of Congress and newspapers began speculating whether or not the protracted stalemate and squabbling were finally at an end. Representative Lee of Virginia said it best: "This week will decide the fate of the Potomac fever" and perhaps finally signal a "harmonious conclusion of our session." Nevertheless, he also warned, "If it fails I fear we shall break up abruptly in disgust and confusion." There had even been rumblings that New England might leave the union over the matter.[11]

The grand compromise would appease *most* everyone. Thomas Greenleaf, in his influential paper, the *New York Journal*, likely spoke for New Yorkers when he complained about the "prostitute Miss Assumption" and her "bastard twins

Potowmac and Philadelphia." New Yorkers wanted to retain the capital and saw Hamilton's behavior as a betrayal. Indeed, just as Madison angered his fellow Virginians, Hamilton angered his fellow New Yorkers. Emotions ran high; thus was the nature of the capital debate. Greenleaf's newspaper criticized the deal that took the capital from New York City and Washington's aides, opining anonymously, "The rude behavior of certain gentlemen, who are near the person of the P____t of the US . . . I mean their sneering conduct on that day to the virtuous minority."[12]

A New Yorker himself, the charges hurt Hamilton, who wanted the temporary capital to remain in New York City. The treasury secretary had the difficult task of attempting to heal the bad blood resulting from losing the capital. In an effort to heal the contentious wound, Hamilton reminded his critics, "The funding system including the assumption is the primary national object. All subordinate points which oppose it must be sacrificed." He also tried to justify his tactic of joining the two contentious issues, explaining, "Agreeing to New York and Baltimore will defeat [debt assumption], so that in the present state of things nothing but Philadelphia or Philadelphia and Potomac will ensure it. Massachusetts therefore will not agree to New York and Baltimore, because her object is the assumption."[13]

Of course, the dour and cranky William Maclay could be counted on to complain: "The President of the United States has (in my opinion) had great influence in this business. The game was played by him and his adherents of Virginia and Maryland." Critical of Washington's manipulative fingerprints on the deal, he admitted, "But I did not then see so clearly that the abomination of the funding system and the Assumption were so intimately connected with it. . . . The President has become in the hands of Hamilton the dishcloth of every dirty speculation, as his name goes to wipe away blame and silence all murmuring."[14]

Others realized what Senator Maclay had pieced together—that the two contentious issues were linked in the bargain. An editorial in the *New York Journal* complained, "The true reason of the removal of Congress from this city will be explained to the people in the course of a very few days. To the lasting disgrace of the majority in both houses it will be seen, that the Pennsylvania and Patowmack interests have been purchased with twenty-one and one-half million dollars." (The amount of the state debts assumed by the federal government.)[15]

A comical political poem from the time discusses the topic by way of an imagined conversation between a New York maid and her friend in Philadelphia.

The ode "The New York House Maid to Her Friend in Philadelphia," included the lines

> This Congress unsettled is, sure a sad thing,
> Seven years, my dear Nancy, they've been on the wing,
> My master would rather saw timber, or dig
> Than see them removing to Conococheague [a tributary of the Potomac]—
> Where the houses and the kitchens are yet to be framed,
> The trees to be felled and the streets to be named.[16]

For his part, Washington was delighted with the dinner deal, which also seemed to help buoy his recovery from his pneumonia. He wrote cheerfully to Lafayette that his great "anxiety and perplexity" over the issues were settled.[17] Still, Washington remained concerned about the tone of the debate and general lack of civility and national unity. Writing to David Stuart, his friend and soon-to-be commissioner for the capital city, he warned, "The questions of assumption, residence, and other matters have been agitated with warmth [meaning heated emotion] and intemperance, with prolixity and threats."[18] They were not out of the woods yet.

Jefferson realized he had been manipulated and complained of it the rest of his life, admitting, "Of all the errors of my political life, this has occasioned me the deepest regret." Unfortunately, only Jefferson's account of the dinner has survived history, and his version of the events does not completely square with other facts, suggesting that his remembrance was self-serving. Joseph Ellis, his Pulitzer Prize–winning biographer, even claimed flatly that Jefferson's account contained "misleading and self-serving features."[19] His level of dislike for the man that had just bested him was such that the Sage of Monticello likely placed himself in a more favorable position in his writings.[20]

For example, Jefferson described the dinner meeting without his usual flourishing detail, writing in blandest terms, "They came. I opened the subject to them, acknowledged that my situation had not permitted me to understand it sufficiently but encouraged them to consider the thing together. They did so." Of the deal, he alleges, "It was observed, I forget by which of them, that as the debt assumption pill would be a bitter one to the Southern states, something should be done to soothe them; and the removal of the seat of government to the [Potomac] was a just measure." Finally, regarding the terms of the deal, Jefferson tried to avoid responsibility, claiming implausibly, "I could take no part in it, but an exhortatory one, because I was a stranger to the circumstances which should govern it." He even pushed responsibility to his fellow Virginian, writing, "It ended in Mr. Madison's acquiescence in a proposition that the question should be again brought before the house by way of amendment from the Senate, that he would not vote for it, nor entirely withdraw his opposition, yet he would not be strenuous, but leave it to its fate."[21]

Two years later Jefferson admitted to Washington that Hamilton had outmaneuvered him. Defending himself, he griped, "It was unjust . . . and was acquiesced in merely from a fear of disunion, while our government was still in its infant state." Jefferson also believed his foe had acted only to amass personal power. However, he told his neighbor and ally James Monroe that at least there "will be something to displease and something to soothe every part of the Union except New York, which must be content with what she had."[22]

Madison famously observed, "Those who are most adjacent to the seat of legislation will always possess advantages over others." Everyone got something out of the dinner bargain, but this time the advantage was Hamilton's.[23] Hamilton knew of Washington's vision for the capital (although history is not sure to what extent Washington counseled Hamilton about the dinner deal). No surviving letter exists, but it seems rather obvious that the secretary of treasury was at least acting in the interests of the president, if not on his counsel.

Washington, for all his integrity, favored such quiet discretion, once writing, "In a government which depends so much in its first stages on public opinion, much circumspection is still necessary for those who are engaged in its administration." It is also clear that the two friends had, for many years, collaborated and exchanged ideas to the extent that Hamilton was frequently negotiating on behalf of his mentor. It came down to deal making and a trick up Hamilton's sleeve, one he described as having the potential to "change the political complexion of the government." And so it did. After hearing about the results of the dinner and signing the residence bill, Washington took his family to Mount Vernon for some much-needed rest and relaxation, and presumably a bit of celebrating.

The "Compromise of 1790" can be understood in historic context as the first of three great compromises between leaders in the northern states and those in the southern states that probably saved the nation. The next two would occur in thirty-year increments—the Missouri Compromise in 1820 and the Compromise of 1850. No deal, it seemed, could prevent the destructive forces of disunion in 1861.[24]

Hamilton's financial plan ended up passing. Washington, Vice President Adams, Jefferson, and the Speaker of the House signed the "Act Making Provision for the Debt of the United States." After the initial act passed in August 1790, it would take four additional acts of Congress to implement the complex and comprehensive measure. The debt assumption along with Hamilton's other financial reforms would end up being a roaring success. In the ensuing years US bonds began selling, trade picked up with Europe, the government was able to meet much of its financial obligations, stock markets opened in New York and Philadelphia in 1792, and the country's debt would be paid off.

Years later the eloquent congressional leader Daniel Webster would herald Hamilton's reforms, boasting, "The whole country perceived with delight and the world saw with admiration." Webster went so far as to deify the effort, placing Hamilton on terms with the Roman goddess of wisdom when he added, "The fabled birth of Minerva from the brain of Jove was hardly more sudden or more perfect than the financial system of the United States as it burst forth from the conception of Alexander Hamilton."[25] Equally important in Washington's mind, because state debts had become federal debts, it helped to promote nationhood.

CHAPTER 19

The Residence Act of 1790

*The site is the most beautiful I have ever seen . . . it is much
like that of Constantinople. . . . The country round rises in all
the diversity of hill and dale that imagination can paint.*
William Thornton, Architect of the Capitol

The Constitutional Convention of 1787 produced a long-awaited agreement that a federal district, not to exceed "ten Miles square," would be
established for a capital. Subsequently, the Jefferson-Hamilton dinner bargain
placed the capital city by the Potomac River. These arrangements remained intact in the final bill on the location of the capital, which was passed just days
after Jefferson's dinner party.

The Residence Bill passed in the Senate on July 1, 1790, on a close vote of
14–12. The measure went to the House on July 2. Debate in the House on the
Residence Bill began on July 6. Perhaps not surprisingly, on July 8 and 9, several
amendments were introduced in a final effort to seek locations other than the
Potomac and in an attempt to postpone a vote. The amendments failed.

Of course, it was not certain the Residence Act of 1790 would pass *despite*
all the negotiating that led to this moment—or perhaps *because* of the amount
of debate and compromise behind the bill. Virginia's congressional delegation
continued to make its case for the Potomac throughout the process of drafting
the final bill on the capital, even up to the hour of the vote. "On the banks of the
river Patowmack," the Virginians reminded their colleagues, was a site "above
tide water, in a country rich and fertile in soil, healthy and salubrious in climate,

and abounding in all the necessaries and conveniences of life."[1] The Virginia delegates had been aided all along by a powerful trump card up their sleeve. Although part of the proposed site for the capital was in Maryland, the remainder of it was in the home state of three influential Founders: "the Father of His Country," "the Father of the Constitution," and the author of the Declaration of Independence.

Throughout early July, speculation swirled as to whether Washington would support or veto the bill. A surprising amount of newspaper coverage thought the president would veto the bill, suggesting he was in a tough bind.[2] He had been annoyed and preoccupied, to say the least. Washington even observed on the eve of the Residence Act's passage that his fellow Virginians, despite getting what they had always wanted, "seem to be more irritable, sour and discontented than . . . any other State in the Union, except Massachusetts."[3] However, critics and the press entirely misread Washington and his long-held preferences and vision. For him, there was ever only one site for the capital city.

Years of debate and anti-federalist obstructionism came down to a vote on July 9, and the House passed the Residence Act by a narrow 32–29 margin. The Congress, like the new republic, remained divided. Once again, sectionalism defined the debate, with no representative north of New Jersey voting for the bill.[4]

Washington had sought the counsel of Jefferson and Hamilton throughout the process and used Representative James Madison as his "floor manager" for the bill. Madison's convincing legislative leadership, Hamilton's clever maneuvering, and Jefferson's dinner party and its "grand compromise" helped ensure the bill's passage.[5] But mostly it was Washington's far-reaching vision, considerable gravitas, and subtle lobbying that produced a capital city.[6] Even though the president had, in the words of Pulitzer Prize–winning Washington biographer Douglas Southall Freeman, largely maintained an "almost monarchical detachment" to many of the Founding debates, he had used his extraordinary discreet influence to advocate for the Potomac site.[7]

The president proudly signed the measure officially titled *An Act for Establishing the Temporary and Permanent Seat of the Government of the United States* into law on July 16, 1790.

Washington was able to exhale—for the moment. He had taken a few short trips, one of them to Long Island for five days to take in the sights. He also invited Hamilton and Jefferson for what must have been a tense three-day fishing trip and one that did not improve their relationship. When Congress adjourned after concluding the capital city business, Washington toured Rhode Island.

He had earlier avoided visiting the state while in New England because it had not yet ratified the Constitution. However, the last holdout finally ratified the document on May 29, 1790. Now that it was a part of the union, a presidential visit was in order.[8]

The Residence Act identified Philadelphia as the new temporary capital. The move would be immediate, and Congress was instructed to prepare to relocate for the session commencing in December 1790. Ten years hence—December 1, 1800—was the deadline specified for having the new federal city completed or, more realistically, at least having a hall for Congress and residence for the president ready. This timetable was per Washington's desires but also implausibly ambitious.

The new government was certainly not out of the woods yet. It would also take Hamilton's financial plan, including debt assumption, a few years before the nation was on solid financial footing, and the exact location of the capital city had not yet been determined, much less built. After the passage of the Residence Act, debate shifted to questions of financing the capital, the types of buildings suitable for the city, the design of the city, and, of course, the exact boundary of the new city.

From a public perspective, Washington had largely managed to remain behind the scenes through the years of debate, but suddenly, the spotlight was on him. Speculation abounded as to the exact location. Newspapers, local leaders, and citizens wondered where the president would place the exact boundaries for the federal district and federal city as specified in the Residence Act. Soon, speculation turned to advocacy, and once again, debate ensued as landowners and land speculators were eager to make money off the new capital, buying and selling based on the possible location.

The legislation gave the president broad powers to organize the city and to supervise its construction and allocated specific authority, such as siting and constructing forts and governmental buildings. Amusingly, toward the end of the lengthy ordeal, one newspaper editorial mused of the site for the seat of government, "The usual custom is for the capital of new empires to be selected by the whim or caprice of a despot." The writer reasoned that George Washington "has never given bad advice to his country," so why not simply "let him point to a map and say '*here*?'"[9] This quip was not far off the mark, as Congress ended up delegating nearly all of its authority to Washington.[10]

As to where along the Potomac the permanent capital would be sited, the legislation specified only that it would be "located as hereafter directed on the river Potomac, at some place between the mouths of the Eastern Branch [the Anacostia River] and Connogochegue."

Over the next few months the problem, as Washington saw it, was that Alexandria was presently just outside the limits defined by the Residence Act. To bring the important town into the federal district, Washington would have to convince Congress to let him move the boundaries a bit farther south of the original map than those allowed by the Residence Act, downriver in the direction toward his home at Mount Vernon. He also had other ideas and changes for the boundaries.

Washington did not want to have to appeal to Congress to revoke or revise the law. It would be easier to ask for a slight tweaking of the map to include the new site. Sure enough, he ultimately did not officially request that Congress rewrite the law or extend him new authority in the legislation. Rather, he parsed the matter by offering Congress the "opportunity" to "consider an extension" to the lower limit of the district boundary, one that would include Alexandria. The "10 Miles square" designation along the Potomac would still be intact.

Senator Charles Carroll of Maryland, cousin of Washington's capital commissioner, proposed another bill that would function as a supplemental act supporting Washington's proposed new boundaries for the capital city that had evolved to include Alexandria, parts of Maryland south of the Anacostia River, and other areas in Virginia to the northwest of Alexandria. Senator Maclay of Pennsylvania grumbled that Washington should have let the commissioners select the exact boundaries, but Senator Carroll's measure convinced those who stood to benefit from the new borders to consider supporting the bill.[11]

Washington thus sent a letter to Congress the same day the measure passed, with a request to alter slightly the designated boundary, moving it somewhat to the south and including Alexandria and lands nearer to his home. This brazen decision was rife with problems. It could have reopened debate as to the location of the capital city, or it could have been the mistake Washington's critics needed to charge him with a conflict of interest and abuse of his power. After all, Virginia had ceded land farther up the river from the site Washington selected, which happened to include roughly a thousand acres he owned near Four Mile Run and another thousand acres his wife's grandson owned at the present site of Arlington National Cemetery.[12] Even Vice President Adams scoffed, pointing out that this decision would increase Washington's property values "1,000%," while Charles Nisbet, the president of Dickinson College, claimed such self-interest went beyond reason.[13]

Nevertheless, Congress approved Washington's request to include Alexandria in the federal city. The city, including Washington's adjusted boundaries, would adhere to the "ten Miles square" mandate, hug the banks of the Potomac, and extend from Alexandria through parts of Maryland.

Maryland ceded land along the northern bank of the Potomac, and Virginia ceded land along the southern bank of the river, including the port city of Alexandria. The lands donated included long stretches of the Potomac, its tributary the Anacostia, and an abundance of farm fields, orchards, forests, and marshlands, but all with ample access to waterways. Public buildings were to be on the Maryland side of the river.

Separate from the Residence Act and mindful of the lessons from the Philadelphia mutiny in June 1783, the legislation established the federal district as an autonomous area. When the government relocated to the new site in the late fall of 1800, Congress would have complete authority "to exercise exclusive Legislation in all Cases whatsoever, over the District" as stated in Article I, Section 8 of the Constitution. As Madison noted in the *Federalist Papers*, without jurisdiction, the government's "authority might be insulted and its proceedings interrupted with impunity."[14] It was not only a logical answer to a host of potential problems and, in the words of Madison, an "indispensable necessity," but it was an arrangement largely without precedent around the world.[15]

There was enough agreement among members of Congress to grant the president the authority to appoint a board of three commissioners to help survey, plan, and supervise the new federal district and capital city. They were also empowered to accept money and donations of land for the project. Known as the Commission for the Federal District, they were to set the exact boundaries for the federal district and federal city.

Once again, the president was aware that he needed to exercise caution in making his appointments, especially since he had already begun moving forward unilaterally with his plans for the city in the late summer and fall of 1790. The Residence Act did not require Senate confirmation for the appointments to the commission, but the second part of the law was vague on specifics. Did the commissioners have discretionary power? If so, might they not be influenced by local interests or the lobbying of Jefferson, Madison, and the decentralist faction, or even from northerners opposed to the Potomac and still hoping to keep the permanent capital in Philadelphia? Others worried about the appearance if all three commissioners were from Virginia. Washington understood, however, that the legislation granted him sole authority to both select the commissioners and decide on the boundaries for the federal district and federal city.

On January 21, 1791, the president announced his picks. Two of the commissioners would be from Maryland and one from Virginia. All three men were respected politicians and eminently qualified. Not surprisingly, they were also fellow landowners along the Potomac, stockholders in the Potomac Company, and, most important, good friends of Washington. Yet through the selections, Washington opened himself up to obvious allegations of a conflict of interest. It is of note that Vice President Adams had tried but failed to get Washington to select one member from his home state of Massachusetts. Also of note is that all three were slave owners, reflecting the prevalence of the abysmal institution in the region and prominence of it among southerners in nearly every political debate and issue.[16]

The first commissioner was related to Washington by marriage. David Stuart of Virginia had married the widow of John Park Custis, Mrs. Washington's eldest son from her first marriage. Stuart, a Scot, had studied medicine at the University of Saint Andrews in Scotland and was a practicing physician and member of the Virginia House of Delegates.

The second commissioner was Thomas Johnson of Frederick, Maryland, who served as the state's first governor and had been a delegate to the Continental Congress, where he was one of the men who forwarded the motion to select Washington as the commander of the Continental Army. Washington later appointed Johnson to the Supreme Court. However, he had to resign after only a few months on the bench because of poor health. In fact, as of this writing, Johnson still has the dubious distinction of being the shortest-serving justice on the high court. His health was such that, when Jefferson later stepped down as secretary of state, Washington offered his friend the position, but Johnson declined because of his fragile constitution. Most important regarding the work of the commission, Johnson was a skilled attorney with expertise in land disputes. Washington correctly anticipated that the effort to get residents along the Potomac to buy and sell plots would end up in legal entanglements.

The final commissioner was Daniel Carroll of Rock Creek, Maryland, a wealthy friend of Washington's. Carroll's extended family included many influential leaders. Carroll's brother, John, was a founder of Georgetown University and the first Catholic bishop in America, and his cousin Charles had signed the Declaration of Independence. Daniel Carroll was educated at a Jesuit college in Europe and went on to a distinguished political career as a member of the Continental Congress, signer of the Articles of Confederation, and delegate to the Constitutional Convention. Interestingly, during the Convention, the issue of whether the president should be selected by Congress was raised, and it was Carroll who first suggested the leader be elected "by the people." Like the other commissioners, he owned land by the Potomac and helped Washington promote the Potomac Company (then spelled "Potowmack").

The commissioners served without pay. In 1794 Washington made three new appointments. They would be compensated for their service. The first was Gustavus Scott, a member of the Maryland legislature and fellow stockholder in the Potomac Company. He too was a slave owner.

Senator Tristram Dalton of Massachusetts expressed interest in serving on the commission, but Washington wanted another Virginian and selected Alexander White, a former member of Congress who was also involved in the Potomac Company. Interestingly, Senator Dalton was later selected to serve on the same commission by President John Adams. The second president's pick was controversial, as it was one of his outgoing "midnight" appointments in 1801, an act that would anger Jefferson, the incoming president, and his supporters. In another interesting twist Dalton would lose most of his fortune in real estate deals in the capital city.

Washington had initially offered the final position on the commission to Tobias Lear, his longtime trusted aide and investor in the Potomac Company. However, Lear respectfully declined, perhaps sensing the questionable appearance of his appointment. Washington replaced Lear with Dr. William Thornton, a Maryland physician who had treated the Washington family and Lear. Washington had also appointed the physician's friends and relatives to various government positions.[17]

Thornton was a landowner along the Potomac and a particularly accomplished man. Born in the West Indies and educated in Scotland, Thornton arrived in America in 1787 and became a citizen the following year. Thornton was both a physician and architect who would go on to design the Library Company of Philadelphia, the famous Octagon House in the capital city, and many other homes and buildings, along with the homes of some of Washington's relations. His plan for the US Capitol Building would later form the basis for its design. He too, however, was a slave owner.

The natural alliance between Washington and "his" commissioners was not lost on Jefferson and Madison, or on the president's critics. One man who could always be counted on to fume was Senator Maclay of Pennsylvania, who wrote that Washington assumed all authority on the matter. To Maclay and others, "The commissioners are now only agents of demarcation, mere surveyors to run four lines of fixed courses and distances."[18]

Maclay's criticism was warranted. The Residence Act was vague on details regarding the exact location of the new capital city within the federal district, financing for the project, the means for constructing public buildings, and other questions. These issues would all end up in Washington's capable hands. The president announced the exact location of the planned capital just three days after appointing the original commission, giving credence to the criticism that he alone had made all the decisions.

Senator Maclay complained, "I really am surprised at the conduct of the president. . . . To take on him to fix the spot by his own authority, when he might have placed the three commissioners in the post of responsibility, was a thoughtless act." Maclay had favored his native Pennsylvania as the site of the capital and was appalled by the manner by which the issue had been resolved. He fumed at what he saw as uncompromising and hypocritical tactics of the southerners. "Alas! That the affection, nay, almost adoration of the people should meet so unworthy a return. Here are their best interests sacrificed to the vain whim of fixing Congress and a great commercial town (so opposite to the genius of the southern planter) on the Potomac."[19]

Likewise, even though southerners would get their capital, Representative William Smith of South Carolina maintained the bill was unconstitutional. His argument was that Congress, not the president, should have the power to make the final decisions pertaining to the capital. Smith wrote (somewhat anonymously as "Junius Americanus") a scathing letter directed at Washington in a New York newspaper and later in a Charleston newspaper.[20] Smith was not alone. Other papers and critics alleged the bill was unconstitutional and tore into the president about his new responsibilities and the unilateral nature of his power and actions. There were also concerns about Washington's obvious conflict of interest as a landowner at the Potomac location.[21]

Nonetheless, after more than two dozen possible cities and towns had been considered for the new capital, it was decided that the city and federal district would be created entirely from scratch on land ceded by Virginia and Maryland. The location balanced geographic interests and was placed by a navigable waterway. All this, of course, mirrored Washington's long-held vision for the nation, his hope that the federal city would help unite the country, and his personal preferences for the Potomac.[22]

In late March 1791 Washington set off on a misty day from Suter's Tavern in Georgetown (which was then in Maryland) to inspect the site. He rode through the heavy fog with his three new commissioners, crossing Rock Creek. They contemplated the locations of buildings, took in the landscape, and listened to Washington's plans for the next phase of his vision.

Despite the contentious debate, the Potomac was a good site. It was a growing region, the westward bend of the river along with various newly built trails, roads, and expanding canals offered the promise of linking the Eastern Seaboard with inland communities as far west as the Ohio River valley. Numerous internal improvements promoted by Washington had also helped improve the river's navigability.

Yet in a portent of things to come, one of the first projects for the new capital city went awry. A bridge was needed to cross Rock Creek. Regrettably, the commissioners hired a general builder named Leonard Harbaugh, when they should have selected an engineer with experience in bridge design and construction. The project ran behind schedule, and the completed structure was not wide enough to accommodate the wagons and loads of supplies that needed to be brought into the city.[23] It immediately started to sag. Soon, the bridge appeared ready to collapse, prompting the commissioners to write to Harbaugh on October 16, 1794, with orders to repair the overpass. That December James Hoban, the man chosen by Washington to design and build the president's house, was still complaining that the bridge had yet to be fixed.

Eventually, Washington and his commissioners established a system for building and funding bridges, roads, and other "internal improvements." It would be a painful process of trial and error, and the initial bridge debacle was an "inauspicious beginning" for the new capital.[24]

CHAPTER 20

Philadelphia

I would as soon pitch my tent beneath a tree in which was a hornet's nest, as I would, as a delegate from South Carolina, vote for placing the government in a settlement of Quakers.

Congressman Aedanus Burke

When the president departed New York City, it would mark the last time in his life that he would ever step foot in the city. Federal Hall just off Wall Street had functioned as the interim seat of Congress from March 4, 1789, until August 12, 1790, when Congress departed the city.

New Yorkers gave the president a regal farewell complete with a parade and artillery salutes, even though some were not happy with his decision to sign the Residence Act. Large crowds and the city's newspapers hailed him as a hero, and people wept openly as he passed by. Newspapers described Washington as being "sensibly moved" and Mrs. Washington as "greatly affected" by the outpouring of support.[1]

Before moving to Philadelphia, the Washingtons rode to Mount Vernon for some much-needed rest. As the president noted to his advisers, he preferred "to have my mind as free from public care as circumstances will allow."[2] Although he needed a break from politics, the president did receive visitors as well as regular, long reports from Alexander Hamilton.[3] He also ordered thirty-six bottles of port for his homecoming, clearly a sign that he intended to enjoy the successful conclusion to the long, bitter debates over the nation's finances and capital. Not surprisingly, the break helped Washington recover his health and reinvigorate his spirits.[4]

Washington's Farewell to Officers, by Henry Alexander Ogden, 1893.
Here Gen. George Washington is depicted saying goodbye to his
officers of the Continental Army at the end of the Revolutionary
War at Fraunces Tavern in New York City, December 1783.
Library of Congress.

The West Front of Mount Vernon painted by Edward Savage, c. 1787–92.
Washington returned to his beloved plantation after the Revolutionary
War for what he thought would be his retirement.
George Washington's Mount Vernon, bequest of Helen W. Thompson, 1964.

Federal Hall in New York City, which housed the first Congress,
Supreme Court, and Executive Branch offices in 1789 when
New York was the capital of the new nation.
Library of Congress.

An 1800 view of financier Robert Morris's home on Chestnut Street in Philadelphia. President George Washington rented this large, rambling, unfinished house in November 1790 as his residence while Philadelphia was the nation's seat of government. Library of Congress.

The small port city of Georgetown, Maryland, on the Potomac River was transformed as Washington, DC, grew around it. The Georgetown waterfront is seen here in 1795 after construction of the new capital had begun. Library of Congress.

A portrait of Major Pierre (Peter) Charles L'Enfant, French immigrant, Revolutionary War soldier, and original architect of the plan to develop Washington, DC. Library of Congress.

First Lady Martha Washington. Library of Congress.

George Washington is seen here at the end of his second term as president
in the famous *Lansdowne Portrait* by Gilbert Stuart, 1796. Washington
declined to seek a third term as president, but he continued his
work overseeing the construction of the federal city.
National Portrait Gallery, Smithsonian Institution; acquired as a gift to the
nation through the generosity of the Donald W. Reynolds Foundation.

Waxen bas-relief on glass portrait of James Hoban, attributed to John Christian Rauschner. Hoban was an Irish immigrant to America who became a noted architect of buildings in Charleston, South Carolina, and Washington, DC, none more famous than the White House. White House Historical Association/ White House Collection.

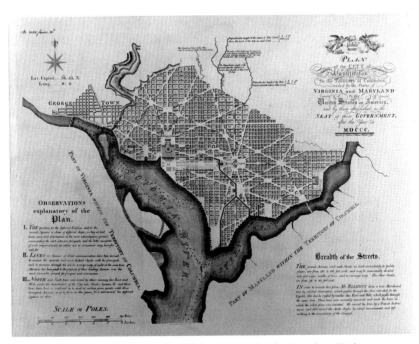

Andrew Ellicott's 1792 plan for Washington, DC. After President Washington dismissed L'Enfant, Ellicott took over and made modifications to the L'Enfant Plan for the city. Ellicott had also surveyed the boundaries for the Territory of Columbia. Library of Congress.

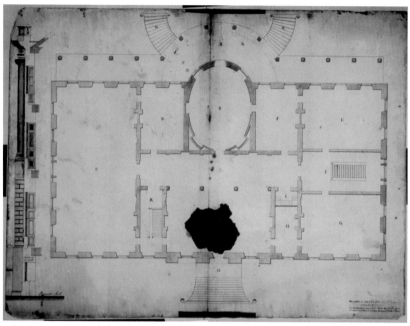

James Hoban's White House Floor Plan, 1792.
White House Historical Association/Massachusetts Historical Society.

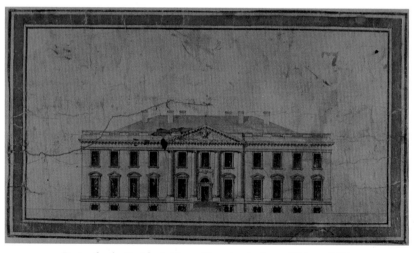

Design for the President's House, Elevation, by James Hoban, 1792.
White House Historical Association.

Washington and Hoban inspect DC, 1798 by N. C. Wyeth, 1932. This is an imagined view of the first president after he left office inspecting construction of one of the most iconic buildings in the new federal city. White House Historical Association.

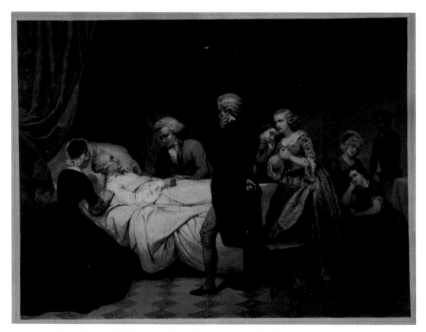

Life of George Washington: The Christian Death by Junius Brutus Stearns; lithograph by Régnier, Paris, c. 1853. Library of Congress.

When Congress reconvened on a frigid Monday morning on December 6, 1790, it would be in Philadelphia, the same city where Washington would later be inaugurated for a second term in 1793. Once again, rudimentary transportation and communication systems, along with the weather, limited the opening of the new session. Only fifteen of the twenty-six members of the Senate arrived in time. They met in Congress Hall, a lovely two-story Georgian brick building that complemented the nearby State House, also known as Independence Hall. The second floor housed the Senate chambers and had been prepared to impress the senators. It did. Rich mahogany desks sat in semicircles around a large Axminster carpet featuring an elegant and imposing Great Seal of the United States. Thirteen large windows trimmed in green and wooden Venetian blinds along with white candles atop each desk provided ample light for the meetings.[5]

Washington's journey to the new interim capital that November was anything but pleasant, however. Heavy rains had washed out roads and made crossing small ravines and creeks troublesome. There was another problem: the coachman following Washington's carriage and transporting the family's personal possessions was apparently under the influence of the bottle. He overturned the wagon twice, spilling luggage onto the muddy roads. At least the president was unharmed during the harrowing journey. Four members of the Massachusetts congressional delegation were not so lucky. They were injured when their carriage toppled over. Thus were the pitfalls of traveling in the late eighteenth century.

The president and his family arrived on November 27 only to discover the renovations to the home Congress would be renting for Washington from Robert Morris on the south side of Market Street were incomplete. His secretary of war, Henry Knox, discovered that much of his furniture was lost during the trip, while the wife of his vice president had her trunks full of dresses and clothing ruined by a leaky ship that transported the second family's possessions. Philadelphia, Mrs. Adams lamented, was not what she had hoped. Of the city's river, she observed, "The Schuylkill is no more like the Hudson than I to Hercules!" In anticipation of the arrival of the new government, the city had undertaken numerous public improvements, but this also had the effect of filling the streets with the sights and sounds of construction.[6]

Members of Congress, tempers and alliances frayed by the previous session's grueling fight over the capital and Hamilton's financial reforms, found plenty to gripe about in the new capital city. The government buildings were unfinished and unorganized. Relatedly, the new government was still struggling for legitimacy. Members of Congress arrived late for sessions and often departed early.

Their business, both to themselves and to their states, was seen as just as important, if not more of a priority, as service to the new nation. As a result, the turnover rate in Congress during the decade Philadelphia hosted the government was shocking. Of the eighty-six senators who served in the first congresses, for instance, fully one-third of them resigned their seats before the completion of their six-year terms. The numbers were only slightly less abysmal in the House. Challenges remained.[7]

The city was also far more expensive than New York, and there were labor and housing shortages. Opportunistic businessmen had quickly set up shop in the new capital city, gouging the local residents and members of Congress alike. "The city seems at present to be mostly inhabited by sharpers," observed Senator James Monroe of Virginia.[8] Similarly, Representative Jeremiah Smith of New Hampshire wrote home, "The Philadelphians are, from the highest to the lowest, from the parson in his black gown to the *fille de joie*, or girl of pleasure, a set of beggars. . . . You cannot turn around without paying a dollar!" William Smith of South Carolina complained, "What a serious business it is to move the seat of government, summed up the mood of many members of Congress. . . . The Quakers wish us at the Devil. I need not tell you where I wish them."[9]

Others commented that the city was, in fact, quite English, which was a mixed blessing in 1790. Nonetheless, many Englishmen and Europeans continued to look down their noses at America and the new, temporary capital. One French visitor dismissed Philadelphia. "The men are grave, the women serious, no financial airs, no libertine wives . . . no agreeable walks." A Parisian, he surmised quite colorfully, would not be amused "because he could not strut upon a boulevard, babble in a coffeehouse, or seduce a pretty woman by his important airs and fine curls."[10]

Yet the noted historian Henry Adams, great-grandson of John Adams, described Philadelphia and Pennsylvania as assets to the young republic: "Too thoroughly democratic to fear democracy and too much nationalized to dread nationality, Pennsylvania became the ideal American state, easy, tolerant, and contented. If its soil bred little genius, it bred still less treason. With twenty different religious creeds, its practice could not be narrow, and a strong Quaker element made it humane."[11]

Back in July 1788 the city had hosted a grand parade in honor of the state's ratifying the Constitution, with crowds of citizens marching in the parade and celebrating throughout the city. The parade was also designed to send a message to Congress that it would be a good site for the capital—waving at the head of the parade was a large flag with the image of a capital city being built with a deity-like sun shining down on it. Philadelphia was now proud to host the government, and city elders and residents alike hoped the capital would remain beyond its interim status. They rolled out the proverbial red carpet: public buildings were being completed and improvements in roads, water, and lighting were underway, and the city had even constructed a "president's house." However, Washington never used it, instead remaining in the home from his friend Robert Morris in order to avoid giving the appearance that he and the new government would permanently stay in Philadelphia.

In many ways, given its history and symbolic significance—it was the site of the First and Second Continental Congresses and the city where the Declaration of Independence and Constitution were produced—Philadelphia was a natural site for government.[12] It was also one of the largest cities in the young nation with a population in the 25,000–33,000 range. With the new government now in the city, the numerous visiting merchants and traders, and growing communities ringing Philadelphia, as many as 45,000 people lived and worked in and around the city in late 1790.

The new interim seat of government was not only now larger than New York City or Boston; it claimed to be more cosmopolitan. It boasted wide cobblestoned roads, organized squares throughout the city, numerous large brick homes, and of course, the celebrated Benjamin Franklin and both his Philadelphia Library Company and American Philosophical Society. Next to Washington, Franklin perhaps most embodied the image of the new republic. One visitor to the city remarked that the locals "believe themselves to be the first and finest people in America as well in manners as in arts and like Englishmen, they are at no pains to disguise this opinion."[13]

The president, knowing the myriad problems that awaited him in Philadelphia, was not eager to resume his duties, with the notable exception of planning the permanent seat of government. The partisan rancor had only temporarily subsided during the recess, and he was presently preoccupied with a "lost" military expedition into western Indian territory (Cdr. Josiah Harmar's patrol had not been heard from for weeks). Yet not everything was worse in Philadelphia, and some legislators applauded the move. In a decade they would discover that the move to the new federal city would be far more problematic.[14]

As was mentioned earlier, the forty-one days Washington vacationed at Mount Vernon did him well. The president described himself upon his arrival in Philadelphia as "perfectly re-established."[15] Washington took up residence in Robert Morris's mansion on Market Street. It was just steps away from Independence

Hall. His residence was known simply as "the President's House." The home agreed with him; Washington had stayed there during the Constitutional Convention a few years prior and would remain at the Morris home from November 27, 1790, until March 10, 1797, after he had completed his second term as president. John Adams would live there with his wife, Abigail, from March 1797 until late May 1800.

Although the home was elegant and spacious for any family, it was too small for a large bustling staff and the demands of the office, which included hosting numerous guests at social events. In addition, according to Washington, a guest or aide had to climb "two pairs of stairs and pass by the public rooms" just to meet with him. This was unacceptable. Moreover, the presidential family included President and Mrs. Washington, her two grandchildren, and at times, other members of the extended family. After Washington's brother Samuel had died, he agreed to help raise his niece, Harriet, who was difficult and lazy. Another two nephews—George and Lawrence—also came to Philadelphia to attend college but proved to be equally troublesome. Washington found himself having to devote a lot of time, energy, and money to the three overly indulged relatives. And he lacked the physical space in the house.[16]

The presidential household also consisted of twenty servants and cooks, clerks, and slaves who had been brought from Mount Vernon, including Washington's personal attendant and cook, Hercules, who insisted that his son, Nathan, join them. The president also received a steady stream of visitors that included his former officers from the war, members of Congress, visiting foreign dignitaries, and friends from Virginia. Accordingly, the president was forced to have his longtime aide, Tobias Lear, prepare plans for expanding the home. Two extra rooms were added to the home and a few of the square walls were replaced with bowed walls in order to better receive guests, reflecting a design feature that anticipated the oval rooms in the White House. Washington made sure, however, that all the redecorations and changes to the house met with the approval of Mrs. Morris.[17]

The French intellectual, writer, and politician François-René, Vicomte de Chateaubriand, visited Philadelphia and recorded his observations regarding the president, the city, and Washington's rented home. As to the presidential home, Chateaubriand admitted, "I was not greatly moved." The aristocrat was expecting a palace in the European tradition. He described his visit as follows: "A small house, just like the adjacent house, was the palace of the President of the United States; no guard, not even a footman." It was not just the simple home; it was the simplicity and lack of protocol that surprised the Frenchman. He noted,

I knocked; a young maid servant opened the door. I asked her whether the general was at home; she answered that he was. I added that I had a letter for him. The girl asked for my name; it is not an easy one to pronounce in English and she could not repeat it. She then said gently, "Walk in, Sir. *Entrez, Monseir,*" and she walked ahead of me through one of these narrow passageways which form the vestibule of English houses. Finally she showed me into a parlor and bade me wait for the general.

The informality alarmed the Vicomte de Chateaubriand.[18]

Although palatial by American standards, the home was simple by European standards, especially for a head of state. Of course, others criticized the home. One Pennsylvanian wrote inaccurately that "instead of a dwelling for the first servant of a republican people you see a palace seemingly designed for Louis XIV." Despite Washington's popularity, he certainly shared something with all his successors—that his every action and decision were subject to criticism.[19] Chateaubriand, however, found the interim capital city to be pleasant, describing a "fine town, with wide streets, some planted with trees, intersecting at right angles in regular patterns." Yet he added that it was not comparable to the grand capitals of Europe.[20]

The Vicomte de Chateaubriand's most emphatic comments were for Washington himself. Watching the president pass by in his carriage, Chateaubriand was reminded of "Cincinnatus in a chariot." At the site of "the soldier-citizen, the liberator of the world," the aristocrat claimed he "re-discovered the simplicity of the ancient Romans." The French visitor was granted an audience with the president, who was, in his words, "tall in stature, with a calm, cool air rather than one of nobility, he looked like his portraits." Overwhelmed by the president's power and charisma, the vicomte paid him a lofty compliment: "But it is less difficult to discover the North-West passage than to create a nation as you have done." Washington was obviously pleased with the praise, chuckling, "Well, well, young man!" then inviting his guest to dine with him.

At dinner they discussed an array of topics from the new nation to the French Revolution. Chateaubriand would look back on the moment years later, recalling that he felt "happy that his gaze should have rested on me! I have felt warmed by it for the rest of my life: there is a virtue in the gaze of a great man." The aristocrat went so far as to describe the experience as akin to being filled with "glory."[21]

While in Philadelphia the Washingtons were regulars at the South Street Theater, where they maintained their own private box. The president particularly enjoyed farcical comedies, a preference seemingly at odds with the outward aloofness and image of stoicism for which he was famous. The first couple also attended the first circus in America, which was held in the interim capital city. They regularly attended church on Sundays, reserving a pew at the Old Christ Church, a beautiful and enormous brick building nestled on a scenic, tree-lined, cobblestone street in the downtown. The high steeple atop the church that beckoned the family to service each Sunday made the building the tallest in the United States until 1856.

Crowds of well-wishers and curious residents regularly gathered to watch the president arrive for services in his coach pulled by four or six horses. One account fawned, "His noble height and commanding air . . . his patient demeanor in the crowd . . . his gentle bendings of the neck, to the right and to the left, parentally, and expressive of delighted feelings on his part; these, with the appearance of the awed and charmed and silent crowd of spectators, gently falling back on each side, as he approached, unequivocally announced to the gazing stranger behold the man!"[22]

The president cut a dashing image. Tall and immaculately dressed, he was always conscious of the aura of heroism from the war and ever aware that all eyes were on him. In public Washington often wore a regal, long blue cape with its scarlet interior lining visible. At other times he was dressed head to toe in black velvet with knee and shoe buckles, gloves, and a long sword on his hip in a polished white scabbard. His hair was powdered and pulled back in a large silk bow, at times under a hat adorned with a cockade or feathers. Of course, some critics decried such instances of "court etiquette" as unacceptable for a simple republic.[23]

Although Washington was still a vigorous and strong man when he entered the presidency, the demands of his schedule and two bouts with a serious illness left him "completely fatigued."[24] Fortunately, the president recovered both times. For exercise, he enjoyed walking the streets of Philadelphia with his close aide Tobias Lear.

Washington especially valued the company of Samuel and Elizabeth Willing Powel. Both George and Martha Washington held the Powels in highest regards, and "the Patriotic Mayor" of the city and his wife, who was often exceedingly warm and flirtatious with Washington, quickly emerged as among the president's closest confidantes. He spent more time with the opinionated, blunt, and social Mrs. Powel than perhaps any woman other than his wife. The city's premiere *saloniste* provided him with invaluable advice about the symbolic importance of his presidency. He listened.[25]

The first couple was well prepared for the challenge of heading the new government in Philadelphia and carving out social customs. The Washingtons were known for being gracious hosts to the many guests they entertained. To be sure, their Mount Vernon home often resembled a boarding house more so than a private home. At one point Washington even quipped that, as the dinner hour approached and no guests had yet arrived, he and Mrs. Washington might do something they had not done in years: "dine alone." The habit continued at their rented home in Philadelphia.[26]

One visitor for two days described the experience thus: "I have been treated as usual with every most distinguished mark of kindness and attention. Hospitality, indeed, seems to have spread over the whole its happiest, kindest influence." The warmest praise was reserved for the first couple themselves: "The President exercises it in a superlative degree, from the greatest of its duties to the most trifling minutiae, and Mrs. Washington is the very essence of kindness. Her soul seems to overflow with it like the most abundant fountain, and her happiness is in exact proportion to the number of objects upon which she can dispense her benefits."[27]

The Washingtons were aware that their every action and inaction forged important precedents for both the inaugural presidency and the new nation. There were no blueprints for what they faced, leading Washington to confess, "I walk on untrodden ground. There is scarcely any part of my conduct which may not hereafter be drawn into precedent."[28] As Washington carved out protocols, he considered the actions of European monarchs—how they would act but also what they would not do—yet fashioned an entirely new kind of office.

Indeed, the challenge for the Washingtons was that they needed to design a social atmosphere and protocol befitting the new experiment in popular governance yet one that earned for the upstart nation the respect and credibility of old Europe. Every event hosted and custom would send important signals to not only their foreign allies but perhaps more importantly to their fellow citizens. Washington knew the eyes of his countrymen, the world, and history were on him and that his anti-federalist foes waited to pounce on any social or political misstep as being too monarchical or royalist. He also knew that the opportunity permitted him to use social events and ceremonies to promote his dream of unity and a national identity.

Washington took great care in recrafting his social protocols with an eye to his image and that of the nation. These events, after all, were forging precedents and a national identity. He thus continually sought the advice of Congressman James

Madison, Chief Justice John Jay, and Hamilton, who was serving as his treasury secretary. He rarely consulted Vice President John Adams, thus establishing the precedent of that office being little more than a potential president-in-waiting that lasted until the late twentieth century. Washington wondered whether he should host weekly socials and whether this would make him too accessible—or alternatively, not accessible enough. Would it promote a sense of republican informality for the new nation? Who should be invited? How should the invitations be made? How should he receive his guests? The answers, they knew, would help to establish an identity for the new nation.[29]

Washington had always been keen on "forms, ceremonies and punctilious etiquette."[30] So one of the first things he did after his inauguration was to have his trusted aide, Alexander Hamilton, draw up a set of proposals to govern social protocol, including social hosting. Typical of Hamilton, he responded with verbosity and detail:

1. The President to have a levee once a week for receiving visits; an hour to be fixed at which it shall be understood that he will appear, and consequently that the visitors are to be previously assembled.

    The President to remain half an hour, in which time he may converse cursorily on indifferent subjects, with such persons as shall invite his attention, and at the end of that half hour disappear. . . . No visits to be returned.

2. The President to accept no invitations, and to give formal entertainments only twice or four times a year, the anniversaries of important events in the Revolution. If twice on the day of the Declaration of Independence, and that of the Inauguration of the President, which completed the organization of the Constitution, to be preferred. . . .

    The President on levee days, either by himself or some gentleman of his household to give informal invitations to family dinners on the days of the invitation. Not more than six or eight to be invited at a time, and the matter to be confined essentially to members of the legislature and other official characters. The President never to remain long at the table.[31]

Washington took Hamilton's advice but welcomed a wide array of guests and visitors at the beginning of his term. He quickly discovered that this was neither practical nor the best use of his time. He complained, "From the time I had done breakfast and thence till dinner and afterwards till bedtime, I could not get relieved from the ceremony of one visit before I had to attend to another." Mrs. Washington was more blunt, writing to friends and relatives back home, "I live a very dull life here. . . . Indeed I think I am more like a state prisoner than anything else."[32]

For instance, the president's visitation guidelines were announced in the *New York Federal Gazette of the United States* when Washington set up his household in New York City. It read,

> We are informed that the President has assigned every Tuesday and Friday, between the hours of 2 and 3 for receiving visits; that visits of compliment on other days and particularly Sunday, will not be agreeable to him. It seems to be a prevailing opinion that so much of the President's time will be engaged by various and important business imposed on him by the Constitution that he will find himself constrained to omit returning visits, or accept invitations to entertainments.

The public and the anti-federalists complained about the limitations.[33]

The first couple settled on Friday night socials with tea. These events were hosted by Mrs. Washington, held at 8:00, and popularly referred to as "drawing rooms." The First Lady sat next to Abigail Adams while tea, cake, and candied fruit were served to the guests, who milled about the large reception room. The drawing rooms were marked by their informal nature, with Mrs. Washington even occasionally serving the tea herself. The president hosted more formal and ceremonial affairs open only to men, per the custom of the times. They were known as "levees," named for the French expression "to rise." In New York City the weekly levees began at 2:00, but the time was moved to 3:00 when the capital was relocated to Philadelphia.

The format for the levee was described as follows: "[Washington] always stood in front of the fireplace, with his face towards the door of entrance. The visitor was conducted to him, and he required that their names be pronounced such that he could hear it. He had the very uncommon faculty of associating a man's name and personal appearance so durably in his memory as to be able to call any one by name who made him a second visit." Guests noted that the president's demeanor remained distinguished, if a bit guarded. One noted, "He received his visitor with a dignified bow, while his hands were so disposed of as to indicate that the salutation was not to be accompanied with shaking hands. This ceremony never occurred in those visits, even with his most near friends, that no distinction might be made."[34]

From surviving letters it seems that Washington typically held his hat and kept his other hand on the handle of his sword as an excuse not to shake so many hands. Another account of the afternoon levee also described the formal tone: "As visitors came in, they formed a circle around the room. At a quarter past three, the door was opened and the circle was formed for that day. He then began on the right and spoke to each visitor, calling him by name and exchanging a few words with him. When he had completed his circuit, he resumed his first position, and the visitors approached him, in succession, bowed and retired. By four o'clock this ceremony was over."[35] Not surprisingly, these events were described as "stiff, formal, and intermittently silent" affairs.[36]

The Washingtons also presided over a number of dinners, dances, and other social events, which sometimes ran until late in the evening and appear to have been livelier than the dour meetings with the president. Washington's dinners were served at a dining room measuring roughly thirty feet in length and, like the evening events, commenced with the First Lady receiving visitors in one of two parlors on the second floor.[37] During Mrs. Washington's evening programs, the president did not consider himself to be functioning in an official capacity, so he did not wear his hat or sword. Rather, he casually moved about the room and chatted with guests. Mrs. Washington, for her part, went to bed early and, like clockwork, announced, "The General retires at nine o'clock, and I always precede him." It was at that moment that inhibitions lessened. The president was a talented dancer, and the queues of women lining up for his favor were impressively long, especially after Lady Washington departed.[38]

As was the case when she was in France, Abigail Adams remained shocked by the libertine behavior at the parties and the fashions worn by the female guests. They seemed, she observed, to be inspired by Parisian sensibilities. She grumbled, "The style of dress . . . is really an outrage upon all decency." Mrs. Adams described it as follows: "Most [women] wear their cloathes too scant upon the body and too full upon the bosom for my fancy, not content with the Show which nature bestows, they borrow from art, and literally look like Nursing Mothers." And to think that Philadelphia had been under the influence of Quakers! Yet for all the concern and controversy, not all the social events were so memorable. One snowy Christmas Day, for instance, Washington donned his ceremonial sword and fine suit only to discover that no one had showed up.[39]

Overall, Washington's social experiment in Philadelphia was a success. His appearances, protocols, events, and image were having the desired effect—a nation was forming, ever so slowly but deliberately. He was playing a role that he had long prepared to fulfill. However, there was a darker side to the years spent in the interim capital.

John Adams described summers in Philadelphia as a "bake oven." Accordingly, many people in a day and age without air conditioning, refrigeration, mosquito control, or proper storm drainage abandoned the city in summers. There was another reason to get away—disease.[40] Scourges such as yellow fever often plagued the city in summer. Yellow fever was a particularly painful and gruesome malady. Its symptoms were positively medieval and included a high fever, continuous vomiting, a repugnant black mucus, blood hemorrhaging through the nose and mouth, and a jaundiced appearance of the skin. Bodies piled up and were carried out of Philadelphia in carts. Without a medical answer to the affliction, city leaders frequently burned barrels of tar. Rather than remove the disease from the air, however, it only fouled and blackened the sky.

The summer of 1793, which marked the beginning of Washington's second term as president, was particularly bad. Disease tore through the city, claiming many lives. One of them was Tobias Lear's wife, Polly, who passed on July 23. The death toll in the city weighed heavily on the president, but the loss of Polly—who was related to Mrs. Washington and had been treated like a daughter to the family—underscored the tragic nature of that summer. As a rule, the president did not attend funerals, but he organized Polly's as if it were a state funeral. The procession included Washington's cabinet members and Supreme Court justices and would end up being the only funeral the president attended during his time in office.[41]

In the midst of the outbreak that August, the First Lady wrote to a relative, sharing a view held by most everyone in the city: "I am truly sorry to hear of so many deaths—the wet raney season has made it sickly every where—I shall be glad when the frost comes to clear the air."[42]

Government ceased to function, as people—including members of Congress and public employees—abandoned the city. Even the bitter fights between the factions in Congress were largely put aside each summer, leading one observer to quip, "Nothing but the yellow fever . . . could have saved the United States from a total revolution of government."[43]

Washington had planned to leave the city during the contagion of 1793; however, the Powels announced that they would remain in Philadelphia. Washington tried to get them to take refuge at Mount Vernon. Mrs. Powel, however, would not leave her husband, writing to Washington, "The conflict between duty and inclination is a severe trial of my feelings, but, as I believe it is always best to adhere to the line of duty, I beg to decline the pleasure I proposed to myself in accompanying you to Virginia at this time."[44]

To inspire his fellow citizens and stand in solidarity with Mayor Powel, Washington symbolically remained behind. He sent his household staff and Mrs. Washington's grandchildren back to his home in Virginia and tried to get his wife to leave, but she too, like Mrs. Powel, remained steadfast and loyal in the city. Sadly, Mayor Powel contracted the disease and died on September 29. Several staffers in the Departments of War, Treasury, Customs, and the Post Office were also lost. Hamilton contracted the malady but survived and fled the city with his wife for her family home in Albany. Jefferson sent the employees at the State Department home and rode to Monticello.

Washington did not leave Philadelphia until mid-September, putting his war secretary and longtime friend Henry Knox in charge of the federal government. It is interesting to note that the vice presidency, as an office, was so insignificant and viewed primarily as the president of the Senate, that Washington did not select John Adams for the responsibility. Likewise, the president's decision reflected both his close relationship with Knox and the severity of the threat that it was a matter of security.

General Knox sent the remaining government workers away and wrote to Washington with updates from the city, claiming that "100 people a day" were dying. "The streets," described Knox, "are lonely to a melancholy degree. The merchants generally have fled . . . as if an army of enemies had possessed the city without plundering it." Knox would be the last to leave Philadelphia, which had been rendered a ghost town.[45]

The credibility of the government was dealt a severe blow that summer. In addition to losing key personnel, confidence in the new government suffered. The disease was affecting the debate about the location of the capital city and threatened to undermine Philadelphia's chances to host the permanent capital. If the president convened a meeting outside the city, it might be misconstrued as an abandonment of Philadelphia and reopen the entire messy affair. Moreover, Washington was cognizant that any relocation of the government could also damage the deal for the permanent capital to be built along the Potomac. Furthermore, constitutional questions were again being raised about whether to move the capital.

A deeply concerned Washington sought the counsel of his cabinet as to whether he should or could call a meeting of the government and Congress outside the interim capital. Writing to Hamilton, the president confided that no one else could "take a more comprehensive view and . . . a less partial one on the subject than yourself. . . . I pray you to dilate fully upon the several points here brought to your consideration."[46] Hamilton, ever the federalist, consulted the Constitution and informed the president that he had the power to recommend an emergency meeting but that he should not order such a meeting. Jefferson, ever the decentralist with a far stricter and limited view of the document, believed such a meeting was unconstitutional.

As was often the case, Washington went with his treasury secretary's advice, although he remained opposed to another move and interested only in a meeting in order to keep government functioning. A crisis in governance and public panic threatened as members of Congress, newspapers, and other voices began discussing the need to move the temporary capital that same month. Sites such as Annapolis, Reading, Trenton, and Wilmington were proposed. Hamilton suggested Germantown, site of the bloody Revolutionary battle, which was only a few miles outside the city.

Washington needed to trod carefully, lest his decision be interpreted as an abandonment of Philadelphia, a nod to Germantown being the new capital, or an argument against a Potomac site. Washington convened his cabinet in Germantown in early November, arriving in the town on November 1. The crowded town was full of refugees from Philadelphia.

Washington's actions, however, prevented the situation from deteriorating further when he declined to act in an autocratic or fearful manner during the crisis. His stoic calm prevailed. To move again would undermine the legitimacy of the fledgling government. He was aided by the weather, which more than any government policy brought the capital back to Philadelphia. A cooler fall and cold winter ended the scourge.

Washington arrived back in the interim capital that December and thoughtfully announced that he would be providing funds to yellow fever widows and their children. Mrs. Washington noted of the capital that "black seems to be the general dress in the city. Almost every family has lost some of their friends." With the disease abated, the city eventually returned to normal, but confidence in the new government had been dealt a blow and Philadelphia's hopes of retaining the capital were all but ended.[47]

CHAPTER 21

The City of Washington

Ambition must be made to counteract ambition.
James Madison

Another explosive matter remained for Washington. Both physically and symbolically, the size and composition of the capital would influence the development of the nation. The grand city envisioned by Washington would reflect the power of the federal government, which worried limited-government advocates.

Accordingly, Washington invited Thomas Jefferson, as his influential secretary of state, to play a role in the project. Both Virginians were experienced surveyors and prominent landowners who enjoyed renovating and tinkering with their homes and properties. Jefferson had frequently offered Washington advice on such matters, once writing him while in Europe, "In Paris it is forbidden to build a house beyond a given height, and it is admitted to be a good restriction. It keeps down the price of ground, keeps the houses low and convenient, and the streets light and airy. Fires are much more manageable where houses are low." Of course, Jefferson was only too happy to help with the city's construction and advocated a simple, small design for the city and its buildings as a way of advancing his pastoral aesthetic, anti-federalist politics, and limited role for government.[1]

Jefferson and his supporters proposed that the new capital be a simple "town" with a few small, brick buildings covering only a few hundred acres.[2] The Residence Act, after all, did not specify an exact size for the capital city within the "ten Miles square" district. Therefore, the next phase of the debate began in earnest. Georgetown landowners publicly estimated the city would require four hundred acres. Daniel Carroll, one of the three commissioners Washington later selected who also owned land by the Potomac, guessed that 160 acres were needed.[3] However, Washington and Hamilton had a vastly different and far grander vision for both the city and nation.[4]

Washington met with Jefferson and Madison on August 29, 1790, to begin formal discussions on the city. The two friends warned the president not to center his plans for the city on Alexandria. To do so would create a stir because the president owned property there. They encouraged him to focus on Georgetown and then add additional lands to the federal city as the process moved forward. However, the president knew that, for political reasons, he would need to include the town of Alexandria within the district and city. It was the county seat of government and a thriving port, it would help to raise revenues for the city, and it would balance the power of the area's other leading town—Georgetown.[5]

The next steps in the plan would unfold in four stages. The first involved weighing the options for the exact location and then fixing the boundaries. The second would be a design competition for the architects of the city, Capitol Building, and presidential home. The third challenge involved selling plots to finance the city. Finally, there was the matter of physically constructing the city and its many buildings.

After the Residence Act passed, Washington headed to Mount Vernon for a much-needed break, but soon thereafter he began an official tour of the region to select the sites for the buildings.[6] In advance of Washington, Jefferson and Madison set off for the Potomac that September. Although Jefferson and Madison were pleased that the capital included land in Virginia, they worried that Washington, their rival Hamilton, and the commissioners would exert their influence and plan a grand city. They were also concerned that, in the event Washington failed to secure the necessary plots of land and revenues, the unpredictable and bitterly divided Congress might vote to select another site for the capital.

Thus, the two friends began working on their own plan for acquiring land, selling plots, and marking the borders of a far less ambitious city. They had also advised Washington that the commissioners "be men who prefer any place on the Potowmac to any place elsewhere."[7]

The problem arose when Jefferson and Madison also "went public" by circulating a plan for the exact location and size of the city in advance of Washington's official report and began lobbying key individuals in hopes of influencing the outcome. They preferred a location near Georgetown that encompassed only about one-twentieth of the city that L'Enfant would envision. Washington was not pleased.

Washington had spent his life along the Potomac and knew the river and region as well as anyone. He had also worked as a surveyor and was eager to map the boundaries for the district and city. In fact, he started surveying the sites even before selecting the commissioners and before having the formal authority to do so.[8] Washington handled the details of the exact boundary for the federal district and capital city with the utmost discretion. Back in October 1790, for instance, when he traveled from Mount Vernon for his first "official" inspection of the lands to be included in the capital, one newspaper covering the trip announced excitedly that the purpose was "to fix upon a proper situation for the Grand Columbian Federal City!"[9] This prompted civic leaders from Georgetown and elsewhere to offer elaborate receptions and a hero's welcome for the purpose of boosting each town's chances of being included within the boundaries of the new capital. As the alcohol flowed at these events, Washington was treated to earfuls of boasts about the exceptional climate, soil, and people of each community.[10]

Yet Washington was well aware of the need for discretion on this twelve-day trip along the Potomac and on subsequent surveys. When local dignitaries hosted him, for instance, Washington responded with professional courtesies but also with generic toasts of "To the town we are in" or "To the prosperity of its residents." He was careful not to show his hand and spark a real estate grab; indeed, some of his trips were but smoke screens. The most explicit the president ever was about publicly acknowledging a location was when he once toasted, "To the River Patowmac! May the residence law be perpetuated and Patowmac view the Federal City!"[11]

In an earlier letter to Madison, Washington admitted an ulterior motive for his tour. He would, claimed the president, "inform himself of the several rival positions; leaving among them inducements to bid against each other in offers of land or money." This would help hold down the price of land. Consequently, he toured sites such as Sharpsburg, Williamsport, Alexandria, Georgetown, and other communities in order to throw speculators and the press off his scent.

Indeed, Washington's every move was followed by the public and land speculators eager to parse each word and site visited as a possible sign that Washington had made up his mind as to the exact boundary of the city. They were left wanting, however. Washington maintained a professional neutrality everywhere he went, disappointing communities through his poker-faced elusiveness to the extent that some communities were left thinking they would not be included within the capital's boundaries.

Washington and his commissioners had until 1800—only ten years—to have the new capital ready for Congress and the executive branch, which, given the dire financial situation in the nation and the paucity of trained architects, brick masons, and master builders, was not much time. For the time being Washington's "City for the Ages" would exist only on paper and in the president's mind; in practicality it was little more than forests, marshland, and pastures.

It was expected that the president would announce the decision for the exact boundaries in his annual message that year. To be sure, Washington was eager to move the project forward as quickly as possible. Nevertheless, in order to give the appearance of neutrality, he did not make the announcement in his annual message. Rather, he announced it at the very first opportunity afterward—on January 24, 1791, only days after selecting his picks for the commission. The format used by Washington was a "Proclamation by the President" with news that Maryland and Virginia had donated land and he had selected the site by the Potomac. Jefferson was asked to draft the proclamation, although it was released under the president's signature. It stated,

> By the President of the U. States of America. . . . Now therefore, In pursuance of the Powers to me confided, and after duly examining and weighing the advantages and disadvantages of the several situations within the Limites aforesaid, I do hereby declare and make known, that the location of one part of the said district of ten mile square, shall be found . . . is now fixed upon, and directed to be surveyed, defined, limited and located for a part of the said district accepted by the said act of Congress for the permanent seat of the Government of the United States.[12]

Not long afterward, in his typical matter-of-fact style, Washington noted in his diary that he and his surveyors were already fixing the boundaries: "Whilst the Commissioners were engaged in preparing the Deeds to be signed by the Subscribers this afternoon, I went out with Majr. L'Enfant and Mr. Ellicott to take a more perfect view of the ground, in order to decide finally on the spots on which to place the public buildings." He was eager to get to work helping to select sites for the "Congress House," "President's House," and government buildings.[13]

The president worked with L'Enfant to locate the city within the "ten Miles square" and on ceded land from Maryland and Virginia. The federal city would be within the diamond shape of this boundary and include Georgetown. Beyond that Washington offered little explanation or detail, yet encouraged Congress to approve his plans quickly, saying, "Let them be published in the News-Papers, put up in public places and otherwise so disposed as to answer my object as fully as possible."[14]

For the site of the Capitol Building, L'Enfant and Washington picked a scenic hill—then known as Jenkins' Hill—with views of the river and covered by a forest. Of the latter point Jefferson complained, "I wish I were a despot, that I might save those noble trees!"[15] As usual, Senator Maclay complained, this time groaning, "The matter, I believe, stands thus in fact: Virginia is not fully satisfied without having half of the ten miles square."[16]

Two months hence, on April 15, Commissioners Carroll and Stuart were on hand in the new federal district to lay the cornerstone for its boundary. With the necessary land transferred and the announcement made, Washington began publicly referring to the city as the "Federal City." This raised yet another debate—the public wondered about a name, with some suggesting "Washingtonople." On September 9, 1791, the commissioners met to pick a name to put on the maps and plots. They decided, without input from Washington, who kept his distance on the question of a name, that the federal district would be known as the "Territory of Columbia," a reference to the explorer and "discoverer" of the New World. Appropriately, they also announced that the new capital city would be named in Washington's honor.[17] It would be known as "the City of Washington."[18] Most everyone expected the city would be named for Washington, including Washington himself.

For the president, it had been an incredibly taxing but successful two years. With the location fixed, a new name, and the final pieces of the financial puzzle shaping up, Washington would now begin building "his" capital city where there had been none. Treasury Secretary Oliver Wolcott perhaps said it best. He wondered why the government would "leave the comforts of Philadelphia to go to the Indian place with the long name in the woods on the Potomac."[19] It must have seemed to many to be a mad idea.

CHAPTER 22

Financing the Capital

A national debt, if it is not excessive,
will be to us a national blessing.
Alexander Hamilton

Any plans for financing the construction of the capital city and ensuring the stability of the federal government required additional financial reforms—Hamilton's bank bill. While Hamilton's plans for debt assumption and his programs for paying veterans, establishing public credit, and obtaining loans were moving forward, Congress had yet to pass the final, major piece of the puzzle for his financial and economic program, one that would, along with the sale of lots, be necessary to finance a bank.

A central bank modeled on the Bank of England, Hamilton assured Washington, would both promote the nation's economy and help to stabilize the value of paper currency. With Washington's support, the secretary of the treasury began making his case for a National Bank in January 1790. The debate was not entirely new, however; with the government and nation in dire financial straits in 1789, Hamilton had arranged loans from the only two banks in the country at the time, the Bank of North America and the Bank of New York. The new plan, however, was far more complicated, and Hamilton had burned most of his political capital on the deal to pass the Residence Act and have the federal government assume states' debts.

Once again, sectionalism, ideology, and political self-interest drove the debate, which began in earnest in January 1791. The issues of the government's role in the economy, power of the federal government, and ability to construct a grand capital city were at stake. Northern merchants and traders had supported much of Hamilton's financial and economic program and now backed the National Bank proposal, although many of them were still angry at him for having abandoned the effort to make New York City the temporary capital. Advocates of limited government, especially southerners, remained staunchly opposed to a central bank and Hamilton's vision for the national economy. They were leery of banks in general but also saw the National Bank as an instrument to promote northern economic and political interests while subverting their own. Northern merchants, with the bank doing their bidding, they claimed, would gain privileges, and this would prompt a marked shift northward in the political balance of power. Many southern planters even opposed his proposal for a uniform national currency.

Another point of debate was the proposed twenty-year charter for a central bank to be located in Philadelphia. The ensuing squabble brought up old competitions and jealousies among the states and emboldened some Pennsylvanians to again make the case for keeping the temporary capital in their city. Like the debt assumption debate, the issues of the National Bank and capital city had become, for better or for worse, conjoined. The bank was linked in another explosive way: it was associated with Hamilton.

The secretary of the treasury had managed to pass the other facets of his economic program over southern and anti-federalist opposition and had badly duped Jefferson in the dinner party bargain. In the process, Hamilton had collected more than his fair share of powerful enemies. The fight over the bank bill was a personal feud and took on symbolic importance to its foes; Hamilton, as much as the bank itself, was the focus of anti-federalist and southern anger and fear.

Hamilton's bank bill was put forward in January through a Senate committee and was first heard in the House on January 21. Jefferson, Madison, and their allies in Congress immediately claimed the bank was unconstitutional. The debate on the floor began on January 31. The next day Congressman William Smith of South Carolina, a planter, proposed postponing the measure and sending it back to the committee of the whole, complaining that the bill was "taken up rather unexpectedly yesterday." Supporters of the bank noted that Smith and the bill's opponents had known about the bill for weeks. Others used the Jefferson-Madison position against them, maintaining that, if the constitutionality of the measure was in question, then further debate was needed.[1]

James Madison weighed in, saying, "At this moment it was not of importance to determine how it has happened that the objections which several gentlemen now say they have to offer, against the bill—were not made at the proper time." He argued for more time to raise objections and discuss the constitutional ramifications of the bill. Representative Fisher Ames, a federalist from Massachusetts, said it was "absurd" to permit the entire Congress to "determine whether the bill is constitutional or not." The committee that brought the bill forward should have attended to such sensitive matters. Madison countered, "There was the greatest propriety in discussing a constitution question" before the entire House. A motion to recommit the bill was defeated 34–23. Debate continued.[2]

Over the next several days Madison treated the House to a lengthy assessment of the relative merits and drawbacks of a national bank. He conceded that the bank would help merchants, provide capital, support the federal government's work, prevent currency fraud, and perhaps make it more practical to use paper currency than to exchange gold and silver. However, he argued that paper money should not be substituted for precious metals and that the charter for the Bank of England had been for only eleven years and was paid for by a loan to the government on favorable terms, although the future renewals occurred at a "very high price." Madison's principal objections were that Hamilton's bank bill "exposed the public and individuals to all the evils of a run on the bank" and that he doubted whether "establishing an incorporated bank among the powers vested by the constitution in the legislature" was legitimate.

Madison also digressed into a philosophical treatise on how to interpret the government's powers and when they should be limited. He took issue with Hamilton's "general welfare" and implied powers arguments for a bank. In other words, where in the Constitution do such powers derive? He set out nuanced guidelines for interpreting constitutional powers that continue to be debated to the present day. Madison concluded that the Constitution did not grant the power to establish a national bank. Yet unlike some southerners and anti-federalists, he did not object to all banks but "did not approve of the plan now under consideration."[3]

The debate remained heated, which angered Hamilton, who saw the bill as part of his legacy and critically necessary to the nation's financial health and his president's capital city. Moreover, Washington was growing impatient with the setbacks. On February 11 Madison rose again to speak in opposition to the bank in the House of Representatives. This time he was far less constrained, decrying the northern investors and bankers as "money changers" who would fleece the public just as did "the social parasites whom Jesus had symbolically driven from the temple." The House, however, voted down Madison's proposal to scrap the plan in a 36–13 rare legislative defeat for him.[4]

The fate of the bank bill was tied to Washington's proposed boundaries for the capital city, which was both good and bad news for Hamilton. Should one of these measures fail, it would likely lead to the defeat of the other, and Washington's opponents had numbers on their side. Fortunately, the earlier debt assumption debate ended favorably for Hamilton. Yet the president asked Madison to draft a possible veto message for him; he was contemplating sacrificing the bank bill to save his capital boundaries.[5]

The president also wrote to Hamilton about the bank's constitutionality and the veto process, asking, "To what precise period, by legal interpretation of the constitution, can the president retain it in his possession, before it becomes a Law by the lapse of ten days?"[6] Hamilton was floored by the question and began to worry that Washington would side with the anti-federalists in opposition to his bank bill.[7] He responded with a deluge of detailed economic, philosophical, and constitutional arguments for the bank and his advocacy of the Constitution's "implied powers."[8]

As to the bank bill's constitutionality, the president admitted, "I do not pretend to be very competent." He solicited the opinion of his attorney general, Edmund Randolph.[9] Washington also asked Madison to draft a possible veto message for him and asked Jefferson for his opinion on the bill's constitutionality. The president sent Jefferson's opinion that it was unconstitutional to Hamilton and asked for his opinion. Hamilton maintained that the bill was constitutional, but the attorney general concurred with Jefferson that the bank was unconstitutional. Both Virginians pointed out that the Constitution did not expressly mention a central bank. Like the rest of the country, Washington's cabinet was fractured over the issue.

Then in February, Senator Charles Carroll introduced a bill to expand the district's boundaries so that Washington could include Alexandria, as he had suggested to Congress. The two bills were now conjoined. Hamilton delivered a brilliant and impassioned case for the bank and constitutional "implied powers."[10] However, behind strong anti-bank challenges, the measure languished for two days. Then, on February 25, the bank bill was postponed in a narrow 14–12 vote in the Senate. Washington was, understandably, angered by the inaction in the Senate. The Senate was playing hardball with the president for the first time: if you want Alexandria, you had better sign the bill. He had come to share his close aide's opinion that the bank bill was essential to the economic prosperity of the country. At the urging of Hamilton, he finally showed his hand in public.

After considering the counsel of his cabinet, the president sided with Hamilton and lobbied the Senate to have a re-vote later that very same day. After

Washington's intervention, Robert Morris of Pennsylvania, John Langdon of New Hampshire, George Read of Delaware, and Philip Schuyler of New York, who was both Washington's close friend and Hamilton's father-in-law, changed their positions that afternoon and voted for the bill. It passed on sectional lines by the same count, 14–12, leaving Senator Maclay to fume, "It is plain the President has bought them. I know not their price, but that is immaterial."[11]

On March 2 the House passed the bill 39–18, again largely on sectional and partisan lines. Washington signed the bill as soon as the House finished business. The supplemental act supporting Washington's new boundaries for the capital city passed as well. Hamilton had his bank and Washington had his boundaries. The National Bank would also help strengthen the government and the nation's economy, and the difficulty of financing the capital city was now a bit less problematic—all thanks to Washington's enormous political influence.

The next steps for the president included completing the survey of the federal city and district's boundaries, hiring an architect, and meeting with landowners to buy and sell plots in the new City of Washington. Washington looked forward to the first two but preferred not to meet directly with private citizens to negotiate for land for the capital. He soon realized that he would be forced to do so. The success or failure of this city was contingent on convincing landowners in the area to cooperate, and he, more than anyone else, stood a better chance of obtaining the necessary plots at an acceptable price.

Writing in March 1791, Washington offered an insight into the challenges he faced: "Finding the interests of the Landholders about George Town and those about Carrollsburgh much at variance and that their fears and jealousies of each were counteracting the public purposes and might prove injurious to its best interests, whilst if properly managed they might be made to subserve it, I requested them to meet me at six o'clock this afternoon at my lodgings, which they accordingly did."[12]

During the meetings held at Suter's Tavern in Georgetown in late March and early April, residents erupted into disagreement. The lack of cooperation was not helpful, Washington warned them, for "whilst they were contending for the shadow they might lose the substance."

He assured those living within the proposed boundary of the capital that everyone would benefit but threatened to go elsewhere for the land if necessary. Everyone at the meeting knew Washington had a trump card: in November of 1790, the Maryland legislature had passed an act allowing the federal government to employ eminent domain over 130 acres per owner if any refused to voluntarily transfer ownership. Washington described his approach to a colleague, writing,

> Other arguments were used to show the danger which might result from delay and the good effects that might proceed from a Union. . . . I represented that the contention in which they seemed engaged, did not in my opinion comport either with the public interest or that of their own; that while each party was aiming to obtain the public buildings, they might by placing the matter on a contracted scale, defeat the measure altogether; not only by procrastination but for want of the means necessary to effect the work.[13]

Washington's message wherever he went was that landowners needed to cooperate. He appealed, "That neither the offer from Georgetown or Carrollsburgh, separately, was adequate to the end of insuring the object. That both together did not comprehend more ground nor would afford greater means than was required for the federal City." Therefore, Washington suggested to his audiences, "Instead of contending which of the two should have it they had better, by combining more offers make a common cause of it, and thereby secure it to the district."[14]

Although Washington was often successful in these negotiations, he found it difficult to entertain so many different interests and felt the process was beneath the dignity of the presidency. This was especially the case when it came to one man in particular—David Burnes.

Burnes owned land between the desired location of the Capitol Building and presidential home. Washington repeatedly tried negotiating with him and made numerous offers, but "the obstinate Mr. Burnes" as the president called him, refused each time. After the project had been delayed yet again on account of Burnes's refusal to sell, Washington dispatched a letter notifying Burnes in blunt terms that his land would be purchased by the government: "I have been authorized to select the location of the National Capital. I have selected your farm as part of it, and the government will take it at all events. I trust you will, under the circumstances, enter into an amicable arrangement."[15] That ended the standoff.

Another tactic employed by the president was to identify and negotiate for land for the federal district through proxies. Washington discreetly dispatched Benjamin Stoddert and William Deakins Jr. to function as his agents in purchasing "in the most perfect secrecy" the necessary land near Georgetown. He trusted both men, especially Stoddert, who, like Washington, owned land near the Potomac River, was a loyal federalist, and had served in the war. Washington would later name Stoddert the first secretary of the navy. Stoddert and Deakins drew up terms for residents to cede property to the federal government in return for just compensation, reducing Washington's burden. But the feint had to be abandoned when L'Enfant arrived at Georgetown in early March and began surveying the same lands despite Washington's instructions not to do so.[16]

Throughout the land deals, the president masterfully balanced the political need for secrecy in negotiations with the corresponding desire to build public support for the project and location. In such instances Washington encouraged newspapers to publicize the events, and they typically responded and did so with praise. The *Maryland Journal* crowed that the new capital city would be an "inconceivable improvement over all other cities in the world." The *Georgetown Weekly Ledger*, *General Advertiser*, and others followed suit. Some of the articles were even written with pen names such as "Americanus" and "Spectator," as if on cue. This helped calm nervous investors, rally landowners, and build political support for Washington's city.[17]

Washington also knew he could not give the appearance that he alone was overseeing all negotiations.[18] It would undermine his "renown as Cincinnatus incarnate—his unique reputation as an incorruptible leader that extended throughout the western world."[19] He understood the situation only too well; he was aware not only of the overwhelming admiration shown to him by his countrymen but of the outsize expectations that now followed his every action. Washington was naturally sensitive about his image and reputation and had become painfully conscious that history was watching his every decision.

In a letter to his fellow Virginian, Henry Lee, Washington alluded to the paradox of his unique position, writing, "I am conscious that I fear alone to give any real occasion for obloquy, and that I do not dread to meet with unmerited reproach. And certain I am, whensoever the good of my country requires my reputation to be put in risque; regard for my own fame will not come in competition with an object of so much magnitude."[20] He still needed to tread carefully, perhaps more at this stage of the capital project than ever before.

Washington worked his magic, and deals were struck. Ultimately, Washington and his negotiators secured approximately 6,100 acres—a tract of land larger than Boston and Philadelphia. Landowners donated their land and received approximately half the land back after it had been platted into lots for sale, minus that which was purchased for streets and federal reservations, including the Capitol and executive mansion grounds. The land was transferred to the government by being passed to trustees.[21] Washington was pleased with the land, predicting, "The federal city . . . will, I have no doubt, from the advantages given to it by nature, and its proximity to a rich interior country, and the western territory, become the emporium of the United States."[22]

Washington celebrated the success of the "ten Miles square" agreement, the Residence Act, Hamilton's debt assumption and finance bills, and the new bank bill. By spring of 1791 the capital project was moving forward in just the way Washington had hoped, although with far more contentiousness. It was abundantly clear who was in charge of the capital.

However, just as progress was being made on the new city, the president learned that Philadelphia was planning a new public building in hopes of enticing the government to remain. To quell any speculation about a deal to stay in Philadelphia, Washington had refused to live in the presidential mansion the city had built for him, preferring instead to remain in the home of Robert Morris. Later, when the government encountered delays in printing maps for the permanent capital, Washington suspected a plot by Philadelphians to throw another monkey wrench into the process of relocating the seat of government.

The president even threatened to hire a London printer for the task and fired off a letter to one of his commissioners, complaining, "There is a current in this city which sets so strongly against everything that related to the federal district that it is next to impossible to stem it."[23] Even as late as 1792, Philadelphia was attempting to rewrite the Residence Act and retain the capital city beyond its decade-long mandate. That February, when Washington turned sixty, the city hosted a grand ball in his honor, which one newspaper dubbed "one of the most brilliant displays of beauty ever exhibited in the city." The next day New Jersey threw him another party.[24] Washington was gracious, but his attention remained on the next capital.

Elsewhere in 1791, the president was wrestling with a number of domestic problems, such as western affairs and Native American land disputes. Partisan bickering had resumed and Congress was again gridlocked. Then, while touring sites for the capital that spring, Washington's carriage nearly wrecked in the Ocquoquam Creek near the Potomac and Alexandria in Virginia. This scare unnerved some of Washington's closest friends and aides, who realized that the president was the lynchpin of not just the prospects of a new capital but of the continuity of government.

Only weeks later Washington himself was jolted when he learned that King Louis XVI of France and the entire royal family had unsuccessfully attempted to flee Paris in disguise. Blood was being spilt in France, and Washington worried about Lafayette, a man he considered as a son, who had been accused of plotting to arrest the royal family. Disturbing reports on the blood-soaked revolution were transmitted to Washington by his secretary of state, prompting him to write, "The, tumultuous populace of large cities are ever to be dreaded."[25] The situation in France must have weighed heavily on the president's mind, as he was also dealing with domestic strife and turmoil in Congress. Many worried that France was not the only country facing mob rule.

The sale of lots in October 1792 raised a paltry and embarrassing $2,000. A sense of desperation resulted over the realization that there were insufficient funds to begin construction. Washington tasked his commissioners with approaching the Maryland legislature, Congress, Dutch banks, and others for financing. The situation was such that plans had to be scaled back and some of the construction delayed. Construction on the capitol building had to be pushed to 1793.

Such challenges only deepened Washington's desire to serve only one term and return home to Mount Vernon in early 1793. Yet it was clear that he was still needed; the tasks of uniting the nation and building the capital required his guiding hand and several more years. In fact, at times it seemed to Washington and others that the only thing holding the government together was Washington himself. His trusted aide, Tobias Lear, worried, "I fear more from the election of another President, whenever our present great and good one quits his political or natural career, than from any other event." Lear prayed for the president's health, asking God to "incline his heart to retain his present station."[26]

The country needed Washington, and the president, who was proceeding with the project as methodically and quickly as possible, now needed for his city a survey, maps, and most important, an architect capable of realizing his ambition and vision.

PART V

BUILDING
THE CAPITAL

CHAPTER 23

The Architect

*I have made of my talents and fortune particularly in the business
of the city of Washington as also in other services constantly
volunteered to this country for these twenty five years past.*

Pierre Charles L'Enfant

Quite simply, the new nation had few trained architects. Washington
would turn to a polymath named Pierre Charles L'Enfant, who had been
born in Paris on August 2, 1754, and traveled to America in 1777 at the age of
twenty-two on a ship filled with weapons and supplies for the Revolutionary
War. Along with a few other young French aristocrats, he seems to have sought
fame and glory by crossing the Atlantic to fight the British.

In addition to fighting, L'Enfant's wit, artistic skill, and indefatigable spirit
helped bolster the army's sagging morale. For instance, the architect produced
sketches of the Continental Army and a painting of Washington, completed
during the frigid winter encampment at Valley Forge. He was also a driving
force behind the establishment in 1779 of a corps of engineers for the army.
L'Enfant, who began referring to himself as "Peter" after arriving in America and
from then on signed his name "P. Charles L'Enfant," rose to the rank of major
and caught the attention of Washington and Hamilton.[1]

L'Enfant had fought alongside General Washington, as well as other noted
leaders, and endured years of fighting, including being wounded in the Savannah
campaign and captured in Charleston. In doing so, he engendered for himself
Washington's respect. The general would later bestow on the Frenchman the

honor of designing the badge for the new Society of Cincinnati. The order, dedicated to preserving the ideals of the revolution, was founded by Continental Army officers in 1783 and named for Washington's hero, the ancient Roman general and statesman. L'Enfant was even sent back to France by the society in order to present French officers from the Revolutionary War with commendations. Relatedly, with Hamilton's endorsement, he designed some of the fledgling nation's earliest coins and other medals. After the war the architect moved to New York City and adopted the United States as his new home. In an 1820 census he referred to himself as a citizen of the United States.[2]

L'Enfant cut a dashing figure in New York society. The war hero was tall, charismatic, and intelligent. His thick French accent behind a rich baritone voice had distinguished him among prominent New Yorkers. He was also not above promoting himself at every opportunity. The architect was appointed by New York City to redesign City Hall, turning it into Federal Hall, which would later serve as the inaugural seat of Congress. Inspired by the Roman Senate, L'Enfant reimagined Federal Hall as the grandest building in the new nation, and this project established him as one of the country's most celebrated architects. He also designed buildings in Philadelphia, remodeled the venerable St. Paul's Chapel in New York, proposed a grand park spanning lower Manhattan, and organized parades and public events for the government, including an elaborate celebration on the eve of New York's ratification of the Constitution, replete with costumed revelers, a warship on wagon wheels, and cannonade salutes.[3] In short, L'Enfant, like his projects, was memorable.

L'Enfant was well prepared for these projects. His father served as a court painter for King Louis XV and sent his son to study painting and architecture at the Royal Academy at the Louvre. There he came to the attention of Silas Dean, an American agent working in France, who offered him a commission in the Continental Army with the rank of lieutenant.

Thus, L'Enfant was a known entity to Washington and had more than demonstrated his genius and commitment to the new republic and its president.[4] As early as September 11, 1789, the architect had even written to the new president requesting permission to submit a plan for a magnificent capital city "of this vast empire." In fact, since at least 1784 L'Enfant had yearned for a commission as the designer of any capital city and the supervisor of its construction.[5] He boldly informed his former commander that he "will not be surprised that my ambition and the desire I have of becoming a useful citizen should lead me to wish to share in the undertaking." He enticed the president with a vision that "the plan should be drawn on such a scale as to leave room for that aggrandizement and embellishment which the increase of the wealth of the nation will permit it to pursue at any period however remote."[6]

Intentionally or inadvertently—and most likely the former—the architect played to Washington's grand vision for the capital city and his understanding of the role it would play in strengthening the struggling new government. Indeed, L'Enfant shared both a political persuasion and ambitious prospects for the capital city and new nation with Washington and his close advisers, including Alexander Hamilton, John Jay, and Henry Knox.[7]

L'Enfant ended his letter to Washington confidently, saying, "I now presume to sollicit the favor of being employed in this Business." It worked. Washington commissioned L'Enfant, most likely in January 1791, and charged him with designing the new federal city.[8] The thirty-six-year-old architect was Washington's first and only choice for the task.

Wrote the president of his decision and new architect, "I have received him not only as a scientific man, but one who added considerable taste to his professional knowledge. . . . He [is] better qualified than any one who come within my knowledge in this country, or indeed, in any other, the possibility of obtaining whom could be counted upon." The Georgetown newspaper announced excitedly that the architect was in town "to survey the lands contiguous to Georgetown, where the Federal City is to be built." The paper also shared Washington's assessment of L'Enfant's abilities, writing, "His skill in matters of this kind is justly extolled by all disposed to give merit its proper tribute of praise. He is earnest in the business and hopes to be able to lay a plan of that parcel of land before the President on his arrival in this town."[9]

He also won over George Walker, a prominent booster of the Potomac capital, who described the architect in glowing terms and convinced him to lay his plan over all the land between Georgetown and the Anacostia and not only on the part identified by Washington at the time. L'Enfant, wrote Walker, "exhibits such striking proofs of an exalted genius, elegance of taste, extensive imagination and comprehension, as will not only produce amazement in Europe, but will meet the admiration of all future ages."[10]

Of course, not everyone was pleased. Too much was at stake. Some antifederalists hoped that Jefferson would serve as the new architect, as his vision for the capital as a simple "town" would reflect their beliefs about a limited role for government, whereas L'Enfant shared Washington's ambitious vision for a capital on a grand scale and in the European tradition. Therefore, Washington's critics claimed the commissioners and Congress would be reduced to "mere surveyors" who would "fix on the spot" the monarchical president's every whim and fancy. Senator Maclay of Pennsylvania warned that Washington was overstepping his authority in a way "that opposition may find a nest to lay its eggs in."[11]

Mindful of the criticism but undaunted, in March the president asked his secretary of state to have the architect come to the Potomac to begin his survey. Jefferson complied, stating matter-of-factly in a letter, "You are desired to proceed to Georgetown where you will find Mr. Ellicott employed in making a survey and maps of the Federal Territory."[12]

Around the same time Washington also instructed his secretary of state to hire Andrew Ellicott, a talented thirty-seven-year-old surveyor (who later taught Meriwether Lewis surveying before his famous expedition), to mark the boundary for the federal district. Ellicott was an excellent choice. Despite his pacifist Quaker upbringing, the Pennsylvanian had fought in the Revolutionary War and risen to the rank of major. After the war Major Ellicott traveled extensively, preparing surveys of much of the new nation, mapping state borders, and surveying the likes of everything from the "Mason-Dixon line" to Niagara Falls to the lands on Washington's beloved Potomac.[13] He too was eminently qualified, arguably the most experienced surveyor in the country.

Ellicott was instructed to provide L'Enfant with his initial maps and then assist him in completing the more detailed surveys of the city. The two planned to meet in March 1791 in Georgetown to begin the task. Ominously, L'Enfant's stagecoach broke down, forcing him to walk to the town.[14] This would turn out to be the least of his problems. L'Enfant's charge, as set out in the letter from Jefferson, stated, "The special object of asking your aid is to have drawings of the particular grounds most likely to be approved for the site of the Federal town and buildings." Jefferson ended by reminding the architect that, on behalf of the president, "I will beg the favor of you to mark to me your progress about twice a week, by letter, say every Wednesday and Saturday evening."[15] Too much was at stake; the secretary of state was determined to play a role in the city's design and, in the process, function from within the system to mitigate the grand plans of the Frenchman and the president.

A small team of surveyors assisted L'Enfant, including Major Ellicott and his crew. Yet Ellicott had needed twenty men to survey the massive area but was able to obtain only six. Even if he had found enough trained surveyors, there were insufficient funds to pay them. Maryland and Virginia were slow in providing the promised funds, and too few lots were sold to cover the expenses of the extensive survey. Therefore, Ellicott worked without pay.[16] Not long afterward, one of his best surveyors died when a tree fell on him. Ellicott was doing the work of several men and began to believe the project could not be completed. Utterly exhausted, he wrote to his wife, "Do not my dear send me any bad news, my present frame of mind would only suffer extremely by it."[17]

One of Ellicott's surveyors was a free black scientist. Benjamin Banneker was a sixty-year-old grandson of a slave and was a highly regarded astronomer, mathematician, and surveyor who had been born in 1731 near Baltimore. His grandfather had been a slave but gained his freedom; his grandmother was a white woman named Mollie Welsh, who had been an indentured servant from England. It was Mollie who taught a young Benjamin to read and saw that he attended school.[18] For his role in assisting Ellicott and L'Enfant in conducting the preliminary survey of the district lines that spring, Banneker was paid sixty dollars for three months' work.[19]

Banneker's race appears, surprisingly and refreshingly, not to have been an issue. Ellicott was an abolitionist and considered the descendant of slaves as being more than up for the task. Even the *Georgetown Weekly Record* expressed its pleasure at having the black scientist as part of the surveying project. It did so while also taking a shot at the secretary of state, writing in March 1791 that Banneker was an "Ethiopian whose abilities as a surveyor and astronomer clearly proved that Mr. Jefferson's concluding that race of men were void of 'mental endowment' was without foundation."

As to the reference to Jefferson, Banneker actually wrote to the famous Founder that August "correcting" him about his comments on African inferiority, noting that such beliefs were flawed because of "the injustice of a state of slavery, and in which you had just apprehensions of the horrors of its condition." The black scientist even reminded Jefferson of his own declaration—"We hold these truths to be self-evident, that all men are created equal." He also appealed to the secretary of state that he had a responsibility "to extend their power and influence to the relief of every part of the human race, from whatever burden or oppression they may unjustly labor under."[20]

The two men struck up an unlikely correspondence on matters of equality. Wrote Banneker to the secretary of state,

> I have long been convinced, that if your love for yourselves, and for those inestimable laws, which preserved to you the rights of human nature, was founded on sincerity, you could not but be solicitous, that every individual, of whatever rank or distinction, might with you equally enjoy the blessings thereof; neither could you rest satisfied . . . in order to their promotion from any state of degradation, to which the unjustifiable cruelty and barbarism of men may have reduced them.

Jefferson responded, "Nobody wishes more than I do to see such proofs as you exhibit, that nature has given to our black brethren, talents equal to those of the other colours of men, & that the appearance of a want of them is owing merely to the degraded condition of their existence both in Africa & America."[21] Interestingly, the capital city would be surveyed and built with considerable black labor—slave, indentured, and free.

Despite "heavy rain and thick mist" that March, L'Enfant and Ellicott were undeterred and immediately began their tour of the area, meeting with the mayor of Georgetown, riding throughout the region to study the natural features, observing possible challenges posed by the tidal marsh and rivers, and contemplating the layout of the city. Where others may have seen marshes, pastures, and forests, L'Enfant, like an artist who sees beauty in a slab of marble or empty canvas, saw a perfect site for a glorious capital. To L'Enfant, architecture was a blank canvas on which to create history—which was his intention.[22]

Writing to Jefferson on March 10, he mused, "As far as I was able to judge through a thick fog. . . . I passed on many spots which appeared to me really beautiful and which seem to dispute with each other who command in the most extensive prospect on the water. The gradual rising of the ground . . . present[s] a situation most advantageous to run streets and prolong them on grand and far distant point of view."[23] That same month Jefferson loaded L'Enfant with maps of such European capitals as Amsterdam, Milan, and Paris, possibly on orders from Washington.

Major Ellicott, however, had a much different impression of the future site of the capital: "For near seven miles, on it there is not one house that has any floor except the earth. We find but little fruit, except huckleberries." In the same letter to his wife, he even expressed concern about Washington's attachment to the bleak area: "As the president is so much attached to the country, I would not be willing that he should know my real sentiments about it. But this country bears no more proportion to the country about Philadelphia, than a Crane does to a stall-fed Ox!" Ellicott also doubted they would sell enough lots to fund a city of Washington's expectations. He closed his letter complaining of the intense work schedule, which he summed up as "hurried my legs and bothered out of my senses."[24]

L'Enfant met with Washington on March 28, and the two set off together to discuss the sites for buildings and boulevards. Once again Washington was careful to include visits to locations that he never intended to be a part of the federal city in order to keep landowners, speculators, and newspapers guessing. The president complained of the rain and bad weather that delayed the project.

He wanted a map produced as quickly as possible.[25] The survey of the district boundary was further delayed when Ellicott came down with the flu, likely because Washington kept him working through cold, rainy days.

The president's enthusiasm for the project and work ethic were such that even the exuberant L'Enfant complained of being "engaged in the most fatiguing work which I ever had to perform." He also wrote to Alexander Hamilton that the weather and delays were such that he "derived no great satisfaction from the review." Despite the weather, fatigue, and illness, Ellicott was tireless and managed to produce an initial hundred-mile boundary for the federal district.[26]

Washington took time away from the capital project to tour the southern states in the spring of 1791. Yet his visits were also designed to build support for his plans. Likewise, a political bone would be given to Pennsylvanians still upset by losing the capital. The main avenue in the new capital city and site of the presidential home would be named for the Keystone State. When Washington returned from his travels, he was eager to continue his work. He requested that L'Enfant join him at Mount Vernon to discuss the plans.

The question now was, What kind of city would they build?

The debate that had existed since the war and the Constitutional Convention over the proper size, role, and scope of government had not faded. It remained as one of the rifts between the federalists and anti-federalists and continued to figure prominently into nearly every political and policy debate of the day, including the size and design for both the capital city and presidential home. Several fundamental questions about the city remained unanswered and were now thrust before the First Congress and president. Would the new seat be a governing city? Would it become the new nation's main city, or would it be a symbolic site for statecraft and a presidential home? What type of buildings would grace the city? What of the design and proper size of the buildings?

Yet little more had been specified or settled than that the city should have "suitable buildings." As has been noted, the answers to these questions would have far-reaching implications, and the role and power of government would now play out in the design of the capital city. Washington's grasp of the importance of the politics of architecture and need for "his" city to promote a sense of national identity and unity is reflected in a letter he wrote to the Marquis de la Luzerne, France's minister to America during the Revolutionary War.

"A spirit for political improvements seems to be rapidly and extensively spreading through the European countries," Washington noted. Yet he bemoaned that the same spirit was not present in America. Rather, too many of his fellow cit-izens were concerned only about "making more haste than good. . . . So much prudence, so much perseverance, so much disinterestedness, and so much pa-triotism are necessary among the leaders of a nation that sometimes my fears nearly preponderate over my expectations."[27] To Washington, it was not only important that the capital city be in the appropriate site but equally vital that it be of a certain size and character.[28]

Washington had long wanted a glorious capital city, one that the nation could grow into and one that would help him accomplish his many and lofty goals for the young republic. In L'Enfant, he found a man who shared his in-spired and glorious vision. The architect imagined a city with a staggering eight hundred thousand residents, a size that would rival Paris and London and is even larger than the current population of the American capital. The brilliant architect's capital would be replete with wide boulevards, bisecting imposing public squares, all adorned with stately public monuments. As he wrote in a letter to Washington, without question "the city must be beautiful."[29]

Perhaps the fait accompli for the project was when the Frenchman proposed to Washington that the crowning achievement of the city would be its "presiden-tial palace." Here the architect was inspired by the grandeur of such palaces as Versailles and informed Washington that the home would reflect "the sumptu-ousness of a palace, the convenience of a house, and the agreeableness of a coun-try seat." Washington wanted the public to be in awe of the presidential house and city. He toured possible sites for the home with L'Enfant and discussed the merits of each location. They identified small crests that could serve for either the Capitol or the presidential home and reminded him of Mount Vernon. The architect agreed with Washington that the president's home should occupy higher ground that would afford a spectacular view of the city and Potomac, and symbolically help place the presidency on a more equal footing with Congress than the Constitution implied.[30]

Soon thereafter Washington wrote to L'Enfant excitedly, "I determined the seat of the presidential palace." The president moved the home slightly to the west to the site they had discussed (it is the site where the White House now sits). He confided in his architect his preference for "the object to adding to the sumptuousness of a palace the convenience of a house and the agreeableness of a country seat situated on that ridge which attracted your attention at the first inspection of the ground."[31] L'Enfant agreed.

A great avenue some 160 feet wide would connect the presidential palace with the Capitol, which, L'Enfant claimed, "will make the long distances of the city seem shorter and promote the growth of the city."[32] Moreover, boasted the architect, "The grand avenue connecting both the palace & the federal House will be most magnificent and most convenient." The home was to be enormous—roughly 700 feet east to west and 350 feet north to south—which would have been roughly five times larger than the current White House.[33]

The sketches produced by L'Enfant included streets intersecting at right angles on a grid and grand avenues crossing diagonally. Philadelphia had also been organized using a grid system, dating to 1682. Its founder, William Penn, and surveyor, Thomas Holme, relied on natural boundaries, such as the Delaware and Schuylkill Rivers, and a system of intersecting roads and five main public squares.[34]

L'Enfant's grand avenues would radiate out from central points to take advantage of the landscape and offer sweeping vistas of the majestic parks, countryside, and river. At each junction there would be large circles or parks boasting heroic monuments. According to L'Enfant, the area known as Jenkins Hill, a wooded crest on a sloping landscape roughly a half mile from the Eastern Branch of the Potomac, was "the most desirable position offer for to Erect the Publique Edifices." The focal point of the city, reflecting its political power, would be two colossal buildings: the "Congress House," at the center of the grid, and the "Presidential Palace," roughly one mile to the west. The two buildings would be connected by a mall with fountains, all the while reflecting the coequal status of the institutions (the judiciary was not yet viewed as being a comparable branch). "The Federal City," predicted L'Enfant, "would soon grow of itself and spread as the branches of a tree do towards where they meet with most nourishment."[35]

L'Enfant's plan for the new capital city was so detailed that it even included the names of the streets and types of statues that would fill the city. According to L'Enfant, the grand boulevards would be named for the states. Anticipating the admission of Vermont and Kentucky to the union, fifteen large public squares were planned, representing each of the states. Additionally, the states could then "improve, or subscribe a sum additional to the value of the land." Each would be filled with statues and monuments "such as the different States may choose to erect." A great statue of Washington on horseback, one modeled on the earlier proposal that never came to fruition, would occupy a prime, central location in the city's grand mall.[36]

Jefferson and many of his republican supporters remained staunchly in opposition to Washington's grandiose view for the capital city and presidential home and thereby were against L'Enfant. They had a much different view of the social, economic, and political future of the nation. Mindful of the importance of political architecture in shaping the nation, Jefferson advocated for a small "Federal *Town*" of a maximum size of less than just fifteen hundred acres, rather than Washington's Grand Columbian "Federal *City*." Pastoral landscapes, farms, and a few understated government buildings would do for the capital. As for the presidential home, a small, one-story brick home would suffice in Jefferson's view.[37]

L'Enfant was aghast at Jefferson's sketches and plans. So were the investors in the new city. Washington "feared that the concept of nation would not take hold, that the rivalries and squabbles of the individual states and of regional interests, so intractable during the Confederation, would destroy the Union."[38] Washington ignored Jefferson's proposals. He selected L'Enfant's grandiose initial plan and provided it to Congress in late August 1791.

L'Enfant's now-famous draft was inspired by the landscape and romanticism—it blended cityscape and landscape. Finding rectangular streets to be too simple and uninspired, L'Enfant's grand radiating grid offered a strict geometric design yet one that allowed for commanding views of the river, hills, and other natural features. He also used the topography to place the two most prominent structures on hills.[39]

The capital was never to be Athens; for Washington, it was Rome. The American Cincinnatus saw his country as the next great republic.[40] Maps and designs were released to the public showing a city with naval yards, numerous churches, residences for diplomats, banks, military barracks and forts, a hospital, theater, and more. Washington was behind many of these ideas and promoted a "national university" and botanical garden located by the future Naval Observatory on what would become Constitution Avenue.

Washington's "Metropolis of America" would be the commercial and cultural capital of the new nation, attracting talent and educating new leaders. Washington even issued a presidential order in October 1791 that all buildings had to adhere to certain design standards. In one of the earliest building codes of its kind in the country, Washington mandated that the "outer" walls of buildings be made of brick or stone.[41]

As early as 1784 the architect suggested that a great federal city would take "decades" to build but later reasoned that such a timeline and scale was "in such a manner as to give an idea of the greatness of the empire as well as to engrave in every mind that sense of respect that is due to a place which is the seat of a supreme sovereignty."[42] While working with an impatient Washington over a year earlier, L'Enfant reminded him, "No Nation perhaps had ever before the opportunity offered them of deliberately deciding on the spot where their Capital City should be fixed, or of combining every necessary consideration in the choice of the situation." Even at the beginning of the process, both men knew that they were creating something unique in history and that the classic design and extraordinary scope of the city would shape not only the nature of the new republic but their own places in history.[43]

Inspired by the ideas of a Roman city with wide avenues and spacious parks that connected to a central political mass, L'Enfant's ambitious vision was truly a "city for the ages."

Washington had found his architect and a plan to match his vision. L'Enfant would prove himself to be creative, talented, and visionary. Yet, the project faced numerous challenges, such as a severe shortage of labor, funds, and skilled architects and builders. However, L'Enfant's own arrogance, hot-headedness, and inability to take orders would soon prove to be the main obstacle.

CHAPTER 24

Intrigues and Injuries

*Distrust naturally creates distrust, and by nothing is good
will and kind conduct more speedily changed.*

John Jay

Washington's three capable but imperious commissioners were charged with overseeing all matters pertaining to the federal district and capital city. They expected their architect to cooperate with them, take their suggestions, and submit regular reports at their monthly meetings, and so did Washington. L'Enfant, however, viewed George Washington's blessing as enough, believing it gave him carte blanche to do as he pleased. The commissioners, according to L'Enfant, had "too narrow a view of the project." Therefore, L'Enfant, for all his genius—or perhaps because of it—would not listen to anyone, especially the three commissioners. Eventually, he even stopped listening to the president of the United States. His tenure as the capital's architect was doomed to fail.[1]

L'Enfant seemed shockingly ignorant of the politics and personal sensitivities surrounding the development of the capital city. Even Commissioner David Stuart began to worry that their architect was "the genius of a Despotic government," not a servant of a republic.[2] In particular, L'Enfant butted heads repeatedly with the wealthy, influential commissioner Daniel Carroll. When Carroll requested feedback and sketches from the architect, L'Enfant failed to comply, maintaining he did not want to unveil the rest of his plan or build the city piecemeal. The final plan would be complete when it was complete and not before, and he would proceed when he was ready.

In early August 1791, Commissioner Carroll notified Washington of the delay, grumbling that it would also delay the government's ability to buy and sell plots of land in the city. "The survey and plan of the city is not in the forwardness we wish," he wrote, adding that "we have hopes still given us that they will be in such a state tho' not complete as to begin the sales the 17th of October."[3] Of course, the commissioners bear some responsibility for the deteriorating relationship.

Fortunately, the city's "assistant" architect, Andrew Ellicott, managed to survey and map several street blocks and marked 40-by-100-foot lots near the planned presidential home. These, the commissioners and Washington believed, would sell for fourteen dollars per acre. Others predicted the value would double by the time construction commenced. The vocal booster of the new city, George Walker, boasted the capital and value of the lots would "grow up with a degree of rapidity hitherto unparalleled in the annals of cities, and will soon become the admiration and delight of the world."[4] The plans for the lot sales were wildly optimistic. The goal was to ultimately sell fifteen thousand lots and raise a whopping $800,000 at the initial auction. Expectations were high; so were the stakes.[5]

The sale was an unmitigated disaster. Lot sales raised a paltry $2,000, so the next auction was of vital importance. Maryland and Virginia had offered $200,000 toward the new capital city, which helped. However, Washington and the commissioners needed to raise the remainder of the finances through selling lots in the federal district. Washington also had to again do damage control.[6] Much depended on the city's investors and stakeholders seeing the details of L'Enfant's plan.

L'Enfant defended his work and his delay in submitting his map as "essential to pursue with dignity the operation of an undertaking of a magnitude so worthy of the concern of a grand empire." In response to complaints by the commissioners in 1791, L'Enfant reminded Washington of the grand scale of the city and grandeur of his vision. "It is in this manner and in this manner only I conceive the business may be conducted to a certainty of the attainment of that success," he wrote.[7]

L'Enfant conducted his survey wherever and whenever he pleased, despite specific requests or orders from the commissioners or Thomas Jefferson. He soon questioned the wisdom of the advice he received and wondered aloud about the fitness of the commissioners to serve. There were other problems. Because of the lack of skilled laborers in Virginia and Maryland, and especially in the South, in

November, the commissioners hired Francis Cabot, brother of Senator George Cabot of Massachusetts, to attempt to procure investors, equipment, materials, and laborers from New England and Europe. Cabot was successful in recruiting skilled brick makers and bricklayers, but L'Enfant announced that he did not want brick; he wanted stone. Before he had even specified the dimensions of his buildings, he demanded the best stone and men to work the nearby Aquia Creek quarry.[8]

The architect ultimately did provide three plans for the city, the first being a mere diagram based on other people's work. However, the latter two were behind schedule and were lacking in detail. Of the second plan, which was mailed to Washington on June 22, L'Enfant apologized, explaining that "due to the shortness of time . . . together with the hurry with which I had it drawn," the survey and plan were incomplete.[9] Nevertheless, Washington liked L'Enfant's ambitious vision, even if he was growing impatient with the delays and his architect's personality. The final plan included a bridge over the Potomac River at Three Sisters Islands upriver from Georgetown and another one over the Eastern Branch (which is today the Anacostia River). Ultimately, the bridge opened six years later on July 3, 1797, and was described in newspapers as a "wooden roofed-in structure" with stone and iron abutments.[10]

Fortunately, Major Ellicott worked reasonably well with L'Enfant despite their many differences in personality and the way they approached their work. Both men managed several assistants on the project, but L'Enfant's expenses were considerably higher than Ellicott's. Most everyone associated with the project found Ellicott to be a harder worker and less contentious in his personal relationships. While Ellicott was somewhat neutral on the location and design for the capital city—which meant he followed orders from Washington and the commission—L'Enfant was consumed with building a magnificent and massive monument to the new nation, and to himself.[11]

Ellicott dismissed L'Enfant's delinquent and deficient plans as "mere fancy work," yet he defended his colleague's talent, noting that the city "would be very different when completed." Still, reassured Ellicott, "it was idle to be alarmed at what was then doing." Unlike the commissioners and others, Ellicott had not yet lost his patience with or confidence in the architect. He soon would.[12]

For his part, Ellicott was making progress in surveying the federal city. On June 27 Washington met with the commissioners and a group of proprietors to finalize the transfer of lands. The president also asked Major Ellicott to alter ever so slightly the boundary for the city and district to ensure it remained consistent with the survey, lot sales, and size permitted in Clause 17 of the Constitution.

Washington was successful in getting landowners to cooperate, and by June 28 the commissioners organized the final deeds. Afterward, Washington, L'Enfant, and Ellicott again toured the site.

In July Washington requested that L'Enfant come to Philadelphia to meet with him as soon as possible. The temperamental architect did not show up, instead offering an excuse to the commissioners, who wrote to Washington on August 2, "L'Enfant purposes to wait on you soon with his drafts for your confirmation."[13] Yet by mid-August L'Enfant had yet to arrive, prompting Jefferson to send him a letter inquiring "when, if at all," he planned to come to Philadelphia.[14] In October a large number of lots were scheduled to be auctioned in Georgetown. The sale would help finance the building of the city and ensure adequate public support for the project. L'Enfant's plans were needed to prepare for the auction. It was an important milestone for the project, but two costly blunders doomed it to failure.

Both Jefferson and Madison were on hand for the sale. Washington intended to preside over the auction, knowing his mere presence would aid in its success. However, he recorded the incorrect date in his calendar and was in Philadelphia that day. Then, L'Enfant failed to provide an updated plan. Without a detailed map or architectural sketches, and without Washington's presence, many speculators and would-be landowners were hesitant to bid.

By the end of October the three commissioners had had it with the difficult architect. Washington blamed L'Enfant for undermining the sale of lots in the city.

Things were about to get worse. On November 20, without even notifying the commissioners and without proper consideration of the homeowner, L'Enfant ordered his aide Isaac Roberdeau to take down a house that jutted into the boundary planned for New Jersey Avenue. His reason: it interfered with his grand boulevard. The politically influential Daniel Carroll of Duddington owned the home, and he was livid. Washington did not approve of L'Enfant's action but had told Carroll to either move and be reimbursed or wait until 1800 and not be paid.

The president was embarrassed, writing flatly to Carroll, "What has been done cannot be undone." There were bigger concerns, as noted by Washington, who was able to temporarily calm the landowner, reminding him, "It would be unfortunate in my opinion, if disputes amongst the friends to the federal city, should arm the enemies of it, with weapons to wound it."[16] Nevertheless, the president told Carroll that he must move the house out of the street (with government compensation) and that if he did not do it now, the federal government would do it in 1800 (without compensation).

Washington then had Jefferson write to L'Enfant with orders "to touch no man's property without his consent, or the previous order of the Commissioners." Washington reiterated his support for the architect's work, but "on condition that you can conduct yourself in subordination to the authority of the Commissioners, to whom by law the business is entrusted, and who stand between you and the President of the United States."[17]

The act of taking down the home was just one more example for Washington of L'Enfant's megalomania and desire to control every aspect of the city. "His aim is obvious. . . . It is to have as much scope as possible for the display of his talents—perhaps for his ambitions."[18] Washington was exasperated, believing L'Enfant to be a highly capable "scientific man." He was beginning to believe, however, that his architect's temperament and ego had become insurmountable obstacles to the project. Washington admitted to Commissioner Stuart, "But I did not expect to have met such perverseness in Major L'Enfant."[19] Washington was risking the entire capital project by retaining L'Enfant, yet he worried that perhaps only the architect shared his vision and only he was able to accomplish the task. The president had put up with far more than could be expected of him.[20]

Jefferson, who never cared for L'Enfant, admitted that Carroll should have cooperated more in the dispute over the location of the home, writing, "Mr. Carroll has acted imprudently, intemperately, foolishly." However, noted the secretary of state, "he has not acted illegally." The ultimate blame for the controversy, believed Jefferson and Washington, rested with L'Enfant.[21]

An exasperated Jefferson pondered what to do about the architect: "I confess, that on view of L'Enfant's proceedings and letters latterly, I am thoroughly persuaded that to render him useful, his temper must be subdued and that the only means of preventing him giving constant trouble to the President, is to submit him to the unlimited control of the Commissioners. We know the discretion & forbearance with which they will exercise it."[22]

By the end of 1791 Jefferson, who had long opposed both L'Enfant and his grand vision for the city, felt he could no longer control the temperamental architect. The commissioners shared his view, so they asked Washington to intervene. The president sent a terse letter to his architect reminding him that he was to report and remain subordinate to the commissioners.[23]

Even when Washington made suggestions, however, L'Enfant would rather focus on what he believed to be best. Though he treated Washington with cordiality and respect, the architect had his own ideas on how to map and build the city. For example, he selected Jenkins Hill to serve as the epicenter of the city. He told Washington and Jefferson of his plan after making up his mind.

"From these hights every grand building would rear with a majestic aspect over the country all around and might be advantageously seen from twenty miles off," he predicted. Jefferson wrote to the ill-tempered architect, informing him that he should cease his plan to center the city on the Eastern Branch, but L'Enfant continued as before, irrespective to the challenges posed by the Eastern Branch flowing through the city and the secretary of state's order.[24]

Such recalcitrance and utter lack of deference was harming the ability of Washington and his agents to buy and sell land in the area. The president's friends, William Deakins Jr. and Benjamin Stoddert, would say one thing, but L'Enfant would do another thing, prompting Stoddert to repeatedly ask for Jefferson's intervention. In exasperation Washington once wrote, "What steps had I best take to bring matters to a close . . . and by declaring at once the site of the public buildings, prevent some inconvenience which I see may arise from the opinions promulgated by Mr. L'Enfant?"[25]

In late November, in a letter to Jefferson, Washington fumed, "He must know there is a line beyond which he will not be suffered to go."[26] That limit was now at hand.

The president informed L'Enfant that his plans for the federal district and federal city must be presented to the commissioners right away. Still, as the end of 1791 approached, the architect had yet to comply. A frustrated Washington, speaking of his architect, complained to Stuart that "men who posses talents which fit them for peculiar purposes" unfortunately sometimes also demonstrate a character of "untoward disposition or are sottish idle or possessed of some other disqualification by which they plague all those with whom they are concerned."[27]

Washington had always admired L'Enfant's talents and appreciated his vision for the city, one that matched his own and would promote a spirit of national unity. Washington needed his grand city to achieve those dreams. He also believed that the architect's military bearing would help move the project forward in a timely manner. L'Enfant, after all, was prone to using military metaphors in his work and daily life; the project was to be "attacked," with surveyors approaching it on the "flank," and so on.

Yet Washington could not lose the three commissioners, local landowners, or support from Congress. The president was upset but also keen on retaining the architect, giving him yet another chance, while also trying to smooth the ruffled feathers of everyone L'Enfant had angered. In December Washington wrote quite diplomatically but firmly to L'Enfant with advice: "Having the beauty and harmony of your plan only in view, you pursue it as if every person and thing was obliged to yield to it, whereas the commissioners have many circumstances to attend to, some of which, perhaps, may be unknown to you."[28]

Washington dispatched a series of letters to the commissioners in December 1791 with instructions on how to deal with L'Enfant and the landowners and how to sooth rankled egos and mend political bridges that had been burnt.[29] He then warned his architect in early December and in no uncertain terms, "In future I must strictly enjoin you to touch no man's property without his consent, or the previous order of the Commissioners." Washington repeated his orders to L'Enfant again in the middle of the month.[30]

Shockingly, L'Enfant did not heed the advice. He even contemplated tearing down another home of a prominent landowner named Notley Young, a relative of commissioner Carroll. L'Enfant then notified Washington of a series of additional steps he would need to take to complete the next phase of the project and stated that the entire construction project needed to be placed under the direction of one person—himself.[31]

Now it was Congress that was asking questions and needed reassuring. The president instructed his architect to bring his plans to Philadelphia in order that Congress might be kept informed and that a movement to abandon the Potomac capital would not take hold. The testy architect sent a lengthy letter to Washington with a litany of excuses and explanations, as well as a promise to "end the business as shortly as possible."[32]

L'Enfant ultimately traveled to Philadelphia, arriving at the end of the month. But rather than provide Washington and Congress with an updated map of the city to be engraved, L'Enfant had French colleagues make a fancy and expensive engraving of his previous sketches, which were little improved or updated from August and lacked the necessary detail requested. The meeting with Congress was an embarrassment.[33]

Things were no better in 1792. Realizing that Washington and Congress were displeased with the lack of progress and discovering that much of Philadelphia still opposed building a new capital city, L'Enfant published a description of the merits of his grand plan in January in the *Gazette of the United States*, which had been drafted in large part by Andrew Ellicott a month earlier.[34] He boasted of planning a great church "intended for national purposes, such as public prayer, thanksgiving, funeral orations, etc., and assigned to the special use of no particular Sect or denomination, but equally open to all." The testy architect assured the public, "It will be likewise a proper shelter for such monuments as were voted by the late Continental Congress for those heroes who fell in the cause of liberty, and for such others as may hereafter be decreed by the voice of a grateful Nation."[35]

Washington still awaited a finished plan for Congress. In January 1792 the president again attempted to console both Congress and his commissioners. To the former, he promised a plan soon; to the latter, he asked for their continued patience with his architect, suggesting, "His pride would be gratified and his ambition excited, by such a mark of your confidence."[36] After the debacle in Philadelphia and article in the newspaper, Jefferson too felt the need to act and requested a meeting with L'Enfant, but the architect declined to meet with him.[37]

L'Enfant alienated the commissioners in other ways. Again, without consulting the commissioners, he sent his assistant architect, Isaac Roberdeau, to begin quarrying stone at a new site, one he preferred. Roberdeau did so despite not having a permit, the necessary funding, or a contract. The commissioners immediately notified L'Enfant with orders "to discharge the hands engaged . . . and employed in digging" immediately. The architect refused, prompting the commissioners to complain to Washington of the "mortifying treatment" they had received.[38]

Roberdeau was arrested and jailed, which created more bad publicity for the entire project. That same month L'Enfant went on the offensive, complaining to Washington about the commission and suggesting, "It is necessary to place under the authority of one single director all those employed in the execution." He then demanded over one thousand workers—hundreds for digging, hundreds working on the canal, hundreds to build bridges, and so on—along with an astonishing $1.2 million as part of his five-year proposal. L'Enfant was so bold as to tell Washington to get another loan from Europe for the funds. All this came on the heels of an earlier bill of $300,000 he had presented to the commission.[39]

Washington reacted with rage, writing to Jefferson, "The conduct of Majr L'Enfant and those employed under him astonishes me beyond measure!" The president instructed Jefferson to give L'Enfant an ultimatum to deliver his completed architectural plan immediately and improve his relationship with the commission. L'Enfant responded in typical fashion—with a long-winded excuse and even more excessive demands. Jefferson conveyed Washington's response to the architect: "The President has not read the Papers, nor is he in any hurry to do so."[40]

The architect's behavior mystified the president to the very end. Writing to his longtime aide Tobias Lear, a perplexed Washington pondered, "Whether it is zeal,—an impetuous temper, or other motives that lead him into such blameable conduct, I will not take upon me to decide—but be it what it will, it must be checked; or we shall have no Commissioners." Washington tried dispatching Lear to meet with L'Enfant and the commissioners in hopes a fresh face and approach might repair the damage. Writing to Lear, the president advised he address L'Enfant "in decisive terms without losing his services." Washington, after all, still worried that the loss of his brilliant ally in the grand scheme for the capital "would be a serious misfortune" for the city. Lear's intervention also failed to change L'Enfant.[41]

The extended deadlines for submitting the plan came and went. Utterly tone deaf, L'Enfant wrote to Washington on February 6, 1792, again demanding complete and independent authority for the city's design and threatening to quit. Ignoring the architect's threat, Washington ordered Major Ellicott to prepare the maps based on the work L'Enfant had thus far completed, but without L'Enfant, which he promptly did. On orders from Washington, Jefferson had it engraved and distributed to Congress. Washington also called a meeting with Jefferson, Madison, Hamilton, and other advisers on February 16 to try to remedy the disastrous situation.

As was expected, news that his plan had been revised and submitted infuriated L'Enfant, who complained bitterly the next day that there were changes in Ellicott's plan that did not reflect his own work or vision. L'Enfant fired off a terse letter to Tobias Lear: "This draft to my great surprise I found in the state in which it now is, most unmercifully spoiled and altered from the original plan to a degree indeed evidently tending to disgrace me and ridicule the very undertaking."[42] L'Enfant maintained arrogantly, "nor must it be expected that anything short of what I proposed will answer that purpose or warrant success." Writing to Jefferson, L'Enfant returned to his familiar refrain that he would not work with the commissioners, for "the determination I have taken no longer to act in subjection to their will and caprice is influenced by the purest principles." In clear language, he concluded, "I cannot nor would I upon any consideration submit myself to it."[43]

Washington, desperate to move forward with the project, approved Ellicott's blueprint and, showing remarkable patience, instructed Jefferson to allow L'Enfant to point out any "radical defects" in the plan. The key was that it had to be done right away.[44]

L'Enfant responded to Jefferson in a letter on February 26. In a huff, he defended his own record, but suggested that the commissioners had not been acting in good faith or the public interest. He complained about the "disfiguration" of his plans by Ellicott at the behest of the commissioners. He concluded by saying that "If therefore the Law absolutely requires without any equivocation that my continuance shall depend upon an appointment from the Commissioners, I cannot, nor would I upon any Consideration submit myself to it."[45]

That same day Washington asked Lear to try one last time to appeal to the architect, but Lear responded that L'Enfant had dismissed him, saying he "had already heard enough of this matter."[46] At the same time Hamilton met with everyone involved to try to save L'Enfant's job, making a desperate and ultimately unsuccessful appeal. The commissioners had long ago lost patience with L'Enfant. Commissioner Stuart gave the ultimatum, informing Washington, Jefferson, and Hamilton that he and his fellow commissioners were prepared to resign "rather than be any longer subject to the caprices and malicious suggestions of Major L'Enfant." A choice had to be made—the architect or the Commission.[47]

It had always been Washington's policy to treat others with dignity and maintain the moral high ground in public life. The president had worked hard to put out the brushfires caused by his architect but eventually grew tired of having to provide excuses for L'Enfant.

On February 27, the politically savvy Washington had Hamilton write the first draft of a response letter that Jefferson would send to L'Enfant. The letter sought to confirm L'Enfant's remarks in his previous letter and in his conversation with Lear, which were to the effect that L'Enfant could no longer continue to work under the commissioners. It was sent to the architect and commissioners under Jefferson's signature and with his slight revisions.[48] Jefferson's letter concluded by stating, "It is understood that you absolutely decline acting under the authority of the present commissioners. I am instructed by the President to inform you that notwithstanding the desire he has entertained to preserve your agency in the business, the condition upon which it is to be done is inadmissible, and your services must be at an end."[49]

Both the commissioners and L'Enfant had made appeals to Washington to dismiss the other, but L'Enfant lost. Likely realizing this, L'Enfant responded immediately to Jefferson's letter but sent it directly to Washington. L'Enfant reiterated that it "is still my resolution" that he could not continue to work under the present system with the commissioners. With regret, he said, "I perceive that all my services are at an End."[50]

Jefferson's letter may have been intended to give L'Enfant an opportunity to back down, but L'Enfant's letter to Washington signaled that he was resolute and would rather resign. L'Enfant resigned before Washington had to formally fire him. On February 28, Washington wrote back acknowledging "your final resolution being taken." Washington went on to blast L'Enfant in the letter, which must have wounded the architect. "The continuance of your services (as I have often assured you) would have been pleasing to me, could they have been retained on terms compatible with the law. Every mode has been tried to accommodate your wishes on this principle, except changing the Commissioners." Washington reminded L'Enfant that the law required the commissioners, that L'Enfant had been obligated to report to them, and he blamed L'Enfant for "many weeks" of delays.[51]

In early March the president notified the commission that L'Enfant's "services are at an end."[52] A week later he informed Jefferson that "no farther overtures will ever be made to this Gentn."[53] Tobias Lear summed up the sad chapter in the building of the capital city: "The President did everything that he could with propriety to retain L'Enfant's service."[54]

Washington asked the commissioners to offer L'Enfant $3,000 for his services. In a rare break with the president, the commission agreed to a payment of only 500 guineas (roughly $1,500) and a lot in the city. The stubborn architect declined both offers, writing proudly, "Without enquiring of the principle upon which you rest this offer, I shall only here testify my surprise thereupon, as also my intention to decline accepting it."[55]

But L'Enfant did not go quietly. After departing in a huff, he publicly belittled the commission. Jefferson worried about the political damage the architect might cause, predicting just days after the firing that "the enemies of the project will take advantage of L'Enfant to trumpet an abortion of the whole."[56]

Sure enough, L'Enfant also had his supporters come to his defense, chief among them were proprietors and political leaders in the area who supported his grand vision for the city and who stood to make a lot of money off it.[57] In March he composed a letter to the landowners and proprietors in the federal district, alleging, "I cannot disguise to you that much has already been attempted by the contrivance of an erroneous map of the city about to be published, which partly copied from the original has afterwards been mangled and altered in a shameful manner in its most essential parts."[58] Shockingly, he also pushed for the removal of Jefferson and the commissioners.

As Washington had fretted, L'Enfant's removal and behavior also undermined support for the entire project. Congressman Egbert Benson, a federalist from New York, announced he was considering proposing legislation to repeal the Residence Act. Public confidence in the project waned and resulted in a growing hesitancy to purchase land and lots in the federal district.[59]

Not fully aware of the countless problems caused by the Frenchman, thirteen of the main proprietors of the city signed a petition demanding L'Enfant be reinstated as principal architect. L'Enfant defended himself by reminding the landowners of the "impossibility" of an undertaking "to change a wilderness" into a glorious capital city. It was no small matter, he boasted, to design a capital equal to the finest cities in Europe "in a country devoid of internal resources and distant from the mass of population from whence hands as well as all materials . . . are to be procured."[60] Washington would have none of it and put his formidable prestige and interpersonal graces to work to reassure the proprietors and end the talk of abandoning the plans for the new capital city; he also pried the landowners away from their defense of L'Enfant.[61]

L'Enfant's reputation was damaged; Washington would not see him again. The temperamental architect refused to visit the city for several years. Then in late 1800, L'Enfant moved to Washington and submitted his first petition to Congress for compensation for his design. His personality traits became more pronounced, alienating his supporters, and the grandiose schemes he pitched only further marginalized him.[62] However, much of L'Enfant's remarkable design and vision for the capital city remained and are, today, still seen in the city. John Adams would recall late in life, "Washington, Jefferson, and L'Enfant were the triumvirate who planned the city, the capitol, and the prince's palace."[63]

L'Enfant passed away penniless in Maryland at age seventy. Late in life, he had attempted to receive full payment for his services but was given the sum of only $3,800 by Congress. In 1909 L'Enfant's body was exhumed and, fittingly, honored in the Capitol rotunda. He was reinterred at Arlington National Cemetery in a spot overlooking the city he loved and inspired. It took roughly a century, but his adopted country rediscovered and paid homage to the brilliant architect, artist, and engineer who helped design the capital city.

CHAPTER 25

A Design Contest

*Man is not made for the State but the State for man and it
derives its just powers only from the consent of the governed.*
Thomas Jefferson

A ndrew Ellicott replaced L'Enfant in 1792 as surveyor general of the capital
city. The Philadelphian had extensive experience as a surveyor and map-
maker, having explored more of the new nation than probably any other person
alive. Although he was never enamored of the Potomac location and questioned
the feasibility of the scope of the city, Ellicott was eager to build Washington's
glorious capital. Unlike his predecessor, Ellicott was more amenable to orders,
requests, and deadlines for completing the survey, maps, and plans.[1]

Yet by the end of 1792, he too was complaining. In a letter to his wife he
grumbled, "I begin to dislike the whole place and have become too ill-natured
to associate with any beings except my four assistants. . . . I eat alone in the office, to which I confine myself as closely as a Bear to his den in the winter."[2] He
also began to run afoul of the commission.

Ellicott too would soon lose the confidence of Washington and the commissioners. The job was turning out to be too big for any one person. Ellicott
gives us a glimpse into the challenges facing the new nation when, later in life
after a nationwide tour in 1796, he again toured the country and expressed
disappointment with it. Most of the towns he visited lacked clean water, bridges
and roads, adequate schools, a trained physician, and other necessary services.
The new nation, he wrote, "does not appear to be in a better state of cultivation

than it was twenty-six years ago." He was particularly appalled by the condition of communities in the South. He labeled them "disagreeable" and blamed them partly on slavery, which was prevalent throughout the region. A Quaker and social reformer, he had always thought "that domestic slavery is wrong in a moral point of view is evident from the ordinary principles of justice."[3]

For the time being, however, Ellicott provided the surveys and maps George Washington needed. The next step was to hire an architect and builder for the presidential home.

Washington envisioned the presidential home being a jewel in the new capital city. He and L'Enfant had surveyed and selected what he believed to be the perfect site for the grand presidential residence. After the departure of L'Enfant in February 1792 further delayed the construction and undermined support from the public for the site of the capital, Washington was eager to move the project forward immediately. He even briefly considered rehiring L'Enfant.[4]

Thomas Jefferson, who disliked the despotic architect and was adamantly opposed to his outsize vision for the capital city, took great pleasure in the architect's departure. With Washington having lost an important ally and precious time, Jefferson realized it was not too late for him to affect a fundamental change in the plans for the city and home. He therefore seized the opportunity to move the project forward, but in a far more modest and simple way. This was his chance to reinsert his decentralist ideology into the debate over the size and nature of the capital city and presidential residence.[5]

Jefferson's "federal town" would be a maximum of only fifteen hundred acres, with just three hundred acres for government buildings. It would contain ordinary brick buildings placed far apart to promote a rural character. Houses would be built between the low, airy public buildings, and much of the town would be made up of parks and undeveloped areas. The presidential residence and "congressional hall" would sit next to one another, both pointing in the same direction and be unassuming and simple in their design.[6]

Such a city, Jefferson believed, would naturally limit the power of government and symbolically reflect the preeminence of the states. A small-town capital would ensure republican simplicity and avoid what Jefferson believed to be the natural corrupting influence of the urban experience. The secretary of state had also long wanted the capital to be built in his native Virginia in order to promote the state's power and reflect the plantation lifestyle. Jefferson now believed momentum had shifted behind his plan; a simple design contest for the presidential residence, one open to the public, would seal the deal.

Therefore, rather than reappoint the temperamental genius, Jefferson proposed another measure: a design contest for the presidential home and capitol building. It would be a fittingly democratic gesture for the new nation. It might, he suggested, have the added benefits of building support for the city and helping to unify the nation. These arguments appealed to Washington.

Washington and Jefferson, though disagreeing on the dimensions for the city and role of the new national government, understood that, in this instance, architecture was politics by other means. One need only to consider Jefferson's elaborate design for his own home, Monticello, and ambitious plans for the University of Virginia or Washington's fondness for the large, stately mansions in New York and Philadelphia with their oval rooms and his constant expansions and restorations of Mount Vernon. They were fellow Virginians, planters, and architectural enthusiasts who delighted in reading about the different styles of the buildings of the age and devoted considerable time and money to renovating their own magnificent homes. They were also both eager to influence the design of the building—just in different ways.

Jefferson preferred a humble structure befitting a republican leader with limited powers. He even had ideas in mind. It would be modeled on the homes in Williamsburg. Back in 1779, when Virginia's leaders decided to move the state capital from Williamsburg further inland to Richmond, they had contacted Jefferson for his input. During the design and construction phase of the new capital in 1785, Jefferson was in Paris but worked through allies and architects to submit plans for the new city consistent with his republican political philosophy of limited government. However, delays in communications and transportation caused Jefferson's proposals to arrive too late.

Worried about further delays in the Richmond project and the threat that the capital might move back to Williamsburg, the state's political leaders decided to rush ahead with the development of the new site before receiving Jefferson's proposal. The author of the Declaration of Independence missed his opportunity to imprint his ideology on his own state's capital. When he finally saw the Richmond capital, he was not pleased. Jefferson did not want to miss another opportunity to influence a capital; time was of the essence.[7]

Washington agreed immediately with the idea of a contest. He had little choice. The entire capital project was moving forward slowly; the government lacked funds for a home, a "congressional hall," and a city on the scale of what Washington and L'Enfant had planned. There were still the problems of enticing the few trained architects in the country to participate and attracting workers and residents. The area remained noticeably undeveloped. It boasted fewer than a hundred brick homes and two hundred small wooden buildings spread across a semi-rural landscape. By 1792 only the cellar for the presidential residence had been dug.

Shortly after the announcement that L'Enfant had left the project, another announcement was issued. The secretary of state was authorized to promptly invite the public to participate in a design contest. And so, on March 14, 1792, ads appeared in newspapers and printed notices were circulated under the auspices of the three commissioners. They read,

> A Premium of 500 dollars or a medal of that value at the option of the party will be given by the Commissioners of the federal buildings to a person who before the fifteenth day of July next shall produce to them the most approved plan, if adopted by them for a President's house to be erected in this city—The Site of the building, if the artist will attend to it, will of course influence the aspect and outline of his plan and its destination will point out to him the number, size and distribution of the apartments—It will be a recommendation of any Plan if the Central part of it may be detached and erected for the present with the appearance of a complete whole and be capable of admitting the additional parts in future, if they shall be wanting—Drawings will be expected of the ground plots, elevations of each front and sections through the buildings in such directions as may be necessary to explain the internal structure, and an estimate of the Cubic feet or brickwork composing the whole mass of the wall.[8]

Jefferson interpreted Washington's order as meaning that he, as secretary of state, would personally oversee the design contest. He immediately began developing his own blueprints for the residence. Jefferson, however, was not the only one worried about further delays; Washington did not wait for proposals to be submitted. He quickly began seeking his own replacement for L'Enfant. Washington wanted more than just an architect. He wanted someone who could also build the home and realize his grand vision for the home, city, and nation.

Back in April 1791, during his southern tour, Washington had met a young Irishman and fellow Freemason in South Carolina named James Hoban. The native of Callan in County Kilkenny, Ireland, was just twenty-nine and had studied architecture at the Royal Dublin Society under the tutelage of the noted architect Thomas Ivory, who specialized in the Georgian neoclassical style and had designed several of Dublin's most celebrated buildings. Hoban immigrated to Philadelphia in 1785, after the end of the Revolutionary War, and then re-located to Charleston, most likely in the year 1787. Two years later, he married Susanna Sewell, with whom he would eventually have ten children.

In a remarkably brief period Hoban had designed and built some of the most majestic homes and public buildings in Charleston and around the state, including the State Capitol Building, which replaced the old statehouse that burned in 1788. Colloquially known as the "Statehouse," this striking neo-classical structure was completed around the time of Washington's visit and, because the state capital was moved to Columbia in 1786, now functioned as the Charleston County Courthouse. During the visit Charleston's city el-ders were so keen on Hoban that they notified the president of his talents and arranged for Washington to view the Statehouse on the northwest cor-ner of Broad and Meeting Streets. Washington was duly impressed by the Anglo-Palladian architecture. His dream was staring him in the face, matching perfectly his preference for a "stately stone structure, rich in architectural em-bellishments; a design similar to an English country seat, built on as palatial a scale as politics would allow." He would never forget the building—or the architect.[9]

Throughout the spring and summer of 1792 submissions to the design contest trickled into the secretary of state's office. Most were based on exist-ing courthouses and mansions. One of them came from Andrew Mayfield Carshore, known as "the Poet of the Hudson River," and another from John Collins, a Richmond builder, who proposed a domed house. It is believed that Jefferson also either submitted his own plan anonymously or had Collins sub-mit the domed residence at his behest. Of the submissions, however, it was said, "most . . . were beneath contempt from an architectural point of view; and many of them have been pronounced wildly absurd structurally and decora-tively." For instance, one plan had an imposing central window over which were two large sculptures of men ready for battle. Another featured a gigantic clock with the letters spelling out "United States" on its face rather than the numbers one through twelve, and with an eagle as the weathercock. Few were feasible architecturally.[10] None of them caught Washington's attention.[11]

Indeed, the announcements failed to produce the deluge of ideas Washington had hoped for, which secretly pleased Jefferson. At one point, shortly before the close of the contest, Washington griped to his commissioners about the poor quality of submissions, "If none more elegant than these should appear . . . the exhibition of architecture will be a very dull one indeed."[12] Timing was now of the essence for Washington. He needed to obtain the right architect and plan during this initial design contest. To again delay construction or reopen the contest would assuredly doom the project.

Washington, desperate for a proposal to his liking, made inquiries in late May as to whether Hoban was still in Charleston and if he might be interested in submitting a design for the contest. The July deadline for the submissions was looming, so Washington reached out to his friend Henry Laurens, one of the most prominent citizens of Charleston. The president trusted Laurens, who had earlier succeeded John Hancock as president of the Continental Congress and whose eldest son, John, had served alongside Alexander Hamilton in Washington's headquarters during the Revolutionary War. The elder Laurens contacted Hoban with the president's personal invitation.

Only one month before the contest ended, Hoban sailed to Philadelphia to meet with Washington. They wasted no time, discussing plans for the home and L'Enfant's designs for the city and visiting the federal district, surveying equipment in hand, to make preliminary sketches. Washington was obviously quite pleased with both Hoban's interest in the project and vision for the home and city. He introduced the Irish architect to the commissioners, who shared the president's high opinion of him. Hoban returned to Charleston with his sketches in order to prepare a detailed submission for the contest.[13]

Aside from Washington's enthusiastic reception of Hoban, he generally tried to keep a low profile during the spring and summer of that year. Though a skilled and experienced surveyor himself and an architectural enthusiast, the president went so far as to give the public appearance that he knew little about architecture and was letting the contest unfold on its own. Of course, Washington was fascinated by architecture. During his extensive travels during the war and throughout his presidency, he made a point of viewing the most architecturally imposing buildings in every town. For instance, he was deeply fond of the governor's residence in Williamsburg, which he had visited often. So, to the public and Congress, it appeared that Jefferson was running the contest, which was just what Washington wanted.[14]

In total, nine entries, including Hoban's sketches, were submitted. Washington and Jefferson then met in Georgetown with the commissioners to review the submissions. One of the proposals was a Palladian-style villa with a rotunda resembling a more modest version of Jefferson's home, Monticello. This was likely Jefferson's own sketch or his by proxy. However, Washington dismissed it, making it abundantly clear to the secretary of state who would be making the decision. Days before the July deadline, the president set off again to look at the site he had selected for the presidential residence. Armed with the designs from the contest, he seems to have wanted to reassure himself that he was making the right decision.

After reviewing all the plans, the president made it known that he liked only one of the proposals—from Hoban. Interestingly, Hoban's design for the building was partly inspired by L'Enfant's design for Federal Hall in New York City. Washington then turned all the submissions over to the commissioners, presumably for appearance's sake and their endorsement of Hoban's design. On July 16 he informed Jefferson and the commission that Hoban had won the contest. The event, it seems, "was not intended [by Washington] to be entirely random."[15]

The commissioners officially announced that James Hoban had won first prize, taking home a gold medal worth $500, a lot in the new District of Columbia, and a commission to build the presidential residence. Second place went to John Collins, the Richmond builder and ally of Jefferson. In the announcement the commissioners said simply of Hoban that he had "been engaged in some of the first buildings in Dublin, appears a master workman, and has a great many hands of his own."[16] The new architect was charged with building a mansion with over a hundred rooms from sandstone quarried nearby at Aquia Creek.

The winning design had been inspired by Washington's appreciation for Federal Hall and two other existing structures, one of which was "plate 51" in a book Hoban had read called the *Book of Architecture*, published in London in 1728 by the architect James Gibbs. The other was the former palace of the Duke of Leinster in Ireland. The mansion sat on Kildare Street on the outskirts of Dublin but was a country home and was well-known throughout Ireland and England. It later served as the headquarters of the Royal Dublin Society and, in modern times, as a parliamentary building for the Irish government.

Built in 1748, the massive, three-story building with prominent colonnades was an elegant example of modernized Greek architecture—a Georgian mansion in the Palladian style or, more simply, a neoclassical country house of the style Washington admired in the architectural books he frequently ordered from London. In fact, Washington knew and admired the Duke of Leinster's family. One son, Edward Fitzgerald, was an acquaintance of Washington's relatives and had been captured and imprisoned in Charleston during the Revolutionary War. Moreover, neoclassicism as an architectural style shared a similar philosophical ideal with the Enlightenment, which had inspired the American Revolution.[17]

L'Enfant's vision for the home would continue to influence Washington and Hoban, but only in principle. As was said of the temperamental architect, his plans always "floated somewhere in the clouds." Borrowing from L'Enfant's "clouds," Leinster's design, and Washington's musings, Hoban had proposed a three-story home in the Anglo-Palladian style of Georgian England. He reduced the size of L'Enfant's palace considerably, which would prove to be one of the president's only concerns with the winning proposal. Before Hoban started construction, Washington simply had his new architect increase the size of the home by one-fifth.[18]

There was a larger kinship between the Irish and Americans in terms of their political views and a shared experience with British rule. So too was there a warmth between Washington and his new architect. Unlike L'Enfant, Hoban met Washington's deadlines, was agreeable, and furnished the president with specific details regarding his work. However, just like L'Enfant, Hoban's "goal was to achieve *Washington's* vision."[19] Perhaps most important, Hoban saw himself building an empire, not just a home. Such visions of grandeur resonated with Washington. The two had quickly developed a comfortable rapport that would turn into a productive working relationship. Accordingly, the architect's work did not end after the design contest. Washington employed him to oversee the building's construction.

After the announcement of the winning design, the two men rode to the site for the home, where they surveyed the grounds and placed the first stakes and markers for what would become the White House. Together, they would preside over every detail of the construction, down to the location of the front door, which Washington dictated should be exactly where L'Enfant had proposed a year earlier. Over the ensuing years, Jefferson and Washington would end up requesting a number of alterations or modifications. The secretary of state, for instance, suggested replacing the stone with brick, while the president asked the architect to include an array of carvings, engravings, and ornamental flourishes for the home. Not surprisingly, the former recommendation was ignored; the latter was accepted.[20]

Although some Jeffersonians criticized the plan as too regal, the home would eventually become the most iconic and recognized symbol of democracy in the world. A few years later, when the Swedish diplomat Baron A. L. Klinckowström visited, he commented to a member of Congress that it was "neither large nor awe-inspiring." The congressman summed it up perfectly, responding quite cleverly: "The building served its purpose, that if it were larger and more elegant, perhaps some President would be inclined to become its permanent resident, which was something to be aware of."[21]

The cornerstone was placed on October 13, 1792, the three hundredth anniversary of Columbus arriving in the Western Hemisphere. Hearing of the event, a bitter L'Enfant dismissed Hoban's design as "hardly suitable for a gentleman's country house [and] wholly inconsistent for a city habitation [and] in no aspect . . . becoming the State Residency of the chief head of a sovereign people."[22] Nevertheless, the public ceremony was marked by speeches, protocols in the masonic tradition, and much anticipation.[23] A brass plate was placed in the ground at the cornerstone, inscribed with the following words, including the Latin verse meaning "Long live the Republic":

> This first stone of the President's House was laid on the
> 13th day of October, 1792,
> and in the 17th Year of the Independence of the
> United States of America.
> George Washington, President.
> Thomas Johnson, doctor Stewart, Daniel Carroll, Commissioners.
> James Hoban, Architect.
> Collen Williamson, Master Mason.
> *Vivat Respublica.*

Washington finally had his architect. Now all he would have to do is see the home built—with virtually no funds, with few skilled builders, and amid continued political bickering.

CHAPTER 26

Building the
President's House

*The sumptuousness of a palace, the convenience of
a house, and the agreeableness of a country seat.*
L'Enfant on the President's House

W ork on the presidential residence began soon after the laying of the cornerstone. James Hoban returned to the capital city with his assistant, Pierce Purcell, and several of his slaves from Charleston—among them three skilled carpenters named Ben, Daniel, and Peter. Hoban immediately showed himself to be highly capable, answering the commissioners' requests, submitting a detailed assessment of the costs for the project, and promising regular updates on his work. Nonetheless, the work was difficult and tedious and the conditions harsh.

For the construction workers, the day began shortly after sunrise with a roll call of names and often lasted until sunset, six days a week. Most workers simply slept at the quarry or construction site and did not return home or see their families until the end of the construction season each year. To avoid the cold of winters, the bulk of the construction occurred between the months of April and October, which posed other problems, namely, the heat, humidity, and prevalence of disease. In mid-to-late October, workers packed their equipment and the wood and stone they cut in straw, and most departed the city, although some remained and found jobs building the homes that were slowly appearing around the city. Those able to work inside, such as carpenters and stonecutters, remained, worked on doorframes and other projects, and were paid through the winter.

The workers were poorly fed from food prepared in a central kitchen and served in a military-style mess. Payments, besides being meager, were doled out weekly, but they were docked if workers were late, failed to follow orders, were drunk (which was often the case), or refused to work atop high ladders and scaffolding arranged against the walls of the building. Work conditions were even worse for those in the quarries. The quarry "swarmed with mosquitos," and the task of digging and cutting rock out of the earth with shovels and picks was backbreaking. The men then had to transport the rock up and out of the quarry and forty-five miles upriver to the construction site. To cope with the brutal conditions, workers at the quarry were given "a half-pint of whiskey" each day.[1]

Materials such as wood and nails were ordered from Boston, but Hoban also cut through the red tape of the era by using his contacts in Charleston to quickly and cheaply furnish him with what he needed. This included a hundred-pound bell that he would ring to notify workers of their break times.[2] The amount of wood required for a project of this size was such that, in December 1792, Hoban wisely secured a five-hundred-acre wooded lot near the river in Westmoreland County, Virginia, for timbering. The arrangement appears to have been kept quiet because the land was owned by William Augustine Washington, one of the president's nephews. He was paid "half up front" and half later and agreed to supervise the axe men, including both slaves and residents of the area whom he hired.[3]

The initial phase of construction in 1792 and 1793 logically focused on the foundation and basement. The second phase included the walls. Once they were completed, the third phase was the roof, and then finally the interior rooms. The work progressed slowly and necessitated numerous alterations owing to a shortage of funds. In general, the commissioners approved most every request made by Hoban. One such example, over Jefferson's objections, was that work on the presidential residence was prioritized over construction of the "congressional house." This, of course, reflected Washington's priorities. Still, it was a frustratingly slow process for the president. The exterior walls were not completed until 1797, and the building was mostly empty inside.[4]

The project continued to attract controversy, even years later. One later critic of the size and suspected opulence of the mansion during the Van Buren administration claimed it was "a Place as splendid as that of the Caesars, and as richly adorned as the proudest Asiatic mansion."[5] As had been the case for years, every aspect of the capital city invited political bickering and harsh criticism from Congress, the press, and advocates of limited government. Most of the debate on the presidential residence shifted from its location and design to its size and cost, although an occasional newspaper editorial or speech in Congress still called for changing the location of the capital.

The Jeffersonian Democratic-Republicans and others in Congress, claiming they were "watch-dogs of the Treasury," threatened cuts.[6] They had a point. Construction of the presidential residence and congressional hall ran over budget. Hoping to avoid cuts or having to ask Congress for additional funds, Washington and the commissioners attempted to generate additional money from selling additional lots in the city. The effort, however, failed to raise the necessary funds.

Much of the opposition came from the Democratic-Republicans and was likely orchestrated by Jefferson, who had wanted the home built next to the "congressional hall" and remained displeased about its size and extravagance. At one point, with the home progressing faster than the Capitol, Democratic-Republicans threatened to have Congress meet in the presidential residence, which prompted the commissioners to propose shifting funds and workers from the home to the Capitol Building. Washington, however, sternly vetoed the change. The priority must be completing the home.[7]

Washington was only too aware that the success of the city depended on him and, conversely, that his esteem was on the line. As Thomas Johnson of Georgetown reminded the president in a letter in 1795, "The Success of the City has now become important to your Reputation." Johnson, former delegate to the Continental Congress, governor of Maryland, and Supreme Court justice, noted of the stakes, "for you will stand as the first Figure confessed to posterity the noblest Reward."[8] As the project lagged in the mid-1790s, Washington was forced to send his commissioners to Congress to request funds to complete the buildings. Instead of receiving funds, they encountered complaints and proposals to change the design of the presidential residence and even to move the capital city. One commissioner recorded the chilly reception they received:

> I had not been long in the city [Philadelphia] when I found . . . the clashing interests that have caused so much discord in Washington. Some proposed that there should be a small house erected near the Capitol for the residence of the President, and that the executive offices should be built in the same vicinity; some wish his house to be the permanent, others the

temporary residence of the President. Those who wish it permanent talk
of making a judiciary of the President's house, and allege that the seat of
justice would be as advantageous to the adjacent proprietors as the residence of the President. Others propose making the President's house the
residence of Congress; and too many on both sides are of the opinion that
only one of these houses should be finished, and that any money granted
should be appropriated to finishing the one which might be preferred.[9]

Ultimately, in January 1796 Washington had the commissioners make a formal request to Congress to borrow more money to complete the federal city
and executive mansion. Congress approved a $300,000 loan guaranteed by the
federal government. The city's opponents seized the opportunity, and all hell
broke loose. There were calls to end all construction and, again, to move the site
of the capital. The *Columbia Herald* published a poem that same month that
captured the mood. It read,

> O ye who sit at helm of state
> Your vast designs you broach too late
> Leave the ship of state on rocky ground
> And fools to pay for Federal Towns![10]

The money was to be appropriated in three installments and was for the purposes of completing the presidential residence, Capitol, and offices for the executive departments, respectively. It was decided to wait on a site for the judiciary.
In the interim the Supreme Court would have to meet in the Capitol. Two
months later, however, the funds for the three projects had yet to be released.

On March 11, 1796, Congress stated that it was waiting to hear from Vice
President John Adams on his plans for construction. Washington was completing his second term in office, and it was assumed that Adams would be the front-
runner in the election that November. While Congress was well acquainted with
Washington's plans and vision for every aspect of the capital city, Adams had remained uncharacteristically quiet on the matter, deferring to the president. Did
he intend to fulfill Washington's project? Would he make changes? If elected,
did he intend to live in the presidential residence if it were completed?

Adams said little except that he preferred the executive departments be
housed near the Capitol Building and that, "with respect to the President's
house, so far as concerns himself, he is perfectly satisfied." He said he would go
"a mile and a half whenever his official duty may require it, as long as he shall

remain in office, or, if he should find it inconvenient, he could hire a house, so far as concerns himself." Congress eventually released the funds.[11]

But a lack of money was not the only problem.

One of the main causes of delay was the inability to find skilled labor. The new capital city was in a sparsely populated region, and the commissioners were repeatedly short on money to recruit and pay workers. They needed stone-cutters and stonemasons, brick makers and bricklayers, carpenters, and men to transport materials by land and up the river. Although some workers from Maryland and Virginia were used, the numbers were insufficient to meet the demand. Therefore, one of the few points of agreement between Washington and Jefferson over the capital city and presidential residence was the need to hire foreign labor. They both felt that the Scots and Germans were the most talented architects, stonemasons, and builders and expressed confidence in their discipline and work ethic. Thus, at Washington's urging, in 1792 the commissioners and Jefferson began recruiting Scottish and German workers. They assigned the Georgetown merchant John Laird the task of recruiting his fellow Scots; meanwhile, Jefferson reached out to Dutch associates about finding German labor.

America was a land of immigrants, and people from across Europe continued to come to the country. However, few of them were skilled laborers; most were desperate and came seeking opportunities. Experienced builders, carpenters, and stonecutters already had better paying work in Europe. In November 1792 Laird notified the commission of bad news. His Glasgow agent had little success, noting that there was "great demand and building going on in all the towns. . . . It is our opinion good men could not be engaged to go to America unless they were assured of near double the wages they get here."[12]

More bad news came in from the Dutch and Germans. Washington proposed sending his commissioners to France to recruit workers, but the idea was rejected because of the lingering effects of the French Revolution. He then asked Philadelphia merchants to have the city's large German population recruit their brethren from across the Atlantic. The efforts bore little fruit.

A panicked Washington wrote to his commissioners the next month that the dilemma "fills me with real concern." He explained why: "For I am very apprehensive if your next campaign in the Federal City is not marked with vigor, it will cast such a cloud over this business and will so arm the enemies of the measure, as to enable them to give it (if not its death blow) a wound from which it will not easily recover."[13]

Eventually, a few skilled Scottish and German workers were found, most of whom had already been living in America. To entice others, the commission agreed to pay for their passage on a ship and offered sixteen-month contracts for skilled workers and twenty-month contracts for unskilled laborers. It seems fitting that the new experiment in self-governance and its ambitious idea of a glorious capital city would be built with immigrant labor. The nation was largely peopled by recent arrivals and those whose parents and grandparents were born overseas. Yet some Americans were displeased that European skill and knowledge was needed for their capital. This included the Democratic-Republicans, who had long wanted a clean break from the Old World.[14]

The chief stonemason was Collen Williamson, a Scot who had apparently immigrated to New York after the war. How he came to be in charge remains uncertain, and the veracity of the story has been questioned, but it appears the commissioners often met at the Fountain Inn, a tavern in Georgetown, to discuss the project. The tavern owner, John Suter, once heard the three men complaining over drinks about the lack of quality stonecutters. He informed them of his cousin, Collen Williamson, who was a trained stonemason.[15] The commissioners offered Williamson the job in 1792.

Williamson had previously overseen the masonry for the renovations of Castle Grant, an imposing stone manor near the town of Granton-on-Spey in the Scottish Highlands, and a large country estate named Moy House, both owned by Sir Ludlow Grant. For three years Williamson would oversee the quarrying, cutting, and placement of stone in the federal city. To assist Williamson, the commissioners recruited additional workers in the fall of 1793. Six stonemasons from Masonic Lodge No. 8 in Scotland—Robert Brown, James McIntosh, Alexander Scott, George Thomson, James White, and Alexander Wilson—arrived to begin work in April 1794. Fortunately, Williamson, the chief stonemason, and his successors knew how to quarry rock and trained the workers in the difficult task.[16]

Both Hoban and Williamson were highly competent, but their personalities clashed. With the project still moving too slowly in 1795, a quarrel between Hoban and his chief stonemason resulted in the Scot being dismissed. Two men replaced Williamson. One of them, George Blagdin, an Englishman, was hired as the chief stonemason for the Capitol building and, at Washington's request, he was also tasked with helping to supervise construction on the mansion. The commissioners also recruited John Adam, a stonemason from Edinburgh who, like Williamson, had worked for Lord Grant. Adam's brothers were also stonecutters and joined the project. Two additional stonemasons were brought from

Scotland to expedite the progress, brothers John and James Williams. This new crew offered another valuable contribution to the home. Washington wanted intricate carvings of roses, garland, leaves, and ribbons with bows to grace the mansion, but few stonemasons outside Scotland and Rome were able to carve those particular designs. Fortunately for Washington, the new workers were both stonemasons and artisans.

According to Washington's instructions, the presidential mansion was to be covered in sandstone rather than red brick, which was more readily available and cheaper. As was mentioned earlier, the source of stone was Aquia Creek, located a few miles south of the city on the Virginia side of the Potomac. The small creek was rich in arkose sandstone from the Cretaceous period. It also flowed into the Potomac, which meant that the cut stone could conveniently be brought up the river by boat. Once the sandstone arrived in the capital city, it was further cut and dressed in a large shed near the construction site.

The Scots were used to working with a harder, superior quality stone; sandstone was highly porous and not the best building material. Quarrying and cutting it were tricky processes. Fortunately, the skilled Scottish stonemasons came up with a technique for quickly sealing the stone as soon as it was set. They used a thick, lime-based whitewash mixed with salt, rice, glue, and water that functioned like mortar. This mix was placed into every crack to strengthen the stone, but the whitewash also resembled paint and gave the mansion a white color. Later, in 1798, the gray Aquia sandstone exterior was "painted" with the material, which would later factor into nicknaming the building the "White House."[17]

The time-consuming and expensive task of quarrying, transporting, cutting, and treating the sandstone forced Washington and Hoban to again alter their plans. The height of the exterior walls would be reduced and stone would be used only for the exterior of the home. Two feet of brick would supplement the stone walls, and the partitions inside the home would now be made of brick. However, that meant that more brick makers and bricklayers were needed.[18]

The chief brick mason was Jeremiah Kale, a capable worker and supervisor who, like Washington and Hoban, was a surveyor. Kale was employed in 1793 and oversaw the crew of brick makers and bricklayers. One of his first tasks was building two large kilns by the construction site that churned out the thousands of 9-x-4½-inch bricks needed for the massive project.[19]

The large construction project also required many carpenters. Two crews of carpenters worked in long shifts, one overseen by the chief carpenter, Peter Lennox, and the other by the master carpenter, Joseph Middleton. The first crew cut and shaped wood for framing the floor and roof; the second built the window frames, doors, and interior. To facilitate the work, a large wooden structure known affectionately as Carpenter's Hall was built at the present-day site of Lafayette Park. It stood until the end of 1798. Similarly, the carpenters erected a building for the stonecutters and brick workers. The crews worked, ate, and relaxed in the two halls, which were also used for Sunday religious services by the workers.

Most of the stonework on the residence was finished by the summer of 1797. At the conclusion of the project, additional skilled workers were needed. In 1798 a slater from Philadelphia named Orlando Cooke was brought in to oversee the completion of the natural stone floors and roof. The plumbing work followed and was supervised by John Emory. The chief plasterer, Hugh Densley, completed the building's main floor, rooms, ceilings, and basement in 1799. It proved to be a massive, expensive, and labor-intensive project.[20]

Aside from the name, about all that remains of the original construction is the stone. During modern renovations of the White House, artisans and preservationists with the National Park Service stripped away an extraordinary forty-two layers of paint and discovered the Scots' original whitewash, which was still preserved in mint condition and proved to be the most difficult to remove.[21] There was another remarkable finding. As the Scots were Masons, they were paid in banker marks rather than directly in wages. According to Masonic protocol, payment was based on cubic volume, and the stonecutters and builders would etch their marks on the building, indicating where to deposit the remunerations. As a result, roughly thirty different Masonic banker marks are preserved on the walls of the White House.[22]

CHAPTER 27

A House Divided

*If your love for your Selves, and for those inesteemable laws which
preserve to you the rights of human nature, was founded on Sincerity,
you could not but be Solicitous, that every Individual of whatsoever
rank or distinction, might with you equally enjoy the blessings thereof.*
Benjamin Banneker to Thomas Jefferson, 1791

espite the talents of Hoban and his European masons, the construction
projects repeatedly ran behind schedule and suffered from continued shortages of laborers. Perhaps aware of the irony of building the capital city with slave
labor, the commissioners "initially planned to import workers from Europe to
meet their labor needs" and avoid the politically sensitive situation of slavery, with
the exception of Hoban using his own three slaves. L'Enfant, after all, although
stating that he would need thousands of laborers, had not planned to use slaves.[1]

It became apparent that "most of the human elements necessary to build a
great city," however, "were missing: there were too few carpenters, bricklayers,
plasterers, or roofers; there were virtually no stone cutters or carvers; and surveyors, architects, and engineers had to be brought in from elsewhere." James
Hoban had to use his contacts back in Ireland to bring workers to the capital
city. Still, it was difficult and time-consuming to advertise for work around
the states and in Europe, and not enough workers were enticed to move to
the Potomac. Few men with the necessary skills, it seemed, were interested
in the low wages offered and in moving to a backwater region. Shortages continued and led to a disturbing development. Ultimately, delays of money and

continued labor shortages prompted the commission to revive the idea of using slaves by paying slave owners in Maryland and Virginia. As a congressional report on the capital city concluded, "The only human resource that the neighborhood could supply in abundance was . . . slaves."[2] Using enslaved laborers was a cheap and readily available, although thoroughly reprehensible, solution.[3]

Therefore, the commission decided to rent slaves from nearby slave owners for an annual fee, paid out per month.[4] Slave owners and non–slave owners throughout the South and along the Potomac had long pursued the practice of renting laborers from neighboring plantations, especially if a particular skill or trade was needed. Often these arrangements were for extended periods. The commission, for example, issued a report on April 13, 1792, stating that they were prepared "to hire good laboring negroes by the year, the masters cloathing them well and finding each a blanket, the Commissioners finding them provisions and paying twenty one pounds a year wages." The financial details included arrangements that "the payment if desired to be made quarterly or half yearly. If the negroes absent themselves a week or more, such time to be deducted."[5]

In 1792 the commission approved a request to hire forty "stought-armed Negro men" to work the quarry.[6] Quarry and stonework were exceedingly difficult, and the workers were forced to toil year-round—in hot, humid, mosquito-infested summers and in freezing winters. Enslaved stonecutters worked long hours with small rations of "pork, beef, and bread" and a "grog" break each day for a "half-pint of whiskey per day to help them cope."[7] Few others would subject themselves to such brutal conditions, prompting one white worker to observe, "The negroes alone work."[8] Indeed, it appears that black laborers were worked harder than the white laborers. For instance, Elisha Williams, hired by the commissioners to supervise Hoban's laborers, recorded that he was ordered "to keep the yearly hirelings at work, from sunrise to sunset, particularly the negroes."[9]

Collen Williamson, the Scottish chief stonemason at the time, quickly trained the slaves for the grueling task of extracting and cutting stone. In January 1793, another twenty-five slaves were rented from nearby slave owners at a price of fifteen pounds per year. They were also sent to quarry sandstone. One year later, with the progress on the "Congress House" moving slowly, the commission decided to double the number of slaves working on the new city.[10] Slave labor had become a primary facet of the effort to build a capital. Yet slave labor did not entirely resolve the financial problem; although it was cheaper than bringing skilled workers from Europe, slave owners needed to be paid for the labor, and slaves needed to be fed, trained, and supervised.[11]

Soon, slaves provided "the bulk of labor" for the city, along with free blacks and indentured servants. The worksite constituted one of the first places in America where slaves worked alongside white men and free men of color. Payroll records show that the commission listed forty-six slaves working on the presidential home and capitol building in August 1795. Slaves toiled in the quarries; were used to transport stone, wood, and supplies; did the cooking for the crews; cut down the trees on Jenkins Hill, where the capitol would be built; and were employed in the full range of construction jobs, including stonecutters, plasterers, painters, carpenters, and brick makers.

All around the capital city, including on the construction grounds of the presidential residence, there would have been the telltale signs of slavery. "Slave pens," for instance, were built on the present site of Lafayette Square beside the White House. Likewise, the boarding house that stood on the northeast corner of Third Street and Pennsylvania Avenue housed "overflow" slaves in the basement, and one of the largest slave auctions in the area was held nearby on Seventh Street. In the words of one historian, "The District of Columbia became a great slave market."[12]

The use of slave labor to build the capital city seems cruelly inevitable. Not only were Washington, Hoban, and all three commissioners slave owners, but the land ceded for the capital was from two slave states. The Potomac region also had the dubious distinction of having one of the largest concentrations of slaves in the nation at this time.[13] To be sure, the Potomac region was very much defined by the institution of slavery. It had existed in the region for generations, and as in much of the South, its economy was tied to slavery: slaves tended the fields, fished, worked on boats, built barns and homes, cleaned streets, served as coachmen and cooks, and were forced to tend to their masters' every need.

As many as 250 slaves worked at Mount Vernon, including while Washington served as president. Seven other American presidents from the South owned slaves during their time in the White House: Thomas Jefferson, James Madison, James Monroe, Andrew Jackson, John Tyler, James Polk, and Zachary Taylor. Four other presidents had slaves at one point or another in their lives: Martin Van Buren, William Henry Harrison, Andrew Johnson, and Ulysses Grant.

Nor was the practice new or unusual. Slave labor had built much of the South, and the new capital was now in the South. Public works projects and large buildings in every city in the South had been built with slave labor, including the manors of Washington, Jefferson, and Madison, as well as much of the city of Williamsburg. Ironically, slave labor helped erect Philadelphia's Independence

Hall, where both the Declaration of Independence and Constitution were debated and signed, and Boston's "Cradle of Liberty"—Faneuil Hall—was donated to the city by a slave owner who made a fortune in the slave trade. Slaves
and former slaves fought at such iconic battles as Lexington, Bunker Hill, and
Yorktown, where, with Alexander Hamilton, they stormed British artillery bat-
teries in a bold attack that secured the victory in 1781 and helped end the war.
Slaves also served George Washington and Thomas Jefferson while they were
planning and building the capital city.[14]

The first census, ordered by Congress in 1790, revealed the new nation's
population to be 3,929,827. Fully 18 percent of the country was enslaved—
over 700,000 people, the lion's share of whom lived in a few southern states,
such as South Carolina, where slaves made up 43 percent of the population;
Virginia, where they were nearly 40 percent; Georgia, where they were 35 percent; and North Carolina, where they were 25 percent. The numbers were
staggering in the South. Even the border state of Maryland's population was
32 percent slave.[15]

Accordingly, the stakes were high for southern plantation owners and politicians to retain the wretched institution, and too few leaders gave a second
thought to employing slaves to build the federal city and president's house.
Accordingly, a sizable workforce of enslaved laborers helped build the capital
city, and several slave owners who furnished laborers made a lot of money off
the construction.[16]

Commissioner William Thornton, who had been born in the British West
Indies and was appointed after the initial commissioners' terms ended in 1794,
proposed in July 1795 that they purchase slaves rather than rent them from
slave owners. The plan was to purchase slaves for a multiyear contract, then
grant them their freedom once the work was completed. Thornton hoped slave
owners would agree to the plan, reasoning, "If Negroes were to be purchased,
to have their liberty at the expiration of 5 or 6 years, it would be perhaps still
better, as no interference of the owners could then take place."[17] Nonetheless,
slave owners who stood to make more money from the rental of slaves defeated
the proposal. They also opposed any talk of emancipation, even if it involved
building the new capital. The issue was simply too politically charged in the
South and risked unraveling all that had been accomplished.[18]

Thornton prided himself on having a progressive view against slavery. He was
also proud of his appointment to the commission and of the new capital city,
gushing about his new position, "The trust reposed in us is so great that I do
not know a more extensive power in any offices of our government, except the

President, or perhaps the Secretary of State, Treasury, and War."[19] The new commissioner was bothered by the contradictions that slaves had been building the
capital city, writing, "I cannot rest when I think what I might have done, and
reflect on what I could have done. . . . I sicken at the idea. . . . God grant grace
to me, and direct me to be, if possible, a benefactor to man! I must do more than
I have ever yet done, or my name too will die." Yet this was not the only con-
tradiction. Thornton also owned slaves and, like Jefferson and Madison, owed
much of his wealth and privilege to the institution.[20]

Even though there was political opposition to any labor-for-freedom arrangement, free blacks did supplement the slave workforce. The historical record men-
tions men named Isaac Butler, Cesar Hall, Jack Fuller, and Jeremiah Holland, all
of whom were hired in 1795 and paid eight dollars per month under the names
"Free Isaac," "Free Cesar," and so on in the payroll. Holland was later hired by
the commission in 1798 to work directly for them. George Planter, another free
black, owned a boat and was hired to transport the stone from the quarry to the
construction site. Hoban also hired a few white indentured servants from their
"employers." A record from February 1795, for instance, shows that indentured
servants Peter Smith and the McCorkill brothers worked for twenty-one days
and earned "six pounds, sixteen shillings, & six pence."[21]

It is almost certain that little will ever be known about the lives of these
slave and free black laborers. Records tell us only that, for instance, "Negro
Peter," along with four slaves named Ben, Daniel, Harry, and Tom, worked as
carpenters on the presidential residence. The records also report that payments
of thirteen dollars for a woman named Nance and twenty-three dollars for slaves
named Charles, Davy, Gabriel, and Harry were made to a slaveholder named
Elizabeth Brent and her sisters, Eleanor, Jane, Mary, and Teresa (the family
owned the Aquia quarry and married into the Carroll family). Renting slaves
was easy money for slave owners and a solution to the labor shortages, and soon
plantations in the region lined up to offer their slaves.

Elsewhere, commission records show that William Beall, a member of a
prominent Georgetown family, hired out his slaves Davy, Frank, and Newton; a
man named Ignatius Boone offered his slaves Charles, Jacob, and Moses; Joseph
Green sent his slaves Clem, Jess, and Moses to work in the federal city; and
Edmund Plowden's slaves Gerald, Jack, and Tony were hired for the project. The
evidence suggests that the commissioners contracted with slave owners for three
workers at a time so as to not give one planation favor or a monopoly on the
work. Then, in 1796, after the commission ordered an astonishing one million
bricks for the capital city, slave children and women were put to work making

bricks, and the number of slaves rented per plantation was increased. Women were also hired to cook and clean.[22]

Southern planters not only obtained the capital city through the famous "dinner bargain" but were now making money off its construction. Of course, the slave laborers who toiled for months on the project did not reap any benefits from their labor.[23]

An incident arose in 1797 that prompted the commission to temporarily ban the use of slave labor from the presidential residence. It seems that the chief stonemason, Collen Williamson, who feuded constantly with Hoban, had been accusing the architect of making extra money off the project. The commissioners were notified that Hoban's slave carpenters were being paid as much as whites, which meant the architect was pocketing the funds usually reserved for white workers. Likely owing to racist jealousies, others complained about slave labor, prompting the commission to announce, "No Negro Carpenters or apprentices be hired at either of the public Buildings and that no Wages be allowed after that day to any black Apprentices without an especial order of the board." Soon thereafter, however, necessity brought slave laborers back to the project.[24]

Throughout the early nineteenth century, slaves worked at the White House and lived on the grounds. Jefferson brought with him approximately one dozen enslaved household servants from Monticello, as did his successor, James Madison. One of the fourth president's slaves, Paul Jennings, who was literate, wrote about his experience in great detail. His account, which marks the first known record of slavery in the White House, began, "When Mr. Madison was chosen President, we came on and moved into the White House; the east room was not finished, and Pennsylvania Avenue was not paved, but was always in an awful condition from either mud or dust. The city was a dreary place."[25]

A few years later, after the British burned the capital city during the War of 1812, enslaved people were used to rebuild public buildings, including the White House and Capitol.[26] Slave labor continued to be used in the city; most every government building continued to rely on slavery in some capacity. Not only was this source of labor cheap and manageable but it was abundant.

In the early 1800s in Virginia and Maryland, tobacco began to be replaced by wheat and other less labor-intensive crops, making slavery less necessary to run a plantation. This coincided with the ban on importing new slaves in 1808, the rise of cotton in the Deep South, and the westward expansion of slavery, all of which put additional pressures on the region's slave owners. The answer for many planters was to lease their slaves as laborers in the capital city. Tragically, the prevalence of slavery became a visible and viable part of the city.[27] This would continue.

Through the nineteenth century, freed blacks came to the city in droves. By the time of President Zachary Taylor's death in 1850, freed blacks in the city outnumbered slaves by almost two to one. That year Congress abolished the slave trade in the District of Columbia as part of the Compromise of 1850. President Lincoln signed the Emancipation Act of April 16, 1862, finally outlawing the "peculiar institution" in the district, freeing an estimated three thousand slaves and prefiguring his more famous proclamation that following January 1.[28]

Historian Bob Arnebeck noted of the problem in determining an exact number of slaves who worked on the city and the extent of their contributions that "not much was written about them."[29] Indeed, an accurate number "cannot be determined due to the scarcity of documentation." However, records do indicate that the building of the capital city relied on slave labor and that their contributions to the city "were essential." A report by the architect of the US Capitol concluded, "There is enough information to know that the role they played had a significant impact on the project." That same 2004 report, commissioned by Congress, concluded, "No one will ever know how many slaves helped to build the United States Capitol—or the White House" because the experiences of most slaves were never recorded. It is, however, undeniable that slaves built many of the public buildings in the city, including the White House and Capitol.[30] It is also undeniable that many whites at the time thought little of the irony of the capital being built by slavery.[31]

The problem of assessing the role of slavery in the capital city continued after the construction. Richard Baker, Senate historian, and Kenneth Kato, associate historian of the House of Representatives, coauthored a foreword to the aforementioned report. In it, they stated, "Indifference by early historians, poor record keeping, and the silence of the voiceless classes have impeded our ability in the twenty-first century to understand fully the contributions and privations of those who toiled over the seven decades from the first cornerstone laying to the day of emancipation in the District of Columbia."[32]

Nevertheless, the task force found records of 385 payments for "Negro hire" from 1795 until 1801. Today, a plaque in the US Capitol Building commemorates the role of slave labor in its construction.[33] Relatedly, in 2016 the outgoing first lady, Michelle Obama, addressed a large animated audience at the Democratic National Convention. In her remarks the first African-American

First Lady shared her feelings about the honor of waking up every morning in the White House but commented on the emotion she felt knowing the home had been built by enslaved workers. Despite the furor occasioned by her comments among her critics, the First Lady was correct. It is undeniable that slave labor built the White House—and the capital city.

PART VI

LEGACY

CHAPTER 28

Washington (Never) Slept Here

The Federal City would soon grow of itself and spread as the branches
of a tree do towards where they meet with most nourishment.
L'Enfant on the capital

W ashington was intimately involved in every facet of the president's house, from the first day of construction through the next seven years. It was his passion. As early as August 2, 1792, he was on hand to rethink the location for the home's foundation because he preferred a better sight line with the building that would become the Capitol. He settled on a small ridge. But the angle of the home would need to be turned slightly, which affected the diagonally aligned boulevards laid out by L'Enfant. The house was no longer on the axis of Pennsylvania Avenue as L'Enfant had preferred. The commissioners suggested a slightly different angle for the home. However, Washington personally drove the stakes into the ground, marking his preferred spot. It would be on the site designated by L'Enfant but on the far northern end of the lot.[1]

Washington and L'Enfant also selected the site for the Capitol Building, which would be situated on the opposite end of the grand boulevard some distance from the home. Four years later he selected the location for the executive buildings, including War, Treasury, and the Navy.

Stonemasons were often given ample latitude during construction. This was the norm in Europe, where chief stonemasons were often also master builders.

While the stonemasons working on the presidential home were permitted minor improvisations, Hoban's only real collaborator in the construction was the president. The two men partnered on all the necessary alterations to the home during its construction. They were in constant contact with one another and worked well together, which is readily apparent from their surviving correspondence. When Washington intervened and requested a change, Hoban complied, but he was also free to make suggestions, and the president often accepted them.[2]

Although the president liked both L'Enfant's vision for the home and Hoban's architectural plans, he made several minor adjustments and a few significant changes. The most obvious was that the home was on a much smaller scale than L'Enfant's palace, although Washington then requested to increase the size of Hoban's plan by a fifth. Second, the home was to be three stories but had to be reduced to two stories. Washington wanted the third story but was told it could be added in the future when the financial situation was improved. Third, Washington also reluctantly eliminated the basement and had to forgo the marble floors.

Another major change was that the stone building became a stone-brick hybrid. Washington felt strongly about the presidential home and "Congress House" being built entirely of stone. Stone was nature's most durable building material, and it would emulate the great ancient structures, providing the city and new nation with the grandeur Washington envisioned. However, the commissioners were told there might not be sufficient stone reserves in the Aquia Creek quarry and that, even if there were an adequate supply, they lacked the funds to continue digging and there were too few stonemasons. Brick was more readily available, less time-consuming, and far cheaper.

As a result, the first floor of the home was made of stone. However, in 1793, Washington agreed to use the Aquia Creek sandstone only as a stone facade for the outer walls of the second floor, which were then backed by a thick layer of brick. He had resorted to similar architectural "bluffs" when renovating and expanding Mount Vernon, once thickening paint with crushed sandstone in order to pass wood off as stone. The president was, however, successful in adding a number of ornamental embellishments to the building despite their costs.

Hoban had estimated the house would cost $200,000, a figure Washington thought was overstated but proved to be the opposite. This was but one example of the larger financial problem. The failure to plan for the funding of an entirely new capital city would repeatedly threaten the project. Congress would not—and could not—continue to authorize sizable loans because Washington and the commissioners had greatly overestimated the amount of funds that could be made by selling lots in the city.

For instance, Commissioner Carroll once boasted to a concerned James Madison, "The sales of lotts will produce at least 300,000 pounds for public use. This with the grants from Virga & Maryland will amt to near a Million of dollars." However, even the initial public auction, with Washington, Jefferson, and Madison all on hand in Georgetown, was a disaster. It rained, L'Enfant refused to bring along the maps of the lots, and only thirty-five plots were sold, raising a paltry $2,000. A hastily organized second auction was also a failure.[3]

Still, Washington and Hoban were undeterred, soldiering on despite the cuts and adapting the scale and construction of the home accordingly. Hoban was even redrawing the home through 1793, after a full year of construction.

The sides of the home were built to resemble one another, but the front and back—or north and south ends—of the building were designed to be different. Both had ornamental cornice trim around the windows and a rusticated basement, but there were structural differences that distinguished them. The north side was conceived as the front, so it would feature the main doorway and contain some of the best stone engravings and carvings in the home.

The home was rectangular and had four attached Ionic columns and a pediment surrounding the entrance, modified from the Corinthian columns of Leinster House. Washington referred to the design as the "frontispiece." Hoban added more engravings, such as an eagle and rays of the sun, carved into the stone of the frontispiece to enhance the home.

Modifications to the home would continue for years to come. Over time, practical additions were added. For instance, Hoban's initial plan lacked the iconic North and South Porticos and the now-famous West Wing. The grounds would later contain the famous Rose Garden and much more. Hoban's original plan called for a raised basement, partially visible above ground, but this was canceled owing to cost overruns. The home's porch was also removed, but 160 years later, the Truman Balcony would be added, to the delight of most every president since then.[4]

Washington visited the construction site for the rest of his life, often expressing impatience with the progress. In June 1797, after he had stepped down from the presidency, he wrote optimistically, "The President's house will be covered in the autumn."[5] However, the building was still behind schedule, and the final work on the walls and roof were not yet complete.

To Washington's disappointment, the mansion remained an object of ridicule. Few people shared Washington's enthusiasm for the building. Oliver Wolcott, the secretary of the treasury, writing to his wife three years later and after the Independence Day celebration in the unfinished city in 1800, commented that the home "will render its occupant an object of ridicule with some and of pity with others." Harsh words! Wolcott would go on to note such practical concerns as "It must be cold and damp in winter, and cannot be kept in tolerable order without a regiment of servants."[6]

That same year Congressman John Cotton Smith of Connecticut recorded his impressions of the home and capital city:

> Our approach to the city was accompanied with sensations not easily described. One wing of the Capitol only had been erected, which with the President's house, a mile distant from it, were shining objects in dismal contrast with the scene around them. Instead of recognizing the avenues and streets portrayed on the plan of the city, not one was visible, unless we accept a road, with two buildings on each side of it, called the New Jersey Avenue. The Pennsylvania leading, as laid down on paper, from the Capitol to the Presidential mansion, was then nearly the whole distance a deep morass covered with alder bushes.[7]

It took time for the people to fall in love with the White House and for it to become the internationally recognized symbol that it is today. The construction would last eight years with a total price tag of a whopping $232,372, the equivalent of over $65 million today, and would be the largest home in the country until the late 1860s.

The White House would be different from any other mansion in the country and any residence of a head of government in the world in several ways, which is still the case. It blended French, English country, Irish, Greek, and neoclassical designs and, in so doing, became distinctly American. It was always Washington's project, just as it was his vision for the city and home that he hoped would help him realize his goals for a strong, stable government and united nation.

Today, the White House functions as a residence, museum, office complex for staff and the press corps, the seat of executive power, the focal point of the US government, and much more. The home has welcomed heads of state from around the world who arrive at the columned North Entrance and then are greeted by the president there or in the Yellow Oval Room on the second floor.

Other guests, including the public and those attending the many events hosted at the building, walk through the East Entrance. Its many ceremonies, from presidential appearances on the grand stairway to salutes of rolling drums and "Ruffles and Flourishes" to welcoming announcements of "Hail to the Chief," all herald the nation and blend architecture, politics, and nationhood.

The building is also the most famous address in the world today. The building's history chronicles the story of the nation and its people. From this residence Thomas Jefferson received news of the acquisition of the Louisiana Territory, doubling the size of the young country, and also prepared the Lewis and Clark expedition to traverse and document the vastness of the continent.

The building was burned in August 1814 when the British invaded the capital city during the War of 1812. Then, with typical American indefatigable spirit, it was rebuilt. It was witness to Abraham Lincoln's trials and tribulations during the Civil War and housed both the Emancipation Proclamation and Gettysburg Address.

From within its walls Franklin D. Roosevelt oversaw Allied operations during World War II and the momentous landings at Normandy on D-Day. And it was within the White House's walls that President Richard Nixon recorded in his diary on July 20, 1969, after watching humanity's first lunar landing, "The President held an interplanetary conversation with Apollo 11 astronauts Neil Armstrong and Edwin Aldrin on the Moon."[8]

The White House has been home to every First Family since 1800, witnessing the birth of presidential children and grandchildren; the passing of presidents, their wives, and their children; and the trials and triumphs of the nation. Yet for all Washington's visionary efforts and the building's grand history, it is one of the nation's historic residences where the Founder would never sleep.

CHAPTER 29

A Pedestal Waiting
for a Monument

E pluribus unum. (Out of many, one.)
Senate Chamber

George Washington and Pierre Charles L'Enfant, the original architect of
the capital city, had worked together to select the site for the Capitol
Building. L'Enfant had decided it was to sit at the east end of the National Mall
on an eighty-foot crest known as Jenkins Hill, described by L'Enfant as "a pedestal waiting for a monument."[1] It was indeed a superb location.

Washington had repeatedly pressed his architect for the designs, but L'Enfant
put him off by saying it was "in my head." L'Enfant was supposed to design and
oversee the construction of the building, so with his resignation and with no architect or firm plans, Thomas Jefferson suggested a design contest.[2] Washington
and the commissioners again agreed to a contest, and the secretary of state announced the event in March 1792.

As they had for the president's house, the commissioners—Thomas Johnson,
David Stuart, and Daniel Carroll—placed advertisements inviting submissions,
which were due "before the 15th day of July, 1792." The commissioners realized
that this job would be far larger and more complicated than a presidential home.
It would be the largest construction project in the country. In addition, they
lacked the money and labor to break ground for the project. The announcement
noted, "Drawings will be expected of the ground plats, elevations of each front,

and sections through the building." In particular, they advised that the new home for the Congress include the following items:

A conference room
A room for Representatives to contain 300 persons each
A lobby or antechamber to the latter
A Senate room of 1,200 square feet of area
An antechamber and lobby to the latter
Twelve rooms of 600 square feet area each for committee rooms and clerks[3]

The winner would receive $250 or a medal and a lot in the city. As was the case with the presidential residence, Jefferson appears to have seen the contest as a way to exert his influence on the design and size of the building. A scaled-down hall for Congress, yet one superior to the executive mansion, would reflect his Democratic-Republican ideology. In fact, anticipating the removal of L'Enfant, the secretary of state had asked his friend and French architect Stephen Hallet to begin preparing designs for the Capitol back in the closing weeks of 1791.[4]

When Jefferson announced the contest for the Capitol, he described an understated brick building with a simple conference room, a place where both chambers could convene. The secretary of state offered few specifications other than the details listed in the public announcement. What he did do, however, was continue to promote his vision for a small "town" with a few modest buildings and an understated house for Congress.[5]

Once again, Washington was displeased with his fellow Virginian's proposal. He envisioned something far larger in scale, a building of Greco-Roman inspiration, and one that included offices for the president. This second major disagreement put a strain on what was otherwise a respectful relationship. Both men were eager to see the submissions, but financial difficulties and fate intervened. In 1791 and 1792 the value of stocks had plummeted, rendering the new nation's currency nearly worthless. The economic downturn was such that Congress even considered putting the entire project on hold. Therefore, and with Washington otherwise engaged in the presidential home, Jefferson pushed to delay and scale back the proposals. Writing to the commissioners, he suggested, "You have certainly heard of the extraordinary crush which has taken place, here at N York and Boston, of persons dealing in paper, & or goods merchants and others who had dealings with paper-men. It has produced a great stagnation of money contracts, which will continue till it is known who stands and who falls, during this crisis. . . . This will oblige you to keep back some of your operations."

Jefferson was only too happy to have the funding reduced, as this would achieve his goal of scaling back the congressional "house" and the entire capital city.[6]

Despite the enormous scale of building a capitol, the contest generated a lot more submissions than the contest for the presidential residence. By mid-July seventeen plans had been received. While there was no obvious front-runner, five of them captured Washington's attention. On July 16 and 17, Washington, Jefferson, and the commissioners began the task of judging the five main contenders.

Jefferson pushed for his friend Hallet's neoclassical design, which was likely organized with his input. Some scholars believe the secretary of state may even have submitted his own plan anonymously, as he had done with the earlier proposal for a simple brick residence for the president. Despite Jefferson's rhetoric about republican simplicity and understated public buildings, Hallet's plan was the fanciest and most expensive. Jefferson's love of architecture seems to have overridden his political ideology and previous opposition to most everything having to do with the capital city. In fact, the Hallet submission was so elaborate that the commissioners requested the architect scale back his design.

In addition to Hallet's plan, there was a submission by Leonard Harbaugh, an architect who had designed and was currently building the "Federal Bridge" from Georgetown into the city. He interrupted his work long enough to submit his design for the Capitol. Another attractive proposal came from a builder in Alexandria named Robert Lanphier. Then, in late July a design was submitted by George Turner, a judge living in the Northwest Territory. The commissioners liked it and had it sent to Washington, who had recently returned home to Mount Vernon.[7]

Samuel Blodget Jr., who had been assigned to engrave the map of the new city and help secure loans to cover its construction costs, submitted the fifth plan. Blodget, a self-taught architect and economist, used the Maison Carèe in Nîmes, France, as his inspiration. One of the best preserved of the ancient Roman temples, it was built around the year 20 BCE under the rule of Augustus. It was certainly ambitious, and its Roman inspiration appealed to Washington.[8] However, during the review of his plan, Blodget lectured the commissioners in a dismissive tone, noting, "I hope I shall be pardoned if I remind you that full elevated columns and the Dome has been admired by all ever since they were invented, so say all the modern connoisseurs. Therefore I hope no new fretters will take the place of noble ancient Grecian and Roman principles, the results of the experiences of ages."[9] The financier even demanded that his design be viewed at the distance of three yards and only in "good light" in order to appreciate its genius.[10]

Blodget's attitude, more than the expense of his design, seems to have doomed his chances, which was a good thing. The financier went on to become embroiled in a real estate scheme in the capital city that landed him in prison in 1802. He later attempted to redeem himself by raising funds for the establishment of a national university. Sadly, most of the submissions for the Capitol have been lost to history, and we are left with only vague descriptions in letters of most of the proposals.

After the second round of reviews, Washington and the commission had yet to make a decision but seemed inclined toward the plan from Judge Turner. Concerned that Turner's design would be selected, Jefferson acted with haste by asking the commissioners to invite Hallet to visit the site for the Capitol. In a surprise twist Washington warmed to Hallet's design, writing to the commissioners that he was "more agreeably struck with the appearance of [the Hallet plan] than with any that has been presented to you."[11]

In typical Washington fashion, he began to make architectural adjustments to the design, "correcting" the outside columns by noting that they should be in a "semicircular projection at the end," adding more committee meeting spaces to the building because "there appears to be a deficiency," and to Jefferson's dismay, increasing the size of the rooms and building. What really caught the president's attention, however, was the proposed dome over the center building. It would, he said, "in my opinion, give beauty & grandeur to the pile; and might be useful for the reception of a Clock – Bell &c."[12] Washington was also considering combining elements of Judge Turner's plan with Hallet's design, only on a larger scale with more columns and colonnades.

With the contest still undecided, the president not fully sold on any one plan, and the process delayed by a lack of finances, a letter arrived in October from the British West Indies from William Thornton, a Scottish physician living there. He requested the opportunity to submit a plan past the contest due date, and the commissioners granted the request, most assuredly on instructions from Washington, who appears to have known of Thornton and admired the man. Washington may even have used back channels to reach out to Thornton, who was friends with Judge Turner and had won a similar design contest to develop the Library Company Building in Philadelphia in 1789.

The following spring the sketch was submitted. Washington instantly liked what he saw, applauding its "grandeur, simplicity and convenience." Thornton's plan, which included a large building in three sections—a central domed building flanked by two rectangular wings, one for each chamber of Congress—was accepted by the commissioners on April 5, 1793, and placed into consideration for the contest. That July Washington made his decision and selected Thornton's plan. He instructed the commission to hire Thornton to assist James Hoban, the architect of the presidential residence. The next month Washington and the commissioners appointed Hoban as the superintendent architect overseeing the construction of the entire city. Washington may also have helped select the surveyors, builders, and supervisors for the Capitol.[13]

Jefferson and L'Enfant had referred to the building as the "Congress House," while others involved called it the "Hall of Congress" or "Congress Hall." However, the massive structure became known as the Capitol Building, a "nod" to Jefferson and Virginians who called their statehouse the "capitol." On September 18, 1793, Washington placed the cornerstone at the southeast edge of the building in a public ceremony.[14]

The next task was to clear Jenkins Hill of trees. The commission requested the "best axe-men" for the task, but cutting down such a large, thickly wooded area and digging out the root systems would be time-consuming and backbreaking work. With workers reluctant to undertake the job, the commissioners assigned the project to a crew of slaves. After the hill was cleared, it was surveyed. Stakes were driven in the ground marking its boundaries, the foundation was set, and more stone was quarried. Without additional funding, however, the actual construction on the building would not begin until February 11, 1795, when a skeleton crew began preparing the foundation in the dead of winter.[15]

Thornton lacked experience with such a monumental project, and progress on construction lagged. Therefore, the commissioners employed two other architects to help him. The assistants included Stephen Hallet (likely a nod to Jefferson by Washington and the commission) and George Hadfield, both of whom had submitted unsuccessful plans for the contest. However, both assistant architects would attempt to make unauthorized changes to the design of the building, which went against Washington's preferences, their charge by the commission, and the winning design. Both were fired. Even though James Hoban had his hands full with the presidential mansion, Washington and the commissioners assigned him responsibility for the Capitol Building as well. A number of problems awaited him.

Construction was far behind schedule, and the lots designated to finance the building remained unsold. The supplies of brick and stone were insufficient for a building of its size, and the stonemasons and crews making bricks were threatening to walk off the job.[16] Amid the threats, the supervisor of all the stone cutting and masonry vanished. He did not just walk off the job; he stole roughly $2,000.[17] Theft on the construction sites was widespread, and after the supervisor had disappeared, workers walked off with tools, supplies, and even wood. Then, when it appeared things could not get worse, in July 1795 the Capitol's foundation wall collapsed. It was so poorly built, what remained had to be knocked down and rebuilt. The embarrassing development seemed to be symbolic of the entire project.

CHAPTER 30

Temple of Liberty

Union, Justice, Tolerance, Liberty, Peace
Rostrum in the House of Representatives

There were other problems delaying progress on the Capitol. A financial scandal erupted in 1795 that further threatened the project. Robert Morris and John Nicholson had purchased hundreds of lots in the federal district, helping to finance the capital and hoping to make money off their resale. However, both speculators had trouble making their scheduled payments when the lots stopped selling. Soon all funds for construction were depleted, and the president worried that the financial crisis and the "endless disputes," as he described them, with landowners and Congress would undermine the entire project. Washington complained to the two men, saying there were "serious consequences, which must inevitably result" if a payment was not made immediately.[1]

Washington called an emergency meeting on August 19 with his commissioners: Gustavus Scott, Dr. William Thornton, and Alexander White, who were appointed to replace their predecessors. "Besides arresting the work in the present critical state, & compelling the discharge of some valuable workmen, who may never be recovered," the government needed money in order to continue construction. Morris and Nicholson's inability to pay, he worried, "would throw such a cloud over the public & private concerns of the City, & would be susceptible of such magnified & unfavorable interpretations, as to give it a vital wound."[2]

Neither man was able to pay the tens of thousands of dollars owed. Morris, the former superintendent of finance during the war, was bankrupt and on his way to debtors' prison. The Capitol project was in limbo.

The project fell even further behind schedule after another year without a full construction crew working on the building. Congress considered whether to abandon the project altogether and simply plan to meet in the president's house whenever it was completed. Fortunately, Washington settled on having the Capitol built in phases.[3]

The crisis prompted Washington and the commission to hire the Italian-born English architect George Hadfield on October 15, 1795, to supervise construction on the building and assist Hoban. Hadfield toured the site and informed the commission and Congress of the state of affairs. It was not pretty. "I find the building begun, but do not find the necessary plans to carry on a work of this importance, and I think there are defects that are not warrantable, in most of the branches that constitute the profession of an architect, Stability—Economy—Convenience—Beauty," he wrote quite candidly. He provided examples such as "deformity in the rooms, chimneys and windows placed without symmetry," and he noted the entire foundation, whose floor plan and heights did not match, was "in a state not to be depended on." It was a shocking assessment. The British architect concluded, "No progress can be made this season or perhaps the next."[4]

By August 1796 the commissioners had instructed Hoban to use any spare funds designated for the mansion and focus all his efforts on the North Wing of the Capitol so that at least something would be finished when Congress arrived in the city after a decade in Philadelphia. Then, in October 1797 the commission ran out of funds and could not pay the construction crews and architects. Questions remained as to what would happen when construction was scheduled to resume in the spring. Fortunately, at the end of 1797, Maryland provided a much-needed loan of $100,000 in order to complete the Capitol and public buildings. The crisis was averted. The commissioners notified the new president, John Adams, on May 7, 1798, to reiterate the earlier proposal: "We consider the existing orders as sufficient authority for us to proceed with the building; but to secure the completion of the North Wing of the Capitol, and the finishing whatever buildings may be commenced, in due season, we mean at present only to contract for one of the executive buildings, and as soon as that shall be undertaken, to discontinue the work on the interior of the President's house."[5]

The massive project had other impacts. The region was sparsely populated. It lacked a sufficient number of homes, beds, supplies, workers, and most everything else needed for the new capital. However, the scope of the Capitol project was such that it produced an economic windfall for residents living in and around the city. It generated jobs—roughly two hundred laborers were hired for the Capitol, making it the largest construction project at the time in the country. Workers rented rooms, local residents sold land, and newcomers opened businesses to accommodate the construction workers and many visitors. Yet, the slight economic boom emboldened some landowners and builders to inflate their costs, gouging the government and workers living in the city. The area also encountered growing pains in other ways.

With the shortage of funds and looming deadline to complete the Capitol and city, the commission and construction supervisors again turned to slave labor. Additional free blacks, white indentured servants, and slaves were hired. Once again, slave owners made money off the construction. So many free blacks and enslaved laborers arrived in the federal district that Georgetown passed racial codes, including one back in 1795 that forbade groups of five or more blacks from congregating together in one location. Harsh penalties and punishments, including public whippings, were doled out to slaves and free black workers for breaking the law—or for being suspected of breaking the law.[6]

The use of slave labor did not subside. Rather, by the end of the project as President Adams prepared to move to the city in 1800, roughly half the workers at the Capitol were slave laborers. So prevalent was the reliance on slavery that the commission did not try to keep it a secret.

Not long after the Capitol was finally completed in the 1820s, the building that had been referred to as the "Palace" or the "Congress House" gained a new nickname. It was called the "Temple of Liberty," an entirely fitting term as it embodied the ideals of freedom and equality, yet an ironic one given its history.[7]

With the new government scheduled to move to the new city in two years, Hoban was forced to prioritize which projects to complete and which ones would remain unfinished. On a shoestring budget and grit, he and his workers rushed to make the deadline. However, more of the same marked the final two years of construction before the 1800 deadline. Partisan rancor would over-shadow the (partial) completion of the Executive Mansion and Capitol and the official move of the seat of government to the City of Washington. The political decay in the late 1790s caused by the two forming political parties was, of course, very discouraging to Washington. He had hoped that the new city would unite the nation. Instead, from his retirement at Mount Vernon, he watched the nation fall further into the grip of bitter political division.

The two opposing political factions that had emerged in the 1790s, the Federalists and Democratic-Republicans, used partisan newspapers to report the "news" from one perspective or another. By the time the government moved to the new capital, there were 184 newspapers functioning across the country, and a good number of them were anything but reliable; indeed, before the journalistic standards of the twentieth century, most papers of the age were little more than hearsay or obviously partisan. Jefferson even kept "reporters" on retainer, ensuring a steady stream of attacks against the Federalists, namely, John Adams and Alexander Hamilton. At the same time, leaders of both factions wrote under pseudonyms attacking one another. They also hired proxies to fight their fights in the pages of the papers.[8]

Some of these battles centered on the capital city and the high costs of construction. Washington's beloved project endured blistering criticisms despite being so close to completion. Some newspapers maintained that the capital should have remained in Philadelphia; others continued the old anti-federalist (now Democratic-Republican) line that the new city was overly extravagant and resembled a European capital. The result was paranoia over an allegedly all-powerful and intrusive government that spilled over into the pages of the opposition press and congressional debates. The Democratic-Republicans peddled fear by going so far as to claim that Washington and the Federalists decreed that portraits of European monarchs be displayed at all government buildings. Of course, this was unfounded rubbish.[9]

They also demonized Alexander Hamilton, who had been Washington's secretary of treasury until 1795, and claimed he would return to the new city, where he would assume power and banish anyone who opposed him. Long before present-day attack ads and yellow journalism, the Jeffersonian Republicans alleged that Hamilton was also planning to bring along one of his whore-mistresses to tell the citizenry what to do. Later, in 1800, when a fire raged through the War Department, the Jeffersonian-leaning press went so far as to use the incident to suggest that Federalists had set the fire in order to destroy the records of their crimes. Despite the sensational nature of the attacks, some people believed them, and partisan rancor again threatened the capital city.[10]

The divisiveness would not get better after the election in November 1800 and debut of the new capital city that same month. In fact, it likely worsened owing to the contested race and controversial vote. It proved to be an election for the history books: the first election without Washington alive, the first election with political parties, and a contest between two of the nation's Founders. The result was even more intriguing: a tie. While Thomas Jefferson bested John Adams, the

Electoral College vote ended in a 73–73 tie between Jefferson and Aaron Burr, his would-be vice president. When Burr opportunistically opposed Jefferson, fully thirty-six ballots were needed in the House of Representatives to break the tie.[11]

Jefferson would assume the presidency, but in a tainted process and only after the surprising support of his sworn enemy, Hamilton, who, believing the former secretary of state to be the lesser of the two evils, helped to swing the final House vote in Jefferson's favor. The "Revolution of 1800" swept the Federalists from office and brought the Jeffersonians and the new Democratic-Republican Party to power. They would go on to enjoy two terms under Jefferson followed by two more terms each by James Madison and James Monroe. Washington's life's work and his capital were again threatened. The capital was open but was far from complete.

The debut of the presidential home and Capitol were, like the new capital city itself, underwhelming. Surprisingly, many newspapers largely neglected the otherwise momentous occasion of the relocation of the seat of government, opting instead to cover alleged scandals and the ongoing feuds and intrigues of the parties.

Hoban barely managed to complete the first phase of the Capitol—the North Wing—in time for the opening of the first session of Congress on November 17, 1800. Yet "complete" meant that there were walls and a roof overhead; few rooms were finished, and both chambers of Congress, the Supreme Court, and the Library of Congress were forced to share the cramped Senate quarters. The condition of the Capitol and other public buildings, along with the challenges of communication and transportation at the time, were such that the final transfer of power from Philadelphia to the federal district could not be completed until June 1801.[12]

The new capital city was also a city in name only; it was still very small town in character with an estimated 366 homes, with just one-third of them made of brick. The population hovered around 3,000, with the census showing 109 "heads of household." The entire federal government boasted only a few hundred employees. There were few lawyers, physicians, pastors, or teachers; few boarding homes and roads; and a general lack of amenities. The mile-long "grand boulevard" connecting the presidential mansion with the Capitol was a rutted dirt path still containing stumps and bushes, while the town was bordered by cornfields, woods, and tidal marshes. The National Mall was still a pasture for cows, a cherry orchard grew just off Pennsylvania Avenue, and locals fished in a pond in the heart of the city.

One amusing account of the city joked that the only way to get to, or travel within, the new capital was by "coach or telescope." It was also nearly impossible to travel at night, and local law enforcement had yet to be fully organized. Despite the primitive conditions, the new Democratic-Republican Congress delayed the allocation of funds for enhancing the roads or streetlamps. One visitor in 1800 from New York described a harrowing experience: "I took a [ride] after dinner to visit Nath'l Maxwell and . . . I considered my life in danger. The distance on straight lines does not exceed half a mile, but I had to ride up and down very steep hills, with frightful gullies on almost every side."[13] Another visitor commented, "I am here in the woods. The works of art not yet numerous enough to conceal those of nature."[14]

Some of Congress and government officials were also less than impressed by their new capital. Senators and representatives arriving in the city had trouble finding housing, and many were forced to share a room and bed at one of the handful of boarding houses in the town. One member even grumbled that Theodore Sedgwick of Massachusetts, because he was the Speaker of the House, was the only one with a bed to himself. Representative Roger Griswold of Connecticut was even less charitable, writing home with a succinct description of the city as "both melancholy and ludicrous."[15]

Indeed, there was little to do socially or culturally in the new city and few restaurants. A theater finally opened in August 1800 but closed the next month. There was even a lack of houses of worship, forcing different denominations to share the Capitol Building on Sundays, with clergy borrowing the podium of the Speaker of the House. One Scottish Presbyterian congregation huddled in the corridor of the Treasury Building to worship, while an Episcopalian priest called his flock to service in a tobacco house.[16]

Fortunately, not all the reports of the new city were negative. A newspaper in New York published a letter from a visitor to the new capital city in 1800 who at least was balanced in his description, writing,

> It is impossible for me to describe, or you to conceive the impression which the first view of this metropolis of our vast empire made on my mind; nature has bestowed here her best gifts. . . . The city is laid out fancifully enough, and if the buildings already erected had been concentrated, it would wear a rich and splendid appearance, but they are widely separated, the intervening spaces are filled with a confused mixture of stumps, trees, huts, lime-kilns and brick yards.[17]

After the capital city opened, the Office of the Commissioners was disbanded in 1802. The commissioners were replaced by a superintendent of the City of Washington, a post filled by Benjamin Henry Latrobe, who trained as both an architect and engineer. The following year Congress finally allocated funds to continue construction on the unfinished Capitol Building. With the new funds, Latrobe added more rooms to the Capitol and streamlined the construction process, making it far more efficient. The building was finally finished under Latrobe's supervision. Members of the House of Representatives were able to move into the South Wing in 1807, and the chambers for both wings were completed in 1811. Latrobe also redesigned the interior, making it far more spacious and useful, and added a chamber for the Supreme Court.

Tragically, the War of 1812 intervened. Just three years later, on August 24, 1814, British forces set fire to the building and parts of the city as retribution for Americans burning the Canadian capital of York a year earlier. A sudden and violent thunderstorm saved parts of the building, while President James Madison and his formidable wife, Dolley, saved the city by pressuring Congress not to relocate the capital.

Latrobe was brought back to oversee the reconstruction of the building in 1815. Congress met in various locations throughout the city, including Blodget's Hotel on Seventh and E Streets NW. More than simply reconstruct the Capitol, the architect refurbished it, changing the interior and making numerous other enhancements, such as adding marble after a rich vein of the precious material was discovered along the upper Potomac. The finished product at long last fulfilled Washington's plans for marble to be used in public buildings.

However, frustrated with a lack of funds and political opposition, Latrobe resigned his position in November 1817. Charles Bulfinch, a Boston architect, replaced him. Bulfinch completed Latrobe's work, including restorations of both legislative chambers, but he also redesigned the central part of the building, made the dome higher, and oversaw the effort to landscape the grounds. He finished his work in 1829.[18]

The crowning glory of the Capitol is a fitting metaphor for the building and nation. Atop it, at a height of 288 feet, sits the *Statue of Freedom*, designed by artist Thomas Crawford. It was commissioned to represent freedom triumphant. Ironically, Crawford had planned three statues to be considered for the project, one of which was a bronze figure of "Armed Liberty," wearing a "liberty cap," which was the symbol of freed slaves. The plan was halted by opposition in the South organized and led by Secretary of War Jefferson Davis, who would later lead the Confederacy during the Civil War and who was in charge of overseeing construction at the Capitol. The secretary of war complained, "Its history renders it inappropriate to a people who were born free and should not be enslaved." Davis threatened to withhold funding unless the statue was changed. The artist acquiesced and, working from his studio in Rome from 1855 to 1857, depicted freedom in female form wearing instead a version of a Roman military helmet. It features "freedom triumphant" with a military helmet (a nod to George Washington's vision), holding a sheathed sword (symbolizing war) in her right hand and a laurel wreath (symbolizing peace) and shield of the United States with thirteen stripes in her left hand.[19]

Davis approved Crawford's third design in April 1856. The project, however, was nearly undone when the sculptor died suddenly a year later, just after completing the statue. His widow had the massive nineteen-and-a-half-foot, fifteen-thousand-pound statue disassembled and shipped across the Atlantic in six crates in the spring of 1858. It almost did not arrive. The ship took on water and was forced to sail to Gibraltar for repairs. Before arriving in America, it again began leaking, and the captain was forced to dock in Bermuda for additional repairs. During the process the crates were unloaded and placed in storage. A lack of funds again undermined the project, along with a mistake regarding the exact location of the statue. It stayed in Bermuda for months.

Finally, a few of the crates arrived in New York's harbor in December; the remainder did not arrive until March 1859. Congress requested assistance in reassembling the figure and placing it atop the dome. They also wanted a plaster replica to be displayed on the grounds of the Capitol. An Italian artist familiar with the project was approached about completing the work but asked for too much money. Yet again, the project was nearly derailed. The figure and model were again placed on hold.

A sculptor from South Carolina named Clark Mills had recently moved to the capital city and opened an iron and bronze foundry. Mills offered to help. A few years earlier he had won a competition and built an equestrian statue of Andrew Jackson for Lafayette Park. The impressive monument caught the attention of Congress and now-senator Jefferson Davis. Mills was hired to reassemble the grand statue and produce a likeness of it. He assigned the job to his slave Philip Reid (sometimes listed as "Reed" in historical sources), whom he had purchased in Charleston for $1,200.

From June 1860 to May 1861, Reid worked seven days a week recasting the enormous statue. However, the commencement of fighting in the Civil War in 1861 put the project on hold yet again. On April 16, 1862, President Lincoln signed the District of Columbia Emancipation Act, which granted all enslaved people in the federal district, including Reid, their freedom. Without Reid, the statue remained incomplete. At the end of 1862, however, Reid, described by his former owner as "smart in mind, a good workman in a foundry," was hired to complete the job.[20] After completing the *Statue of Freedom*, Reid fittingly changed his name to Freed. On December 2, 1863, Lincoln ordered the statue be placed atop the Capitol. A thirty-five-gun salute marked the long-awaited occasion.

It is doubtful that George Washington or members of the early Congress would recognize the Capitol Building of today. It sits at the head of the eastern end of the National Mall on four acres atop an eighty-eight-foot hill with a breathtaking view of two long rows of some of the world's finest museums. It is a majestic 751 feet in length and 350 feet wide (at its widest point) and boasts 540 rooms and 658 windows. Graced by its famous dome, the Capitol is one of the most architecturally impressive buildings in the nation and most recognizable structures in the world.

The Capitol is now a meeting place for Congress, the location of some of the country's finest art and sculpture, a resting place for great Americans, and a museum for the American people that hosts some four million visitors per year. The "Temple of Liberty," despite being burned, rebuilt, renovated, and restored, is a monument to the ingenuity and perseverance of the American people and a tribute to the vision and determination of George Washington.

CHAPTER 31

The Father of His Country

His example was as edifying to all around him,
as were the effects of that example lasting.
Washington Monument

By 1796, his last full year in office, Washington was exhausted. He felt all of his sixty-four years—his hearing, eyesight, and memory had deteriorated—and he believed he was at the end of his life. Usually indefatigable, he had become disillusioned with the relentlessness and bitterness of the opposition to "his" capital city and the rise of partisanship and divisiveness in the new nation's politics. In fact, the political situation was such that Hamilton, Jonathan Trumbull, (the governor of Connecticut), and other Federalists begged Washington to reconsider and remain in office. John Adams, they worried, could not live up to the impossibly high bar set by his predecessor.

The former general declined, even demurring that he no longer had "personal influence." In a rare display of pessimism, he complained that character, accomplishment, and loyalty to the nation no longer seemed to matter in politics. "The line between Parties," he wrote to Governor Trumbull, had become "so clearly drawn" that members of Congress "regard[ed] neither truth nor decency; attacking every character, without respect to persons—Public or Private—who happen to differ from themselves in Politics." Of his "unprincipled" opponents, he said, "Let that party set up a broomstick, and call it a true son of Liberty . . . or give it any other epithet that will suit their purpose, and it will command their votes in toto!" Washington had never sidestepped a challenge or shirked responsibility, but he put an end to any further talk of remaining in office. The principles of republicanism were at stake. Moreover, he reminded his supporters, returning to his pessimistic frustration, "I am thoroughly convinced I should not draw a single vote from the Anti-federal side."[1]

Washington had devoted much of the last decade almost singly focused on building a great capital city in hopes of imbuing his fellow citizens with a sense of unity and nationhood. It appeared to him that he had fallen short. Exactly like his hero, the great Cincinnatus, he would relinquish power and return to his farm, a shining example to his fellow citizens and, if not his entire reputation, at least with his civic virtue intact.

Therefore, the president announced his retirement by way of a Farewell Address given to his Cabinet on September 15. James Madison had composed an early draft of the Farewell in 1792, when the president contemplated stepping down after a single term. However, in the intervening years Washington's relationship with Madison had been tested, in part over the struggle to build the capital city. Thus, the president asked his loyal, longtime aide Alexander Hamilton to assist him in an extensive rewrite. Washington proofed the final version and approved. It was part sentimental—a wistful look back at the founding years—and part hard-headed advice about how to govern. The written announcement opened:

> The period for a new election of a citizen to administer the executive government of the United States being not far distant, and the time actually arrived when your thoughts must be employed in designating the person who is to be clothed with that important trust, it appears to me proper, especially as it may conduce to a more distinct expression of the public voice, that I should now apprise you of the resolution I have formed, to decline being considered among the number of those out of whom a choice is to be made.[2]

In the Farewell, which was published in Philadelphia's *American Daily Advertiser* on September 17, the president reminded his countrymen of the birth of their nation. He also turned the nation's attention to the future, again calling for a national university to be built in the new capital. Washington's main points, however, had less to do with policy or his achievements than with sage advice.

In his Farewell the president cautioned against foreign entanglements and warned that the sectionalism and partisanship that defined the politics of the 1790s threatened unity. Again attempting to stay above the fray and unify his country, Washington did not identify his critics by name or by party. However, the source of his aggravation was the Jeffersonian Republicans who had gained followers and seats in Congress and with their new influence had grown increasingly personal and aggressive in their criticism of the Federalists, government, the capital city and presidential mansion, and even Washington.

Washington knew that many of his countrymen remained far more loyal to their states or regions than to the nation. Still hoping to promote national unity and an American identity, the Founder bemoaned the ugly "spirit of revenge" that was pervasive in the politics of the era, saying instead that the people "must always exalt the just pride and patriotism more than any appellation derived from local discriminations." He cautioned against this brand of "factionalism," as he called it, and the "geographic discriminations, Northern and Southern, Atlantic and Western" that caused citizens to "excite a belief that there is a real difference of local interests and views." All this, he maintained, threatened to supplant service to the common good and the demagogues masquerading as leaders who would use parties "to subvert the power of the people and to usurp for themselves the reins of government."[3]

Relatedly, the president touched on the paranoia about the federal government and attempted to assuage the people's fear by reminding them that it was the union that bonded them together and that their "independence and liberty" were not only dependent on one another but also the by-product of the "common dangers, sufferings, and successes" they had experienced.

With characteristic humility, Washington closed the Farewell by admitting, "I may have committed many errors." He offered his hope for the new nation:

> In offering to you, my countrymen, these counsels of an old and affectionate friend, I dare not hope they will make the strong and lasting impression I could wish, that they will control the usual current of the passions, or prevent our nation from running the course which has hitherto marked the destiny of nations. But, if I may even flatter myself that they may be productive of some partial benefit, some occasional good; that they may now and then recur to moderate the fury of party spirit, to warn against mischiefs of foreign intrigue, to guard against the impostures of pretended patriotism; this hope will be a full recompense for the solicitude for your welfare, by which they have been dictated.[4]

Most important, Washington stated what many Americans thought they would never hear: he would retire at the conclusion of his term in four months.

Although he had said as much at the start of that second term, many of his fellow citizens—and a few of his critics—believed he would continue to serve. Yet Washington was determined to step aside, worried that, should he pass away while in office, his presidency would be seen as a lifetime appointment. Rather, by resigning he would establish the principle of citizen-statesmen. Washington assured the country he was no longer needed; the experiment in self-government and the republic he led would now outlive him, and his two-term limit would eventually be enshrined in the Twenty-Second Amendment to the Constitution.[5]

The Farewell Address remains relevant today, especially the message of unity. Its timeless wisdom set the tone for all future presidential farewells and is unequalled in its merits. For many years it was read aloud on the anniversary of Washington's birth, and it is still recited in the US Senate, a tradition that dates to the Civil War.

That second term in office ended on March 4, 1797, and Washington looked forward to retirement, announcing in grand fashion, "I begin my diurnal course with the Sun." He departed the office to much fanfare and widespread adulation. Large crowds, cannonade salutes, and mounted escorts marked his every move, including on the trip back to Mount Vernon.

Yet not everyone was sad to see the hero of the revolution leave office. Washington's reputation was showing signs of wear and tear after eight years in office and so many difficult political battles, including over the capital city. In fact, even his farewell was not spared. A future president sitting in the congressional chambers refused to applaud or salute the president after his visit to the House—Andrew Jackson, then a young congressman from the new state of Tennessee and still fuming over the Jay Treaty with Great Britain and the growth of the federal government and capital city.[6]

Some Jeffersonian Republicans now mocked the former president as "Old Washington" or "the Royalist," a smear suggesting he was a monarchist. They even began a critical revisionist assessment of his generalship during the war, one utterly divorced from fact. Samuel Adams, the influential former leader of the Sons of Liberty who had come to loath Washington, joined in the condemnation. Another critic was the firebrand Thomas Paine, whose influential pamphlets helped light the spark of revolution. The noted pamphleteer went so far as to call the president "a patron of fraud" and a "hypocrite in public life." One Republican from New Jersey offered the following toast to his departure: "A despot from the South, with Democracy on his lips and tyranny in his heart!"[7]

Several Democratic-Republican newspapers repeated such criticisms. The *New York Journal* chimed in suggesting the president had "aristocratic blood" and cared not for republican government.[8] The *Aurora*, based out of Philadelphia, claimed that Washington had taken far more than his presidential salary of $25,000. Benjamin Franklin Bache, the publisher of that newspaper, had been such a constant critic of the president that famed historian Gordon Wood said of him, "No editor did more to politicize the press in the 1790s."

As Washington departed office, Bache offered a particularly scathing critique of his presidency:

If ever a nation was debauched by a man, the American Nation has been debauched by Washington. If ever a nation has suffered from the improper influence of a man, the American Nation has been deceived by Washington. Let his conduct then be an example to future ages. Let it serve to be a warning that no man may be an idol, and that a people may confide in themselves rather than in an individual. Let the history of the federal government instruct mankind, that the masque of patriotism may be worn to conceal the foulest designs against the liberties of the people.[9]

Another constant critic of the president was the man known as "the Poet of the Revolution," Philip Freneau. While Washington was still in office, Freneau, a friend and political supporter of both Jefferson and Madison, used newspapers to level his attacks. Of the man he called a "monarchical farce," the poet said, "He holds levees like a King, receives congratulations on his birthday like a King, makes treaties like a King, answers petitions like a King, employs his old enemies like a King . . . swallows adulation like a King and vomits offensive truths in your face." Freneau also turned his quill to Washington's beloved capital city, writing cynically,

An infant city grows apace,
Intended for a royal race,
Here capitols of an awful height.
Already boast upon the site,
And palaces for embryo kings,
Display their fruits and spread their wings.[10]

Washington even encountered criticism from his home state. Elected officials in Virginia—though the state had received the honor of hosting the capital city—had opposed their native son on several issues and spoke out viciously against him. When Washington departed the presidency, Federalists in the Virginia House of Delegates promoted the idea of a proclamation thanking the president for a lifetime of service and for his "virtue, patriotism, and wisdom." The Democratic-Republicans in the legislature opposed the congratulatory gesture but later softened their opposition to simply striking the word "wisdom" from it. However, the influential John Marshall, who would soon go on to serve as Chief Justice, successfully reinstated the full description.[11]

Soon a chorus of condemnation appeared in print. The spirit of nationalism and unity Washington had long sought was, at best, turning into mockery amid calls of naiveté and incompetence; at worst, it was being subverted amid allegations of royalism and treason among southerners and Jeffersonian Republicans. Rather than unity, the country seemed in the grips of paranoia and fear over the power of the new federal government and its capital city. At the center of both concerns was Washington, even after his passing. In the 1800 election that brought Jefferson to power, his supporters even used the "unrestrained ambitions" and corrupting evils of the capital city as a campaign issue.[12]

Despite the criticisms it is undeniable that the legacy Washington was leaving behind was nothing shy of remarkable. The federal government was established, executive offices were created, courts were developed, and a new capital city was set to be unveiled. With Hamilton's bank and debt assumption, the nation's financial situation was headed in the right direction. Washington, through his every action and inaction, had produced countless important precedents—social, military, and political—for the new republic and presidential office, most of which are still in use today. The new government had legitimacy in the eyes of the world thanks to Washington's guiding presence. Treaties and trade agreements had been signed and alliances forged.

Washington ended his term and traveled to Mount Vernon with his family. On the way he stopped in the city named for him to inspect the progress. What he saw must have been devastating. The roof on the mansion was incomplete and its floors were wooden rather than the expensive marble he wanted, only a third of the nearby Capitol was nearing completion, temporary shanty homes dotted the landscape, and construction equipment littered the grounds of the unfinished buildings. Despite the condition of the city in front of him and bitter partisanship he left behind in Philadelphia, Washington would have taken solace in the fact that the capital was located on his beloved Potomac and was at least being built.

CHAPTER 32

'Tis Well

First in War, First in Peace, and First in the Hearts of His Countrymen.
Henry "Light Horse Harry" Lee, Washington's Funeral Oration

In retirement George Washington busied himself by putting his home and farms back in order. After years of neglect Mount Vernon was soon buzzing with activity and reaping the benefits of his return. Less than two years after his retirement and just five months before his death, Washington also reworked his will. In it the plantation owner made a detailed, thirty-page inventory of his vast land holdings, accounts, and assets and was careful that his wife would be well off after he was gone. The man who never attended college bequeathed money to educational institutions and arranged to have all 125 slaves under his name freed (others were under the Custis estate of his wife and her grandchildren).[1]

Washington shared his view of being home with his former muse, Sally Fairfax. In a letter written in 1798, he noted, "Five and twenty years, nearly, have passed away since I have considered myself as the permanent resident of this place; or have been in a situation to endulge myself in familiar intercourse with my friends, by letter or otherwise." He added, "Worn out in a manner by the toils of my past labour, I am again seated under my Vine & Fig tree." The former president was understated in summing up the events of the past quarter century with Ms. Fairfax, then a fatigued Washington confided, "My wish is, to spend the remainder of my days (which cannot be many) in rural amusements—free from those cares which public responsibility is never exempt."[2]

Washington's two terms as president ended on March 4, 1797, but his passion for and involvement with the capital city remained for him a priority. He was intimately involved in the details of the capital city's construction. It was his pet project, so to speak, during his retirement. Just as he had done during the turbulent years of debate surrounding the city from 1789 to 1791, he traveled often to the site to inspect the buildings and construction. One of the first items of business after he had left office, for instance, was to visit the capital city, even before arriving home.

The *Washington Gazette* described the affectionate response of soldiers and citizens who "saluted" and welcomed the former president back to the city with open arms. The paper described the president being "followed by repeated *huzzas*, dictated by hearts sensibly alive to his merits."[3] Washington was back in Alexandria in early May—only two months into his retirement—to work with the commissioners and the capital's architects and builders. He returned to the capital a few days after that and was back to inspect the progress on July 17, 1797.

These "inspections" of what he described as the "Fedl. City" continued in 1798, with Washington taking his wife to see the city that May. Again, on September 21 and 22, he was back in the city and "examined in company with the Comrs. some of the Lots in the Vicinity of the Capital and fixed upon No. 16 in 634 to build on." Washington purchased Lot 16 on the west side of North Capitol Street, between B and C Streets, for $535.71 and paid for it in three installments, beginning that year. He planned to build two boarding houses in the city that bore his name. Sadly, the houses were not finished before Washington's passing, and one later burned in 1814 and the other was torn down in 1908. Washington was back in October for three days and continued to dine and communicate with the commissioners and visit "his" city throughout the following year.[4]

The former president continued his correspondence with the builders, leant his powerful voice to the project during possible political setbacks, and offered advice to Hoban, Congress, and others. Washington's interest in the city and visits to the site clearly did not diminish in retirement, which is evidence in both his correspondence and diary. He remained proud of the presidential mansion and city, despite the slow progress and numerous vocal critics of the capital. The latter contributed, however, to Washington becoming somewhat jaded about politics in his final years, although he still believed in the city's potential to unite the people and promote a spirit of nationhood.

On November 9 and 10, 1799, the former president recorded in his diary, "Viewed my building lot in the Fedl. City." Sadly, that would be the final time Washington would ever set eyes on his cherished city. But it did not mark the end of his interest in the capital. In early December Dr. David Stuart, one of the men Washington had appointed to the commission, dined and spent a night at Mount Vernon. The two likely discussed the state of construction on the city, which was nearing completion and the date for the government to relocate from Philadelphia.[5] As late as one week before his death, the former president was still promoting the capital and trying to prompt crews to hurry the work, complaining that, at the current pace, it would take a "full century" to finish the city.

Perhaps Washington's final recorded words on the capital were written on December 8, when he notified the commission, "By the obstructions continually thrown in its way, by friends or enemies, this city has had to pass through a fiery trial. Yet, I trust will, ultimately, escape the ordeal with éclat." Instead of a fiery trial it would have been more appropriate to have said, it has passed, or is on its passage through, "the ordeal of local interest, destructive jealousies, and inveterate prejudices; as difficult, and as dangerous I conceive as any of the other ordeals."[6] It was one last example of a familiar refrain for Washington.

Just four days later, on Thursday, December 12, Washington mounted his horse to inspect his farms at Mount Vernon, a routine he completed every morning and afternoon. Never one to rest on his laurels or be content with his vast land holdings, Washington was planning a new fishpond and improvements to the farms and his home. However, that day the weather took a turn for the worse. A storm kicked up and temperatures dropped. After five hours out, Washington returned home shivering, recording in his diary, "About 1 o'clock, it began to snow—soon after to hail and then turned to a settled, cold rain." Tobias Lear, the family's longtime aide, recalled that his employer "appeared to be wet and the snow was hanging upon his hair." By midday Washington was stiff and hoarse. The weather and his sore throat kept him inside that afternoon, but when the weather cleared before dinner, Washington went back outside to identify some trees by the river to be cut.[7]

With her husband's apparent recovery that afternoon, Mrs. Washington had gone to visit her relative Nelly Custis, who had recently given birth. When the former First Lady returned home, she encouraged her husband to retire early to regain his health. He chose to sit by the fire reading the newspaper and discussing Virginia politics with Tobias Lear. In particular, the two expressed dismay at the growing prestige of James Monroe, another mentee of Jefferson. Washington retired late that evening. Outside the snow was still falling.

Around 2:00 a.m. on the thirteenth, Washington awoke and was having difficulty breathing. He showed the signs of a fever. Mrs. Washington was also awake and concerned. She wanted to summon a physician and called for a servant, but her husband dismissed his situation. Mrs. Washington had recently been ill, and he requested that she not bother herself, as she needed her rest. He would be fine in the morning, he assured her. It is, of course, impossible to think Mrs. Washington would have been able to rest. A natural worrier who had suffered through so many deaths of family members and close friends, she likely spent the night worrying.

Sure enough, by morning Washington's condition had worsened. Mrs. Washington rushed downstairs to fetch Lear and the household servants, one of whom lit the fireplace and opened the blinds. Mrs. Washington sent one of the slaves for a doctor and another to get Albin Rawlins, one of the overseers at Washington's farms. Rawlins arrived and was asked to bleed Washington, a common medical practice at the time. A reluctant Rawlins hesitated but was coaxed by Washington, who groaned, "Don't be afraid . . . cut . . . but small cut." Rawlins barely nicked the president, who responded, "The orifice is not large enough."

A nervous Rawlins managed to get a half pint of blood out of Washington, who was now clearly in the throes of a severe fever and having trouble breathing. Lear swabbed Washington's throat with an ammonium carbonate substance. The president murmured, "Tis very sore." The aide then recommended medicine, but the president whispered, "You know I never take anything for a cold. Let it go as it came."[8]

Dr. James Craik, a Scot and the physician general of the US Army, arrived later that morning around 11:00. Craik and Washington were old friends who had served together in both the French and Indian War and the Revolutionary War. The elderly, overweight physician deemed the ailment to be "an inflammatory infection of the upper part of the wind pipe." Washington dressed and sat by the fireplace for two hours as Craik tried a variety of treatments. One involved a soothing syrup, but Washington choked on it. Another was a concoction of vinegar, butter, and sage tea, but Washington's throat was so swollen and inflamed that he could neither swallow nor speak. He again choked. Seemingly desperate for relief, the doctor used an old technique from apothecaries; he placed the toxin from a "Spanish fly" (an emerald-green beetle) on the inflamed throat. It was all to no avail.[9]

Craik believed his patient would not recover, so he consulted with Mrs. Washington and Lear and recommended they seek the services of Dr. Gustavus Richard Brown, another Scot who lived nearby and was thought to be the best physician in the area. Lear immediately drafted a note saying, "Mrs. Washington's anxiety is great, and she requests me to write you desiring you will come over without delay, as it is impossible for the General to continue long without relief." A rider was dispatched with much haste.[10]

Washington was deteriorating at an alarming rate but managed to record an entry in his diary on the thirteenth: "Morning snowing and about 3 inches deep. Wind at northeast and mercury at 30. Continuous snowing till 1 o'clock and about 4 it became perfectly clear." It would be his final diary entry.[11]

By evening the scene in the bedroom was worrisome. Dr. Brown arrived and recommended Washington be bled again and administered a medicine designed to reduce the swelling in Washington's throat. Rawlins was instructed to cut into the president again. Mrs. Washington squeamishly protested, but her husband gave his consent, and they continued to bleed him until a full pint of blood was removed. Neither remedy worked. Dr. Brown then had the servants bring a steaming kettle to the room and had his patient breathe the vapors. The tall, powerful president was unresponsive and was soon covered in blood and sweat from the "treatments." Everyone in the room began to realize Washington would not recover.

Hoping to find an elusive cure that was escaping them, and as a final effort, the physicians sent for Dr. Elisha Cullen Dick of Alexandria. The noted physician had studied medicine under the illustrious Benjamin Rush, the most famous medical doctor in the country. Dr. Dick arrived and proceeded with a third round of bloodletting; twice poured calomel, a white, tasteless chemical compound used as a purgative, down his patient's throat; and held a vinegar vapor to his nose. Washington vomited and choked violently. The physicians then administered an enema to clear their patient's bowels.[12]

The primitive state of medicine at the turn of the eighteenth century was taking its toll on Washington and most certainly contributed to his premature demise. Indeed, had nothing at all been done, he would have stood a far better chance and likely would have recovered. The president was now gravely weak and unable to speak or breathe.

Dr. Dick proposed an emergency tracheotomy, arguing that the small incision in Washington's throat would allow him to breathe, but the two other doctors opposed the little-known procedure. The effort was abandoned on a two-to-one vote. Dr. Dick always maintained that the tracheotomy would have saved Washington, later commenting, "I shall never cease to regret that the operation was not performed." Washington's fever worsened.[13]

As the inevitable was at hand, Tobias Lear tried to remain positive for everyone gathered around the bed. However, Washington alone seemed to accept what was happening, "with perfect resignation," as Lear described. With Lear holding Washington's hand, the former president rasped, "I feel myself going" and gave his final orders in a weak and strained gasp. He wanted riders to bring Lawrence Lewis and his grandson, but they were traveling and not expected home for a few days. Lear was instructed to "arrange and record all my late military letters and papers. Arrange my accounts and settle my books . . . and let Mr. Rawlins finish recording my other letters." Mrs. Washington was sent downstairs to get the will from Washington's desk. There were two copies, and she was advised to burn the old one.[14]

To his old friend from the war, Washington whispered in a faint and strained voice, "Doctor, I die hard, but I am not afraid to go. I believed from my first attack that I should not survive it." It was time. The servants, physicians, and family gathered to bid farewell. Washington, in great discomfort, resigned himself to his situation, saying, "I thank you for your attentions, but I pray you to take no more trouble about me. Let me go off quietly. I cannot last long."[15]

Drs. Brown and Dick stepped out of the room, while Dr. Craik remained with friends and family. Then, to tears and sobs, at 10:00 Washington whispered to Lear "I am just going. . . . Have me decently buried, and do not let my body be put into the vault in less than three days after I am dead. Do you understand me?" The aide responded in the affirmative. Interestingly, Washington did not, through the ordeal, ask for a minister or last religious rites. Stoic until the end, Washington simply reached over and took his own pulse and groaned, "Tis well." The man who had survived many battles, close calls with enemy bullets, and years of living outdoors in Spartan conditions was gone at 10:34 in the evening of December 14. He was sixty-seven.[16]

Of the scene in the room, Lear recorded simply that "the general's hand fell from his wrist. I took it in mine and put it into my bosom. Dr. Craik put his hands over his eyes." Washington, he noted, "expired without a struggle or a sigh." Mrs. Washington, who remained at the foot of the bed crying, asked, "Is he gone?" When Lear confirmed, she managed to repeat her husband's words, "'Tis well," adding, "All is now over. I shall soon follow him. I have no more trials to pass through." The widow moved out of the bedroom the couple had shared for four decades, never to step foot in it again.[17]

As word spread of the loss, there was a nationwide outcry of emotion and grieving. Cities held parades, and Philadelphia staged an elaborate display with a mock funeral. Congress made a request of Mrs. Washington to have the president's body interred in the Capitol. Martha Washington had been as dutiful as her husband, always complying with the countless requests that came from being the wife of Washington. She too shared a sense of duty and service. But in a rare gesture, the former First Lady did not comply with the congressional proposal. Her husband would be buried at the family vault at Mount Vernon.

Other gestures of remembrance and commemoration poured forth. In May 1800, with the new government preparing to move to the City of Washington, Representative Henry Lee of Virginia promoted the idea of a marble monument for the great Founder's remains and requested that a large statue of Washington on horseback be placed in front of the Capitol. Representative Robert Goodloe Harper of South Carolina suggested a mausoleum in the shape of a pyramid be erected to house Washington's remains. Representative Roger Griswold of Connecticut supported the grand gesture. Reflecting Washington's long-held vision, he hoped the memorial would promote patriotism and unity in the nation. "The grandeur of the pile will impress a sublime awe on all who behold it," Griswold announced. "It will survive the present generation. . . . It will receive the homage of our children and our children's children; and they will learn that the truest way to gain honor amidst a free people is to be . . . virtuous."[18]

The Jeffersonian Republicans who came to power through the 1800 election, however, disregarded these tributes and others. Insulted by the lack of appreciation, Representative Lee, who had served in the war with Washington and was known affectionately as "Light-Horse Harry" for his service, thundered that European monarchs built better memorials to their mistresses. What one scholar referred to as "monument mania" ensued, with proposals and counter-proposals in Congress. No one wanted to look unpatriotic. Under mounting pressure, Jefferson's party proposed a few modest recognitions. The House of Representatives also narrowly passed a measure in January 1801 for a mausoleum and appropriated $200,000 for its construction.[19]

However, once again, the unity was only fleeting, and partisan bickering ensued. The cost of the tribute was also quite high for a nation still on shaky footing. The Scottish rabble rouser, James T. Callender, who wrote for a pro-Jefferson newspaper, lashed into the proposals. Later, in a rare moment of poignancy and honesty, he argued that the money would be far better spent on "the survivors of the old continental army."[20]

The controversy even spilled over into the political campaigns of 1800 and 1802, when the Jeffersonian Republicans used criticisms of the bank, capital city, presidential mansion and Capitol, and now the planned memorial for Washington to energize voters. The attacks outraged Hamilton, who came to the city's defense, reminding the public it was "a favorite of the illustrious Washington."[21] The tributes were all either defeated or, after endless debate, resigned to inaction.

Despite his party's position, Jefferson, whose complicated relationship with Washington had nonetheless been one of mutual respect and civility, praised the great Founder's life and deeds. A few years earlier Jefferson attributed the successful struggle for independence to Washington, writing that the "moderation & virtue of a single character has probably prevented this revolution from being closed as most others have been, by a subversion of that liberty it was intended to establish." Jefferson added that, even when the famous Founder was wrong, he alone erred with integrity, reminding his colleagues that Washington "did not sacrifice the public good in order to maintain his own fame and popularity." The former secretary of state also remembered that the general "often declared to me that he considered our new constitution as an experiment on the practicability of republican government, and with liberty man could be trusted for his own good; that he was determined the experiment should have a fair trial, and would lose the last drop of his blood in support of it."[22]

Jefferson was not alone in his praise. The *Connecticut Courant* celebrated not just the leader but the man, stating, "Many a private man might make a great President; but will there ever be a President who will make so great a man as WASHINGTON?" Indeed. Perhaps no words ring out over the years quite like those of Washington's friend, the noted Henry Lee, who, in his famous funeral oration after the president's passing, described him as "First in war, first in peace, and first in the hearts of his countrymen."[23]

Professor Gordon Wood, the foremost scholar of the Revolutionary era, said of the Founder's legacy, "Washington was an extraordinary man who made it possible for ordinary men to rule. There has been no president quite like him and we can be sure that we shall not see his like again." Of the tribute by Lee, Professor Wood observed that the description should not have "ever-weakening meaning" over time. It is too easy to forget just how great a leader Washington was, just as many Americans today take for granted the privileges of living in a nation he, more than any other, forged. Rather, Wood suggested, "Washington ought to be first in the hearts of all Americans, even two centuries later."[24]

Revolutions often beget tyrants. Even the French Revolution, which broke out the year Washington took the oath of the presidency, resulted in Napoleon declaring himself emperor. But the American Revolution was a historical exception. It produced the concept of popular sovereignty and a republic led by a man uncorrupted by ambition and riches, a leader who twice stepped away from power. That man who rose from humble beginnings adopted as his motto words from Joseph Addison's famous play *Cato*, "'Tis not in mortals to command success." Yet ironically, he did. Washington employed his political skills and influence, but not for the purpose of making himself a king; rather, he devoted his considerable gifts to building a capital from which the government could operate, one intended to inspire and unify the people and promote a commitment to the principles of liberty and self-government.[25]

Washington was, as was pointed out early in the book, in many ways an unlikely leader. Yet in other respects he was a natural leader. Perhaps none of the other Founders, for all their gifts, but Washington could have managed to win the Revolutionary War, preside over a constitutional convention, forge a new nation, and build a capital city that would give the fledgling government credibility, unite the fractious country, and unify the people under a spirit of nationhood. Washington was a man of seeming contradictions: he exuded a kingly demeanor yet was the father of liberty; he wore the trappings of power and command with ease but had enjoyed neither a privileged nor inspired upbringing; he exuded leadership, though was prone to insecurities about his intellect and oratory; he was intensely private but rose to fame as the foremost public man of his times; he is heralded as "the Father of His Country," although he remains somewhat unknowable to us even today; he has been lauded for roughly two and a half centuries for his courage, integrity, and judgement, but history has largely ignored the "other" side of Washington as a man of great vision, political savvy, and the ability to take bold risks.

Tragically, George Washington did not live to see the government move to the city he envisioned, dying only months before the new capital's unveiling. On his passing the capital was still quite controversial. Unfinished, underfunded, behind schedule, and but a smattering of houses and buildings, it was an object of ridicule by many.

The government of the United States was only a decade old when Washington passed. It was, more than any other factor, his staunch, unwavering advocacy for the federal government, capital city, and nation, along with his vision for all three that allowed the fledgling experiment in self-government to succeed. As the historian of the capital city Robert James Kapsch concluded, "It was Washington's vision that triumphed."[26]

Washington had envisioned, then planned almost every aspect—its location, size, design, buildings—of the new capital city that would house the republic. Without Washington there would have been no capital city. But for Washington, the visionary architects Pierre Charles L'Enfant and James Hoban would not have been hired. Absent his powerful presence and ceaseless advocacy, the promise of a unifying symbol for the new nation would not have been realized. Even the memory of Washington after his death continued to inspire the construction and completion of the capital.

As one scholar stated unequivocally, "There is no mistaking it, George Washington himself was building the city."[27] The capital was Washington's life's work. Even the radical notion of inviting newspapers, the public, and Congress to weigh in on questions about the construction of a capital city was a unique phenomenon in history. Nearly alone in his grand ambitions for the city, he recognized that the design of the capital and its buildings would ultimately shape the nation and help to unify the people in a spirit of nationhood. The rural, sparsely populated country would, in Washington's vision, be a great power, just as his capital would serve "beyond the present day" as his "city for the ages." And it would.[28]

Washington had long been the public face of the nation and government, and his example served as the very image, if not epitome, of republican virtue and service. He accomplished much more than could have been expected and in a remarkably brief period and against all odds.

Poetically, after years of bitter debate about where to locate the capital and the importance of "geographic centrality" to the decision, it turned out that Washington's Mount Vernon home was the virtual epicenter of the new nation. His preferred site along the banks of the Potomac sat equidistant between North and South and, thanks to his beloved Potomac, helped to connect the Atlantic Seaboard with the emerging West. Yet as the old saying suggests of his extensive travels, Washington slept in many homes, tents, and villages around the land but never slept at the presidential home in the city he built.

The capital city remained in the forefront of the general's thoughts and priorities until his death, and had he lived a bit longer, he surely would have been on hand for the inaugural festivities for the government's official relocation to the mansion, Capitol, and city. Those privileges would be for John Adams, who disappointingly played virtually no role in any pomp and pageantry surrounding the investiture of the new city and its public buildings.

Martha Washington lived two and a half years beyond her husband, passing on May 22, 1802. During that time and in the years that followed, Congress continued to request to have the body of the man who helped create the nation. However, family descendants refused. The body would remain at Mount Vernon, where it rests today. Ultimately, Washington would get his much-debated and postponed memorial. It would be in the form of a 555-foot-tall obelisk begun in 1848 and completed in two phases. When it was opened in 1884, it was the tallest building in the world, and appropriately, it sits in the center of the National Mall in the city that is his lasting memorial.

The Building Is in a State to Be Habitable

*May none but Honest and Wise Men
ever rule under This Roof.*

John Adams

Six months after Washington's death, President John Adams met in Philadelphia with the three new commissioners for the federal district. The president and Congress were scheduled to officially move to the new capital in the late fall of 1800, which was just a few months away. It was time to start making plans for the relocation of the government. Adams also had to tend to such practical matters as shipping his personal furnishings. The commissioners assured the president that his personal items and office would be moved and that the presidential home would be completed in time.

Adams, who had taken virtually no role in the capital's design or development, decided to visit the city before returning home for the summer. It was his first visit to the site. After the June meeting with the commissioners, he traveled to the soon-to-be capital to inspect the progress. Joining Adams were his wife's nephew William Shaw, who served as a presidential secretary, two footmen, and a coachman. As the coach traveled outside Philadelphia, they had their first taste of what was to come. The roads turned into bumpy dirt trails, and it appeared to Adams's party that they were heading into an area filled with little more than agricultural land and woods.

On the outskirts of the federal district, they were met by an escort who took them to the Union Tavern in Georgetown. After a small ceremony there in the president's honor, the Adams entourage continued its journey the next day across Rock Creek Bridge into the City of Washington. The scene before them was one of disorder. Buildings in various stages of construction stood along dirt trails and partially cleared fields and forests. Construction and debris were strewn across the grounds of each building. Workers seemed to outnumber residents, and the presidential home and Capitol were nowhere near completion.

The president observed optimistically that "a sufficient number of rooms" were under construction in the mansion, but none were finished, meaning he could not stay at the presidential mansion. Adams and his party had trouble finding a suitable place to sleep. He ultimately found rooms at Tunnicliff's City Hotel, where he entertained visitors and attended a few social ceremonies. All told, Adams was eager to leave the area. He saw no possible way that the presidential mansion and Capitol would be ready for the November deadline, but the commissioners again assured him the city would be ready. They were planning, it appeared, for a very productive summer and fall. On the way to Massachusetts, Adams detoured to Mount Vernon to pay his respects to Mrs. Washington, then set off for Quincy to see his wife and family.[1]

After a pleasant and extended visit to Massachusetts, Adams bid a temporary goodbye to his wife and family, who would join him later, and departed on October 13, 1800, for the new capital city. One can only imagine his anxiety about moving into the new presidential mansion and wondering if it was even ready. Moreover, the presidential election was pending the next month.

The commissioners knew that Adams would be leaving Massachusetts on October 13 and guessed he would arrive in the capital city around November 3. They therefore inspected the presidential mansion in the morning of November 1 and, to their horror, observed that it was not ready for its first resident. In fact, it was not even close to being ready.

The first family had shipped furnishings, china, and clothing, which had arrived before them, so the commissioners had the items quickly delivered to the mansion. There was, however, no place to have them stored. Nor were the items unpacked and arranged. The commissioners assumed they had another day or two. As they scrambled to figure out what to do, President Adams arrived unannounced that very afternoon—a Saturday, at 1:00. His coach was accompanied unceremoniously by only his longtime steward John Briesler, on horseback.[2]

What the president saw was troubling. The idea of the United States was not quite a quarter century old, and the government had been formed just over one decade earlier. The census that year would show that only 3,210 people—mostly men, with a male-to-female ratio of 18 to 1—lived in the City of Washington, including roughly 620 slaves and 120 free blacks. Only 14,093 people resided in Alexandria, Georgetown, and the rural areas that made up the ten-mile-square federal district. There had been little progress made on the city since the president's inspection that June. Consequently, he was welcomed by unpaved streets, rutted trails, tree stumps, bushes, few people, and still fewer homes, businesses, or boarding houses. It was certainly not yet the metropolis, center of commerce and culture, governing capital, or "City for the Ages" Washington had envisioned.

The mansion was large and its exterior impressive and promising, but it was unfinished. The building was cold, damp, unlit, unstaffed, and sat in the middle of a dirty construction site. Only twenty-six rooms had walls and about half were plastered. Only a few had wallpaper, which was still drying. Consequently, buckets of wall paste made of white flour and beer, along with plaster thickened with hair from hogs and horses, still sat about the place. Not surprisingly, it smelled as awful as one might expect. The family furnishings and clothing, which had been shipped by sea, then up the Potomac, were still in their containers sitting about the house unpacked. Some of it had been broken or lost en route.[3]

Making matters worse, Adams had arrived alone and understood that he was now to govern in a city that bore his predecessor's name from a home conceived by his predecessor. Indeed, Washington's shadow had loomed large for Adams since the day he took office, and it promised to be ever more the case in the new capital. Always cognizant of his lack of the very traits that endeared Washington to many and the inevitable comparisons to Washington, Adams had lamented, "I expect to be obliged to resign in six months."[4]

Newspapers were particularly unkind to Adams, which was made all the worse by the growing influence and power of the opposition party and his hotly contested bid for reelection against Jefferson. It did not help matters that Adams was perhaps even more thin-skinned and sensitive to criticism than Washington and had aged poorly, though he would live a very long life. Sixty-two when he entered the office, Adams was having difficulty speaking and writing and suffered from frequent colds and an array of maladies. He had also lost his teeth. Yet the stubborn Adams refused to wear dentures. Around the time he moved to the new capital city, he grumbled, "I am old, old, very old. . . . I shall never be very well—certainly while in this office, for the drudgery is too much for my years and strength."[5]

The press and his critics constantly pointed out that he was not Washington, and the *Aurora*, printed by the rabid Democratic-Republican Benjamin Franklin Bache, went so far as to describe him as "the old, querulous, bald, blind, crippled, toothless Adams." Others called him "His Pomposity" and "His Rotundity." At 5′6″ in height, Adams had gained an unhealthy amount of weight and even referred to himself in his diary as "puffy, vain, conceited."[6] So too could he be prickly and argumentative, and he was ever conscious that he lacked Washington's natural charm and charisma, admitting that there are "few people in this world with whom I can converse. I can treat all with decency and civility, and converse with them, when necessary, on points of business. But I am never happy in their company."[7]

He also worried about the office bankrupting him. Unlike his predecessor or his successor, he was not extremely wealthy. For instance, when hosting an Independence Day party in Philadelphia, Adams purchased $500 worth of cakes, rum, wine, and other celebratory items, but the cost set him back dearly. Now, the prospects of living in the unfinished mansion were unsettling. Adams immediately realized he would need to purchase everything, as "There is not a chair fit to sit in. . . . The beds and bedding are in a woeful pickle."[8]

However, it was not all bad. Word of his arrival spread quickly throughout the city and region. Numerous well-wishers showed up at the mansion to welcome the capital's most famous resident, and soon, spontaneous ceremonies broke out throughout the city. Despite the state of the city, Adams received a warm and enthusiastic—if informal—welcome to the new capital. It bolstered his confidence in being reelected a few days hence.

After dinner that night and utterly exhausted from the long journey and many visitors, the president climbed the only completed staircase in the mansion, candle in hand, to the second-floor residence. It too was unfinished. He went to bed early. The next morning Adams gathered his thoughts and wrote a two-page letter to his wife back in Massachusetts. The letter, penned on November 2, 1800, would become famous, not just because it was the first letter written from the mansion but because of the brief benediction he included.

Writing to "My dearest friend," Adams touched on family matters and then shared a few vague details about the home, including an underwhelming invitation to come to the new city, saying, "The building is in a state to be habitable and now we wish for your company." Cryptically, the president said only that, of the prospect of living in the mansion, his wife would soon "form the best idea of it." However, Adams added a profound wish. It was there that he wrote the famous invocation: "I pray Heaven to bestow the best of the blessings on this house, and on all that shall hereafter inhabit it. May none but honest and wise men ever rule under this roof." Indeed.[9]

Adams's words were published in 1841. Roughly a century later, President Franklin Roosevelt ordered the prayer be placed on the fireplace mantel in the State Dining Room, where it has been ever since.

Abigail Adams was traveling to the federal city when her husband wrote the famous letter. She had departed roughly one week after him but stopped in New York to visit their second son, Charles. The First Lady decided to take Charles's four-year-old daughter, Susanna, with her to the capital city. It was a fortuitous decision, as we shall soon see. Mrs. Adams and her granddaughter then traveled to Philadelphia, where they stayed briefly in the former presidential home. The First Lady and her nine-person entourage then continued on to Baltimore, where a celebration was organized in her honor. The trip to the capital city would be her first visit to not only the city but the region, and she was shocked by what she saw.

The journey took her through the countryside on unpaved trails. At one point her coachman turned on the wrong trail, and they became lost, requiring aides to hack their way through the thick underbrush before being "rescued" by a man traveling on the trail. As Mrs. Adams described the ordeal, "fortunately, a straggling black came with us, and we engaged him as a guide to extricate us from our difficulties."[10]

To say the First Lady was not happy with the capital city is an understatement. She abhorred both the city and president's house. She described her experience, writing to her daughter, "Woods are all you see from Baltimore until you reach the city, which is only so in name. Here and there is a small cot[tage], without a glass window, interspersed amongst the forests, through which you travel miles without seeing any human being. . . . In the city there are buildings enough, if they were compact and finished . . . but they are not, and scattered as they are, I see no great comfort for them."[11]

Mrs. Adams's description of the new capital was echoed by Connecticut congressman John Cotton Smith, who arrived in the city around the same time. He noted, "One wing of the Capitol only had been erected, which, with the president's house, a mile distant from it, both constructed with white sandstone, were shining objects in dismal contrast with the scene around them. Instead of recognizing the avenues and streets portrayed on the plan of the city, not one was visible, unless we except a road with two buildings on each side of it."[12]

Like her husband days before, Mrs. Adams arrived quite fatigued from the difficulties of travel in the year 1800 and found the grounds and home cluttered

with construction debris. The living quarters upstairs were only partially completed, and it was nearly as cold inside as it was outside. The frigid, damp breeze
that blew through the unfinished sections of the home caused her rheumatism
to flare up.[13]

Of the effort to warm the cavernous home, she wrote, "Surrounded with forests, can you believe that wood is not to be had, because people cannot be found
to cut and cart it!" Mrs. Adams ended up sending the family aide, Briesler, to
purchase from their own pockets "nine cords" of wood and two hundred bushels
of coal to light the fireplaces. She later recalled that her main pastime was to
"shiver, shiver" and listen to the sounds of saws, hammers, and construction.

There was no yard, no fencing, and no source for water. Aides were sent to
cart buckets of water back to the home from a spring. Then, when inquiring
about her furnishings and china, she discovered "many things were stolen, many
things were broken." Nor were there accommodations for cooking or doing the
laundry. Mrs. Adams and a servant resorted to hanging laundry in the unfinished East Room to dry—the very site of what would become the most elegant
room in the White House, one used for state affairs.

The first couple was forced to convert the Diplomatic Reception Room to
a living quarter for their aide, Briesler, and his wife, who served as the housekeeper. The president had earlier requested servants, stables on the grounds,
a garden, and other amenities to be available for his wife's arrival. However,
nothing had been provided, and the president soon learned that Congress had
not appropriated funds. While George Washington's mansion in Philadelphia
had uniformed servants and the Adams's had enjoyed thirty staffers there, they
now had to manage the cavernous residence with four staffers whom they paid
out of their own pockets; the staff was neither adequate in number nor elegantly
attired. On top of all that, the roof leaked. It was not the reception Mrs. Adams
had hoped for.[14]

Mrs. Adams described the presidential mansion in detail and not with
affection:

> The house is upon a grand and superb scale, requiring about thirty ser-
> vants to attend and keep the apartments in proper order, and perform the
> ordinary business of the house and stables. . . . The lighting the apart-
> ments, from the kitchen to parlours and chambers, is a tax indeed; and the
> fires we are obliged to keep to secure us from daily agues is another very
> cheering comfort. To assist us in this great castle, and render less atten-
> dance necessary, bells are wholly wanting, not one single one being hung

through the whole house, and promises are all you can obtain. This is so great an inconvenience, that I do not know what to do, nor how to do.[15]

Speaking for herself and her husband, Mrs. Adams stated stoically, "I could content myself almost enywhere three months." But she found living in the new mansion and city a dreary and impossible experience. It seemed, to them, that "we have indeed come into a new country." Yet ever the politician, Mrs. Adams reminded her daughter, "You must keep all this to yourself, and, when asked how I like it, say that I write you the situation is beautiful."[16]

It was about to get a lot worse. News of the most disturbing variety arrived. The couple learned that their son Charles had died soon after Abigail's visit. Ruined by financial speculation and ill with a chronic cough and liver disease from a long bout with alcoholism, he succumbed to cirrhosis of the liver. It was a cruel twist of timing in yet another way—the president and First Lady received word of their twenty-nine-year-old son's passing at the same time news arrived that Adams had lost the 1800 presidential race to his former friend and current foe Thomas Jefferson. Fortunately, Mrs. Adams had decided to bring their son's four-year-old daughter with her to the capital city. The young girl was thus spared the brunt of being at home when her father died.

Truth be told, the First Lady missed Massachusetts and simply did not like living in the South. She grumbled often with a trace of Yankee pride, such as when she wrote, "If the twelve [actually ten] years in which this place has been considered as the future seat of government had been improved, as they would have been in New England, very many of the present inconveniences would have been removed." Similarly, while watching impatiently the unhurried pace of construction, she could not help but gloating of her New England and Federalist leanings:

The four carts are all loaded at the same time, and whilst four carry this rubbish about half a mile, the remaining eight rest upon their shovels. Two of our hardy New England men would do as much work in a day as the whole 12, but it is true Republicanism that drive the slaves half fed, and destitute of clothing . . . to labour, whilst the owner watches about Idle, tho his one slave is all the property he can boast.[17]

She also found "the want of punctuality" and excessive social customs of the genteel southern ladies irritating, groaning that "yesterday I returned fifteen calls." The First Lady was not happy.[18]

But one of the main sources of shame and contempt for the region was the prevalence of slavery. Both the president and First Lady opposed the practice. It was on their mind constantly. That winter Adams wrote, "My opinion against it has always been known . . . never in my life did I own a slave." Likewise, in the momentous year 1776, Abigail had written to her husband about the work of the Founders, "I have sometimes been ready to think that the passion for Liberty cannot be Eaquelly Strong in the Breasts of those who have been accustomed to deprive their fellow Creatures of theirs."[19]

Indeed, in the new capital the sight of many slaves, auction blocks, chains, and unforgiving overseers was inescapable. They saw it when they went out to eat, to meet friends, to travel. Deeply bothered, Abigail noted, "The effects of slavery are visible everywhere; and I have amused myself from day to day in looking at the labour of 12 negroes from my window, who are employed with four small horse carts to remove some dirt in front of the house."[20]

Abigail could not wait to leave the building she called the "great castle." Yet she did not want it to occur in the manner forced on them. Adams lost his bid for reelection. He did not take it well. Still keen on his work, the Founder was not prepared emotionally for the rejection or for retirement after "a life of long journeys and distant voyages, in one or another of which I have been monthly and yearly engaged for two and forty years." He dreaded the coming "routine of domestic life." Rather, he needed to be in the public arena and in the thick of its politics and debates to the extent that, in the years to come, he would become animated whenever he received a request for advice from a politician.[21]

Abigail recognized her husband's dejection, sharing with their son Thomas, "I wish your father's circumstances were not so limited and circumscribed, as they must be, because he cannot indulge himself in those improvements upon his farm, which his inclination leads him to, and which would serve to amuse him, and contribute to his health."[22]

The shocking tie in the November election between Jefferson and Burr was not settled until February 16 after three dozen contested ballots. Mrs. Adams had known since November that her husband would not be serving a second term. She therefore packed quickly and departed as soon as the House of Representatives announced the decision. With her daughter-in-law Louisa Catherine Adams, she worried about traveling such a great distance and to the federal district alone, but they were determined to put the unpleasant city and politics behind them at first opportunity.

Still upset, the First Lady observed that the roads and trails were just as rutted on the way out, but she boasted independently that she "was accustomed to get through many a trying scene and combat many difficulties alone." She was already in Baltimore during the balloting but arrived in Philadelphia just as church bells were signaling Jefferson's victory. Despite the difficult experience, the couple appreciated Washington's vision and recognized that the city and home were "built for the ages to come" on such a "grand and superb scale."[23]

On November 22, 1800, President Adams delivered the Annual Message to Congress. It would be his final one and, because his successor started the practice of writing rather than delivering the address, the last spoken annual message until Woodrow Wilson's in 1913. Adams dedicated much of his address to congratulating Congress and the people on the new "permanent seat of their Government." He acknowledged the "accommodations are not now so complete as might be wished, yet there is great reason to believe that this inconvenience will cease with the present session." Adams called for Congress to help make it "the capital of a great nation."[24]

The president stayed behind with his aide, appointing several Federalists to office and the courts—including John Marshall as Chief Justice—until the final moment. These actions angered Jefferson and his party, who had swept into power through the election, and also prompted the famous Supreme Court case of *Marbury v. Madison* in 1801. Still angry and embarrassed, Adams slunk out of the city under cover of darkness just hours before Jefferson's inaugural.

After the bitter election of 1800, the new president symbolically wore unassuming clothing, and rather than ride in a fancy coach with regally adorned footmen and horses to the inaugural ceremony, as Washington and Adams had, he walked to the Capitol. Jefferson delivered his inaugural address in a hushed and hesitant voice. Afterward, he walked to Conrad's boarding house, where he had been staying, and dined with a few guests.

The mansion and capital city were the by-products of Washington's vision and the Federalist Party. Yet Washington did not live to see its completion, and Adams spent but a few miserable weeks in the home. It would be turned over to the Democratic-Republicans for twenty-four years through three of the most ardent critics of the home and city: Jefferson, Madison, and Monroe. Some of Washington's supporters worried the city and home, in the hands of the new Democratic-Republican Party, would be reduced in size, redesigned, or even moved to a new location. The opposite occurred.

Jefferson moved into the mansion he had long opposed on March 19. With him were three servants, a housekeeper, and his longtime French steward, Joseph Rabin. When Congress recessed the next month, he returned to Monticello and brought back several slaves to staff the home. Like Washington, Jefferson loved architecture and was always remodeling and experimenting on new improvements for his home, habits that continued at the presidential mansion.

Rather than reduce the executive residence to a small, humble brick structure, as he had long advocated, Jefferson ordered that workers dig a well on the grounds; organize tin reservoirs in the attic to store rainwater; build a fence with gates; erect a high stone wall on the south side of the home; construct an elaborate, deep wine cellar lined with clay bricks; and procure modern stoves for the building. He also had the old wooden outhouse torn down and replaced with two "modern" water closets inside the home, with pipes running through the building and onto the grounds.

Jefferson also brought the architect Benjamin Latrobe to oversee other major projects on the home. These included installing a sheet-iron flat roof and a grand arch on the grounds, tearing out the south stairway and installing a new staircase for guests on the north side of the building, designing a regal horseshoe-shaped staircase to the second floor, and placing a terrace and four majestic columns by the entrance. Gardens were planted and bouquets of roses and geraniums graced the home. Soon, Jefferson and Latrobe began developing the initial proposal for East and West Wings on the mansion. These were hardly the actions of a man who opposed even the idea of having a presidential home, let alone a grand mansion. Likewise, his party, which had spent years obstructing Federalist plans for the home and city, suddenly seemed less concerned with his costly and stately upgrades. Yet there were complaints about Jefferson's elaborate modifications to the home.[25]

It was not the physical enhancements to the home that caused an uproar in the city; rather, it was Jefferson's conversion of the room used for social receptions into a library and the levee room into his office. Jefferson canceled the popular weekly levees and instituted new social and political protocols, announcing "the principle of equality, or of *pêlemêle*" would govern—meaning there would be no more galas or recognition of social rank at events. Politicians and affluent residents were upset to learn that the new president intended to host an open house only on Independence Day and New Year's Day.

Jefferson also abandoned Washington's practice of wearing white gloves and standing on a dais for receptions. He donned a simple ponytail rather than a powdered wig, ended the custom of accepting gifts, and even opted to be called "Mr. Jefferson" rather than "Mr. President."[26] Change had come to the home and now to the city, just not in the way people expected. In these respects Jefferson was being true to his ideals. Moreover, in his effort to promote

"Republican" values, Jefferson went so far as to welcome guests at the front door wearing slippers.

One visitor, Sir Anthony Merry, an English diplomat who joined the president for dinner in November 1803, was highly offended by the informality, taking it as a snub. As if the entire city was not bad enough for the English aristocrat—"a thousand times worse than the worst parts of Spain," in Sir Anthony's words—Jefferson greeted him wearing "usual morning attire." The president was at the door, Sir Anthony fumed, "standing in slippers . . . and both pantaloons, coat, and underclothes, indicative of utter slovenliness and indifference to appearances, and in a state of negligence actually studied." The diplomat was, of course, dressed royally and accompanied by a large entourage of dignitaries and servants. He concluded, "I could not doubt that the whole scene was prepared and intended as an insult not to me personally, but to the sovereign I represented."[27]

Defending his relaxed rules of etiquette, Jefferson reminded his guests of the principles of the new nation: "When brought together in society, all are perfectly equal, whether foreign or domestic, titled or untitled, in or out of office."[28]

Yet when Jefferson did dine and entertain friends in the mansion, it was a lavish affair. He served multiple-course meals of the finest foods and wines imported from France, Italy, and Spain. His slaves Edy and Fanny were taught the art of French cuisine, and guests sampled the first waffles in the country, brought from Holland; the first ice cream and anchovies direct from France; and the first macaroni imported from Italy. He installed oval tables to facilitate dinner conversation and built revolving doors connected to the dining room to enhance the meal service. Fancy yet functional door shelving held stacks of wines, and a large wait staff supplemented a bustling team of slaves from Monticello.

Soon, Jefferson was hosting far more dinners and events than his predecessors. With his wife deceased and eldest daughter married with children, the president often called on the wife of his secretary of state to preside. Dolley Madison soon became known for her grace and hosting prowess and organized elaborate affairs. Surprisingly, Jefferson came to enjoy the mansion, stating, "We find this a very agreeable country residence, good society and enough of it, and free from the heat, the stench, and the bustle of a close built town."[29]

The mansion during Jefferson's presidency was becoming the lavish, aristocratic center of social life and culture that he and his party had warned against. Interestingly, later, after the British burned government buildings in the city in the War of 1812, then-president James Madison and his wife fought naysayers who called for the capital to be moved, demanding that it remain in its present location and be rebuilt. Madison's successor, James Monroe, even had it rebuilt to the original plans and then enhanced the attractiveness of the mansion with French-inspired embellishments.

Amusingly, a member of the party of Jefferson, Madison, and Monroe visited the presidential mansion after a quarter century of Democratic-Republican rule. Expecting to see the simple home his party had always advocated, Senator Thomas Hart Benton of Missouri was surprised and a bit conflicted at what he encountered. Writing after the New Year's Day reception of 1827, he described,

> This being the day on which the President's house is thrown open to all visitors, I went among others to pay my respects to him, or rather, I should fairly confess, I went to see the East Room, for the furnishing of which we had voted $25,000 at the last session of Congress. I was anxious to see how that amount of furniture could be stowed away in a single room, and my curiosity was fully satisfied. It was truly a gorgeous sight to behold; but had too much the look of regal magnificence to be perfectly agreeable to my old Republican feelings.[30]

Although he generally enjoyed the experience of being president and came to appreciate the mansion and capital city, Jefferson, like his two predecessors, had had enough. He would describe the final years of his presidency as "a splendid misery," one that brought "nothing but unceasing drudgery and the daily loss of friends." After the inaugural festivities of James Madison in 1809, Jefferson was eager to return to Monticello, a place where he spent roughly a quarter of his days while serving as president. Upon arriving home, a relieved Jefferson admitted, "Never did a prisoner, released from his chains, feel such relief as I shall on shaking off the shackles of power."[31]

The government was profoundly changed by the Democratic-Republicans in several ways, just not as expected. Jefferson ended up presiding over the construction of additional public buildings in the city and even advocated grand monuments be erected in the city's parks, a gesture that Washington had hoped would help to inspire a sense of nationhood and patriotism. He promoted America's national development beyond the Potomac, just like Washington. Through his treasury secretary, Albert Gallatin, he built roads, bridges, canals, and other public improvements, also in the manner of Washington and the Federalists. Jefferson also presided over the Louisiana Purchase of 1803, which doubled the size of the nation, and sent Meriwether Lewis and William Clark west the following year on their epic journey of discovery.

Thanks to Hamilton's financial reforms and secretary of the treasury Albert Gallatin's penny-pinching, by 1806 the government was no longer operating in debt. Of course, Jefferson and his party received the credit, despite their ardent opposition to it years prior. In fact, the efforts of Jefferson's avowed enemy worked so well that the president was now confronted with what to do about the surplus. Echoing the president and treasury secretary he once opposed, Jefferson announced in his annual message to the Democratic-Republican Congress that same year that the surplus would be used for the very purposes his party had long opposed: the government would build "roads, rivers, canals, and such other objects of public improvement as it may be thought proper to add to the constitutional enumeration of Federal powers." It was in the public interest, Jefferson and the Democratic-Republicans reasoned, yet again sounding a lot like Washington and the Federalists. "By these operations new channels of communication will be opened between the States, the line of separation will disappear, their interests will be identified, and their union cemented by new and indissoluble ties."[32]

When Jefferson stepped down in 1809 after two terms, the presidential mansion was vastly improved and had become much closer to the grand home Washington had long advocated. The outgoing president conducted a detailed inventory of every item in the home, including the lavish furnishings he had installed. He also disbanded the commission and hired a superintendent of public buildings. Rather than select James Hoban, Jefferson appointed Latrobe. After the British had burned the mansion a few years later, Hoban rejoined Latrobe. Together, they restored the home now known as the White House, completed the Capitol, and finished construction on the capital city—just as George Washington had envisioned.

Chronological List of Temporary Capitals

First Continental Congress

Carpenter's Hall in Philadelphia, Pennsylvania (September 5–October 24, 1774)

Second Continental Congress

Pennsylvania State House (Independence Hall) in Philadelphia, (May 10, 1775–December 12, 1776)

Henry Fite's house in Baltimore, Maryland (December 20, 1776–February 27, 1777)

State House in Philadelphia, Pennsylvania (March 4–September 18, 1777)

Courthouse in Lancaster, Pennsylvania (September 27, 1777)

Courthouse in York, Pennsylvania (September 30, 1777–June 27, 1778)

Pennsylvania State House in Philadelphia (July 2, 1778–March 1, 1781)

Congress under the Articles of Confederation

Pennsylvania State House in Philadelphia (March 1, 1781–June 21, 1783)

Nassau Hall in Princeton, New Jersey (June 30–November 4, 1783)

State House in Annapolis, Maryland (November 26, 1783–August 19, 1784)

French Arms Tavern in Trenton, New Jersey (November 1–December 24, 1784)

City Hall in New York, New York (January 11, 1785–Fall 1788)

Congress under the Constitution

Federal Hall in New York, New York (March 4, 1789–August 12, 1790)
Congress Hall in Philadelphia, Pennsylvania (December 6, 1790–May 14, 1800)

Congress in the Permanent Capital City

The US government moved to the City of Washington, and Congress to the
Capitol (November 17, 1800)

List of Proposed Locations for the Capital

Cities and Towns

Delaware: New Castle, Newark, Wilmington

Maryland: Annapolis, Baltimore, Charlestown, Cumberland, Ft. Frederick, Georgetown,[1] Hagerstown, Hancock, Havre de Grace, Head of Elk River, Little Falls, Sharpsburg, Williamsport

New Jersey: Bordentown, Burlington, Elizabeth, Howell's Ferry, Lamberton, New Brunswick, Newark, Princeton, Trenton

New York: Brooklyn, Kingston, Morisania (the Bronx), New Windsor, Newburgh, Poughkeepsie

Ohio: Marietta

Pennsylvania: Bethlehem, Carlisle, Easton, Germantown, Harrisburg, Lancaster, Middletown, Morrisville, Philadelphia, Pittsburgh, Reading, Wright's Ferry (Columbia), York

Virginia: Alexandria, Fredericksburg, Norfolk, Shepherdstown, Williamsburg

Locations by Waterway

Chesapeake Bay	Potomac River
Delaware River	Schuylkill River
Hudson River	Susquehanna River

NOTES

Preface

1. Most people referred to Washington, DC, as the "seat of government" rather than the capital prior to the Civil War. This reflected republican norms of the time that although DC was the location of the federal government, states' rights balanced central authority. However, I prefer to use "capital" throughout most of the book because I believe George Washington's vision was always for it to be a grand national capital. Using the term "seat of government" also becomes cumbersome to read, and the distinction may not be significant to present-day readers.

Introduction: The "Other" Founding Debates

1. Bordewich, *Washington*, 2.
2. Kapsch, *Building Washington*, 6.
3. See Law, "Reply to Certain Insinuations."
4. Bordewich, *Washington*, 2; see also First Federal Congress Project.
5. "Thomas Jefferson's Explanations of the *Anas*," February 4, 1818, in Founders Online, https://founders.archives.gov/documents/jefferson/01-22-02-1033-0001.
6. See Articles of Confederation.
7. Henry Knox, quoted in Wood, *Creation of the American Republic*, 431.
8. I use the lowercase terms "federalist" and "anti-federalist" beyond the period 1787–90 to describe, respectively, those who favored a relatively strong federal government and those who advocated for a decentralized government with more authority left in the hands of individual states.
9. These factions were not new. There were factions in the First and Second Continental Congress that debated whether to declare independence and how. The Federalist and Anti-Federalist Parties had not yet officially formed, so I will use the terms in lowercase in order to denote factions, rather than parties, until such time as they became parties.
10. Fitzpatrick, *Writings of Washington*, 30:5.

11. George Washington to David Stuart, July 14, 1787, in Fitzpatrick, vol. 29.

12. See Madison in Federalist No. 10, November 23, 1787, in Congress.gov Resources, https://www.congress.gov/resources/display/content/the+federalist+papers #TheFederalistPapers-10.

13. "Differences between Federalists and Antifederalists," Gilder Lehrman Institute of American History, https://www.gilderlehrman.org/content/differences-between -federalists-and-antifederalists.

14. Flexner, *Washington*, 155–56; see also Kenyon, "Men of Little Faith," 3–4.

15. Morales-Vazquez, "Imagining Washington," 15; see also *Journals of Congress*, 25:647–54, 707–8; and Bowling, *Creation of Washington*, 54–57.

16. Bowling, *Creation of Washington*, 21.

17. Flexner, *Washington*, 55.

18. Kapsch, *Building Washington*, 1.

19. Kapsch, 3.

20. Kapsch, 2–3.

21. Wood, *Creation of the American Republic*, 620.

22. The best-selling author Doris Kearns Goodwin is credited in her book *Team of Rivals* with revealing Lincoln's political genius and ability to get rivals to work with and for him.

23. Chernow, "George Washington," 42.

24. The noted presidency scholar Fred I. Greenstein, in his book *The Hidden-Hand Presidency: Eisenhower as Leader*, is credited with changing the way historians viewed the thirty-fourth president.

25. Fred I. Greenstein's book *The Presidential Difference: Leadership Style from FDR to Barack Obama* is one of the leading scholarly works to examine the admirable traits and effective approaches by presidents. Washington, in many ways, embodies nearly all of them.

26. Carroll and Ashworth, *George Washington*, 433.

1. Surveying a Future

1. George Washington to Sir Isaac Heard, May 2, 1792, in Sparks, *Life of Washington*, 504–5.

2. Rhodehamel, *George Washington*, 12.

3. Chernow, *Washington*, 4; see also Anderson, *George Washington Remembers*, 30–32.

4. Wiencek, *Imperfect God*, 31.

5. Chernow, *Washington*, 4–6.

6. The home has long since been lost to fire, so history knows very little about it.

7. George Washington's siblings were half brothers Lawrence and Augustine from the father's first marriage, along with a sister who died, and Betty Lewis, Samuel, John Augustine, and Charles from the second marriage.

8. The date fell under the old Julian calendar, which failed to accurately calculate the actual time it took Earth to circle the sun or to consider the effect of leap years. The Gregorian calendar is named for Pope Gregory XIII, who in 1582 decreed that dates be dropped to more accurately reflect the year. When it was adopted in North America in 1752, dates such as Washington's birthdate had to be adjusted.

9. George Washington to Marquis de Lafayette, December 8, 1784, in Abbot et al., *Papers of Washington*, 2375.

10. Abbot et al.

11. Watson, *Affairs of State*, 16–18.

12. "The Rules of Civility," George Washington's Mount Vernon, https://www .mountvernon.org/george-washington/rules-of-civlity.

13. Watson, *Affairs of State*, 57–59.

14. Freeman, *George Washington*, 2:389.

15. Freeman.

2. Western Adventures

1. The "West" at the time included the western reaches of Virginia and Pennsylvania as well as the Ohio and Kentucky Territories.

2. Washington would never see George or Sally Fairfax again. Fairfax passed in 1787, but Washington appears to have continued to write to Sally until a year prior to his death.

3. Rhodehamel, *Washington*, 13.

4. Bowling, *Creation of Washington*, 1.

5. The complete title is "The Journal of Major George Washington, Sent by the Hon. Robert Dinwiddie, His Majesty's Lieutenant Governor, and Commander in Chief of Virginia, to the Commandant of the French Forces on Ohio." The report from 1754 is available in the Huntington Library, document 18718.

6. Chernow, *Washington*, 39.

7. Different spellings of the chief's name exist, including Tanacharison.

8. The Mingo were an Iroquoian-speaking Seneca tribe that migrated to the Ohio region in the mid-eighteenth century. Though technically called the "Mingwe," the name was misunderstood as "Mingo."

9. Lengel, *General George Washington*, 33–37; see also Trudel, "Jumonville Affair," 331–73.

10. George Washington, "Expedition to the Ohio, 1754," March–June 1754, letter, in Twohig, *George Washington's Diaries*, 49. See also "Expedition to the Ohio, 1754: Narrative," Founders Online, https://founders.archives.gov/documents/Washington /01-01-02-0004-0002.

11. Robert Dinwiddie to George Washington, June 1, 1754, in Abbot et al., *Papers of Washington*, 1:119.

12. Flexner, *Washington*, 1:89.

13. For a helpful discussion, see Bruce L. Brager, "The Start: Jumonville's Glen and Fort Necessity," *Military History Online*, https://www.militaryhistoryonline.com /18thcentury/articles/thestart.aspx.

14. George Washington to John Augustine Washington, May 31, 1754, in Founders Online, https://founders.archives.gov/documents/Washington/02-01-02-0058.

15. The war between the British and French also included Austria, Prussia, Spain, and others. See Fort Necessity National Battlefield, https://www.nps.gov/fone /jumglen.html.

16. George Washington to Robert Dinwiddie, July 3, 1754, in Fitzpatrick, *Writings of Washington*, 73.

3. The Dispensations of Providence

1. Watson, *Affairs of State*, 62–63.

2. In 1803 Meriwether Lewis followed the same path to go to Pittsburgh to purchase boats for his famous expedition.

3. For a helpful discussion, see "Braddock Pathway," National Park Service, https:// nps.gov/fone/planyourvisit/upload/fone-braddock-pathway-2-pdf.

4. Rhodehamel, *George Washington*, 25.

5. George Washington, memorandum, July 18–19, 1755, in Founders Online, https://founders.archives.gov/documents/Washington/02-01-02-0168.

6. For a helpful discussion, see "Braddock Pathway."

7. George Washington to John A. Washington, July 18, 1755. Founders Online, https://founders.archives.gov/documents/Washington/02-01-02-0169.

8. For a helpful discussion of Rev. Davies's sermon and Washington's reputation after the French and Indian War, see "French and Indian War," George Washington's Mount Vernon, www.mountvernon.org/library/digitalhistory/digital-encyclopedia /article/french-and-indian-war/.

9. Dinwiddie's proclamation was issued on February 19, 1754, from Williamsburg; see the Huntington Library, item #19867.

10. Prussing, *Estate of George Washington*, chap. 7, 25–27; see also Clark, *Washington's Western Lands*; and Freeman, *George Washington*, 6:388–92.

11. Rhodehamel, *George Washington*, 37–39.

12. Quoted in Higginbotham, *George Washington Reconsidered*, 206; and Fitzpatrick, *Writings of Washington*, 1:4.

13. Fitzpatrick, *Writings of Washington*, 1:4.

14. Fitzpatrick, 1:30.

4. Potomac Fever

1. Livengood, *Philadelphia-Baltimore Trade Rivalry*, 1–20.

2. The notion of Washington having "Potomac Fever" is a reoccurring theme in Bowling, *Creation of Washington*.

3. Costanzo, *George Washington's Washington*, 14.

4. Bowling, *Creation of Washington*, 106.

5. Smyth, *Tour in the United States*, 2:144–45.

6. See Costanzo, *George Washington's Washington*, 14.

7. Edward Savage's famous 1796 painting *The Washington Family* is in the National Gallery of Art (www.ngp.gov/collection/art-object-page.561.html).

8. Sometimes referred to as Anacostans; see Tilp, *This Was Potomac River*, for stories of the early settlers along the river.

9. For a helpful discussion, see Peck, *Potomac River*.

10. For a helpful discussion of the first residents of the Potomac, see "Native American Tribes and the Indian History in Potomac, Maryland," American Indian, www.americanindiancoc.org/native-american-tribes-the-indian-history-in-potomac -maryland/.

11. "Native People of Washington, DC," National Park Service, https://www.nps .gov/people/native-peoples.html.

12. Bowling, *Creation of Washington*, 107.

13. Costanzo, *George Washington's Washington*, 14.

14. Bowling, *Creation of Washington*, 111–12.

15. James, *Ohio Company*, chaps. 2 and 3.

16. Nite, "Washington and the Potomac," 502.

17. Hutchinson, Rutland, and Hobson, *Papers of Madison*, 8:9–20.

18. Boyd et al., *Papers of Jefferson*, 7:16–50.

19. Fitzpatrick, *Writings of Washington*, 28:55, 75.

20. Morgan, *Genius of Washington*; see also Morgan, *Meaning of Independence*, 30.

21. George Washington to James Anderson, December 21, 1797, in Founders Online, https://founders.archives.gov/documents/washington/06-01-02-0406.

22. Bowling, *Creation of Washington*, 111.

23. Arnebeck, *Through a Fiery Trial*, 34.

24. For a helpful source on the natural history of the Potomac, see "Potomac: America's River," American Rivers, www.americanrivers.org/river/potomac-river/.

5. Cincinnatus

1. Flexner, *Washington*, 101–6.

2. See "Martha Washington," Center for the Study of the American Constitution, www.csac.history.wisc.edu/multimedia/founders-on-the-founders/martha -washington/.

3. "Martha Washington."

4. See "Farm Reports," November 26, 1785–April 15, 1786, in Founders Online, https://founders.archives.gov/documents/washington/04-03-02-0454; and "George Washington and Slavery," George Washington's Mount Vernon, www.mountvernon .org/george-washington/slavery/ten-facts-about-washington-slavery/.

5. George Washington to John Francis Mercer, September 9, 1786, Item GLC 3705, Gilder Lehrman Collection, Pierpont Morgan Library, New York.

6. George Washington to Tobias Lear, May 6, 1704, HM 5229, Huntington Library.

7. George Washington to Robert Dinwiddie, March 10, 1757, in Founders Online, https://founders.archives.gov/documents/washington/02-04-02-0062.

8. Rhodehamel, *George Washington*, 46.

9. See "Fairfax County Resolves," July 18, 1774, Constitution Society, https://constitution.org/bcp/Fairfax_res.htm.

10. Philander D. Chase, "A Cryptic Record of a Family Tragedy: The Unhappy Progression of Patsy Custis's Epilepsy," *Washington Papers* (November 28, 2018), http://gwpapers.virginia.edu/a-cryptic-record-of-a-family-tragedy-the-unhappy-progression -of-patsy-custiss-epilepsy/; see also George Washington's diary entries for June 19, 1773, and George Washington to Burwell Bassett, June 20, 1773, in Founders Online, https://founders.archives.gov/documents/Washington/02-09-02-0185.

11. George Washington to Eliza Parke Custis, September 14, 1794, George Washington's Mount Vernon, www.mountvernon.org/library/digitalhistory/quotes/article /love-is-a-mighty-pretty-thing.

12. The story of Parson Weems and his book on Washington is told in "Parson Weems," George Washington's Mount Vernon, www.mountvernon.org/library /digitalhistory/digital-encyclopedia/article/parson-weems/.

13. The Houdon statue now graces the Virginia State Capitol in Richmond, the Ball statute can be found in Boston's Public Garden, and Greenbough's 1832 statue, after having been moved from the Capitol Rotunda and other locations, now sits in the Smithsonian Museum of American History.

14. Chernow, *Washington*, vii.

15. Quote is from Burns and Dunn, *George Washington*, 58.

16. Barratt and Miles, *Gilbert Stuart*, 137.

17. Thomas Jefferson to Walter Jones, January 2, 1814, in Founders Online, https://founders.archives.gov/documents/Jefferson/03-07-02-0052.

18. Custis, *Recollections*, 418.

19. Peter R. Henriques, "George Washington: America's Atlas," *HistoryNet*, November/December 2016, https://www.historynet.com/george-washington-americas-atlas.htm.

20. Chernow, "George Washington," 42.

21. Rhodehamel, *George Washington*, viii.

22. George Washington to Bushrod Washington, January 15, 1783, in Founders Online, https://founders.archives.gov/documents/Washington/99-01-02-10429. Letter was written while in camp at Newburgh, New York.

23. Thomas Jefferson to Dr. Walter Jones, January 2, 1814, in Boyd et al., *Papers of Jefferson*, vol. 54; see also Founders Online, https://founders.archives.gov/documents /Jefferson/03-07-02-0052.

24. Resolution of the House of Burgesses, February 26, 1759, in Founders Online, https://founders.archives.gov/documents/washington/02-06-02-0156.

25. Rhodehamel, *George Washington*, 15.

26. The full title of the booklet is *Rules of Civility and Decent Behavior in Company and Conversation*. It is based on sixteenth-century codes of behavior.

27. For a helpful discussion, see W. W. Abbot, "An Uncommon Awareness of Self," *Prologue Magazine*, Spring 1989, www.archives.gov/publications/prologue; see also Washington Papers, University of Virginia, http://gwpapers.virginia.edu/resources /articles/an-uncommon-awareness/.

28. Chernow, "George Washington," 39.

29. Gleaves Whitney, "George Washington, the Greatest Man," *Ask Gleaves*, September 6, 2007, https://scholarworks.gvsu.edu/ask_gleaves/18/.

30. When the war ended in 1783, a group of American and French officers from the army founded the Society of the Cincinnati, named in honor of Lucius Quinctius Cincinnatus, the man Washington so admired and emulated, just as the members of the fraternal order so admired Washington.

6. Swords in Their Hands

1. Born into an aristocratic family in 1738, Charles Cornwallis, the First Marquess Cornwallis, also carried the titles Viscount Brome and Earl Cornwallis. Cornwallis served as the second in command of British forces under General Clinton. He died in 1805.

2. Charles Earl Cornwallis to George Washington, October 17, 1781, Item MA 488, Pierpont Morgan Library and Museum, New York.

3. The largest loss of colonial troops occurred in the battle for Charleston, which lasted through April and early May 1780 and resulted in the death or capture of roughly three thousand colonials. British forces in South Carolina were commanded by Sir Henry Clinton and Lord Cornwallis.

4. For a helpful discussion, see Watson, *Ghost Ship*.

5. "Surrender of the British General Cornwallis to the Americans," Gilder Lehrman Institute of American History, October 19, 1781, www.gilderlehrman.org/history-now /spotlight-primary-source/surrender-british-general-cornwallis-americans-october-19 -1781.

6. For a helpful discussion, see Wensyel, "Newburgh Conspiracy."

7. The British would hold New York City until the very end of the war, abandoning the city roughly two months after the peace treaty was signed.

8. The nationalist faction favoring a stronger government would later be known as the Federalists. The anti–national government faction would later be known as the Anti-Federalists or the Democratic-Republicans or simply as the Republicans.

9. George Washington to James McHenry, October 17, 1782, Item HM 128, Huntington Library.

10. Rhodehamel, *Great Experiment*, 73.

11. George Washington to John Laurens, January 30, 1781, Item HM 5391, Huntington Library.

12. Kohn, "Inside History," 203.

13. George Washington to Joseph Jones, December 14, 1782, in Rhodehamel, *George Washington*.

14. George Washington to William Health, February 5, 1783, in Rhodehamel, *George Washington*.

15. Kohn, *Eagle and Sword*, 16–35.

16. Rhodehamel, *Great Experiment*, 81.

17. Fleming, *Perils of Peace*, 263.

18. Chernow, *Alexander Hamilton*, 179.

19. Kohn, "Inside History," 202.

7. Mutiny!

1. Before his death Martha's son from her first marriage, Jacky, and his wife, Eleanor Calvert, had seven children, four of whom lived to maturity. Martha adopted the youngest two. Martha Washington's two adopted grandchildren were Eleanor "Nelly" Parke Custis and George Washington Parke Custis.

2. George Washington to William Heath, June 6, 1783, in Fitzpatrick, *Writings of Washington*, vol. 10.

3. "Biography of George Washington," George Washington's Mount Vernon, www .mountvernon.org/george-washington/.

4. George Washington to William Heath, February 5, 1783, in Rhodehamel, *George Washington*; see also Chernow, *Washington*, 430.

5. Kohn, "Inside History," 188–220.

6. Fitzpatrick, *Writings of Washington*, 26:227, 298, 334.

7. For a helpful discussion, see Skeen and Kohn, "Newburgh Conspiracy Reconsidered."

8. For a helpful discussion, see Wensyel, "Newburgh Conspiracy."

9. There are several good sources for Washington's speech, including Rhodehamel, *American Revolution*; and Rhodehamel, *George Washington*, 497; see "Speech to the Officers of the Army," March 15, 1783, and "To the Genls. Fields, & Other Officers Assembled," March 15, 1783, Item HM 1607, Huntington Library.

10. Fleming, *Perils of Peace*, 271.

11. For a helpful discussion, see Wensyel, "Newburgh Conspiracy."

12. For a helpful discussion, see Flexner, *Washington*.

13. Kohn, "Inside History," 211.

14. Chernow, *Washington*, 433–36.

15. Chernow.

16. May 27, 1783, entry in *Robert Morris Diary*, Robert Morris Papers.

17. George Washington to Theodorick Bland, April 4, 1783, in Fitzpatrick, *Writings of Washington*, 26:285–96.

18. "George Washington General Orders," June 2, 6, and 11, 1783, in Fitzpatrick, 26:463–72.

19. Bowling, "New Light," 424.

20. James Madison to Edmund Randolph, February 25, 1783, in Hutchinson, Rutland, and Hobson, *Papers of Madison*, 6:286.

21. See National Constitution Center, "How Philly Lost the Nation's Capital to Washington," *Constitution Daily* (blog), May 15, 2018, https://constitutioncenter.org/blog/how-philly-lost-the-nations-capital-to-washington.

22. Benjamin Rush was a Founding Father, signer of the Declaration of Independence, educator, social reformer, and a surgeon for the Continental Army.

23. For a helpful discussion, see Collins, *Continental Congress*; and Henderson, *Party Politics*; see also Alexander Hamilton to John Dickinson, July 1, 1783, in Syrett, *Papers of Hamilton*, 3:438–58; and the writings of John Dickinson, in Logan, *Colonial Records of Pennsylvania*, 13:654–66 and in Dickinson Papers, Historical Society of Pennsylvania, Philadelphia.

8. The Day the War Ended

1. John Jay to George Washington, January 7, 1787, in Johnston, *Correspondence and Public Papers of Jay*, 3:227.

2. George Washington to John Jay, August 15, 1786, in Johnston, *Correspondence and Public Papers of Jay*, 3:208–9.

3. Williamson, *History of North Carolina*, 2:56.

4. *Pennsylvania Packet*, October 14, 1786. See https://www.newspapers.com/title_1194/the_pennsylvania_packet/.

5. Wood, *Creation of the American Republic*, 394.

6. For a helpful discussion, see Fowler, *American Crisis*; and George Washington, "Circular Letter to the States," George Washington's Mount Vernon, https://www.mountvernon.org/library/digitalhistory/digital-encyclopedia/article/circular-letter-to-the-states/.

7. George Washington to Mesech Weare and others, June 8, 1783, and "Circular Farewell to the Army," June 8, 1783, both in Washington Papers, Library of Congress.

8. "Circular Farewell to the Army."

9. "Circular Letter to the States," June 8, 1783, in Fitzgerald, *Writings of Washington*, 26:483–96.

10. Elias Boudinot to Elisha Boudinot, June 23, 1783, Boudinot Papers, 7:195; Elias Boudinot to William Livingston, June 23, 1783, Boudinot Papers, Morgan Library, New York; see also Boyd, *Elias Boudinot*, introductory pages.

11. It must be remembered that the idea of self-government was novel at the time and the structure for the new government was without precedent.

9. A Singular Destiny

1. Washington referenced "Under their vine and fig tree," which is found in 1 Kings 4:25 and elsewhere in the Hebrew scriptures.

2. George Washington to James McHenry, August 22, 1785, in Abbot et al., *Papers of Washington*, 3:197–99.

3. Washington to McHenry, August 22, 1785.

4. George Washington to John Washington, May 31, 1776, in Fitzpatrick, *Writings of Washington*, 5:20.

5. Quoted in Morales-Vasquez, "Imagining Washington," 13; see also Davis, "Abbé Correa in America," 105.

6. These early books are Weems, *Life of George Washington* (1800); Marshall, *Life of George Washington* (1838); and Irving, *George Washington* (1856–59).

7. Chernow, "George Washington," 46.

8. Abbot, "George Washington in Retirement."

9. Scott, "L'Enfant's Washington Described."

10. George Washington to John Jay, August 15, 1786, in Johnston, *Correspondence and Public Papers of John Jay*, 3:208–9.

11. Wood, *Creation of the American Republic*, 295.

10. Fixing the Seat of Government

1. See Jon Roland, "Albany Plan of Union," Constitution Society, August 10, 1997, last updated September 8, 2019, www.constitution.org/bcp/albany.htm.

2. Jensen, "Origin of the First Continental Congress."

3. The quip is originally attributed to John Adams but was used by those who tired of Virginians' allegedly stating that their colony/state was better than the others.

4. Bowling, *Creation of Washington*, 15.

5. Bowling, 16.

6. The debate was covered in the *Pennsylvania Evening Post*, March 5, 1776, in Library of Congress.

7. John Adams to Abigail Adams, June 4, 1777; see also Benjamin Irvin, "Streets of Philadelphia," *Pennsylvania Magazine of History*, vol. 129, no. 1 (Jan. 2005), 7–43.

8. Washington's army lost roughly twenty-five hundred men to disease, malnutrition, and exposure that bitter winter.

9. Wood, *Creation of the American Republic*, 83–90, 233–37.

10. Bowling, *Creation of Washington*, 76.

11. Elias Boudinot to Robert Livingston, August 29, 1783, New York Historical Society; see also Bowling, *Creation of Washington*, 49–50.

12. See Letter from James Madison to Edmund Randolph, July 28, 1783, Founders Online, National Archives, and Letter from James Madison to Edmund Randolph, October 13, 1783, Founders Online, National Archives.

13. Bowling, 45.

14. Bowling, 43–44.

15. Bowling, 45.

16. Bowling, 45. In 1783 George Lux Jr. wrote the anonymous letter.

17. Elizabeth, throughout its history, was referred to as "Elizabethtown," "Elizabeth Town," or "Elizabethport." For a helpful discussion, see Hatfield, *History of Elizabeth*.

18. The article appeared in the *New Jersey Gazette* on December 23, 1783, in Library of Congress.

19. Bowling, *Creation of Washington*, 44.

20. Daniel Carroll to Thomas S. Lee, May 20, 1783, Manuscript #1974, Maryland Historical Society, Baltimore.

21. Hutchinson, Rutland, and Hobson, *Papers of Madison*, 7:219.

22. Bowling, *Creation of Washington*, 48–54.

23. Bowling, 77–79.

24. For a helpful discussion, see "Nine Capitals of the United States," US Senate, https://www.senate.gov/reference/reference_item/Nine_Capitals_of_the_United_States.htm. See also Bowling, 62–65.

25. "Letter, George Washington to Richard Henry Lee, February 8, 1785" and "Letter, George Washington to William Grayson, June 22, 1785," both in Founders Online, National Archives, https://founders.archives.gov.

26. R. N. Smith, *Patriarch*, 42–43.

11. Political Architecture

1. Bowling, "New Light," 420–22; for a helpful discussion, see also Brunhouse, *Counter-Revolution*, chaps. 2–3.

2. Morales-Vasquez, "Imagining Washington," 14.

3. Morales-Vazquez, "Imagining Washington," 15–16; see also Zall, *Comical Spirit*, 151–53.

4. Houdon was a neoclassical sculptor who gained fame for his busts and statues of prominent political figures of the Enlightenment, such as Benjamin Franklin and Jean-Jacques Rousseau. He was born in Versailles, France, in 1741 and died in Paris in 1828.

5. In his book *Peter Charles L'Enfant*, Kenneth Bowling notes that L'Enfant used "Peter" rather than "Pierre" while living in America. Because most sources refer to him as Pierre and because most people recognize that name, it will be used in this book.

6. For a helpful discussion, see Stephenson, *Plan Wholly New*.

7. Stephenson, 10.

8. Boorstin, *Hidden History*, 97–98.

9. Quoted in Wood, *Creation of the American Republic*, 6.

10. Daniel Leonard, "Daniel Leonard's Letter of January 9 1775," American History: From Revolution to Reconstruction and Beyond, 2012, http://www.let.rug.nl/usa/documents/1751-1775/daniel-leonards-letter-of-january-9-1775.php.

11. Rowland, *Life of Mason*, 123.

12. Oliver, quoted in Adair and Schutz, *Peter Oliver's Origin*, 159.

13. Boorstin, *Hidden History*, 97–98.

14. Young, *Washington Community*, 26–27.

15. Wood, *Creation of the American Republic*, 6. See also Boorstin, *Hidden History*, 97–98.

16. Wood, *Creation of the American Republic*, vii.

17. Von Clausewitz was a Prussian general and military strategist who was born in 1780 and lived in Germany and Poland. He wrote about the moral and political facets of warfare.

18. Bickford et al., *Documentary History*, 11:1338.

19. Greenberg, *George Washington, Architect*, 95. Wren lived from 1632 to 1723.

20. Speer, *Inside the Third Reich*, 82.

21. Mahan, "Political Architecture," 31.

22. Singleton, *Story*, viii.

23. For a helpful discussion, see "Q&A: Have You Ever Wondered," White House Historical Association, https://www.whitehousehistory.org/questions/.

24. Quoted in Singleton, *Story*, x.

25. "Recorded Speeches and Utterances of Franklin D. Roosevelt, 1920–1945," Franklin D. Roosevelt Presidential Library and Museum, 2016, https://fdrlibrary.org/utterancesfdr.

12. Convention

1. For a good source on Shays and the rebellion, see Richards, *Shays's Rebellion*.

2. For a helpful discussion, see Richards.

3. George Washington to David Humphreys, October 22, 1786, in Crackel, *Papers of Washington Digital Edition*.

4. For a helpful discussion, see Richards, *Shays's Rebellion*.

5. George Washington to Henry Knox, February 25, 1787, in Crackel, *Papers of Washington Digital Edition*.

6. *New York Morning Post*, August 4, 1789, https://www.genealogybank.com/explore/newspapers/all/usa/new-york/new-york/new-york-morning-post; see also DePauw et al., *Documentary History*.

7. Washington to Knox, February 25, 1787.

8. Rhodehamel, *George Washington*, 103.

9. George Mason to George Washington, October 7, 1787, in Rutland, *Papers of Mason*; see also the Elbridge Gerry correspondence in Elbridge Gerry Papers, Massachusetts Historical Society, Boston; and the letters of Hugh Williamson.

10. Grayson to James Monroe, May 29, 1787, in Monroe Papers.

11. *New York Daily Gazette*, June 14, 1790, in Library of Congress.

12. Farrand, *Records of the Federal Convention*, 2:127–28, 260–63.

13. Bowling, *Creation of Washington*, 76.

13. Ten Miles Square

1. James Madison, Federalist No. 43, in *The Federalist Papers*, https://www.congress.gov/resources/display/content/the+federalist+papers#TheFederalistPapers-43.

2. Pelatiah Webster [Citizen of Philadelphia], "Essay on the Seat of the Federal Government and the Exclusive Jurisdiction of Congress over a Ten Miles District," *Pennsylvania Mercury and Universal Advertiser*, 1789, 15–29; see also Percy L. Greaves, "Our Republic's First Economist," Bellevue University Economics Department, July 4, 1951, http://jpatton.bellevue.edu/pelatiah-webster-economist.html.

3. Bowling, *Creation of Washington*, 5.

4. Charles Willson Peale to George Washington, June 27, 1790, in George Washington Papers, Library of Congress; see also Madsen, *National University*; and Bowling, *Creation of Washington*, 6.

5. Costanzo, *George Washington's Washington*, 13–17; Kapsch, *Building Washington*, 255.

6. The quote comes courtesy of Dr. James McHenry, a delegate from Maryland to the convention. Some sources omit Franklin's use of "Madam," while others suggest he was not addressing just Mrs. Powel but a crowd.

7. Bowling, *Creation of Washington*, 75, 83.

8. Hutchinson, Rutland, and Hobson, *Papers of Madison*, 9:417; see also Patrick Henry, "Common Sense," *American Herald*, May 8, 1788, in Library of Congress.

9. Kenyon, *Antifederalists*, lxix.

10. Bowling, *Creation of Washington*, 6.

11. See "What Was the Three-Fifths Compromise?," 2017, https://constitution.laws.com/three-fifths-compromise.

12. "New York Ratifying Convention," July 15, 1788, in Founders Online, https://founders.archives.gov/documents/Hamilton/01-05-02-0012-0069.

13. Syrett, *Papers of Hamilton*, 5:189.

14. Main, *Antifederalists*, 151–52.

15. Hillary S. Kativa, "Capital of the United States (Selection of Philadelphia)," *Encyclopedia of Greater Philadelphia*, 2015, https://philadelphiaencyclopedia.org/archive/capital-of-the-us-selection/.

16. See *Pennsylvania Packet*, July 9, 1788, in Library of Congress.

17. News of the states ratifying was published in *New York Daily Advertiser*, July 14, 1788; *New York Packet*, August 12, 1788; *New York Weekly Museum*, July 29, 1788; see also Syrett, *Papers of Hamilton*, 5:160.

18. Quote appears in Washington's "Circular Letter of Farewell to the Army," June 8, 1783.

14. An Inauguration

1. Arnebeck, *Through a Fiery Trial*, 12.

2. See, for example, articles in *New York Packet* (February 10, 1789), *New York Daily Advertiser* (January 21, 1789), and *New York Daily Gazette* (January 16, 1789).

3. See the so-called Philadelphia letter in *New York Daily Advertiser*, December 8, 1790, in Library of Congress.

4. Tobias Lear to George Washington, April 24, 1791, June 5, 1791, in Founders Online, https://founders.archives.gov/documents/Washington/05-08-02-0099.

5. Bowling, *Creation of Washington*, 89–90.

6. For a helpful discussion, see Davis, *Sectionalism in American Politics*.

7. George Washington to Henry Lee, September 22, 1788, in Fitzpatrick, *Writings of Washington*, 30:95–96.

8. George Washington to James McHenry, July 31, 1788, in Fitzpatrick, 30:29.

9. David Stuart to George Washington, July 14, 1789, in Washington Papers, Library of Congress; see also Boyd et al., *Papers of Jefferson*, 19:51.

10. *Federal Gazette* (Philadelphia), March 6, 1789, in Library of Congress.

11. Humphreys, "Remarks," 47–48.

12. Chernow, *Washington*, 644; see also George Washington to John Greenwood, January 20, 1797, in Rhodehamel, *George Washington*, 985–86.

13. John Greenwood to George Washington, December 28, 1798, in Abbot et al., *Papers of Washington*, 3:289.

14. Chernow, *Washington*, 643.

15. For a helpful source, see Erick Trickey, "George Washington's Congress Got Off to an Embarrassing Start," *Smithsonian Magazine* (April 28, 2017), www.smithsonian.com/history/congress-embarrassing-start-and-how-madison-kicked-it-gear-180963079/.

16. Fitzpatrick, *Writings of Washington*, 30:267–69.

17. George Washington to Henry Knox, April 1, 1789, file #GLC 2437 LIII, p. 69, Gilder Lehrman Collection, Pierpont Morgan Library.

18. George Washington to Lafayette, January 29, 1789, in Founders Online, https://founders.archives.gov/documents/Washington/05-01-02-0198.

19. See "President-Elect George Washington's Journey to the Inauguration," George Washington's Mount Vernon, https://www.mountvernon.org/george-washington/the-first-president/inauguration/.

20. See "Presidential Election of 1789," George Washington's Mount Vernon, https://www.mountvernon.org/library/digitalhistory/digital-encyclopedia/article/presidential-election-of-1789/.

21. "The Inauguration of George Washington," in Jackson and Twohig, *Diaries of Washington*, 445–49.

22. George Washington, "First Inaugural Address," April 30, 1789, Center for Legislative Archives, National Archives, https://www.archives.gov/legislative/features/gw-inauguration.

23. Rhodehamel, *George Washington*, 119.

15. New York City

1. Martha Washington to Elizabeth Ramsay, December 30, 1775, in Fields, "*Worthy Partner*."

2. For a discussion of the scene, see Bass, *Description of the Diorama*.

3. Flexner, *Washington*, 171.

4. George Washington to Catherine Macaulay Graham, January 9, 1790, in Founders Online, https://founders.archives.gov/documents/Washington/05-04-02-0363.

5. For a helpful discussion, see "10 Facts about President Washington's Election," George Washington's Mount Vernon, http://www.mountvernon.org/george-washington/the-first-president/election/10-facts-about-washingtons-election/.

6. "President-Elect George Washington's Journey."

7. See "Teaching with Documents: America Votes," Educator Resources, National Archives, last updated August 15, 2016, https://www.archives.gov/education/lessons/vote.html; and "Presidential Election of 1789: A Resource Guide," Library of Congress, October 23, 2018, https://www.loc.gov/rr/program/bib/elections/election1789.html.

8. Martha Washington to Fanny Bassett Washington, October 23, 1789, George Washington's Mount Vernon, www.mountvernon.org/education/primary-sources-2/article/letter-martha-washington-to-fanny-bassett-washington-october-23-1789/.

9. George Washington to John Adams, May 10, 1789, in Founders Online, https://founders.archives.gov/documents/Washington/05-02-02-0182; see also George Washington to David Stuart, July 26, 1789, in Founders Online, https://founders.archives.gov/documents/Washington/05-03-02-0180.

10. See Tagg, "Benjamin Franklin Bache's Attack."

11. Flexner, *Washington*, 155.

12. Thomas Jefferson to Mrs. Eppes, June 13, 1790, in Randolph, *Domestic Life of Thomas Jefferson*, 184.

13. See Page, Washington in New York in 1789.

14. See *New York Morning Post and Daily Advertiser*, in Library of Congress; for criticism, see T. E. V. Smith, *New York*; and Monaghan and Lowenthal, *This Was New York*.

15. Bowling, "Neither in a Wigwam nor the Wilderness," 163–79.

16. Bowling, *Creation of Washington*, 131.

17. Bowling, 129.

18. Boyd et al., *Papers of Jefferson*, 19:6.

16. The Great Debate

1. For a helpful discussion, see Bowling, *Creation of Washington*.

2. Bowling, *Creation of Washington*, 134–38.

3. 1 Annals of the Cong., 819 (1789); DenBoer et al., *Documentary History*, 1:97–100.

4. Bowling, *Creation of Washington*, 211.

5. The vote is discussed in a letter in Boyd et al., *Papers of Jefferson*, 16:449.

6. Bowling, "Dinner at Jefferson's"; see also "The First Federal Congress Exhibit Teacher's Guide," Birth of the Nation: First Federal Congress, 1789–1791, 2000, http://www2.gwu.edu/~ffcp/exhibit/lessonplans/approach3.html.

7. See "How Philly Lost"; and Riley, "Philadelphia, the Nation's Capital."

8. Flexner, *Washington*, 155.

9. Bowling, *Creation of Washington*, 88.

10. *Pennsylvania Gazette*, March 18, 1789, in Library of Congress.

11. Bowling, *Creation of Washington*, 142.

12. DenBoer et al., *Documentary History*, 4:274–77; see also *New York Daily Advertiser* (April 15, 1789), *New York Daily Gazette* (May 22, 1789), and *New York Journal* (April 2, 1789), available in the Library of Congress newspaper archives.

13. Bowling, *Creation of Washington*, 142.

14. Elias Boudinot to John Caldwell, May 17, 1790, in Special Collections, Rutgers University Library (historians are not completely sure if the letter was to Caldwell).

15. Boyd et al., *Papers of Jefferson*, 18:163–83.

16. Cutler, *Explanation of the Map*.

17. Bowling, *Creation of Washington*, 12.

18. Bowling, *Creation of Washington*, 9.

19. The article, written under the pseudonym "X," appeared in *New York Journal* on September 3, 1789. Other satirical pieces appeared in *New York Daily Advertiser* on June 2, 1790.

20. 1 Annals of Congress 868–69 (1789).

21. Boyd et al., *Papers of Jefferson*, 19:19.

22. See "1790 Overview," US Census, www.census.gov/history/www/through_the _decades/overview/1790.html.

23. See *New York Daily Gazette* (May 26, 1789) and *New York Daily Advertiser* (June 5, 1789), both in Library of Congress.

24. Morris to his wife, September 15, 1789, in Morris Papers, Huntington Library; see also Boyd et al., *Papers of Jefferson*, 19:7, 9.

25. Robert Morris to Mary Morris, May 23, 1789, in Morris Papers, Huntington Library.

26. P. Muhlenberg to Benjamin Rush, September 9, 1789; see also Hartley to Jasper Yeates, September 20, 1789, Historical Society of Pennsylvania, Philadelphia.

27. Bowling, *Creation of Washington*, 149.

28. Grogg, "Introduction: Where Oh Where"; see also Alan Taylor, "The New Nation, 1783–1815," *History Now*, https://www.gilderlehrman.org/history-now/new -nation-1783–1815.

29. Wilkinson, *Land Policy and Speculation*, 9; see also Bowling, *Creation of Washington*, 145.

30. Bowling, *Creation of Washington*, 11; see also Charles Carroll, "Reasons against Moving the Seat of Government," Manuscript no. 215, in Carroll Collection, Maryland Historical Society.

31. George Washington to David Stuart, March 28, 1790, in Fitzpatrick, *Writings of Washington*, 31:28–30.

32. George Washington to Alexander Hamilton, in Syrett, *Papers of Hamilton*, 4:225.

33. George Washington to Bushrod Washington, November 10, 1787, in *Documentary History of the Constitution*, 4:373–74.

34. James Madison to Thomas Jefferson, October 17, 1788, in Boyd et al., *Jefferson Papers*, 14:18.

35. Ketcham, *James Madison*, 309.

36. Alexander Hamilton to John Jay, November 13, 1790, in Syrett, *Papers of Hamilton*, 12:149.

37. September 4 and 21, 1789, in Hutchinson, Rutland, and Hobson, *Papers of Madison*, 12:373–79.

38. Boyd et al., *Papers of Jefferson*, 19:14; see also Bowling, *Creation of Washington*, 154.

39. Beverley Randolph to the Governor of Maryland, December 16, 1789, in Virginia State Library, Richmond.

40. Boyd et al., *Papers of Jefferson*, 19:7.

41. Hutchinson, Rutland, and Hobson, *Papers of Madison*, 12:128, 343.

42. See John O'Connor, *Political Opinions Particularly Respecting the Seat of the Federal Empire*, October 1789, Georgetown, 43–44.

43. *Maryland Journal and Baltimore Advertiser*, March 24, 1789, in Library of Congress; see also a story on this topic in the *Maryland Historical Magazine* 71, 310–21.

44. See, for example, *Maryland Journal and Baltimore Advertiser*, January 23, 1789, and April 8, 1791, in Library of Congress.

45. See, for example, articles in *Virginia Gazette* (May 6, 1790), *Massachusetts Centinel* (May 22, 1790), *American Mercury* (May 24, 1790), and *Cumberland Gazette* (May 31, 1790).

46. Bowling, *Creation of Washington*, 142.

47. Fisher Ames to Theodore Sedgwick, October 6, 1789, in Sedgwick Papers.

48. Clymer to Peters, September 9, 1789, in Pennsylvania Historical Society, Philadelphia.

40. Hutchinson, Rutland, and Hobson, *Papers of Madison*, 12:419.

50. Robert Morris to Mary Morris, September 9, 1789, Morris Papers, Huntington Library; see also David Stuart to George Washington, September 12, 1789, in Fitzpatrick, *Writings of Washington*, 30:147; the letters are also in the Washington Papers, Library of Congress.

51. R. N. Smith, *Patriarch*, 22.

52. R. N. Smith, 40.

53. William Grayson to Patrick Henry, September 29, 1789, in Henry Papers.

54. Fisher Ames to Theodore Sedgwick, October 6, 1789, in Sedgwick Papers.

55. See *New York Packet* (September 10, 1789), *New York Journal* (September 17, 1789), and *New York Daily Advertiser* (September 8, 1789), available in Library of Congress newspaper archives.

17. The (Second) Most Famous Dinner in History

1. Rhodehamel, *American Revolution*, 128.

2. Chernow, *Washington*, 630.

3. W. Maclay, *Journal of Maclay*, 374, 395–98.

4. Chernow, *Washington*, 620. See also "Report Relative to a Provision for the Support of Public Credit," in Syrett, *Papers of Hamilton*, 6:52–168.

5. Flexner, *Washington*, 249.

6. Flexner, 246.

7. Horton, "Alexander Hamilton."

8. Hamilton, *Writings*, 56–57.

9. Elkins and McKitrick, *Age of Federalism*, 77–92.

10. Hamilton's views were published by his friend John Fenno in *Gazette of the United States*, while Jefferson's views were published as a pamphlet by Childs and Swaine, for example. See also Boyd et al., *Papers of Jefferson*, 19:xxxii.

11. George Washington to David Stuart, June 15, 1790, in Rhodehamel, *George Washington*, 761.

12. Fitzpatrick, *Writings of Washington*, 31:52–53.

13. Flexner, *Washington*, 248.

14. George Washington to James Madison, May 20, 1792, Document MA 505, Washington Papers, Pierpont Morgan Library.

15. Bowling and Veit, *Diary of Maclay*, 269.

16. Ford, *Writings of Jefferson*, 5:168.

17. Fitzpatrick, *Writings of Washington*, 31:46.

18. R. N. Smith, *Patriarch*, xx–xxi.

19. Flexner, *Washington*, 246.

20. Rogers, "Letters of William Loughton Smith," 116; see also Boyd et al., *Papers of Jefferson*, 17:206; for information on the votes and gridlock, see DenBoer et al., *Documentary History*, 4:417, 432.

21. Bowling, *Creation of Washington*, 179.

22. R. N. Smith, *Patriarch*, 40–41.

23. Risjord, "Compromise of 1790," 309–14.

24. Bowling, *Creation of Washington*, 184; DePauw et al., *Documentary History*, 6:1767–91; Boyd et al., *Papers of Jefferson*, 17:206; Hutchinson, Rutland, and Hobson, *Papers of Madison*, 13:246.

25. See Chernow, *Hamilton*.

26. Joanne B. Freeman, "Jefferson and Hamilton, Political Rivals in Washington's Cabinet," n.d., Mount Vernon, https://www.mountvernon.org/george-washington/the-first-president/washingtons-presidential-cabinet/jefferson-and-hamilton-political-rivals/.

27. Thomas Jefferson, "Memorandum on Assumption of State Debts," 1790, in Library of Congress.

28. Chernow, *Alexander Hamilton*, 328.

29. Flexner, *Washington*, 247.

18. The Grand Compromise

1. Ellis, *Founding Brothers*, 50.

2. Thomas Jefferson to James Monroe, June 20, 1790, in Boyd et al., *Papers of Jefferson*, 16:536–38; and James Monroe to Thomas Jefferson, July 3, 1790, in Boyd et al., 16:596–97.

3. Boyd et al., *Papers of Jefferson*, 17:205–7; see also Risjord, "Compromise of 1790," 309–14.

4. Thomas Jefferson, "Explanations of the Three Volumes Bound in Marbled Paper" (aka "Anas"), February 4, 1818, in Founders Online, https://founders.archives.gov/documents/Jefferson/03-02-0343-0002.

5. Ellis, *Founding Brothers*, 70.

6. Ellis, 53–54; see also McCoy, *Last of the Fathers*, xiii.

7. Flexner, *Washington*, 248; see also Bowling, *Creation of Washington*, 186.

8. Theodore Sedgwick to Pamela Sedgwick, June 22 and June 27, 1790, Sedgwick Papers; see also Boyd et al., *Papers of Jefferson*, 17:207.

9. James Madison to Pendleton, June 20, 1790, in Rutland and Mason, *Papers of Madison*, 13:252.

10. Henry Lee to James Madison, March 4, 1790, and April 3, 1790, in Rutland and Mason, 13:87–90, 136.

11. Bowling, *Creation of Washington*, 188.

12. *New York Journal*, July 13, 1790 (written by "Civis"), in Library of Congress.

13. See Hamilton's New York letter in *American Mercury*, July 12, 1790, in Library of Congress; see also Cooke, "Compromise of 1790," 523–45; and June 30, 1790, in DePauw et al., *Documentary History*, 6:1767–91. For a good discussion, see Bowling, *Creation of Washington*, 187.

14. July 15, 1790, entry in W. Maclay, *Journal of Maclay*.

15. See *New York Journal*, July 27, 1790, in Library of Congress; see also Boyd et al., *Papers of Jefferson*, 17:182.

16. *Documentary History of the First Federal Congress*, vol. 20, 2137.

17. Fitzpatrick, *Writings of Washington*, 31:45; see also Chernow, *Washington*, 630.

18. George Washington to David Stuart, June 15, 1790, in Rhodehamel, *George Washington*, 761.

19. Ellis, *Founding Brothers*, 49.

20. Boyd et al., *Papers of Jefferson*, 17:205–7; see also a later version, apparently written around 1818, of the account in Sawvel, *Complete Anas*.

21. "X. Jefferson's Account of the Bargain on the Assumption and Residence Bills," 1792, in Founders Online, National Archives, https://founders.archives.gov /documents/Jefferson/01-17-02-0018-0012; see also Boyd et al., *Papers of Jefferson*, 17:205–8.

22. Thomas Jefferson to George Washington, September 9, 1792, in Abbot et al., *Papers of Washington*, 11:98; see also Ford, *Writings of Jefferson*, 5:187–89.

23. Miller, *Alexander Hamilton*, 248–49.

24. Bowling, *Creation of Washington*, x–xi.

25. Daniel Webster, "Hamilton, the Financier" (speech, March 10, 1831), in Stedman and Hutchinson, *Library of American Literature*, vol. 4, *Literature of the Republic*, pt. 1, "Constitutional Period."

19. The Residence Act of 1790

1. Mellon, *Book of the United States*, chap. 4.

2. *Old New York*, July 20, 1790.

3. George Washington to David Stuart, June 15, 1790, in Fitzpatrick, *Writings of Washington*, 31:50.

4. Kapsch, *Building Washington*, 7.

5. Several letters were exchanged between Washington and Jefferson, and Washington and Madison during the debate on the bill. They are in Madison Papers, Library of Congress; Boyd et al., *Papers of Jefferson*; Stagg, *Papers of Madison*; and Jackson and Twohig, *Diaries of Washington*. See also Bowling, *Creation of Washington*, 193.

6. Bowling, x–xi.

7. Freeman, *George Washington*, 6:265.

8. Bordewich, *Washington*, 196.

9. Ellis, *Founding Brothers*, 60.

10. Costanzo, *George Washington's Washington*, 4.

11. Bowling and Veit, *Diary of Maclay*, 385–86; see also Boyd et al., *Papers of Jefferson*, 19:35.

12. Fitzpatrick, *Writings of Washington*, 30:408, 31:24–26.

13. For Adams's quote, see Janson, *Stranger in America*, 206; see also Schutz and Adair, *Spur of Fame*, 174–85. For Nisbet, see Bowling, *Creation of Washington*, 213.

14. James Madison, Federalist No. 43, in *The Federalist Papers*, Library of Congress, guides.loc.gov/federalist-papers/full-text.

15. Costanzo, *George Washington's Washington*, 1.

16. Fitzpatrick, *Writings of Washington*, 31:176–77; see also Clephane, "Writings of Washington," 32.

17. See letters of March 18, 1799, and April 22, 1799, in Thornton Papers, Library of Congress; see also Jackson and Twohig, *Diaries of Washington*, 6:343–44.

18. W. Maclay, *Journal of Maclay*, 376.

19. E. S. Maclay, *Diary of Maclay*, 368; see also William Maclay to Benjamin Rush, July 10, 1790, in W. Maclay, *Journal of Maclay*.

20. Daily Advertiser, July 13. *Columbian Herald* (Charleston, SC), August 10, 1790, in Library of Congress.

21. *New York Daily Gazette*, July 10, 1790, in Library of Congress.

22. Hening, *Statutes at Large*, 13:43–44.

23. Kapsch, *Building Washington*, 9.

24. Kapsch, 85.

20. Philadelphia

1. Act Ceding Land in Virginia to the Federal Government, December 3, 1789.

2. Boller, *Presidential Diversions*.

3. Fitzpatrick, *Writings of Washington*, 31:91.

4. Flexner, *Washington*, 269.

5. See "The Senate Moves to Philadelphia," US Senate, https://www.senate.gov /artandhistory/history/minute/The_Senate_Moves_To_Philidelphia.htm.

6. See Abigail Adams, letter, December 12, 1790, in Letters of Abigail Adams, American Antiquarian Society, http://americanantiquarian.org/abigailadams/exhibits /show/letters/item/745.

7. "Senate Moves to Philadelphia."

8. Griswold, *Republican Court*, 251–52.

9. Griswold.

10. R. N. Smith, *Patriarch*, 32.

11. H. Adams, *History of the United States*; see also Schachner, *Founding Fathers*, chap. 2.

12. Riley, "Philadelphia, the Nation's Capital," 369.

13. "Senate Moves to Philadelphia."

14. The letter from James Monroe is quoted in Griswold, *Republican Court*, 252; the other quotes are found in Christman, *First Federal Congress*, 196–97.

15. Fitzpatrick, *Writings of Washington*, 31:142.

16. For a description of Harriet, see Harriet Washington to George Washington, April 2, 1790, in Founders Online, https://founders.archives.gov/documents/Washington/05-05-02-0199; and George Washington to David Stuart, September 21, 1794, in Founders Online, https://founders.archives.gov/documents/Washington/05-15-02-0289.

17. Described in Flexner, *Washington*, 270; see also Fitzpatrick, *Writings of Washington*, 37:570–71.

18. Quoted and discussed in Chernow, *Washington*, 645.

19. Bowling, "Foreboding Shadow," 7.

20. Chateaubriand, *Memoirs*, bk. vi, chap. 7, sec. 1, 1822.

21. Chateaubriand, sec. 2, 1822.

22. Decatur, *Private Affairs*, 311.

23. Singleton, *Story*, 23.

24. Flexner, *Washington*, 269.

25. Watson, *Affairs of State*, 70–72.

26. Parsons, "George Washington."

27. Flexner, *Washington*, 270.

28. Graff, *Presidents*, 5.

29. Whitcomb and Whitcomb, *Real Life*, 2.

30. Singleton, *Story*, 19.

31. Alexander Hamilton to George Washington, May 5, 1789, in Founders Online, https://founders.archives.gov/documents/Hamilton/01-05-02-0128.

32. Martha Washington to Fanny Bassett Washington, October 23, 1789, George Washington's Mount Vernon, https://www.mountvernon.org/education/primary-sources-2/article/letter-martha-washington-to-fanny-bassett-washington-october-23-1789.

33. Seale, *White House*, 1:5.

34. Singleton, *Story*, 23.

35. Singleton, 24.

36. Whitcomb and Whitcomb, *Real Life*, 2.

37. Singleton, *Story*, 23.

38. Wentworth, *Ladies' Repository*, 499.

39. Abigail Adams to Mary Smith Cranch, 1800.

40. Whitcomb and Whitcomb, *Real Life*, 8.

41. Chernow, *Washington*, 700.

42. Martha Washington to Fanney Basset Washington, August 4, 1793, in Fields, *"Worthy Partner,"* 250.

43. Letter about J. A. Snidely, in Cappon, *Adams-Jefferson Letters*, 347.

44. Elizabeth Willing Powel to George Washington, September 1793, in Abbot et al., *Papers of Washington*, 14:36, 54.

45. Henry Knox to George Washington, September 18, 1793, in Abbot et al., *Papers of Washington*, 14:113.

46. Chernow, *Alexander Hamilton*, 452.

47. Unger, *Unexpected George Washington*, 222.

21. The City of Washington

1. Boyd et al., *Papers of Jefferson*, 17:460–61.

2. Thomas Jefferson to Charles L'Enfant, March 2, 1791, in Founders Online, https://founders.archives.gov/documents/Jefferson/01-19-02-0093; see also Verner, "Surveying and Mapping."

3. Jackson and Twohig, *Diaries of Washington*, 6:105.

4. Boyd et al., *Papers of Jefferson*, 17:460–63.

5. Thomas Jefferson to George Washington, August 29, 1790, in Founders Online, https://founders.archives.gov/documents/washington/05-06-02-0174.

6. Boyd et al., *Papers of Jefferson*, 19:32.

7. "James Madison's Advice on Executing the Residence Act," August 29, 1790, in Boyd et al., *Papers of Jefferson*, 19:58–60.

8. Thomas Jefferson to George Washington and James Madison to George Washington, August 1790, in Boyd et al., *Papers of Jefferson*, 17:460–61.

9. *Maryland Journal and Baltimore Advertiser*, October 26, 1790, in Library of Congress.

10. Thomas Jefferson to George Washington, October 27, 1790, in Founders Online, https://founders.archives.gov/documents/washington/05-06-02-0278; see also George Washington to Elizabethtown Citizens, October 20, 1790, in Founders Online, https://founders.archives.gov/documents/washington/05-06-02-0269.

11. See "Fixing the Seat of Government on the Potomac," in Boyd et al., *Papers of Jefferson*, 17:452–60.

12. "The Proclamation by the President," January 24, 1791, in Founders Online, https://founders.archives.gov/documents/jefferson/01-19-02-0001-0015.

13. Boyd et al., *Papers of Jefferson*, 19:25.

14. Fitzpatrick, *Writings of Washington*, xxxi, 204–5; see also Flexner, *Washington*, 271.

15. Boyd et al., *Papers of Jefferson*, 19:26.

16. W. Maclay, *Journal of Maclay*, 375 and 384.

17. Seale, *White House*, 77–79.

18. Federal Commissioners to L'Enfant, September 9, 1791, in Padover, *Thomas Jefferson*, 47; see also Fitzpatrick, *Writings of Washington*, xxxi; and Chernow, *Washington*, 663.

19. Boyd et al., *Papers of Jefferson*, 19:65–66.

22. Financing the Capital

1. "The Bank Bill," February 1 and 2, 1791, in Founders Online, https://founders
.archives.gov/documents/Madison/01-13-02-0282.

2. "Bank Bill"; see also *General Advertiser*, February 7, 1791, and *Gazette of the United States*, February 23, 1791, both in Library of Congress.

3. "Bank Bill."

4. Ellis, *Founding Brothers*, 57.

5. See "Philadelphia Letter," *Cumberland Gazette*, March 14, 1791, in Library of Congress; see also Boyd et al., *Papers of Jefferson*, 19:35.

6. George Washington to Alexander Hamilton, February 23, 1791, in Syrett, *Papers of Hamilton*, 8:134–35.

7. George Washington to Alexander Hamilton, February 16, 1791; Alexander Hamilton to George Washington, February 23, 1791, in Syrett, *Papers of Hamilton*, 8:62–63.

8. See George Washington to Alexander Hamilton and Alexander Hamilton to George Washington, January and February 1791, in Syrett, *Papers of Hamilton*, 8:50, 134–36.

9. Ford, *Writings of Jefferson*, 5:187–89.

10. *American Daily Advertiser*, February 16, 1791, in Library of Congress.

11. W. Maclay, *Journal of Maclay*, 401.

12. See the letter, March 29, 1791, in Fitzpatrick, *Writings of Washington*, 31:153–54.

13. Clephane, "Writings of Washington."

14. Clephane.

15. Whitcomb and Whitcomb, *Real Life*, 6.

16. George Washington to Deakins and Stoddert, February 3, 1791, and George Washington to Deakins and Stoddert, February 17, 1791, in Clephane, "Writings of Washington"; the letters are also available in Founders Online, https://founders
.archives.gov/documents/Washington/05-07-02-0214.

17. See *Georgetown Weekly Ledger* (July 2, 1791), *General Advertiser* (July 12, 1791), and *Maryland Journal* (September 30, 1791), all in Library of Congress.

18. George Washington to Arthur Young, December 12, 1793, in Fitzpatrick, *Writings of Washington*, 33:175–76.

19. Boyd et al., *Papers of Jefferson*, 19:47.

20. George Washington to Henry Lee, September 22, 1788, in Fitzpatrick, *Writings of Washington*, 30:95–96.

21. Bowling, *Creation of Washington*, 222.

22. George Washington, letter, December 12, 1793, in Boyd et al., *Papers of Jefferson*, 27:5; see also Fitzpatrick, *Writings of Washington*, 35:328–29.

23. See Clephane, "Writings of Washington," 51–52.

24. Dunlop's *Daily Advertiser*, February 21, 1792, in Library of Congress; see also R. N. Smith, *Patriarch*, 128.

25. Chernow, *Washington*, 661.

26. Lear papers and diary; see also Tobias Lear to Samuel Powell, September 20, 1791, in Fisher Family Papers, and Tobias Lear to George Washington, April 24, 1791, in Founders Online, https://founders.archives.gov/documents/Washington/05-08-02 -0099.

23. The Architect

1. See Bowling, *Peter Charles L'Enfant*, for a detailed discussion of the architect's name.

2. See Bowling, 1.

3. Bowling, 2.

4. Seale, *White House*, 2–3.

5. Bowling, *Peter Charles L'Enfant*, 21.

6. Pierre L'Enfant to George Washington, September 11, 1789, in Kite, *L'Enfant and Washington*, 14.

7. Kite, 1.

8. No letter survives about the hiring of L'Enfant, but a letter from Jefferson to the commissioners on January 29, 1791, alludes to the hiring of the architect by Washington. See Kite, *L'Enfant and Washington*, 33.

9. *Georgetown Weekly Ledger*, March 12, 1791, in Library of Congress.

10. Bowling, *Peter Charles L'Enfant*, 29.

11. March 4, 1789–March 3, 1791, in Bowling and Veit, *Diary of Maclay*, 368.

12. Thomas Jefferson to Pierre Charles L'Enfant, March [2,] 1791, in Founders Online, https://founders.archives.gov/documents/Jefferson/01-19-02-0093.

13. Kite, *L'Enfant and Washington*, 32. Washington wrote to Ellicott on February 4, 1791.

14. Arnebeck, *Through a Fiery Trial*, 38.

15. Kite, *L'Enfant and Washington*, 35.

16. Arnebeck, *Through a Fiery Trial*, 56–57.

17. Andrew Ellicott to Sally Ellicott, August 9, 1791, in Matthews, *Andrew Ellicott*, 90.

18. Arnebeck, *Through a Fiery Trial*, 39; see also Cerami, *Benjamin Banneker*; and Bedini, *Life of Benjamin Banneker*.

19. Weatherly, *Benjamin Banneker*, 75–76.

20. See the *Georgetown Weekly Record*, March 12, 1791; Benjamin Banneker to Thomas Jefferson, August 19, 1791, in both Cerami, *Benjamin Banneker*; and Bedini, *Life of Benjamin Banneker*, 136.

21. Cerami, *Benjamin Banneker*; and Bedini, *Life of Benjamin Banneker*, 164. The twelve-page letter was later published in Banneker's almanac.

22. Padover, *Thomas Jefferson*, 42.

23. Pierre L'Enfant to Thomas Jefferson, March 10, 1791, in Boyd et al., *Papers of Jefferson*.

24. Andrew Ellicott to Sally Ellicott, June 26, 1791, in Alexander, "Sketch of the Life," 173–75.

25. Dabney, "George Washington Reconsidered," 83–89.

26. Pierre L'Enfant to Alexander Hamilton, April 8, 1791, in Syrett, *Papers of Hamilton*, 8:253–56.

27. See R. N. Smith, *Patriarch*, 23.

28. Bowling, *Peter Charles L'Enfant*, 26.

29. Pierre L'Enfant to George Washington, August 27, 1791, in Kite, *L'Enfant and Washington*, 16.

30. L'Enfant to George Washington, March 1791, in Kite, 45.

31. Twohig, *George Washington's Diaries*, 8:290; see also Whitcomb and Whitcomb, *Real Life*, 3.

32. Arnebeck, *Through a Fiery Trial*, 51.

33. Pierre Charles L'Enfant to George Washington, August 19, 1791, in Twohig, *George Washington's Diaries*, 8:440.

34. National Constitution Center, "Why Did the U.S. Capital Move from Philadelphia to D.C.?," *Constitution Daily* (blog), https://blog.constitutioncenter.org/2011/07/philly-asks-why-did-you-leave-me-for-dce2809d.

35. L'Enfant to George Washington, March 1791, in Kite, *L'Enfant and Washington*, 52–58.

36. Caemmerer, *Life of L'Enfant*, 162.

37. Thomas Jefferson, memorandum, September 14, 1790, in Founders Online, founders.archives.gov/documents/washington/05-06-02-0209; see also Harris, "Washington's 'Federal City.'"

38. Harris, 51.

39. Costanzo, *George Washington's Washington*, 23–24.

40. See Kite, *L'Enfant and Washington*, 35–58; see also Stephenson and Sibley, "Delineation of a Grand Plan," 207–78.

41. See "The L'Enfant & McMillan Plans," National Park Service, n.d., www.nps.gov/nr/travel/wash/lenfant.htm; see also Harris, "Washington's Gamble."

42. Bowling, *Creation of Washington*, 6.

43. Pierre L'Enfant to George Washington, September 11, 1789, in Washington Papers, Library of Congress.

24. Intrigues and Injuries

1. Bob Arnebeck, "The Use of Slaves to Build the Capitol and White House, 1791–1801," Slaves in Early Washington, http://bobarnebeck.com/slavespt5.html.

2. Harris, "Washington's Gamble," 527–64.

3. Commissioners to George Washington, August 2, 1791, in Founders Online, https://founders.archives.gov/documents/washington/05-09-02-0142.

4. Daniel Carroll to James Madison, April 23, 1791, in Kite, *L'Enfant and Washington*, 51; see also Arnebeck, *Through a Fiery Trial*, 66.

5. Arnebeck, *Through a Fiery Trial*, 64.

6. Commissioners to George Washington, August 2, 1791.

7. Pierre L'Enfant to George Washington, August 19, 1791, in L'Enfant Papers; see also Kite, *L'Enfant and Washington*.

8. Arnebeck, *Through a Fiery Trial*, 80–81.

9. Pierre L'Enfant to George Washington, June 22, 1791, in Jackson and Twohig, *Diaries of Washington*, 6:166.

10. See the *National Intelligencer*, March 16, 1808, and *Columbian Mirror*, August 12, 1797, both in Library of Congress.

11. Arnebeck, *Through a Fiery Trial*, 54.

12. Arnebeck, 56–57.

13. Commissioners to George Washington, August 2, 1791.

14. Thomas Jefferson to Pierre Charles L'Enfant, August 18, 1791, in Boyd et al., *Papers of Jefferson*, 22:47–48.

15. Kite, *L'Enfant and Washington*, 23.

16. George Washington to Daniel Carroll, December 2, 1791, in Founders Online, https://founders.archives.gov/documents/Washington/05-09-02-0145.

17. Arnebeck, *Through a Fiery Trial*, 77; Padover, *Thomas Jefferson*, 78–86; see also Clephane, "Writings of George Washington," 34–50.

18. Clephane, 34–35.

19. George Washington to David Stuart, November 20, 1791, in Founders Online, https://founders.archives.gov/documents/Washington/05-09-02-0118.

20. See both Arnebeck, *Through a Fiery Trial*, 87–88; and Bowling, *Peter Charles L'Enfant*, 30–33, for a discussion of Washington's patience and views on L'Enfant's ability to complete the project.

21. Padover, *Thomas Jefferson*, 78–86.

22. Padover.

23. George Washington to Pierre L'Enfant, December 13, 1791, in Founders On-line, https://founders.archives.gov/documents/Washington/05-09-02-0170.

24. Pierre L'Enfant to Thomas Jefferson, in Caemmerer, *Life of L'Enfant*, 136.

25. See George Washington to Thomas Jefferson, March 16, 1791, in Founders Online, https://founders.archives.gov/documents/Washington/05-07-02-0327; and Thomas Jefferson to Pierre L'Enfant, March 17, 1791, in Founders Online, https://founders.archives.gov/documents/Washington/05-07-02-0333; see also Padover, *Thomas Jefferson*; see also George Washington to William Deakins and Benjamin Stoddert, February 3, 1791, in Founders Online, https://founders.archives.gov/documents /Washington/05-07-02-0179; and George Washington to William Deakins and Benjamin Stoddert, March 17, 1791, in Founders Online, https://founders.archives.gov /documents/Jefferson/01-20-02-0001-0006.

26. George Washington to Thomas Jefferson, November 30, 1791, in Abbot et al., *Papers of Washington*, 9:239.

27. George Washington to David Stuart, November 20, 1791.

28. George Washington to Pierre L'Enfant, December 2, 1791, in Founders On-line, https://founders.archives.gov/documents/washington/05-09-02-0146.

29. George Washington to the Federal Commissioners, December 1, 18, and 27, 1791, in Founders Online, https://founders.archives.gov/documents/Washington/05-09 -02-0183; see also https://founders.archives.gov/documents/Washington/05-09-02-0207.

30. George Washington to L'Enfant, November 28, 1791, December 2, 1791, and December 13, 1791, in Founders Online, https://founders.archives.gov/documents /Washington/05-09-02-0136; see also https://founders.archives.gov/documents /Washington/05-09-02-0146; and https://founders.archives.gov/documents /Washington/05-09-02-0170.

31. L'Enfant to George Washington, January 17, 1792, and February 6, 1792, in Kite, *L'Enfant and Washington*, 89–91.

32. Pierre L'Enfant to George Washington, December 7, 1791, in Founders On-line, https://founders.archives.gov/documents/Washington/05-09-02-0157.

33. Chernow, *Washington*, 664.

34. Pamela Scott, "L'Enfant's Washington Described: The City in the Public Press, 1791–1795," *Washington History* 3 (1991): 103.

35. *Gazette of the United States*, January 5, 1792, in Library of Congress.

36. George Washington to Pierre L'Enfant, December 2, 1791, in Abbot et al., *Papers of Washington*, 9:425.

37. George Washington to Thomas Jefferson, January 15, 1792, in Founders Online, https://founders.archives.gov/documents/Washington/05-09-02-0261; see also Padover, *Thomas Jefferson*. Washington also wrote to his commissioners, see the letter on January 17, 1792, in Fitzpatrick, *Writings of Washington*.

38. Commissioners for the District of Columbia to George Washington, January 7, 1782, in Founders Online, https://founders.archives.gov/documents/washington/05 -09-02-0235.

39. Berg, *Grand Avenues*, 175.

40. Thomas Jefferson to Pierre L'Enfant, January 7, 1792, in Founders Online, https://founders.archives.gov/documents/Jefferson/01-23-02-0021; see also Boyd et al., *Papers of Jefferson*.

41. George Washington to Thomas Jefferson, January 18, 1792, in Abbot et al., *Papers of Washington*, 9:469.

42. Pierre L'Enfant to Tobias Lear, February 17, 1792, in Kite, *L'Enfant and Washington*.

43. Pierre L'Enfant to Thomas Jefferson, February 22, 1792, Founders Online, founders.archives.gov/documents/Jefferson/01-23-02-0153; see also Boyd et al., *Papers of Jefferson*.

44. Kite, *L'Enfant and Washington*, 143–45.

45. Pierre L'Enfant to Thomas Jefferson, February 26, 1792, in Founders Online, https://founders.archives.gov/documents/Jefferson/01-23-02-0148. The letter is also discussed in Kite, *L'Enfant and Washington*, 146–50.

46. Reps, *Making of Urban America*, 256.

47. Kite, *L'Enfant and Washington*, 137.

48. Hamilton wrote the first draft, which was changed ever so slightly in the Jefferson draft. See Thomas Jefferson to Pierre L'Enfant, February 27, 1792, nn. 1, 2, and 3, in Founders Online, https://founders.archives.gov/documents/jefferson/01-23-02-0153.

49. Jefferson to L'Enfant, February 27, 1792.

50. Letter from L'Enfant to Washington, February 27, 1792, Founders Online.

51. Washington to L'Enfant, February 28, 1792; see also Thomas Jefferson to Pierre L'Enfant, in Syrett, *Papers of Hamilton*, 11:50.

52. Thomas Jefferson to George Walker, March 6, 1792, in Padover, *Thomas Jefferson*, 120.

53. George Washington to Thomas Jefferson, March 14, 1792, in Padover, *Thomas Jefferson*, 121.

54. Tobias Lear to David Humphreys, February 1792, in R. N. Smith, *Patriarch*, 128.

55. Pierre L'Enfant to Commissioners, March 18, 1792, in Kite, *L'Enfant and Washington*, 174.

56. Thomas Jefferson to the Federal Commissioners, March 6, 1792, in Founders Online, https://founders.archives.gov/documents/Jefferson/01-23-02-0186.

57. Arnebeck, *Through a Fiery Trial*, 78–79.

58. Pierre L'Enfant to the proprietors, March 10, 1792, in Kite, *L'Enfant and Washington*, 166.

59. Bordewich, *Washington*, 90–92; Bowling, *Peter Charles L'Enfant*, 34.

60. See Arnebeck, *Through a Fiery Trial*, 101.

61. Arnebeck, *Through a Fiery Trial*, 4.

62. See Bowling, *Peter Charles L'Enfant*, 34; and Kite, *L'Enfant and Washington*, 174–76.

63. Chernow, *Washington*, 665.

25. A Design Contest

1. Matthews, *Andrew Ellicott*, 90–93.

2. Andrew Ellicott to Mrs. Ellicott, December 14, 1792, Ellicott Papers.

3. Ellicott, *Journal*, 27.

4. See "Residence Construction: 1792–1800," White House Museum, www.white housemuseum.org/special/renovation-1792.htm.

5. Harris, "Washington's 'Federal City,'" 49–50.

6. Twohig, *George Washington's Diaries*, 7:549.

7. Boyd et al., *Papers of Jefferson*, 9:45; see also Kennon, *Republic for the Ages*, 109.

8. "Building the President's House," White House Historical Association, https://www.whitehousehistory.org/construction-of-the-white-house/building-the-presidents-house; see also Seale, *White House*, 26–27.

9. Whitcomb and Whitcomb, *Real Life*, 1.

10. Singleton, *Story*, 5.

11. Seale, *White House*, 5.

12. George Washington to David Stuart, July 9, 1792, in Clephane, "Writings of George Washington."

13. Seale, *White House*, 2; see also Arnebeck, *Through a Fiery Trial*, 125.

14. See "Washington's Southern Tour: An Interview with Warren Bingham," George Washington's Mount Vernon, https://www.mountvernon.org/george-washington/the-first-president/george-washingtons-1791-southern-tour/; see also "George Washington in Charleston, 1791," Charleston County Public Library, https://www.ccpl.org//charleston-time-machine/george-washington-charleston-1791.

15. Historian Ed Lengel, quoted in "New 1600 Sessions Podcast: "Exploring the Legacy of White House Architect James Hoban," White House Historical Association, May 25, 2018, www.whitehousehistory.org/press-room/press-releases/new-1600-sessions-podcast-exploring-the-legacy-of-white-house-architect-james-hoban; see also Seale, *White House*, 28.

16. Commissioners to George Washington, July 19, 1792, in Butler, *Competition 1792*.

17. Seale, *White House*, 6.

18. Seale.

19. "James's Hoban's Observations on William Thornton's Design for the Capitol," July 10, 1793, in Founders Online, https://founders.archives.gov/documents /Jefferson/01-26-02-0408.

20. Whitcomb and Whitcomb, *Real Life*, 1.

21. Deak, *Picturing America*, 217.

22. Caemmerer, *Life of L'Enfant*, 402–3.

23. See "Residence Construction."

26. Building the President's House

1. Arnebeck, "Use of Slaves."

2. James Hoban to Commissioners, December 1, 1792, in Kapsch, *Building Washington*, 58–60.

3. W. A. Washington to Commissioners, December 11, 1792; and Commissioners to W. A. Washington, January 2, 1793, in Arnebeck, *Through a Fiery Trial*, 142.

4. Seale, *White House*, 33.

5. See Singleton, *Story*, xxii.

6. Singleton.

7. Singleton.

8. Letter from Thomas Johnson to George Washington, February 28, 1795. Founders Online, National Archive, founders.archives.gov.

9. See Singleton, 7, for the quote and discussion of the issue.

10. The *Columbia Herald* article ran on June 6, 1796, quoted in Stewart, *Opposition Press*, 77.

11. John Adams's comments were recorded by Commissioner A. White; see Singleton, *Story*, 8–9.

12. John Laird to the Commissioners, November 15, 1792, in Arnebeck, *Through a Fiery Trial*, 142.

13. George Washington to the Commissioners, December 18, 1792, in Founders Online, https://founders.archives.gov/documents/Washington/05-09-02-0183; see also Padover, *Thomas Jefferson*, 163.

14. Arnebeck, *Through a Fiery Trial*, 122.

15. Arnebeck, 181; see also the White House Museum, "A White House of Stone," https://www.whitehousehistory.org/1600-sessions/a-white-house-of-stone.

16. Arnebeck, *Through a Fiery Trial*, 20; see also "Designing the White House: 1792–1830," White House Historical Association, www.whitehousehistory.org/teacher -resources/designing-the-white-house-1792-1830.

17. Arnebeck, *Through a Fiery Trial*, 23.

18. See "Designing the White House," White House Museum, https://www .whitehousehistory.org/teacher-resources/designing-the-white-house-1792-1830.

19. Seale, *White House*, 32.

20. See "Residence Construction."

21. "Residence Construction."

22. Seale, *White House*, 26.

27. A House Divided

1. "Q & A: Did Slaves Build the White House?," White House Historical Association, www.whitehousehistory.org/questions/did-slaves-build-the-white-house.

2. Allen, *History of Slave Laborers*, 3.

3. Arnebeck, *Slave Labor in the Capital*.

4. Allen, *History of Slave Laborers*, 9.

5. Allen, chap. 2.

6. See Commissioners to Thomas Jefferson, January 5, 1793, in Founders Online, https://founders.archives.gov/documents/Jefferson/01-25-02-0022; and "Did Slaves Build?"

7. Allen, *History of Slave Laborers*, 5–6; see also Commissioners to Thomas Jefferson, January 5, 1793.

8. The quote is by Julian Niemcewicz in 1798; see Arnebeck, *Slave Labor in the Capital*, 2.

9. Arnebeck, "Use of Slaves."

10. Allen, *History of Slave Laborers*, 7; see also Arnebeck, *Through a Fiery Trial*, 262.

11. Arnebeck, "Use of Slaves," part 5.

12. Clephane, "Local Aspect of Slavery," 235; see also Lusane, *Black History*, 119.

13. Wilkins, *Jefferson's Pillow*, 11.

14. Allen, *History of Slave Laborers*, 1.

15. See "History: 1790 Overview," US Census, www.census.gov/history/www/through_the_decades/overview/1790.html; see also L. W. Brown, *Free Negroes*, 17.

16. Lusane, *Black History*, 105–20.

17. William Thornton to Commissioners, July 18, 1795, in Harris, *Papers of Thornton*, 320.

18. Lusane, *Black History*, 114; see also Arnebeck, "Use of Slaves," part 5.

19. William Thornton to John Coakley Lattsom, December 22, 1794, in Harris, *Papers of Thornton*, 286; see also his letter on November 26, 1795, on p. 340.

20. William Thornton to John Coakley Lattsom, January 8, 1795, in Harris, *Papers of Thornton*, 295.

21. See Lusane, *Black History*; Arnebeck, "Use of Slaves," part 5; and Wilkins, *Jefferson's Pillow*, for detailed discussions of slave labor in the capital city.

22. See Records of the Commissioners.

23. Arnebeck, *Through a Fiery Trial*, 138; see also Arnebeck, "Use of Slaves"; and Holland, *Black Men*, 4.

24. Arnebeck, *Through a Fiery Trial*, 456; see also Lusane, *Black History*, 109.

25. Paul Jennings's story was first published in 1865 as *A Colored Man's Reminisces of James Madison*.

26. Watson, *America's First Crisis*, chap. 28.

27. Lusane, *Black History*, 116.

28. The Thirteenth Amendment outlawed slavery in 1865.

29. Arneback, *Through a Fiery Trial*, 4.

30. "Slave Labor Commemorative Marker," Architect of the Capitol, last updated September 11, 2018, https://aco.gov/art/commemorative-displays/slave-labor-commemorative-marker.

31. Allen, *History of Slave Laborers*, 2.

32. The congressional task for report was issued in 2005 and titled "History of Slave Laborers in the Construction of the United States Capitol."

33. See "Residence Construction."

28. Washington (Never) Slept Here

1. Janke, "President's Park."

2. Seale, *White House*, 22; see also Whitcomb and Whitcomb, *Real Life*, 5.

3. See Fitzpatrick, *Diaries of Washington*, 142–43; see also Daniel Carroll to James Madison, April 23, 1791, in Rutland and Mason, *Papers of Madison*.

4. Seale, *White House*, 294.

5. See "Building the New Nation's Capital," George Washington's Mount Vernon, www.mountvernon.org/george-washington/the-first-president/building-the-new-nations-capital/.

6. Wolcott and Gibbs, *Memoirs of the Administrations*, 1:377.

7. See Singleton, *Story*, 10.

8. "Telephone Conversation with the Apollo 11 Astronauts on the Moon," July 20, 1969, doc. P-690714, Richard Nixon Presidential Library and Museum, Yorba Linda, CA.

29. A Pedestal Waiting for a Monument

1. Berg, *Grand Avenues*, 103. Note that some sources list the quote as "a pedestal waiting for a superstructure."

2. "History of the US Capitol Building," Architect of the Capitol, https://www.aoc.gov/history-us-capitol-building.

3. See *Gazette of the United States*, March 24, 1792, in Library of Congress; see also Cullen, *Papers of Jefferson*, 23:224–28.

4. "Jefferson's Plans for a Capitol Building," Library of Congress, www.loc.gov/exhibits/jefferson/jeffed.html#102; see also G. Brown, "History of the United States Capitol," 51–54; and Bennett, "Stephen Hallet," 1–31.

5. Harris, "Washington's 'Federal City,'" 49–53.

6. Thomas Jefferson to the Commissioners, April 20, 1792, in Padover, *Thomas Jefferson*.

7. "History of the U.S. Capitol Building."

8. Samuel Blodget Jr. to Thomas Jefferson, June 25, 1792, in Founders Online, https://founders.archives.gov/documents/Jefferson/01-24-02-0120.

9. Samuel Blodget Jr. to Thomas Jefferson, July 10, 1792, in Founders Online, https://founders.archives.gov/documents/Jefferson/01-24-02-0188.

10. Samuel Blodget to the Commissioners, July 11, 1792. For a discussion of the letter, see Founders Online, https://founders.archives.gov/documents/Jefferson/01-24 -02-0198.

11. George Washington to James Hoban and Stephen Hallet, July 1, 1793, in Founders Online, https://founders.archives.gov/documents/Washington/05-13-02 -0117.

12. George Washington to the Commissioners, July 23, 1792, in Clephane, "Writings of Washington"; see also Butler, *Competition 1792*.

13. "History of the U.S. Capitol Building."

14. Seale, *White House*, 2.

15. Allen, *History of Slave Laborers*, 8–10.

16. Bordewich, *Washington*, 198.

17. Sakolski, *Great American Land Bubble*, 160–63.

30. Temple of Liberty

1. Freeman, *George Washington*, 7:266–67.

2. George Washington to the Commissioners, July 22, 1795, in Washington Papers, Library of Congress; see also Jackson and Twohig, *Diaries of Washington*, 6:205.

3. Bordewich, *Washington*, 227.

4. Bordewich, 198–99.

5. Singleton, *Story*, 9–10.

6. See Arneback, "Use of Slaves"; and Lusane, *Black History*, 117.

7. Allen, "History of Slave Laborers."

8. Bowling, "Foreboding Shadow," 4; see also Palsy, *Tyranny of Printers*, for a helpful overview of the early partisan press.

9. See "Press Attacks," *Digital Encyclopedia*, George Washington's Mount Vernon, www.mountvernon.org/library/digitalhistory/digital-encyclopedia/article/press -attacks/. Such criticisms appear in the *National Gazette* newspaper, edited by ardent anti-federalist Philip Freneau.

10. For a helpful discussion, see Everly, "Local Impact," 8–11; see also Main, *Antifederalists*.

11. For a helpful discussion of the intriguing election, see Larson, *Magnificent Catastrophe*; and Ferling, *Adams vs. Jefferson*.

12. "Washington, D.C. History," Historical Society of Washington, DC, www .dchistory.org/publications/dc-history-faq.

13. "Washington, D.C. History."

14. Bowling, "Foreboding Shadow," 5.

15. Bowling, "Foreboding Shadow."

16. Whitcomb and Whitcomb, *Real Life*, 6–7.

17. See "Letter from Washington, D.C.," *Albany Gazette*, December 15, 1800; reprinted in *Ostego Herald*, December 25, 1800, in Library of Congress.

18. "History of the U.S. Capitol Building."

19. See "The Statue of Freedom," Architect of the Capitol, last updated October 19, 2018, https://www.aoc.gov/art/other-statues/statue-freedom.

20. See Holland, *Black Men*, 5; and Lusane, *Black History*, 128; see also "The Statue of Freedom."

31. The Father of His Country

1. George Washington to Jonathan Trumbull Jr., July 21, 1799, in Gilder Lehrman Collection, www.gilderlehrman.org/sites/default/files/inline-pdfs/05787_fps.pdf.

2. George Washington, Farewell Address, 1796. See the Avalon Project at the Yale Law School for a complete transcript: https://avalon.law.yale.edu/18th_century/washing .asp; a transcript of Washington's Farewell Address can also be found at George Washington's Mount Vernon: www.mountvernon.org/library/digitalhistory/digital-encyclopedia /article/george-washingtons-farewell-address/. An early draft of the address was published in Claypoole's *American Daily Advertiser* out of Philadelphia on September 19, 1796, and that copy is available as GLC 185, in Gilder Lehrman Collection.

3. Washington, Farewell Address.

4. Washington, Farewell Address.

5. Washington, Farewell Address.

6. Unger, *Unexpected George Washington*, 236.

7. R. N. Smith, *Patriarch*, 252.

8. Lynch, "Great Deal of Noise."

9. *Philadelphia Aurora (General Advertiser)*, December 31, 1796, in Library of Congress.

10. Freneau, "Lines on the Federal City," December 18, 1800, in Hiltner, *Newspaper Verse*, 634.

11. Chernow, *Washington*, 765.

12. Morales-Vazquez, "Imagining Washington," 21.

32. 'Tis Well

1. George Washington's Last Will and Testament, July 9, 1799, in Founders Online, https://founders.archives.gov/documents/washington/06-04-02-0404-0001.

2. "Letter, George Washington to Sally Fairfax, May 16, 1798," Founders Online, National Archives, founders.archives.gov.

3. See, in order, March 15, 1797, in Fitzpatrick, *Writings of Washington*, 4:255; *Washington Gazette*, March 15, 1797, in Library of Congress; Kennon, *Republic for the Ages*, 62.

4. There are numerous diary entries, but see Fitzpatrick, *Writings of Washington*, 4:257, 284.

5. See the entries in Fitzpatrick, 257, 277, 284–86, 305, 315, 317.

6. George Washington to William Thornton, December 8, 1799, in Founders Online, https://founders.archives.gov/documents/Washington/06-04-02-0397; see also Fitzpatrick, *Writings of Washington*. An "éclat" is a wonderful achievement.

7. December 12, 1799, in Twohig, *George Washington's Diaries*, 428.

8. See "The Death of George Washington" and "Cause of Death," in George Washington's Biography, George Washington's Mount Vernon, www.mountvernon.org /george-washington/death/.

9. Twohig, *George Washington's Diaries*, 429.

10. See "Tobias Lear Journal," December 1799 entries for a detailed account of the death at the Historical Society of Pennsylvania: https://hsp.org/history-online/digital -history-projects/tobias-lear-journal-account-death-george-washington.

11. "George Washington's Diary Entry," December 13, 1799, in Founders Online, https://founders.archives.gov/documents/washington/01-06-02-0008-0012-0013.

12. For accounts of the death, see "Tobias Lear Journal" and "Death of George Washington."

13. Chernow, *Washington*, 806–7.

14. Abbot et al., *Papers of Washington*, 4:548; see also Lear and Washington, *Letters and Recollections*, 129–41; and Twohig, *George Washington's Diaries*, 430.

15. Twohig, *George Washington's Diaries*, 430.

16. Dr. James Craik, statement, *Alexandria Gazette (and Columbian Mirror)*, December 21, 1799, in Library of Congress; see also Wells, "Last Illness and Death."

17. Twohig, *George Washington's Diaries*, 430–31.

18. See Morales-Vazquez, "Imagining Washington," 24.

19. Morales-Vazquez.

20. See Callender, *Prospect before Us*.

21. Alexander Hamilton, March 21, 1801, in Syrett, *Papers of Hamilton*, 25:358.

22. Thomas Jefferson to George Washington, April 16, 1784, in Founders Online, https://founders.archives.gov/documents/jefferson/01-07-02-0102; see also Thomas Jefferson to William Branch Giles, December 31, 1795, in Boyd et al., *Papers of Jefferson*, 19:48.

23. See the "Funeral Oration on the Death of General Washington," discussed in "First in War, First in Peace, and First in the Hearts of His Countrymen," George Washington's

Mount Vernon, www.mountvernon.org/library/digitalhistory/digital-encyclopedia
/article/first-in-war-first-in-peace-and-first-in-the-hearts-of-his-countrymen/.

24. See the *Connecticut Courant*, June 20, 1791, in Library of Congress; and
Rhodehamel, *Writings of Washington*, vii–xii.

25. For information on Cato and its influence, see Joseph Addison, "Cato (A Tragedy in Five Acts)," Constitution Society, https://www.constitution.org/addison/cato
_play.htm.

26. Kapsch, *Building Washington*, 256.

27. Mahan, in Watson, *Life in the White House*, 40.

28. Watson.

Epilogue: The Building Is in a State to Be Habitable

1. Whitcomb and Whitcomb, *Real Life*, 8.

2. Whitcomb and Whitcomb, 9.

3. Mahan, "Political Architecture," 45.

4. John Adams to Abigail Adams, April 1, 1797, in Adams Family Papers, http://
www.masshist.org/digitaladams/archive/doc?id=L17970401ja; see also John Adams to
James Warren, July 27, 1776, in C. F. Adams, *Works of Adams*, 428, for a sense of his
self-identity compared to the public view of George Washington.

5. DeGregorio, *Complete Book*, 19.

6. Means, *Women in the White House*, 46.

7. DeGregorio, *Complete Book*, 19.

8. See C. F. Adams, *Works of Adams*; see also Whitcomb and Whitcomb, *Real Life*, 11.

9. Levin, *Abigail Adams*, 387; see John Adams to Abigail Adams, Adams Family
Papers, www.masshist.org/digitaladams/.

10. Whitcomb and Whitcomb, *Real Life*, 9–10; see also Levin, *Abigail Adams*, 388;
and Hurd, *White House Story*, 30.

11. Abigail Adams to her daughter, November 21, 1800, in Founders Online,
https://founders.archives.gov/documents/adams/99-03-02-0795.

12. J. C. Smith, *Correspondence and Miscellanies*, 204–7.

13. Adams to her daughter, November 21, 1800.

14. There are many descriptions of the building. See Singleton, *Story*, 13; Seale,
White House, 33; and "Residence Construction."

15. Adams to her daughter, November 21, 1800.

16. Singleton, *Story*, 11–13.

17. Abigail Adams to Cotton Tufts, November 28, 1800, in Founders Online,
https://founders.archives.gov/documents/Adams/99-03-02-0799.

18. A variety of descriptions and complaints from Abigail exist. See Singleton,
Story, 11–13; Levin, *Abigail Adams*, 389; P. Smith, *John Adams*, 1050; Whitcomb and
Whitcomb, *Real Life*, 6.

19. Abigail Adams to John Adams, March 31, 1776, in Founders Online, https://founders.archives.gov/documents/adams/04-01-02-0241.

20. John Adams to George Churchman and Jacob Lindley, January 24, 1801, in C. F. Adams, *Works of Adams*, 9:92–93; Abigail Adams to John Adams, March 31, 1776, Founders Online, https://founders.archives.gov/documents/adams/04-01-02-0241; also in Adams Family Papers.

21. John Adams to Joseph Ward, February 4, 1801, in Founders Online, https://founders.archives.gov/documents/Adams/99-02-02-4791.

22. Adams to Ward, February 4, 1801. See also L. E. Richards, "Vexatious Honors."

23. Levin, *Abigail Adams*, 390; see also Singleton, *Story*, 12.

24. President John Adams, Fourth Annual Message to Congress, November 22, 1800. Miller Center, University of Virginia. www.millercenter.org.

25. Seale, *White House*, 43–45.

26. M. B. Smith, *First Forty Years*, 32.

27. A. Jensen, *White House*, 17; see also Malone, *Jefferson*, 378; and Singleton, *Story*, 34–37.

28. Randall, *Thomas Jefferson*, 554.

29. Thomas Jefferson to Thomas Mann Randolph, June 4, 1801, in Founders Online, https://founders.archives.gov/documents/Jefferson/01-34-02-0213.

30. Singleton, *Story*, xxiv–xxv.

31. Singleton, 53; see also Malone, *Jefferson*, 18; and Whitcomb and Whitcomb, *Real Life*, 18.

32. Jefferson's Annual Message, December 2, 1806, in *Presidential Speeches: Thomas Jefferson Presidency*, Miller Center, https://millercenter.org/the-presidency/presidential-speeches/December-2-1806-sixth-annual-message.

Appendix B: List of Proposed Locations for the Capital

1. The city was, at the time, in Maryland.

BIBLIOGRAPHY

Historic Documents

Abbot, W. W., Dorothy Twohig, Philander D. Chase, David R. Hoth, Christine Sternberg Patrick, and Theodore J. Crackel, eds. *The Papers of George Washington*. 27 vols. Charlottesville: University of Virginia Press, 1983–97.

Adams, Charles Francis. *Letters of Mrs. Adams, The Wife of John Adams*. 4th ed. Boston: Wilkins, Darer, 1848.

———. *The Works of John Adams, Second President of the United States*. Boston: Little, Brown, 1854.

Adams, Henry. *History of the United States of America during the Administration of Thomas Jefferson*. New York, 1889–1891. Reprint edited by Earl Harbert. Boone, IA: Library of America, 1986.

Adams Family. Papers. Massachusetts Historical Society, Boston. www.masshist.org /digitaladams/archive/.

Ames, Fisher. "The Letters of Fisher Ames." Benjamin Vaughn Papers. American Philosophical Society, Philadelphia.

Articles of Confederation. November 15, 1777. Papers of the Continental Congress, 1774–1789. Record Group 360. National Archives and Records Administration, Washington, DC. www.ourdocuments.gov/doc.php?flash=false&doc=3#.

Baker, William Spohn. *Washington after the Revolution, 1784–1799*. Philadelphia, 1897.

Bass, Eduard. *Description of the Diorama Representing the First Inauguration of George Washington*. London: Forgotten Books, 2017. First printed in 1789.

Bedini, Silvio A. *The Life of Benjamin Banneker: The First African-American of Science*. Annapolis: Maryland Historical Society, 1999.

Bickford, Charles Bangs, Kenneth R. Bowling, William Charles di Giacommantonio, and Helen E. Veit, eds. *Documentary History of the First Federal Congress of the United States, March 4, 1789–March 3, 1791*. 15 vols. Baltimore: Johns Hopkins University Press, 1992–96.

Boudinot, Elias. Papers. Historical Society of Pennsylvania, Philadelphia.

———. Papers. Morgan Library, New York.

Bowling, Kenneth, and Helen Veit, eds. *Diary of William Maclay and Other Notes on Senate Debates*. Baltimore: Johns Hopkins University Press, 1988.

Boyd, Julian P., et al., eds. *The Papers of Thomas Jefferson*. 44 vols. Princeton, NJ: Princeton University Press, 1950–65.

Callender, James T. *The Prospect before Us*. Richmond, VA: M. Jones, S. Peasant, T. Field Publishers, 1801.

Cappon, Lester J. *The Adams-Jefferson Letters: The Complete Correspondence between Thomas Jefferson and Abigail and John Adams*. Chapel Hill: University of North Carolina Press, 1988.

Carroll, Charles. Collection, 1757–1967. Maryland Historical Society. http://mdhs .org/findingaid/charles-carroll-carrollton-collection-1757-1967-ms-1893.

Chateaubriand, François-René de. *Memoirs (from Beyond the Grave, 1768–1800)*. 42 vols. Translated by Alex Andriesse. New York: NYRB Classics, 2018.

Clephane, Walter C. "The Writings of George Washington Relating to the National Capital." *Records of the Columbia Historical Society* 17 (1914): 25–40.

Crackel, Theodore J., ed. *The Papers of George Washington Digital Edition*. Charlottesville: University of Virginia Press, 2008. https://www.upress.virginia.edu/content /papers-george-washington-digital-edition.

Cullen, Charles T., ed. *The Papers of Thomas Jefferson*. Princeton, NJ: Princeton University Press, 1900.

Cutler, Manasseh. *Explanation of the Map Which Delineates That Part of the Federal Lands*. Salem, MA: Dabney and Cushing, 1787. Reprint, Farmington Hills, MI: Gale ECCO, 2010.

Custis, George Washington Parke. *Recollections and Private Memoirs of Washington*. New York: Derby & Jackson, 1860.

DenBoer, Gordon, Lucy T. Brown, Merrill Jenson, and Robert A. Becker, eds. *The Documentary History of the First Federal Elections, 1788–1790*. 4 vols. Madison: University of Wisconsin Press, 1976–90.

DePauw, Linda Grant, Charlene Bickford, Kenneth Bowling, and Helen Veit, eds. *Documentary History of the First Federal Congress*. Washington, DC: George Washington University, 1972–96.

Documentary History of the Constitution of the United States of America, 1786–1870. Vol. 1. Washington, DC: US Department of State, 1894.

Ellicott, Andrew. *The Journal of Andrew Ellicott*. Philadelphia: Budd & Bartram, 1803. Reprint, New York: Arno Press, 1980.

Ellicott, Andrew. Papers. Library of Congress, Washington, DC.

Farrand, Max. *The Records of the Federal Convention of 1787*, 3 vols. New Haven, CT: Yale University Press, 1911.

Fields, Joseph E., ed. *"Worthy Partner": The Papers of Martha Washington*. Westport, CT: Greenwood Press, 1994.

First Federal Congress Project. George Washington University, Washington, DC. https://www2.gwu.edu/~ffcp/.

Fisher Family Papers. Historical Society of Pennsylvania, Philadelphia.

Fitzpatrick, John C., ed. *The Diaries of George Washington, 1748–1799*. New York: Houghton Mifflin, 1925.

———. *The Writings of George Washington from the Original Manuscript Sources, 1745–1799*. 8 series. Washington, DC: Government Printing Office, 1931–44.

Foner, Philip S., ed. *The Complete Writings of Thomas Paine*, 2 vols. New York: Citadel Press, 1945.

Force, Peter, ed. *American Archives: Containing a Documentary History of the English Colonies in North America*. Washington, 1837–46. Reprint, London: Forgotten Books, 2017.

Ford, Paul Leicester, ed. *The Writings of Thomas Jefferson*. New York, 1892–99. Reprint, Lexington: Ulan Press, 2012.

Founders Online. National Archives and Records Administration, Washington, DC. https://founders.archives.gov.

Gerry, Elbridge. Papers. Massachusetts Historical Society, Boston.

Hamilton, Alexander. *Writings*. New York: Library of America, 2001.

Harris, C. M., ed. *The Papers of William Thornton*. Charlottesville: University of Virginia Press, 1995.

Hening, William Waller, ed. *The Statutes at Large: Being a Collection of All the Laws of Virginia*. 13 vols. Richmond, VA: Franklin Press / W. W. Gray, Printer, 1809–23.

Henry, Patrick. Papers. Library of Congress, Washington, DC.

Hutchinson, William T., Robert A. Rutland, and Charles Hobson, eds. *The Papers of James Madison*. 17 vols. Charlottesville: University of Virginia Press, 1976.

Irving, Washington. *George Washington: A Biography*. New York: G. P. Putnam, 1856.

Jackson, Donald, and Dorothy Twohig, eds. *The Diaries of George Washington*. 6 vols. Charlottesville: University of Virginia Press, 1979.

Johnston, Henry P., ed. *The Correspondence and Public Papers of John Jay*, 4 vols. New York: G. P. Putnam's Sons, 1890–93.

Kline, Cameron L., comp. *Tobias Lear Journal*. Harrisburg: Historical Society of Pennsylvania, 2018.

Law, Thomas. "A Reply to Certain Insinuations." *Quarterly Review*, no. 68 (1827): 1–27.

Lear, Tobias. Diary. Historical Society of Pennsylvania, Philadelphia.

———. Papers. Library of Congress, Washington, DC.

———. Papers. William Clements Library, University of Michigan, Ann Arbor.

Lear, Tobias, and George Washington. *Letters and Recollections of George Washington: Being Letters to Tobias Lear and Others*. New York: Doubleday, 1906.

L'Enfant, Pierre Charles. Papers. Library of Congress, Washington, DC.

Logan, R. R., ed. *Colonial Records of Pennsylvania*. 16 vols. Philadelphia: Jo. Steverns, 1852–53.

———. Dickinson Papers. Historical Society of Pennsylvania, Philadelphia.

Maclay, Edgar S., ed. *The Diary of William Maclay and Other Notes on Senate Debates*. New York: D. Appleton and Company, 1890.

Maclay, William. Journal of William Maclay, United States Senator from Pennsylvania, 1789–1791. American Memory Collection, Library of Congress, Washington, DC. http://memory.loc.gov/ammem/amlaw/lwmj.html.

Madison, James. Papers, 1723–1859. Manuscript Division, Library of Congress, Washington, DC.

Marshall, John. *The Life of George Washington*. Philadelphia: James Crissy, 1838.

Matthews, Catharine van Cortlandt. *Andrew Ellicott: His Life and Letters*. New York: Grafton Press, 1908.

Monroe, James. Papers, 4 series. Library of Congress, Washington, DC.

Morris, Robert. Diary. Manuscript Division, Library of Congress, Washington, DC. https://www.loc.gov/item/mm78033605/.

———. Papers. Huntington Library, San Marino, CA.

Morse, Jedidiah. *The American Geography; or, A View of the Present Situation of the United States of America*. Elizabeth Town, NJ: Shepard Kollock Printer, 1789.

O'Connor, John. *Political Opinions Particularly Respecting the Seat of the Federal Empire*. [Georgetown, MD?], 1789. https://books.google.com/books?id=Vqxb AAAAQAAJ.

Page, John. Washington in New York in 1789. Baker Collection. Pennsylvania Historical Society, Philadelphia.

Parsons, Eugene. *George Washington: A Character Sketch*. Milwaukee, WI: H. G. Campbell Publishing Co., 1898. https://hdl.handle.net/2027/loc.ark:/13960/t3bz6mn6h.

Prussing, Eugene E. *Estate of George Washington, Deceased Boston*. Boston: Little, Brown, 1927.

Randolph, Sarah N. *The Domestic Life of Thomas Jefferson: Compiled from Family Letters and Reminiscences by His Great-Granddaughter*. New York: Harper & Bros., 1871.

Records of the Commissioners for the District of Columbia. National Archives and Records Administration, Washington, DC.

Rhodehamel, John, ed. *The American Revolution: Writings from the War for Independence*. Boone, IA: Library of America, 2001.

———. *George Washington: Writings*. New York: Library of America, 1997.

Rutland, Robert A., ed. *The Papers of George Mason, 1725–1792*. Vol. 1. Chapel Hill: University of North Carolina Press, 2011.

Rutland, Robert A., and Thomas A. Mason, eds. *The Papers of James Madison*. Charlottesville: University of Virginia Press, 1984.

Sedgwick, Theodore. Papers. Massachusetts Historical Society, Boston.

Smith, John Cotton. *The Correspondence and Miscellanies of the Hon. John Cotton Smith, Formerly Governor of Connecticut.* New York: Harper & Bros., 1848.

Smith, Paul, Gerald Gawalt, Rosemary Fry Plakas, and Eugene R. Sheridan, eds. *Letters of Delegates to Congress, 1774–1789.* 26 vols. Washington, DC: Government Printing Office, 1921–38.

Smyth, John Ferdinand D. *A Tour in the United States of America: Containing an Account of the President Situation of That Country.* London, 1784. Royal Collection Trust, Vol. 2.

Speer, Albert. *Inside the Third Reich.* New York: Macmillan, 1970.

Stedman, Edmund Clarence, and Ellen Mackay Hutchinson, eds. *A Library of American Literature: From the Earliest Settlement to the Present Time in Eleven Volumes.* New York: Charles Webster, 1891.

Syrett, Harold C., ed. *The Papers of Alexander Hamilton.* 26 vols. New York: Columbia University Press, 1961–79.

Thornton, William. Papers, 1741–1865. Library of Congress, Washington, DC.

Twohig, Dorothy, ed. *George Washington's Diaries: An Abridgement.* Charlottesville: University of Virginia Press, 1999.

Van Horne, John, ed. *Correspondence and Miscellaneous Papers of Benjamin Henry Latrobe.* 3 vols. New Haven, CT: Yale University Press, 1984–88.

Washington, George. Papers. Huntington Library, San Marino, CA.

———. Papers. Library of Congress, Washington, DC.

———. Papers. Pierpont Morgan Library and Museum, New York.

Weems, Mason Locke. *The Life of George Washington: With Curious Anecdotes, Equally Honourable to Himself and Exemplary to His Young Countrymen.* Philadelphia: Joseph Allen, 1800. https://archive.org/details/lifeofgeorgewashweem/page/n6.

Williamson, Hugh. Papers, 1778–1815. North Carolina State Department of Archives and History, Raleigh.

Wolcott, Oliver, and George Gibbs, ed. *Memoirs of the Administrations of Washington and John Adams.* 2 vols. New York: W. Van Norden, 1846.

Wynkoop, Henry, and Joseph M. Beatty, Jr. "The Letters of Judge Henry Wynkoop, Representative from Pennsylvania to the First Congress of the United States." *Pennsylvania Magazine of History and Biography* 38, no. 1 (1914): 39–64.

Books

Adair, Douglass, and John A. Schutz, eds. *Peter Oliver's Origin and Progress of the American Rebellion: A Tory View.* Stanford, CA: Stanford University Press, 1963.

Aikman, Lonnelle. *The Living White House.* Washington, DC: White House Historical Association, 1991.

Allen, William C. *History of Slave Laborers in the Construction of the U.S. Capitol.* Washington, DC: Architect of the Capitol, US House of Representatives, 2005.

Anderson, Fred. *George Washington Remembers: Reflections on the French and Indian War*. Lanham, MD: Rowman & Littlefield, 2004.

Arnebeck, Bob. *Slave Labor in the Capital: Building Washington's Iconic Federal Landmarks*. Charleston, SC: History Press, 2014.

———. *Through a Fiery Trial: Building Washington, 1790–1800*. Lanham, MD: Madison Books, 1991.

Barratt, Carrie Rebora, and Ellen G. Miles. *Gilbert Stuart*. New Haven, CT: Yale University Press, 2004.

Berg, Scott W. *Grand Avenues: The Story of Pierre Charles L'Enfant, The French Visionary Who Designed Washington, DC*. New York: Pantheon Books, 2007.

Boller, Paul F., Jr. *Presidential Diversions: Presidents at Play from George Washington to George W. Bush*. New York: Harcourt, 2007.

Boorstin, Daniel J. *Hidden History: Exploring Our Secret Past*. New York: Vintage Books, 1987.

Bordewich, Fergus M. *Washington: The Making of the American Capital*. New York: HarperCollins, 2008.

Bowling, Kenneth. *The Creation of Washington, D.C.: The Idea and Location of the American Capital*. Fairfax, VA: George Mason University Press, 1991.

———. *Peter Charles L'Enfant: Vision, Honor and Male Friendship in the Early American Republic*. Washington, DC: George Washington University Libraries, 2002.

Boyd, George Adams. *Elias Boudinot: Patriot and Statesman, 1740–1821*. Princeton, NJ: Princeton University Press, 1952.

Brodie, Fawn. *Thomas Jefferson: An Intimate History*. New York: W. W. Norton, 1975.

Brown, Letitia Woods. *Free Negroes in the District of Columbia, 1790–1846*. New York: Oxford University Press, 1972.

Brunhouse, Robert. *The Counter-Revolution in Pennsylvania, 1776–1790*. Harrisburg: Pennsylvania Historical Commission, 1942.

Burns, James MacGregor, and Susan Dunn. *George Washington*. New York: Henry Holt, 2004.

Butler, Jeanne F. *Competition 1792: Designing a Nation's Capitol*. Washington, DC: US Capitol Historical Society, 1976.

Caemmerer, Paul H. *Life of Pierre Charles L'Enfant*. New York: Da Capo Press, 1970.

Carroll, John, and Mary Ashworth. *George Washington, First in Peace*. Vol. 7 of *The Biography of Douglas Southall Freeman*. New York: Charles Scribner's Sons, 1957.

Cerami, Charles A. *Benjamin Banneker: Surveyor, Astronomer, Publisher, Patriot*. Hoboken, NJ: John Wiley, 2002.

Chernow, Ron. *Alexander Hamilton*. New York: Penguin Press, 2004.

———. *Washington: A Life*. New York: Penguin, 2010.

Christman, Margaret C. S. *The First Federal Congress, 1789–1791*. Washington, DC: Smithsonian Books, 1989.

Clark, Roy Bird. *Washington's Western Lands*. Strasburg, VA: Shenandoah Publishing House, 1930.

Collins, Varnum Lansing. *The Continental Congress at Princeton*. Princeton, NJ: Princeton University Press, 1908.

Costanzo, Adam. *George Washington's Washington: Visions for the National Capital in the Early American Republic*. Athens: University of Georgia Press, 2018.

Davis, Joseph. *Sectionalism in American Politics, 1774–1787*. Madison: University of Wisconsin Press, 1977.

Deak, Gloria Gilda. *Picturing America: 1497–1899*. Princeton, NJ: Princeton University Press, 1988.

Decatur, Stephen, Jr. *Private Affairs of George Washington: From the Records and Accounts of Tobias Lear*. Boston: Houghton Mifflin, 1933.

DeGregorio, William A. *The Complete Book of U.S. Presidents: From George Washington to George Bush*. 5th ed. Fort Lee, NJ: Barricade Books, 2001.

Elkins, Stanley, and Eric McKitrick. *The Age of Federalism: The Early American Republic, 1787–1800*. New York: Oxford University Press, 1993.

Ellis, Joseph J. *Founding Brothers: The Revolutionary Generation*. New York: Vintage Books, 2000.

Ferling, John. *Adams vs. Jefferson: The Tumultuous Election of 1800*. New York: Oxford University Press, 2005.

Fleming, Thomas. *The Perils of Peace: America's Struggle for Survival after Yorktown*. New York: Smithsonian Books, 2007.

Flexner, James Thomas. *Washington: The Indispensable Man*. Boston: Little, Brown, 1974.

Fowler, William W., Jr. *American Crisis: George Washington and the Dangerous Two Years after Yorktown, 1781–1783*. New York: Walker Books, 2011.

Freeman, Douglas Southall. *George Washington: A Biography*. 7 vols. New York: Scribner's Sons, 1948–57.

Goldberg, Vicki. *The White House: The President's Home in Photographs and History*. New York: Little, Brown, 2011.

Graff, Henry F., ed. *The Presidents: A Reference History*. New York: Charles Scribner's Sons, 1997.

Greenberg, Allan. *George Washington, Architect*. London: Andreas Papadakis, 1999.

Greenstein, Fred I. *Hidden-Hand Presidency: Eisenhower as Leader*. 1982. Reprint, Baltimore: Johns Hopkins University Press, 1994.

———. *The Presidential Difference: Leadership Style from FDR to Clinton*. New York: Free Press, 2000.

Griswold, Rufus Wilmot. *Republican Court, or American Society in the Days of Washington*. New York, 1854.

Hatfield, Edwin F. *History of Elizabeth, New Jersey*. New York: Carlton & Lanahan, 1868.

Henderson, James H. *Party Politics in the Continental Congress*. New York: McGraw–Hill, 1974.

Higginbotham, Don, ed. *George Washington Reconsidered*. Charlottesville: University of Virginia Press, 2001.

Hiltner, Judith R., ed. *The Newspaper Verse of Philip Freneau*. Troy, NY: Whitson Publishing, 1986.

Holland, Jesse J. *Black Men Built the Capitol: Discovering African-American History in and around Washington*. Guilford, CT: Globe Pequot, 2007.

Hurd, Charles. *The White House Story*. New York: Hawthorne Books, 1966.

James, Alfred P. *The Ohio Company: Its Inner History*. Pittsburgh: University of Pittsburgh Press, 1959.

Janson, Charles William. *Stranger in America*. London, 1807. Reprint, New York: Press of the Pioneers, 1935.

Jensen, Amy. *The White House and Its Thirty-Four Families*. New York: McGraw-Hill, 1965.

Kapsch, Robert James. *Building Washington: Engineering and Construction of the New Federal City, 1790–1840*. Baltimore: Johns Hopkins University Press, 2018.

Kearns Goodwin, Doris. *Team of Rivals: The Political Genius of Abraham Lincoln*. New York: Simon & Schuster, 2005.

Kennon, Donald R. *A Republic for the Ages*. Charlottesville: University of Virginia Press, 1999.

Kenyon, Cecilia, ed. *The Antifederalists*. Indianapolis: Bobbs-Merrill, 1966.

Ketcham, Ralph. *James Madison: A Biography*. Charlottesville: University of Virginia Press, 1971.

Kite, Elizabeth S. *L'Enfant and Washington, 1791–1792*. Baltimore: Johns Hopkins University Press, 1929.

Kohn, Richard H. *Eagle and Sword: The Federalists and the Creation of the Military Establishment in America, 1783–1802*. New York: Free Press, 1975.

Larson, Edward J. *A Magnificent Catastrophe: The Tumultuous Election of 1800, America's First Presidential Campaign*. New York: Free Press, 2007.

Lengel, Edward G. *General George Washington: A Military Life*. New York: Random House, 2005.

Levin, Phyllis. *Abigail Adams*. New York: St. Martin's Press, 1987.

Livengood, James W. *Philadelphia-Baltimore Trade Rivalry, 1780–1860*. Harrisburg: Pennsylvania Historical and Museum Commission, 1947.

Longmire, Paul K. *The Invention of George Washington*. Berkeley: University of California Press, 1988.

Lusane, Clarence. *The Black History of the White House*. San Francisco: City Lights Books, 2011.

Madsen, David. *The National University: Enduring Dream of the USA*. Detroit: Wayne State University Press, 1966.

Main, Jackson. *The Antifederalists: Critics of the Constitution, 1781–1788*. Chapel Hill: University of North Carolina Press, 1961.

Malone, Dumas. *Jefferson the President: Second Term, 1805–1809*. Boston: Little, Brown, 1974.

McCoy, Drew R. *The Last of the Fathers: James Madison and the Republican Legacy*. Cambridge, UK: Cambridge University Press, 1991.

Means, Marianne. *The Women in the White House*. New York: Random House, 1963.

Mellon, Greenville, ed. *The Book of the United States: Exhibiting Its Geography, Divisions, Constitution, and Government*. Hartford, CT: A. C. Goodman, 1852.

Miller, John C. *Alexander Hamilton: Portrait in Paradox*. New York: Harper & Row, 1959.

Mitchell, Broadus. *Alexander Hamilton: Youth to Maturity, 1755–1788*. New York: Macmillan, 1957.

Monaghan, Frank, and Marvin Lowenthal. *This Was New York: The Nation's Capital in 1789*. New York: Doubleday, 1943.

Morgan, Edmund S. *Genius of Washington*. New York: W. W. Norton, 1980.

———. *The Meaning of Independence: John Adams, George Washington, and Thomas Jefferson*. Charlottesville: University of Virginia Press, 1976.

Padover, Saul K. *Thomas Jefferson and the National Capital*. Washington, DC: Government Printing Office, 1942.

Palsy, Jeffrey L. *The Tyranny of Printers: Newspaper Politics in the Early American Republic*. Charlottesville: University of Virginia Press, 2002.

Peck, Garrett. *The Potomac River: A History and Guide*. Charleston, SC: History Press, 2012.

Randall, Willard. *Thomas Jefferson: A Life*. New York: Henry Holt, 1993.

Reps, John William. *The Making of Urban America: A History of City Planning in the United States*. Princeton, NJ: Princeton University Press, 1965.

Rhodehamel, John. *The Great Experiment: George Washington and the American Republic*. New Haven, CT: Yale University Press, 1998.

Richards, Leonard L. *Shays's Rebellion: The American Revolution's Final Battle*. Philadelphia: University of Pennsylvania Press, 2003.

Rowland, Kate M. *The Life of George Mason, 1725–1792*. New York: G. P. Putnam's Sons, 1892.

Sakolski, Aaron M. *The Great American Land Bubble: The Amazing Story of Land-Grabbing, Speculation, and Booms from Colonial Days to the Present Time*. Eastford, CT: Martino Fine Books, 2011. First published in 1932.

Sawvel, Franklin B. *The Complete Anas of Thomas Jefferson*. New York, 1903. Reprint, South Yarra, Victoria, Australia: Leopold Classic Library, 2016.

Schachner, Nathan. *The Founding Fathers*. New York: Putnam, 1954.

Schutz, John A., and Douglass Adair, eds. *Spur of Fame: Dialogues of John Adams and Benjamin Rush*. Indianapolis: Liberty Fund, 2001.

Seale, William. *The White House: The History of an American Idea*. Washington, DC: White House Historical Association, 2001.

Singleton, Esther. *The Story of the White House*. New York: Benjamin Blom, 1907.

Smith, Margaret Bayard. *The First Forty Years of Washington Society*. New York: Frederick Unger, 1965.

Smith, Page. *John Adams, 1785–1826*. Vol. 2. Garden City, NY: Doubleday, 1962.

———. *The Shaping of America: A People's History of the Young Republic*. New York: McGraw-Hill, 1980.

Smith, Richard Norton. *Patriarch: George Washington and the New American Nation*. Boston: Houghton Mifflin, 1993.

Smith, Thomas E. V. *New York in the Year of Washington's Inauguration*. New York, 1899. Reprint, London: Forgotten Books, 2015.

Sparks, Jared. *The Life of George Washington*. Boston: Little, Brown, 1860.

Stagg, J. C. A., ed. *The Papers of James Madison Digital Edition*. Charlottesville: University of Virginia Press, 2010. https://rotunda.upress.virginia.edu/founders/JSMN.html.

Stephenson, Richard W. *A Plan Wholly New: Pierre Charles L'Enfant's Plan of the City of Washington*. Washington, DC: Government Printing Office, 1993.

Stewart, Donald H. *The Opposition Press of the Federal Period*. Albany: State University of New York Press, 1969.

Tilp, Frederick. *This Was Potomac River*. Alexandria, VA: Self-published, 1978.

Unger, Harlow Giles. *The Unexpected George Washington: His Private Life*. New York: John Wiley & Sons, 2006.

Watson, Robert P. *Affairs of State: The Untold Story of Presidential Love, Sex, and Scandal*. Lanham, MD: Rowman & Littlefield, 2012.

———. *America's First Crisis: The War of 1812*. Albany: State University of New York Press, 2014.

———. *The Ghost Ship of Brooklyn: An Untold Story of the American Revolution*. Boston: Da Capo Press, 2017.

———. *Life in the White House: A Social History of the First Family and the President's House*. Albany: State University of New York Press, 2004.

Weatherly, Myra. *Benjamin Banneker: American Scientific Pioneer*. Mankato, MN: Compass Point Books, 2006.

Wentworth, E., ed. *Ladies Repository*. Chicago: Hitchcock & Walden, 1876.

Whitcomb, John, and Claire Whitcomb. *Real Life at the White House: 200 Years of Daily Life at America's Most Famous Residence*. New York: Routledge: 2000.

Wiencek, Henry. *An Imperfect God: George Washington, His Slaves, and the Creation of America*. New York: Farrar, Straus & Giroux, 2003.

Wilkins, Roger. *Jefferson's Pillow: The Founding Fathers and the Dilemma of Black Patriotism*. Boston: Beacon Press, 2001.

Wilkinson, Norman B. *Land Policy and Speculation in Pennsylvania, 1779–1800*. New York: Arno Press, 1979.

Williamson, Hugh. *The History of North Carolina*. 2 vols. Philadelphia: Fry and Kammerer, 1812.

Wood, Gordon. *Creation of the American Republic*. Chapel Hill: University of North Carolina Press, 1969.

Young, James Sterling. *The Washington Community, 1800–1828*. New York: Harcourt, Brace, and World, 1966.

Zall, Paul M. *Comical Spirit of Seventy-Six*. San Marino, CA: Huntington Library, 1976.

Chapters, Articles, and Speeches

Abbot, W. W. "George Washington in Retirement." Lowell Lecture Series, Museum of Our National Heritage, Lexington, MA, December 5, 1999.

Alexander, Sally Kelly. "A Sketch of the Life of Major Andrew Ellicott." *Records of the Columbia Historical Society* 2 (1899): 165–85.

Arnebeck, Bob. "Tracking the Speculators: Greenleaf and Nicholson in the Federal City." *Washington History* 3 (Spring/Summer 1991): 113–25.

Baker, William S. "Washington after the Revolution, 1784–1799." *Pennsylvania Magazine of History and Biography* 19 (January 1, 1895): 22–50.

Bennett, Wells. "Stephen Hallet and His Designs for the National Capitol, 1791–94." *Journal of the American Institute of Architects* (July–October 1916): 1–31.

Bowling, Kenneth R. "Dinner at Jefferson's: A Note on Jacob E. Cooke's 'The Compromise of 1790.'" *William and Mary Quarterly* 28, no. 4 (October 1971): 629–48.

———. "A Foreboding Shadow: Newspaper Celebration of the Federal Government's Arrival." *Washington History* 12, no. 1 (2000): 4–11.

———. "Neither in a Wigwam nor the Wilderness: Competitors for the Federal Capital, 1787–1790." *Prologue* 20 (1988): 163–79.

———. "New Light on the Philadelphia Mutiny of 1783." *Pennsylvania Magazine of History and Biography* 101 (October 1977): 419–50.

———. "A Place to Which Tribute Is Brought: The Contest for the Federal Capital in 1783." *Prologue* 8 (1976): 129–39.

Brown, Glenn. "History of the United States Capitol." *American Architect and Building News* 52 (May 9, 1896): 51–54.

Buel, Richard, Jr. "Democracy and the American Revolution: A Frame of Reference." *William and Mary Quarterly* 26 (1964): 165–90.

Chernow, Ron. "George Washington." In *The President: Noted Historians Rank America's Best—and Worst—Chief Executives*, edited by Brian Lamb and Susan Swain, 34–46. New York: Public Affairs, 2019.

Clephane, Walter C. "The Local Aspect of Slavery in the District of Columbia." *Records of the Columbia Historical Society* 3 (1900): 220–40.

Cooke, Jacob E. "The Compromise of 1790." *William and Mary Quarterly* 27 (October 1970): 523–45.

Corwin, Edward S. "The Progress of Constitutional Theory between the Declaration of Independence and the Meeting of the Philadelphia Convention." *American Historical Review* 30, no. 3 (April 1925): 511–36.

Dabney, Dick. "George Washington Reconsidered." *Washingtonian* 17 (February 1982): 83–89.

Davis, Richard Beale. "The Abbé Correa in America, 1812." *Transactions* (American Philosophical Society) 45, no. 2 (1955): 87–197.

Everly, Elaine C. "The Local Impact of the War Office Fire of 1800." *Washington History* 12, no. 1 (2000): 8–11.

Grogg, Robert. "Introduction: Where Oh Where Should the Capital Be?" *White House History*, no. 34 (Fall 2013). https://www.whitehousehistory.org/where-oh-where -should-the-capital-be-white-house-history-number-34.

Harris, C. M. "Washington's 'Federal City,' Jefferson's 'Federal Town.'" *Washington History* 12, no. 1 (2000): 49–53.

———. "Washington's Gamble, L'Enfant's Dream: Politics, Design, and the Founding of the National Capital." *William and Mary Quarterly* 56 (July 1999): 527–64.

Horton, James Oliver. "Alexander Hamilton: Slavery and Race in a Revolutionary Generation." *New York Journal of American History* 65, no. 3 (Spring 2004): 16–24.

Humphreys, David. "Remarks." In *The Life of George Washington*, edited by Rosemary Zagari, 47–48. Athens: University of Georgia Press, 1991.

Janke, Lucinda Prout. "The President's Park (Give or Take a Few Acres)." *White House History*, no. 27 (Spring 2010). https://www.whitehousehistory.org/the-presidents -park.

Jensen, Arthur Louis. "The Origin of the First Continental Congress, 1773–74." Master's thesis, University of Wisconsin, 1949. https://minds.wisconsin.edu/handle /1793/31202?show=full.

Kenyon, Cecelia M. "Men of Little Faith." *William and Mary Quarterly* 12 (January 1955): 3–43.

Kohn, Richard H. "The Inside History of the Newburgh Conspiracy: America and the Coup d'Etat." *William and Mary Quarterly* 27 (April 1970): 188–220.

Lynch, Jack. "A Great Deal of Noise, Whipping and Spurring." *Trend and Tradition: The Colonial Williamsburg Journal* (Autumn 2012). https://www.history.org /foundation/journal/autumn12/election.cfm.

Mahan, Russell L. "Political Architecture: The Building of the President's House." In *Life in the White House: A Social History of the First Family and the President's House*, edited by Robert P. Watson, 31–47. Albany: State University of New York Press, 2004.

Morales-Vazquez, Rubil. "Imagining Washington: Monuments and National Building in the Early Capital." *Washington History* 12, no. 1 (2000): 12–29.

Nite, Grace L. "Washington and the Potomac." *American Historical Review* 28 (1923): 497–519.

Parr, Marilyn K. "Chronicle of a British Diplomat: The First Year in the 'Washington Wilderness.'" *Washington Monthly* 12, no. 1 (2000): 78–89.

Richards, Laura E. "Vexatious Honors." Chapter 11 in *Abigail Adams and Her Times.* First published in 1917. https://americanliterature.com/author/laura-e-richards /book/abigail-adams-and-her-times/chapter-xi-vexatious-honors.

Riley, Edward M. "Philadelphia, the Nation's Capital, 1790–1800." *Pennsylvania History* 20 (October 1953): 357–79.

Risjord, Norman K. "The Compromise of 1790: New Evidence on the Dinner Table Bargain." *William and Mary Quarterly* 33 (1976): 309–14.

Rogers, George C., Jr. "Letters of William Loughton Smith." *South Carolina Historical Magazine* 69 (1965): 110–18.

Scott, Pamela. "L'Enfant's Washington Described." *Washington History* 3 (Spring-Summer 1991): 96–111.

———. "Moving to the Seat of Government: Temporary Inconveniences and Privations." *Washington History* 12, no. 1 (2000): 70–73.

Skeen, Edward C., and Richard H. Kohn. "The Newburgh Conspiracy Reconsidered." *William and Mary Quarterly* 31 (April 1974): 273–98.

Stephenson, Richard W., and J. L. Sibley. "The Delineation of a Grand Plan." *Quarterly Journal of the Library of Congress* 36 (1979): 207–78.

Tagg, James D. "Benjamin Franklin Bache's Attack on George Washington." *Pennsylvania Magazine of History and Biography* 100, no. 2 (April 1976): 191–230.

Trudel, Marcel. "The Jumonville Affair." Translated by Donald H. Kent. *Revue d'histoire de l'Amérique Française* 6, no. 3 (December 1952): 331–73.

Verner, Coolie. "Surveying and Mapping the New Federal City: The First Printed Maps of Washington, D.C." *Imago Mundi* 23 (1969): 59–72.

Watson, Robert P. "At Home with the First Families." In *Life in the White House: A Social History of the First Family and the President's House*, edited by Robert P. Watson, 9–29. Albany: State University of New York Press, 2004.

———. "Welcome to the White House." In *Life in the White House: A Social History of the First Family and the President's House*, edited by Robert P. Watson, 3–7. Albany: State University of New York Press, 2004.

Wells, Walter A. "Last Illness and Death of Washington." *Virginia Medical Monthly* 53 (1926–27): 629–42.

Wensyel, James W. "The Newburgh Conspiracy." *American Heritage* 32, no. 3 (April/ May 1981). www.americanheritage.com/content/newburgh-conspiracy.

INDEX

To avoid confusing George Washington with the city bearing his name, subentries refer to "GW."

ABOUT THE AUTHOR

Robert P. Watson, PhD, is an author, historian, professor, and media commentator who has published roughly two hundred scholarly articles, chapters, and essays, three novels, two encyclopedia sets, and over three dozen nonfiction books, including most recently *Affairs of State* (2012); *America's First Crisis* (2014), winner of the Independent Publishers' Gold Medal in History; *The Nazi Titanic* (2016), which is being made into a motion picture; and *The Ghost Ship of Brooklyn* (2017), which won the Commodore John Barry Book Award and received Honorable Mention for the John Lyman Book Award and was the subject of a television special on the National Geographic Channel. He resides in Boca Raton, where he is Distinguished Professor of American History and Director of Project *Civitas* at Lynn University.